ASSESSING
READERS

Qualitative Diagnosis and Instruction

RONA F. FLIPPO

Fitchburg State College
Massachusetts

HEINEMANN
Portsmouth, NH

Heinemann
A division of Reed Elsevier Inc.
361 Hanover Street
Portsmouth, NH 03801-3912
www.heinemann.com

Offices and agents throughout the world

The author and publisher wish to thank those who have generously given permission to reprint borrowed material:

Box 2–3: *Resolution on Misuse of Grade Equivalents* by the Delegates Assembly of the International Reading Association, Newark, DE, April 1981. Copyright © 1981 by the International Reading Association. All rights reserved. Reprinted by permission.

Box 3–1: "A Classification Scheme and Assessment for Emergent Reading" is adapted from "Assessment of Emergent Literacy: Storybook Reading" by Elizabeth Sulzby in *The Reading Teacher*, 44 (7). Copyright © 1991 by the International Reading Association. All rights reserved. Reprinted by permission.

Box 3–2: "Reading Interview" from *Reading Miscue Inventory: Alternative Procedures* by Y.M. Goodman, D.J. Watson, and C.L. Burke. Copyright © 1987. Richard C. Owen Publishers, Inc., Katonah, NY. Reprinted with permission.

Box 3–3: "Informal Reading Inventories" from "Assessment: Informal Reading Inventories" by J.J. Pikulski in *The Reading Teacher*, 43 (7). Copyright © 1990 by the International Reading Association. Reprinted with permission of John J. Pikulski and the International Reading Association. All rights reserved.

Box 3–4: "Graded Word Lists" from *Analytical Reading Inventory, 5th Edition* by M.L. Woods and A.J. Moe. Copyright © 1995. Adapted by permission of Pearson Education, Inc., Upper Saddle River, NJ.

Box 3–5: "A Graded Passage, Narrative Material," Box 3–6: "Student Record Summary Sheet," and Figure 3–1: "Examples and Coding of Miscues" from *Analytical Reading Inventory, 5th Edition* by M.L. Woods and A.J. Moe. Copyright © 1995. Adapted by permission of Pearson Education, Inc., Upper Saddle River, NJ.

Figure 3–2: "Miscue Analysis Coding Form" from *Reading Miscue Inventory: Alternative Procedures* by Y.M. Goodman, D.J. Watson, and C.L. Burke. Copyright © 1987. Richard C. Owen Publishers, Inc., Katonah, NY. Reprinted with permission.

Box 4–1: "Retelling Profile" by Judy N. Mitchell and Pi A. Irwin. Printed by permission of the authors.

Figure 4–2: Figures adapted by permission from *Semantic Mapping: Classroom Applications* by J.E. Heimlich and S.D. Pittelman. Copyright © 1986 by the International Reading Association. All rights reserved. Reprinted by permission.

Box 6–5: "Home Letter Example" adapted from "Encouraging Parent Involvement Through Home Letters" by R.F. Flippo and J.A. Smith in *The Reading Teacher*, 44 (4). Copyright © 1990 by the International Reading Association. All rights reserved. Reprinted by permission.

Box 6–6: "Parent/Family Observation and Evaluation" adapted from "Working with Parents: Involving Parents in the Assessment Process" by A.D. Fredericks and T.V. Rasinski in *The Reading Teacher*, 44 (4). Copyright © 1990 by the International Reading Association. All rights reserved. Reprinted by permission.

A previous edition titled *Reading Assessment and Instruction: A Qualitative Approach to Diagnosis* was published by Harcourt, Inc. in 1997.

Library of Congress Cataloging-in-Publication Data
Flippo, Rona F.
    Assessing readers : qualitative diagnosis and instruction / Rona F.
Flippo.—2nd ed.
      p.   cm.
    Includes bibliographical references.
    ISBN 0-325-00373-4 (alk. paper)
    1. Reading—Assessment. 2. Reading. I. Title.

LB1050.46 .F55 2002
372.41—dc21   2002032875

Editor: Lois Bridges
Production service: Denise Botelho, Colophon
Production coordinator: Sonja S. Chapman
Cover design: Catherine Hawkes, Cat & Mouse
Compositor: TechBooks, Inc.
Manufacturing: Steve Bernier
Photographer: Tara R. Flippo

Printed in the United States of America on acid-free paper
07 06 05 04 03 RRD 1 2 3 4 5

To my family with love and appreciation . . .
my mother, Molly Fleig;
my husband and partner, Tyler Fox;
our daughter, Tara Flippo; our son Todd Graham and his wife Jenne;
and most of all to our wonderful grandbaby, Elena Graham,
whom we all love and cherish dearly and who is already a lover of books!

Elena Graham at seven months with author (Grandma).
Photo by Tyler Fox (Grandpa).

CONTENTS

PREFACE

This book is about reading assessment and instruction in the classroom. It is based on my previous publication, *Reading Assessment and Instruction: A Qualitative Approach to Diagnosis* (1997). Like its predecessor, it provides "the basics" for assessment and instruction, and supports the importance of the individual classroom teacher's knowledge, beliefs, decisions, and role. This new book is intended as a resource for classroom teachers as well as teachers taking certification, graduate, or in-service courses in reading assessment, diagnosis, and instruction.

Equally, it is the intention of *Assessing Readers* to facilitate the development of a **balanced perspective**—one that makes use of the most appropriate ideas from the various philosophies in the field of reading and literacy education—including many traditional assessment and instruction approaches, as well as many contemporary ideas relative to assessment, instruction, and learning (e.g., emergent literacy, cultural and sociocultural considerations, authentic assessment, performance assessment, schemata, metacognition, and portfolios). While many have called for changes in the focus of assessments, I believe these changes in focus must begin with what the teacher knows, believes, and does in her or his classroom. Teachers' understandings and decisions are the most important elements for change; teachers' decisions should be informed, but once made, they also should be valued. This book is dedicated to this idea and to classroom teachers.

The importance of including all **stakeholders,** most usually the children and their parents and families, in assessment and evaluation activities is emphasized throughout this book. Moreover, many of the ideas in it came from working with teachers, children, and their parents and families.

Teachers should find this book easy to understand and practical to use. It contains many specific assessment, instruction, and organization ideas and strategies. Additionally, it contains many suggested readings for those wanting more details or depth of coverage on specific topics. Accordingly, it should serve as a handy reference, resource, and idea book. Distinctive features include the following:

1. It has been developed specifically for the classroom teacher, rather than for the reading specialist, remedial teacher, or learning disabilities teacher.
2. It emphasizes qualitative rather than quantitative assessment.
3. It emphasizes assessment of students' skills, strategies, strengths, interests, motivations, use of cue systems, fluency, schemata, and metacognitive awareness, rather than ability levels.

4. It emphasizes individualization of instruction based on qualitative assessment so that students from all cultural and sociocultural backgrounds, and special learners, have opportunities to learn.

5. It is pragmatic and concise, rather than theoretical and abstract.

6. It offers a style that is easy to read and use, and includes such pedagogical features as:
   - bold-faced contextual definitions and a glossary of terms
   - a listing of focus and goal statements to open each chapter
   - "consider and react" opportunities throughout each chapter for reader interaction
   - questions for reflection and response at the end of each chapter.

7. It provides suggestions for further reading, with separate listings for professional readings and for referenced children's literature.

8. It offers full chapters devoted to such topics as
   - understanding standardized tests and scores, knowing what to look for, and explaining standardized test results to parents/families
   - assessing affective influences and linguistic strategies, including many sample assessments such as a classification scheme for emergent reading, interest/motivation/feelings assessments, informal reading inventories, miscue analysis and running records, fluency considerations, children's writing samples, and information from parents/families and other sources
   - assessing comprehension, metacognition, and other cognitive strategies, including many sample assessments such as retellings, cloze procedures, content reading inventories, and other assessments designed to sample prior knowledge, schemata, metacognition/comprehending strategies, and study skills and strategies
   - collecting assessment data (including use of portfolios and rubrics), analyzing all assessment results, and developing programs of instruction that build on students' existing skills and strategies (including two teacher-developed reports for in-depth purposes and needs)
   - assessing the context of instruction, organizing the classroom, and grouping to facilitate instruction and ongoing assessment (including flexible groupings and cooperative learning possibilities)
   - providing explicit, direct instruction based on assessments, with sample lessons developed by teachers, to enhance and scaffold specific skill and strategy development in word recognition and analysis, comprehension and metacognition, and study skills and strategies.

9. It contains an appendix of portfolio forms that, along with ideas for reflection, ongoing assessment, and organizing for instruction, can be photocopied and used by classroom teachers.

10. Overall, it emphasizes

    - concern for classroom teachers and *all* their students
    - concern for culturally and language diverse learners, and other diverse learners
    - the idea that assessing and teaching are the teacher's responsibilities, and should be done within the context of instruction that the teacher designs
    - practical applications from miscue analysis, and other error analysis possibilities (such as running records) to look at children's reading strategies
    - how students' writing and invented spellings can provide more information about their linguistic and cognitive strategies
    - how portfolios, rubrics, other assessments, and record-keeping ideas can be fashioned to fit the classroom teacher's philosophy and organization
    - how to involve children and their families in assessment, planning, and evaluation
    - how explicit, direct instruction can support development of skills and strategies
    - how selected ideas from various philosophies can be pulled together and utilized by the classroom teacher to form her or his own "balanced perspective," without a need for jargon or labeling.

Assessing Readers aims to encourage the use of information and assessment opportunities from all sources and to inform instruction in the classroom. Its purpose, above all, is to empower its readers and to cause them to think about and value their assessment and instruction choices. One way to make optimal use of this book and the pedagogical aids throughout would be to keep a journal for responses to the "Consider and React" boxes within each chapter. You could also record or discuss your answers and reflections to the "Questions for Reflection and Response" at the end of each chapter with other teachers. Additionally, difficult-to-remember glossary terms and definitions, important chapter focus and goal statements, and suggested readings of particular interest or relevance to the reader can be easily noted for future reference and review.

ACKNOWLEDGMENTS

Numerous individuals have made important contributions to the development of this book. Many of my former students and the classroom teachers with whom I have worked (and from whom I have learned so much) are included and indexed as authors of assessments, skill and strategy lessons, and other ideas in this book. Less visible, perhaps, but equally valuable and appreciated, are the contributions made by many others—among them, Glen Barrett, Jill Black, Ellyn Bourque, Deborah Gregson, Andrea Hall, Migdalia Irizarry, Denise Kalemba, Lisa Fournier Kowaleski, Sovannavy Lim, Robin Murphy, Demetri Orlando, Amy Pottle, Sharon Provencher, Cindy Seferovic, and Trisia Spinney; all of these generously contributed their input to the appendix and the chapters. Special thanks are appropriately due to Denise Kalemba for her meritorious assistance updating the references throughout and for her feedback on the materials in the "Consider and React" and "Questions for Reflection and Response" sections.

Todd Graham of the Minnesota Department of Economic Security developed the data displays to accompany the standardized test examples in Chapter 2 and some of the materials in the appendix as well. Tara Flippo deserves special recognition for the book's wonderful photographs. Thanks also go to Glen Barrett, John Gaumond, and Marcia Haimila at the McKay Campus School, Fitchburg State College and Rosemary Agoglia at The Common School in Amherst, Massachusetts, who let us take photographs in their classrooms; to Tara Flippo and Ron Elbert for developing many of the graphic displays and sample charts in this book; to Ron Elbert for manuscript preparation and editing assistance; and to Tyler Fox for lending his editorial expertise, as well as photographing the priceless image of our grandbaby Elena appearing on the dedication page.

I would also like to extend special thanks to Diane E. Bushner, Salem State College; Kathleen L. Daly, Professor Emeritus, University of Wisconsin, River Falls; Edward J. Dwyer, East Tennessee State University; Marilyn G. Eanet, Rhode Island College; Jacqueline L. Finn, Clark University; Diane L. Lowe, Framingham State College; Richard A. Thompson (retired), University of Central Florida; and June T. Young, Alabama A & M University—all of whom provided insightful suggestions on the teacher-developed assessment ideas and skill/strategy lessons; to Jacqueline Finn, again, for her many children's literature suggestions; to John Gaumond and Marcia Haimila for their help with writing samples; and to Olga Cortés, bilingual teacher at Reingold School, Fitchburg, Massachusetts, for her expertise.

I also owe a debt of gratitude to Jay R. Campbell of the Center for Assessment of Educational Progress, Educational Testing Service, for his assistance in helping me use the

NAEP data; to the staff of International Reading Association for its expert assistance; to Tim Blair, University of Central Florida; Michael McKenna, Georgia Southern University; Alden Moe, Lehigh University; and June Young, Alabama A & M University, whose reviews and input contributed in no small way to giving the contents of this book a better overall balance.

I would, finally, be remiss in not acknowledging the help provided by my wonderful editor, Lois Bridges, and the publishing team at Heinemann for their hard work and their dedication to producing quality educational materials—especially Sonja Chapman and Denise Botelho who brought this book to life using their combined production expertise. Nor could I leave out mention of the help provided me by the Graduate Studies Office at Fitchburg State College with some of the typing expenses for this book. Thank you all.

Rona F. Flippo

PART ONE

ASSESSMENT AND ANALYSIS IN THE CLASSROOM

CHAPTER 1

THE CLASSROOM TEACHER'S ROLE

Focus and Goals of the Chapter

- To provide a general overview of classroom assessment
- To demonstrate the importance of linguistic experience
- To demonstrate the importance of cognitive experience
- To show the power of affective, cultural, and sociocultural influences on the child
- To differentiate between qualitative and quantitative data
- To show the importance of the classroom teacher as a decision maker who will decide what to assess and how to assess it.

Introduction

Classroom teachers must make many decisions as they plan their instructional programs. These decisions will be based on their beliefs of what should be taught and how it should be done, tempered with information from teacher education courses and workshops, professional readings and meetings, teaching experiences, and their own unique classroom situations and demands. This is to be valued. Just like the individual children we teach, classroom teachers are individuals and must be respected to make appropriate decisions. This book is dedicated to that idea.

This chapter presents the importance of the teacher's role in the reading and broader literacy assessment process. One series of decisions that teachers must make relates to what and how they will test or assess children for reading instruction. This chapter discusses aspects of this assessment and decision-making process and describes some areas teachers should consider as they review assessment options. These areas include **linguistic experience** (a child's experience with language), **cognitive experience** (a child's existing knowledge and related experience), **strategy use** (how a child seems to go about trying to figure out a word or the meaning of something the child has read, or how to do an assignment), and **affective influences** (the child's interests, motivations, attitudes, and self-image). All of these areas are also influenced by individual **cultural and sociocultural considerations** (unique qualities, lifestyles, and values). Additionally, teachers will have to devise or select tests or procedures to make assessments of these and other selected areas. This chapter addresses these considerations and suggests a model for the classroom teacher's important decision-making role.

In order to avoid confusion regarding the use of terms, the words *testing* or *reading test(s)* will be synonymous in this book with *assessing* and *reading assessment(s)*. Classroom teachers should be aware, however, that assessment is generally thought of as a much broader term than testing. In fact, assessment encompasses testing but also includes all the informal as well as more formal procedures and observations that teachers use to inform their teaching.

What Is Assessment?

The term **assessment** includes all observations, samplings, and other informal and formal, written, oral, or performance-type testing that a teacher might do in order to gather information about a child's abilities, interests, motivations, feelings, attitudes, strategies, skills, and special cultural or sociocultural considerations. As it relates to reading and other literacy areas, assessment enables a teacher to gather meaningful information (or **data**) concerning or impacting the child's reading of school-related research and assignments, as well as recreational materials. Assessment is an ongoing process and should involve multiple sources, including, but not limited to, the teacher's, students' and parents'/families' observations and efforts. Finally, assessment goes hand in hand with instruction and learning. As teachers teach, they observe and accommodate for students, as well as continually assess and reflect on children's development. As children learn, they self-assess and reflect on their work and their developing strategies. (More discussion regarding the multiple dimensions of valid, fair, and equitable assessment is provided in *Standards for the Assessment of Reading and Writing,* 1994, the publication of the joint Task Force on Assessment sponsored by the International Reading Association [IRA] and the National Council of Teachers of English [NCTE].)

Evaluation involves making use of assessment information to make judgments about the quality of children's work and performance. Evaluation is a natural follow-up to assessment. When we assess over time, we analyze and evaluate the information gathered and observed, and we begin to draw conclusions and make decisions based on that information. Like assessment, evaluation needs to be flexible, reflective, and ongoing so that we are always willing to learn more about students, formulating new judgments and opinions as students develop and learn. In this book the term **analysis** will be used to indicate an open, flexible, reflective, and ongoing type of evaluation process.

Assessment and analysis can be done in so many ways, both formally and informally. In fact, most teachers do assessment and analysis all the time. For instance, when Tara is seen rubbing her eyes while reading, and moving a book closer to her face, the teacher observes, assesses, and decides that Tara might have a vision problem. Or, when Todd is observed looking out the window, yawning, and otherwise looking uninterested whenever the science book is being read, the teacher assesses and concludes that Todd doesn't seem interested in science or, at least, isn't motivated by that science book. Likewise, when the teacher observes Molly reading one word at a time and making tremendous efforts to pronounce each sound in each word, the teacher assesses and analyzes that Molly relies heavily on her phonics decoding strategies. These assessments, though informal and observational, can be just as useful as teacher-made written assessments. For instance, the written test of matching phonic sounds with pictures of objects representing those sounds also may indicate that Molly knows her phonics. Or, the science test covering a recently assigned chapter of the text might indicate that Todd didn't understand the chapter or didn't read it.

Of course, all assessments can miss certain information, and not all assessments are necessarily excellent or even good. For example, perhaps Todd is extremely interested in science, but is turned off by just reading about it in a textbook; for him, doing science hands-on through experiments and other work is best. While the previous examples about Todd (observational and written) indicate a problem with science, the teacher may draw an incomplete or inaccurate evaluation from the data collected because each assessment missed some of what was involved. Would a more formal, standardized assessment have told the teacher more? Maybe, but probably not everything. For instance, at the end of the first half of the school year, suppose the teacher gave Todd a standardized test covering the first half-year of the science curriculum used by the school district for fourth graders. What would the teacher find? Perhaps that Todd wasn't familiar with the topics already covered, but that still doesn't help her figure out why Todd doesn't know the material or help her do a better job of teaching him science.

The point is that teachers need to do many assessments of all kinds to find out what they particularly want to find out about children's abilities, strategies, skills, interests, and motivations. Teachers also need to be open and reflective concerning the assessment information they collect; new information can change the analysis or conclusions reached. Additionally, teachers are making assessments all the time, some planned and many unplanned. No one assessment is likely to give a teacher all the necessary information. No one kind of assessment is probably best or worst. However, professional classroom teachers, who are good decision makers, can design or plan assessments to purposefully find out what they want to find out, if they can first identify the areas or things they wish to assess.

What Should Be Assessed?

This is the big question! In the first paragraph of this chapter, the point was made that classroom teachers will make decisions regarding what they want to teach or emphasize in their classrooms based on their knowledge, experience, and situations. Once teachers know what they want to teach or emphasize, then they can plan how to assess it. Remember, first decide "what," and then you will be able to design "how." Later in this chapter, "A Model for the Classroom Teacher's Decision Making" is presented to help you chart your own course.

Teachers also should consider the following areas that impact children's reading.

Linguistic Experience and Strategies

Linguistic experience, or a child's experience with language, includes all aspects of language development and acquisition: listening, speaking, print awareness, writing, and reading. Children develop their language or linguistic experiences from birth on. A baby learns to identify certain phrases produced by his mother or other caregiver as having meaning: "Are you wet? Here, let me change you." Invariably these phrases lead to a dry diaper and comfort. Or the baby cries and learns that his cries lead to being fed. Later, when the nine-month-old makes certain sounds, like "ma-ma," he's rewarded with his mother's smile and such words as "That's good! Here's ma-ma! Say ma-ma again!" Later, certain print or symbols identify good things to eat. Logos for Burger King, Carvel, or a favorite kind of cookie are easy to spot. (Note, this **environmental print,** or the words on objects and places in our environment, seems to be all around us as we move through our daily lives, routines, and activities.) Mommy leaves a note for Grandma, in case she comes over while we are at the store. When Mother takes a shopping list to the store and refers to it to see what groceries to buy, some of the symbols mean a favorite box of cereal is purchased. At bedtime, the book Mother reads has words on each page; as she turns the pages, a story is told. The young child understands the story because it fits the familiar syntax (structure or phrasing of language), semantic (meaning of language), and phoneme-grapheme (sound and look of language) relationships he has been hearing, speaking, and becoming aware of (in written communications) since birth.

This linguistic experience is powerful. When children begin school they come to kindergarten or first grade with considerable linguistic experience. The classroom teacher can assess to what extent a child is using various linguistic experience or strategies by observing the child read, write, and speak. In Chapter 3, more information will be introduced to help classroom teachers with this assessment, but for now, linguistic experience is suggested as an area it makes sense to assess.

Consider and React 1–1

Consider the following short paragraph, "The Marlup and His Prudat," which was developed as a spin-off of a nonsense story first presented by Kenneth Goodman (1977). This little paragraph illustrates the importance of linguistic experience. Even though it contains nonsense words, your own linguistic experience with English syntax, semantics, and phoneme-grapheme relationships should help you make some sense of it. After you read the paragraph, try answering the literal comprehension questions that follow. How did you do?

The marlup was poving his frump. He was querving very grungy and felt charaffed. Why must things be like grift, he queried himself? Just last gruen I didn't have this prudat. Now I can't robun or zipdig anything.

1. What did the marlup pove?
2. How was the marlup querving?
3. How did the marlup feel?
4. What did the marlup query himself?
5. When didn't the marlup have this prudat?
6. What is the marlup's prudat?

Compare your answers to the answers that follow. You most likely will find that your answers are "correct" because your abilities with linguistic strategies helped you make some sense of this paragraph. The nonsense words that you did not know are comparable to words that your students may not recognize. They, like you, might be able to use **syntax** (structure/phrasing), **semantic** (meaning), and **phoneme-grapheme** (sound and sight, also referred to as graphophonic) clues and strategies to make sense of their reading, even when there are unknown words in the text or story. This is because a person's linguistic experience has a large impact on his or her reading abilities.

Answers to Comprehension Questions on "The Marlup and his Prudat":

1. The marlup poved his frump.
2. He was querving very grungy.
3. He felt charaffed.
4. "Why must things be like grift?" he queried himself.
5. Just last gruen he didn't have this prudat.
6. The marlup's prudat is that he can't robun or zipdig anything. (Or, you might have answered, "The marlup's prudat is his 'problem.'" If you tried to derive a real meaning from this paragraph and answered the question inferentially, you might have guessed that the nonsense word "prudat" sounds and looks [using phoneme-grapheme strategies] similar to the real word "problem." It also makes sense in the text when you substitute it for the word "problem" [using your semantic strategies]. The sentence also remains grammatically correct [using your syntax strategies] when "problem" is substituted for "prudat." In other words, you might have used all of your available linguistic experience and strategies to attempt to make real sense of this paragraph. Your students can do the same when they encounter unknown words if they have good use of their linguistic strategies. Later, you will learn how to assess and analyze this use.)

Cognitive Experience and Strategies

Cognitive experience, or a child's existing or prior knowledge and related experience, includes vicarious experiences (from stories told by others, movies, videos, books, magazines, television, advertisements, and other media) and real life experiences (from real family experience and activities, travel and outings, and other personal experiences and influences). All of these experiences, combined with other prior knowledge, are, conceptualized by an individual into his or her **schema** (**schemata** is the plural of schema) for a given idea, topic, concept, event, person, or thing. In other words, when Anna hears or reads the word "prejudice," her schema (mental picture and mental organization of the information relative to what she knows about "prejudice") is based on all of her cognitive experience with "prejudice." Therefore, someone else's schema for "prejudice" (e.g., Michael's) might be quite different from Anna's. Because cognitive experience varies so much from individual to individual, it must be seriously considered by classroom teachers.

Children interpret information and ideas they read or hear about in school differently from each other and, perhaps, from what an author or teacher might have intended. These differing understandings usually are the result of different cognitive experiences.

Consider and React 1–2

Mrs. Fox, a fourth-grade teacher, is doing a unit on nutrition. In order to develop interest in the unit and to ascertain what the children already know about nutrition, Mrs. Fox asks each child to make one list of all the good/nutritious foods he or she can think of and another list of bad/unhealthy foods. Note the lists made by Jackie and Bobbi. What is your reaction to these lists?

Jackie's Lists:
Good/Nutritious Foods

     meat

     potatoes

     bread

     cheese

     butter

     vegetables

     fruit

     ice cream

     cereal

     eggs

Bad/Unhealthy Foods

     potato chips

     soda pop

     cake

     candy

     cookies

     pizza

Bobbi's Lists:
Good/Nutritious Foods

     vegetables

     fruit

     beans

     meat

potatoes

rice

Bad/Unhealthy Foods

cheese

butter

white bread

cereal

eggs

ice cream

sugar

As you can see, both students made quite different lists. Is one right and the other wrong? Or should their lists be regarded as neither right nor wrong, but instead, as representative of each child's schema for healthy and unhealthy foods based on his or her own cognitive experience? Mrs. Fox will need to consider Jackie's and Bobbi's (and all the other children's) cognitive experiences as she assigns readings and other work in the nutrition unit.

Consider and React 1–3

Sometimes a child may not have a schema for a given idea or topic. This will make it difficult for the child to comprehend information read about that idea or topic. Below is an adaptation from a newspaper article borrowed from Brian Cambourne that illustrates the problem. See how much you understand, then react to the questions that follow it.

KENDALL IN DIRE STRAITS

Kendall was in dire straits against St. Andrew. The opening pair who had been stroking the ball with beautiful fluency on past occasions were both out for ducks. Once again the new ball pair had broken through. Then Yarrow turned on surprising pace and moving the ball off the seam beat Mathie twice in one over. Niland viciously pulled Fraser into the gully but was sent retiring to the pavilion by a shooter from Cochrane.

Brownlee in the slips and Tweddle at silly mid-on were superb and Stewart bowled a maiden over in his first spell. Rothery took his toll with three towering sixes but Lawson had little to do in the covers.

Conder was dismissed with a beautiful yorker and Brownlee went from a brute of a ball. Williams was disappointing. The way he hung his bat out to the lean-gutted Croft was a nasty shock. The rout ended when Melba dived at silly leg and the cry of "Ow's that!" echoed across the pitch.

Do you know what that was about? Were there any clues that gave you some ideas? If you didn't understand it, maybe you lack a schema for the topic. In other words, your cognitive experience does not include this topic. Therefore, even though you are an intelligent person and a good reader, you could not read and understand a fairly simple newspaper article. Your students might have the same problem understanding reading materials that require a schema they may not have or one that isn't fully developed. By the way, the original article was from an Australian newspaper's sports section and was about a game of cricket. You may have thought it was about some kind of ball game. If so, you used your existing schemata for various ball games to ascertain that, although this was an unfamiliar game, it somewhat fit the schema for other games you know. Of course, most Australians would have a schema for cricket and would have little trouble understanding the article.

So where does that leave you? What does this have to do with teacher decision making? Hopefully, you will agree that cognitive experience and children's schemata for various things they read or study about in your classroom are important and should be assessed and considered. In Chapter 4, suggestions for assessing cognitive experience and strategies will be made.

Affective Influences

Affective influences include children's attitudes, interests, feelings, needs, and motivations. This area is extremely important. Most teachers are aware of the need to motivate children, generate their interest, and keep them interested and motivated in the subject or topic under study. But before we can appeal to children's interests and motivations, it is first necessary to ascertain what they are. Each of us is unique. Each is motivated by different things and different needs. Certainly, not everyone in a heterogeneous group of people will be interested in the same things. Because individual interests and needs can be very powerful in motivating us to read and learn, classroom teachers must find out about their students' attitudes, interests, feelings, needs, and motivations. Chapter 3 presents several ideas for doing this.

Cultural and Sociocultural Influences

While each area previously described is important to the reading process, each is also strongly influenced by an individual's cultural and sociocultural background.

For example, if a child grows up in a home where American English is not the first language and culture, the child's linguistic and cognitive experience may be noticeably different from that of the author of his textbook. This would affect the ease with which the child could handle the syntax of the text, as well as the semantic and cognitive cues. In the marlup example, we could make sense of the piece because it was written to model the structure of English syntax. But if our primary language was Spanish, our familiar syntax would be different and we would not be able to rely as much on our previously developed syntax strategies to help us. Certain references in textual material are easier to understand because we can use our semantic strategies and cognitive strategies to figure them out. But if we grew up in a culture different from the author, we might not "get" the meaning clues. Or, we might not have the schema to understand the information presented (remember the cricket excerpt).

Sociocultural factors also greatly influence such affective areas as attitudes, interests, and motivations. Expectations are often very different in different sociocultural groups. If a child's environment de-emphasizes reading as opposed to other activities, such as working, housekeeping, farming, using computers, or playing music or sports, then the teacher must take this into consideration. Overall, a child's cultural and sociocultural background will have an effect on his linguistic, cognitive, and affective attributes. These are all part of the uniqueness and individuality of each person. This uniqueness is something to be appreciated and savored, not changed. However, teachers need to plan assessment and instruction to fairly evaluate and work with each child in their classrooms so that each child is given maximum opportunities and encouragement to succeed. The **cultural difference paradigm** (Banks, 1999) supports the idea of teachers using strategies that are consistent with children's cultural characteristics, showing respect for their cultures, lifestyles, and values. This is very different from a paradigm that views children from certain cultures and socioeconomic groups as deprived and in need of having certain deficiencies corrected.

How Can It Be Done?

That is precisely what this book is all about: sharing with classroom teachers ideas about how reading assessment can be done in their own classrooms, by themselves, without interfering or coming into conflict with their individual beliefs, without taking time away from teaching, and with an instructional approach in mind. The focus is that this classroom assessment is ongoing, it can be done as part of instruction, and in fact it should drive further instruction, which in turn drives further assessment.

Qualitative Data Versus Quantitative Data

Teachers can be inundated with all kinds of data as they review children's cumulative files and standardized test results, observe children as they read and do classroom work, and otherwise teach and assess children. Just as classroom teachers must decide what to teach, and later how to assess children in these selected areas, they also must decide what data are most valuable to analyze and consider. Once again, the teacher's role as decision maker is of utmost importance.

Most of the data that teachers have available to them can be divided into two categories: qualitative and quantitative. **Qualitative data** are data that emerge based on studying the "quality" of children's responses and their work. These data samples often are based on more **informal assessments,** including observations, interviews, and samplings. These samples and analyses tend to be more **process-oriented.** In other words, there is more interest in the skills/strategies, approaches, and processes children use as they read, write, and do their assignments than on the number right or wrong. These samples also tend to contain **naturalistic data,** or data that have emerged from authentic reading, writing, and assignments, and from other real classroom study and work.

On the other hand, **quantitative data** are data that emerge based on counting or extrapolating from the "quantity" of children's correct responses. These data samples often are based on more **formal assessments,** including standardized tests, basal workbooks and tests, and teacher-made objective tests dominated by multiple choice, true/false, and other questions to which there is one correct or acceptable answer. These samples and analyses tend to be more **product-oriented.** In other words, there is more interest in the outcomes, and the number right or wrong, than in the strategies, approaches, or processes children use as they read and do these tests and other assignments. These data collections tend to be more contrived and less naturalistic, since the data usually are collected from test results, as opposed to more informal authentic classroom reading and work.

Assessment Decisions?

Obviously, assessment decisions and subsequent data analysis decisions that affect classroom instruction must be made. What many teachers may not have realized, however, is that these classroom decisions are still almost completely in their hands. Even though your school system probably requires that you give certain standardized tests or basal tests, you must make the ultimate decisions regarding how much you actually use the data from these assessments and to what extent you use other assessments to plan for, group, and otherwise instruct children in reading and reading-related activities.

Your decisions will be based on your professional knowledge and beliefs. You are in the position of selecting and acting on your decisions. Just as other professionals do in their respective fields, you must practice the teaching profession as you see fit within the parameters of acceptable practice and behavior. For example, medical doctors are often inundated with information—from the profession, the insurance providers, and research at large, along with information or data about individual patients. Their decisions to prescribe medication, further assessments, physical therapy, acupuncture, surgery, and so on, are based on the assessments and data they tend to rely on the most. In making decisions, doctors use not only their professional knowledge, but also their beliefs about what is most important and what should be emphasized. Some doctors might use certain data analyses to prescribe medication and continue to observe and monitor a patient, while others would recommend surgery. You, too, must make decisions based on your professional knowledge and beliefs. You will select and act on your decisions as determined by what you believe is best for the children in your classroom.

A Model for the Classroom Teacher's Decision Making

In order to help you make these necessary decisions, a decision-making question and flow chart is provided in Box 1–1. It has been designed to help you specify your beliefs regarding what should be emphasized in your classroom program as it relates to reading and reading-related development. The decisions you make will be tempered by what you have learned from teacher education courses, workshops, professional readings and meetings, experience, and your own unique classroom situations and students. Also, it is hoped that you might be influenced by some of the ideas presented in this book, as well as some of the suggested readings. Consider your options and chart your own course. By personally formulating and implementing your own assessment design, you will gain a sense of professional control over curriculum, assessment, and instruction. The extensive research of Hiebert and Calfee (1992) and others suggests that this informed and reflective approach to classroom teaching is highly desirable. The chapters that follow will help you assess, interpret and analyze, organize/group, and teach your students based on these decisions. Remember, too, that you, as a professional, have the option of modifying decisions as you see a need.

Consider and React 1–4

Review "A Model for the Classroom Teacher's Decision Making." What do you want to assess in your classroom? What do you want to teach or emphasize?

Box 1–1	A model for the classroom teacher's decision making
Question:	What should be assessed?
	Assessment Options
	Linguistic Experience and Strategy Use
	Cognitive Experience and Strategy Use
	Affective Influences
	Cultural and Sociocultural Influences
	Other Options: (Based on individual teacher's professional readings, courses, experiences, etc.)
Question:	What do I want to teach or emphasize in my classroom program as it relates to reading?
Answer:	These are the things (areas, skills, or strategies) that I believe are important and I want to emphasize, develop, and teach in my classroom:

Summary

This chapter has emphasized the importance of the classroom teacher's role in making instruction and assessment decisions. The emphasis also has been on respecting these decisions when they have been made as a result of the individual teacher's beliefs along with her knowledge of the available professional information. Important areas for consideration have been presented, including an overview of linguistic and cognitive experience and strategies and a look at affective influences on reading development. Each area is further influenced by cultural and sociocultural considerations. Finally, the classroom teacher is presented with a decision-making model and is encouraged to list and specify what he believes should be emphasized relevant to reading development and instruction.

Questions for Reflection and Response

1. What is assessment?
2. What should be assessed? Why?
3. What is meant by "qualitative data"? Cite examples from your experience.
4. What is meant by "quantitative data"? Cite examples from your experience.
5. What assessment questions should teachers ask? Why?
6. Which will you ask? Why?
7. How does a teacher make assessment decisions? What do these decisions reflect?

CHAPTER 2

UNDERSTANDING STANDARDIZED TESTS AND QUANTITATIVE DATA

Focus and Goals of the Chapter

- To provide a comprehensive overview of standardized tests and the quantitative data they yield
- To differentiate between the various broad categories of standardized tests and their scores
- To provide information concerning norms, validity, relevance, reliability, passage dependency, and prior knowledge considerations
- To demonstrate how norm-referenced scores are derived and what they show and do not show
- To explain some of the problems with using standardized tests and scores
- To demonstrate how teachers can discuss various criterion-referenced and norm-referenced test scores with parents and families.

UNDERSTANDING STANDARDIZED TESTS
AND QUANTITATIVE DATA

Introduction

In Chapter 1, a distinction was made between qualitative and quantitative data and assessments. To restate that distinction, qualitative data and assessments are more naturalistic, usually gathered and assessed by observing children's performance on authentic reading and writing and on other authentic classroom assignments. Analysis of these data tend to be more concerned with process and the quality of children's approaches and strategies. On the other hand, quantitative data and assessments focus more on the product, or the outcome, such as the number correct or the number wrong. Quantitative assessments are usually contrived—that is, collected from more formal tests rather than from classroom work.

Although many teachers may prefer qualitative measures, it is important that all classroom teachers thoroughly understand and can interpret quantitative tests. There are times when teachers will have to administer standardized and other quantitative measures to students. (**Standardized tests** are commercially prepared formal assessments that are to be given under prescribed conditions.) It is extremely important that teachers know the possible uses and limitations of the test results. It is also important that teachers know how to explain these results to parents and families.

Pikulski (1990b) indicates that although many of us find fault with standardized tests, it is not likely that they will disappear. In fact, he and others (e.g., Andersen, 1994; Strickland & Strickland, 1998; and Valencia & Wixson, 2000) cite evidence that standardized tests are being used now more than ever. Pikulski suggests that one productive thing we can do is to try to curtail some of the misuses and misinterpretations of these tests. If we must give these tests, by our own or by our school system's decision, then we must do our best to ensure that data on our students are not misused or misinterpreted.

The purpose of this chapter is to provide classroom teachers with a thorough, yet concise and easy-to-follow, overview of standardized tests and quantitative data associated with these tests. This overview will include the terminology that is essential to understanding test jargon and test manuals. It also includes a description of the most common types of commercial instruments, a discussion of test usage and applicability considerations, an explanation of the various scores derived from most standardized tests, a discussion of the problems associated with misuse of these tests, and, finally, some scenarios illustrating how to discuss standardized and other quantitative test results with children's parents and families.

Survey, Diagnostic, and Other Commercial Tests

Most commercial quantitative-product tests can be superficially divided into the categories of survey tests, diagnostic tests, and criterion-referenced tests. These are only superficial designations because, in reality, these tests are very similar and yield similar data. Their differences are more in the way they are marketed and in how the scores from the test results are derived, rather than in the tests themselves. Farr and Carey (1986) indicate that reading tests usually do not fall into neat, nonoverlapping categories because test publishers often attempt to develop tests that serve a wide range of uses. Also, test users often try to use a single test for many purposes, even for purposes for which the tests were not developed. Therefore, attempts to classify tests into categories may not be very helpful to consumers (p. 138). Keeping this in mind, readers of this book are given generic descriptions of the most widely mentioned categories and examples pertinent to the classroom teacher. Readers wanting details regarding the many available commercial tests are referred to Harp (2000) and a guide to reading assessments for English- and Spanish-speaking students published by the U.S. Department of Education, International Reading Association, and Health Communications, Inc. (2000). Additionally, Flippo and Schumm (2000) should be consulted for reviews of standardized tests for high school and college-age students. It is also a good idea to consult the latest editions of the best-known authority and reviewer of tests, *The Mental Measurements Yearbook,* which reviews the most current editions of available standardized tests in various disciplines (e.g., see Plake & Impara, 2001). These publications provide a review of specific reading tests, including commercial quantitative-product tests discussed in this chapter, as well as some commercial qualitative informal assessments discussed in the next chapter.

Survey tests are usually marketed as more general tests that give information on a student's overall achievement in reading. Most survey tests have two or three **subtests,** or subparts, that most typically provide a vocabulary score, a comprehension score, and a rate score (usually the rate subtest is only on tests for older youngsters and adults) or instead, literacy concepts or letter-sound correspondence subtests for very young children. Then the subtest scores are averaged to give a student's **total reading score.** The subtest and total scores are based on the number correct. Various procedures are used to standardize and then **extrapolate derived scores** from the number correct. (Extrapolation involves inferring an unknown score from a known score. Derived scores refer to scores—such as percentile ranks, grade equivalents, and stanines—that have been developed or "derived" from raw scores.) Most survey tests come with instructor manuals showing the norm-referenced scores derived from each raw score. (*The Gates-MacGinitie Reading Tests* [MacGinitie, MacGinitie, Maria, & Dreyer, 2000] are widely acknowledged examples of this type of test.)

Commercially developed diagnostic tests can include the more formal group-administered, quantitative product-oriented standardized tests (discussed in this chapter), as well as some of the informal, individually administered commercial assessments (discussed in Chapter 3). (**Diagnostic tests** are designed to assess strengths and weaknesses.) The group quantitative standardized tests are similar to the survey tests previously described. The main difference is that instead of reporting scores on only two or three subtests, the diagnostic tests often have more subtests or report various **item clusters** (groups of items measuring specific objectives) and subcluster scores within subtests, thus providing a more "diagnostic" report of measured test objectives. For instance, rather than reporting just a vocabulary subtest score, the diagnostic test might subdivide the vocabulary score report into clusters, such as listening vocabulary and reading vocabulary, and then further break this down into subcluster information on recognizing word parts, synonyms, relationships among words, and content-area words. These tests usually are marketed as providing more in-depth information about a student's specific reading strengths and weaknesses. However, just like survey tests, the standardized diagnostic tests give little or no information regarding how a student actually goes about reading, or what specific strategies he uses to figure out unknown words or make sense of a piece of literature. (The *Stanford Diagnostic Reading Test* [Karlsen & Gardner, 1995] is a well-known example of this type of test.)

The third commercial test to be discussed is often called a **criterion-referenced test**, although to be more accurate, it should be called a survey or diagnostic test that yields criterion-referenced scores rather than norm-referenced scores. The criterion-referenced test, when developed, really looks similar to survey and diagnostic tests, as previously described. The main difference is that the test developers base the scores for passing the tests on comparisons of students' scores to certain predetermined "criteria," rather than by comparing students' scores to a norm group's scores. This means that if a state, school system, or basal program decides that a passing score for knowledge of word parts or for vocabulary is eighteen correct out of twenty responses, then each student's word parts or vocabulary score will be compared to this criterion. Students who get an eighteen, nineteen, or twenty on the subtest will pass. Students who get a seventeen or less will not.

Criterion-referenced tests are very marketable. Publishing companies and independent testing contractors have "sold" the idea that these tests are better because they can be designed to meet the specific curriculum that a state, school system, or basal series would like to measure. Millions of dollars have been spent to come up with appropriate objectives and items to measure these specific curricula. The reality is that most of these objectives and items look very much the same as the objectives, items, and specifications for the survey and diagnostic tests these criterion-referenced tests are designed to replace. Criterion-referenced tests, like the survey and diagnostic tests previously described, are product-oriented. They are not designed to look at the process children use to read. No information is provided in their scores to tell teachers what strategies children are using to make sense of their reading.

Norm-Referenced Scores

Norm-referenced scores are test scores that have been derived from the quantitative results of standardized survey, achievement, or diagnostic tests by comparing a student's raw score to the derived raw scores of the norm group. (The **norm group** is the group to which your students' scores will be compared.) When the norm group's average raw score on a test or subtest is higher than the raw score of an individual child, the child's derived norm-referenced score will tend to be lower. When the norm group's average raw score on a test or subtest is lower than the raw score of an individual child, the child's derived norm-referenced score will tend to be higher. If a child's raw score is exactly the same as the averaged raw score of the norm group, the child's derived norm-referenced score will be average or "on grade level" or "at age level" or "at the 50th percentile rank."

Two questions probably occur to you: "Who is in the norm group the children I teach will be compared to?" And, "How are these derived norm-referenced scores developed?" These are important questions—questions classroom teachers need answered in order to understand the real meaning and implications of using and interpreting **norm-referenced tests.** These questions will be thoroughly addressed in upcoming sections.

Criterion-Referenced Scores

As previously mentioned, **criterion-referenced scores** are test scores that have been determined from the quantitative results of commercially prepared tests by comparing a student's **raw score** (number correct) to the predetermined passing score for the test/subtest. When a child's number correct is lower than the predetermined passing score, the child does not meet the criterion and does not pass the test. When a child's number correct is the same as or higher than the predetermined passing score, the child meets the criterion and passes. The question that probably occurs to you is "Who sets the criterion to which the children I teach will be compared?" This is an important question, and it will be answered in this section.

The test developers set the criteria for tests they develop, usually in consultation with committees or groups of teachers and administrators who plan to use the test. Test developers for criterion-referenced score tests can include basal reading program publishers, as well as test development contractors. These developers attempt to get consensus from the groups they work with regarding what should be tested and how many correct answers indicate minimum competency. Once consensus is reached, a **cut-off score** and passing score is determined for a particular test. This score becomes the criterion that your students must reach in order to successfully pass the test. Because criterion-referenced scores are fairly simplistic and easy to understand, most of the rest of this chapter is devoted to understanding norm-referenced test development and scores. However, in the sections "Understanding the Problems with Standardized Tests and Their Scores" and "How to Discuss These Test Results with Children's Families," there is more discussion, particularly relating to criterion-referenced measures.

Understanding Test Usage and Applicability

It is likely that classroom teachers will be required to give students standardized tests. It is also likely that classroom teachers will be asked to record the results of these tests. Therefore, it is important that classroom teachers understand how these tests were normed, the assumptions that underlie many aspects of test development, and the terminology frequently associated with evaluating the worthiness of many standardized and commercial tests. The sections that follow provide the basic information that a classroom teacher will need to understand these areas.

Normative Considerations

Remember the previous question, "Who is in the norm group the children I teach will be compared to?" The answer is that test developers try to norm their tests using groups of children from a variety of geographic locations (including urban, suburban, and rural areas), socioeconomic groups, racial and ethnic groups, and so on. Why? If they do not make these attempts, their tests could be considered biased, invalid, and unfair. Just like other commercial enterprises, those who develop, publish, and market tests want to be competitive and to sell a quality product. But even with the best intentions and best test development procedures, it is virtually impossible for a test developer to norm a test on children exactly like those in your classroom. Your children are unique. They cannot be fairly compared to a hybrid mix of children from across the country.

Consider and React 2–1

Let's assume that you teach a third-grade class in a small New England city school system with a high dropout rate and a large population of Latino students and other students of color. You have been asked to give your class a reading test that was normed with the following populations: Twenty-five percent of the students are from a rural, midwestern, farm-belt school system, another 25 percent of the children come from inner-city schools in Los Angeles and New York City, another 25 percent of the children come from a suburban school system in the Southeast, 10 percent of the children come from a Native American reservation school in the Southwest, 10 percent of the children come from a school system in southern California with a high percentage of itinerant farmworkers' children, and 5 percent of the children come from an affluent neighborhood school system in the Northeast. The test publisher will give you the norms from a combination of this entire norming group. Or, the test publisher can give you the norms for any of these individual groups. Do you believe that a comparison of how this entire norm group did on the test, or a comparison between any of these groups and your individual class, would be a fair and accurate comparison?

Even if the norm group and your class are comparable, the norm data must be current. For example, a group tested in the 1970s might be very different from the same population tested today. When you are using a norm-referenced test in your classroom, be sure to read the test manual for teachers/test administrators and the technical manual to see exactly whom your children are being compared to and when the norming was done. Use this information to determine to what extent the norm-referenced scores are applicable to your own students.

Validity and Relevance Considerations

Reports of **test validity** have to do with "what a test is measuring." (Does it measure what it claims to measure?) A test is considered to have **validity** to the extent that it measures what the user is trying to measure. If a test measures the abilities, skills, strategies, and content that a program, school system, or teacher deems as important or relevant for student success, then the test is a valid measure. If other, extraneous variables are also being measured, the test's validity is weakened proportionately. A test cannot be considered valid unless it measures something explicitly relevant to the population being tested, and unless what is being measured is also relevant to the purpose of the testing. This is what is known as **content validity,** and it is the most important type of validity for the classroom teacher to be concerned with. A test that is not reliable cannot be considered valid. (Test reliability considerations are discussed in the next section.)

Flippo and Schumm (2000) point out that validity considerations should also include the extent to which a test is structured appropriately and the extent to which a test uses appropriate materials for the population and purposes of testing. The test format, test directions, item wording, length of passages, readability of passages, and content materials sampled must all be analyzed for the population to be tested and for the specific purposes of that testing. Farr and Carey (1986) emphasize that test use is the most important issue for the test consumer and that test validity can be considered only in relation to the test's actual use.

Although content validity is the most important validity for the classroom teacher's purposes, test developers use other terminology to describe different ways in which their tests are valid. Keep in mind that this different terminology describes different types of validity, usually indicative of different purposes for the same test. It is important to realize that test publishers might report only one or two types of validity for their tests. You cannot generalize one type of validity to another. But if you know why you are testing, what you are testing for, and the needs of the population being tested, you usually can determine the validity of a test for yourself, even when given limited information.

Brown (1983) classifies validity into three main groups:

1. **Criterion-related validity** is a predictive validity measure that involves correlating the test with an accepted index or criterion. The test score is important only in that it predicts a particular variable. An example of criterion-related validity is the use of a scholastic aptitude test to predict a college grade average.

Both **predictive validity** and **concurrent validity** are types of criterion-related validity that are often noted in test or technical manuals. They usually are reported with a validity coefficient. Most testing experts agree that a coefficient of .80 or above is acceptable.

2. Content validity is the most important validity for classroom teachers to be concerned with. True content validity is determined by a thorough analysis by a qualified judge to see whether the test samples what it purports to measure; the adequacy of the item sampling and other aspects of relevance also should be scrutinized. It is not reported with a validity coefficient. **Face validity** is sometimes confused with content validity. (Someone trying to determine face validity might ask: "Does this test look like it measures what it claims to measure?") Because face validity is determined by a more superficial examination of test content, testing experts do not give it much credibility.

3. **Construct validity** focuses on the relationship between the test and a specific trait. An example of construct validity is the development of a test to define a trait such as intelligence. **Congruent validity, convergent validity,** and **discriminant validity** are types of construct validity that are often noted in tests or technical manuals. Like content validity, there is no single quantitative index or validity coefficient of the construct validity of a test. Usually evidence of validity of this type is accumulated through studies of content and criterion-related validity.

Finally, classroom teachers are reminded that if they know what they are testing for, and if they know the skills, strategies, and other important areas they wish to examine, they can carefully review a test themselves to see whether that test has content validity for their own program and purposes. Even if an outside expert indicates a particular reading test has content validity, the teacher must still decide whether it has content validity or relevance for her classroom program. Reading experts, just like classroom teachers, often have different philosophies regarding what should be emphasized in a classroom or school reading program. Ms. Kessler's philosophy of reading might emphasize phonics, correct pronunciation of words, and knowledge of word parts and vocabulary, while Mrs. Galvez might believe strategy use and comprehension are of primary importance. A test with high content validity for Ms. Kessler's classroom program might not be relevant to Mrs. Galvez's program, and vice versa. A test should be both highly relevant and have high content validity for a teacher to really consider and use its results. Later in this chapter a list of questions you might want to consider when reviewing standardized tests for use in your classroom is included. These questions could be helpful to your determining the content validity and relevance of a particular test for your students and program.

Reliability Considerations

Reports of **test reliability** are actually reports of how consistently a test measures whatever it is measuring. This information is usually reported as a **reliability coefficient**. A test is considered to have **reliability** to the extent that the children's test scores are the same each time they take the test. The idea is that test administrators want to be assured that a child's test score is representative of how the child would do if she took the test again. (Reliability coefficients are statistically calculated with the assumption that no learning would take place between administrations and that children would not remember anything about the test when they retake it.) When a test is highly reliable, we are asked to assume that when we give the test, the results will be indicative of a child's performance rather than some "fluke" score. The **coefficient of stability** or a report of **test-retest reliability** is an indication of the test's stability of performance over time.

There are other types of reliability reported for most standardized reading tests. Some report the consistency of performance among various test items (**internal consistency reliability**). Others, like the **coefficient of equivalence**, report parallel or alternate form reliability so that test users can know what to expect if they use an alternate form of the same test.

No test can be one hundred percent reliable. There will always be some variability when you are dealing with human beings. However, the higher the reliability coefficient is for a test, the more confident you can be that the test is accurately measuring children's performance on its content. A reliability of .99 would indicate that a test was 99 percent reliable. Most reading authorities agree that a reliability of .90 or above is a good reliability coefficient, although it is not uncommon for reliabilities to range somewhere between .80 to .90 values. Teachers are warned, however, that even if a test is highly reliable, showing a high reliability coefficient, it may still not be valid for their students. Unless a test is measuring the appropriate skills, strategies, abilities, and content for the children being tested, the test is not indicative of anything.

Therefore, teachers must first determine whether a test has high content validity and relevance for their students. Then, if a test proves to have high content validity, teachers can look at the reliability coefficient to determine how much they can count on the results of the test. A standardized test for use in evaluating children should have high relevance, high validity, and high reliability.

Passage Dependency and Prior Knowledge Considerations

Two other related and important considerations for teachers when evaluating a reading test are passage dependency and prior knowledge considerations. If children can answer certain test items because of their previous knowledge or by the application of logic, rather than by just reading and understanding the passage, then the test items are considered **passage independent**—meaning that the ability to answer is not based on information in the passage alone. If children must read and understand a passage in order to correctly answer the test items, then the test items are considered **passage dependent**—meaning that reading and understanding the passage are essential to getting the items correct and that prior knowledge is not a consideration.

According to the more traditional testing and measurement perspective, developing test items that are passage dependent is desirable. In fact, when items are found to be passage independent, the validity of the test items and the test results are considered questionable. Reading researchers and teachers with this traditional perspective would probably not want children to correctly answer test questions based on their past experience or prior knowledge. They would believe that this approach defeated the purpose for testing reading and would argue that if test items were well developed, children would have to read and understand the test passage to correctly answer questions based on that passage.

On the other hand, other reading researchers (e.g., Johnston, 1984) and teachers would argue that it is desirable to allow prior knowledge to affect reading assessment. Likewise, the IRA and NCTE (1994) publication states: "To assert through a multiple choice test that a piece of text has only one meaning is unacceptable given what we know of language" (p. 10). Because of what we know about the importance of culture, language, schemata, and other prior knowledge and experience, many believe it is not possible to read and understand something without some schemata for the topic and without bringing in our own personal experience and information. Additionally, because readers do use many strategies when reading, it is considered undesirable to try to eliminate some of them (namely, schemata and prior knowledge) from a reading assessment.

Consider and React 2–2

What do you think? In your opinion, is it desirable to allow students' prior knowledge to affect reading assessment? Why or why not? Are there special circumstances when you would (or would not) want your assessments affected by prior knowledge? Why?

Test users must decide for themselves the importance of prior knowledge and the passage dependence issue as each relates to the measurement of reading comprehension. Teachers should try to learn as much as possible about any standardized test they have to use with their students. You can determine test item dependence or independence yourself by trying to answer comprehension items without first reading the test paragraph. If you cannot answer the questions correctly without reading the passage, the items are "passage dependent." If you can answer the questions correctly without reading the passage, the items are "passage independent." Depending on your philosophy, each can be considered undesirable or desirable. When you note students' test results in their cumulative folders or in correspondence or consultation with parents or other teachers, you might want to consider this passage-dependence or independence issue.

Understanding Derived Norm-Referenced Scores

In previous sections, norm-referenced scores were said to be derived scores, and there was discussion regarding the composition of norm groups. However, we still need an answer to the earlier question, "How are these derived norm-referenced scores developed?" This section answers this important question.

Once test publishers select questions and administration procedures for a test, and make arrangements with various schools and districts for the norming groups, the test is administered to the students in those norming groups. Teachers or representatives of the test publisher send the **raw data** (students' responses on their answer sheets with correct, incorrect, or unmarked responses bubbled in, along with information regarding the students' school, grade, date of birth, and the month of testing on each sheet) back to the publisher. These raw data are grouped, collated, regrouped, collated, and displayed in order to extrapolate various norm-referenced scores for the test. Although publishers report various norm-referenced scores in their test manuals, only the most common and frequently used ones are discussed in this section: percentile ranks, grade-level and age-level equivalent scores, and stanine scores.

Before we begin, let's set the stage for a very simplified, but generally accurate, scenario involving the development of norm-referenced scores for The Marion and Asher Reading Test with one hundred questions on it. This test is being normed for use in grades one through six. The publishers have arranged for norming groups from school systems in four regions with different socioeconomic groups. Ideally, teachers or representatives of the publisher spend a good part of one school year gathering the raw data for the test's norming. Here is a description of norming in one school district in a suburban, middle-income area in southern California. This norming activity would supposedly be going on at the same time in the other selected school districts around the country.

In September, all children in the first month of first grade in schools A and B in this southern California district are given The Marion and Asher Reading Test. There are approximately seventy-five first graders in each school, so raw data have been gathered for 150 children in the first month of first grade.

At the same time, all second graders in schools A and B are given the test. There are also approximately seventy-five second graders in each school, so raw data have been gathered for 150 children in the first month of second grade. Also in September, while the publisher's representative is in schools A and B, she goes ahead and tests all third, fourth, fifth, and sixth graders with the same test, giving her raw data for children in the first month of grades three, four, five, and six.

In October, all children in the second month of the first grade in schools C and D take The Marion and Asher Reading Test. Also, children in second through sixth grades in schools C and D are given the test, providing raw data for the second month of school for each grade in these southern California suburban, middle-income schools.

This procedure continues. In November, the publisher's representative gathers the raw data for children in grades one through six from schools E and F; and in December and onward, raw data are gathered from other schools in this large school district. By the middle of June, data have been gathered for every month of school and for every grade for which The Marion and Asher Reading Test is being normed. (Theoretically, the publisher would not be able to test children in the same grade in the same school again, because that would mean the children would take the test more than once, invalidating the norming results. In reality, rather than doing all this time-consuming testing, some publishers take shortcuts and use statistical or other procedures to extrapolate data for some of the grade levels and some of the months of school. Of course, when they do this, the use of the data to make comparisons with children in your class is even more questionable.)

In the next sections, a simplified description of how the raw data are grouped, collated, and displayed illustrates how each of the most commonly used norm-referenced scores are derived.

Percentile Ranks

Percentile ranks are usually reported from 1 through 99. These ranks indicate students' relative positions in a group. When a future student's raw score is converted to a percentile rank, it provides information relative to how that student's raw score compared to the performance of the students in the norming group. For instance, a percentile rank of 50 for a future student on The Marion and Asher Reading Test means that the student's raw score is equal to or better than 50 percent of the norming group's raw scores.

When the test publisher scores and calculates the total raw scores of all the children who took The Marion and Asher Reading Test in the first month of first grade—six hundred in all from all their norming sites—the publisher will display the composite data from the highest to the lowest raw scores. (For an example, see the percentile rank display in Box 2–1.)

The highest raw score, of one first grader (in September) who got fifty-three correct answers out of a possible one hundred, is ranked as the highest for his or her norm group, at the 99-plus percentile rank. The lowest raw scores, of three first graders (in September) who got no correct answers out of a possible one hundred, are ranked as the lowest for their norm group, at the 1 percentile rank. Notice that a difference in one raw score point does not necessarily mean a 1 percentile difference or vice versa. This is because the scores are ranked only from highest to lowest; the difference between each score is not really a factor. For this reason, teachers cannot accurately use percentile ranks to show an increase in a student's reading skill performance.

| **Box 2–1** | The Marion and Asher Reading Test: Percentile norms for first graders in first month of school |

Raw Score	Students with This Score	Percentile Rank	Raw Score	Students with This Score	Percentile Rank
53	1	99+	26	23	73
52	0	99+	25	25	69
51	0	99+	24	28	65
50	1	99+	23	28	60
49	0	99+	22	30	55
48	0	99+	21	31	50
47	1	99+	20	31	45
46	0	99+	19	29	40
45	1	99	18	27	35
44	2	99	17	26	31
43	1	99	16	24	27
42	0	99	15	22	23
41	2	99	14	20	20
40	2	98	13	18	16
39	1	98	12	16	14
38	3	98	11	14	11
37	3	97	10	13	9
36	4	97	9	11	7
35	6	96	8	8	5
34	8	95	7	6	4
33	10	93	6	5	3
32	12	91	5	4	2
31	15	89	4	3	2
30	16	87	3	2	1
29	17	84	2	2	1
28	20	81	1	2	1
27	23	77	0	3	1

Percentile Rank Display

Keep in mind that if the publisher wishes to produce percentile ranks for all first graders (in September) from only suburban, middle-income communities, she would separately group, collate, and display the suburban, middle-income data from the rest of the first-grade (September) data, and do the percentile ranks on that. Thus, once the raw

Box 2–2	The Marion and Asher Reading Test: Grade equivalent norms—grade 1		
Raw Score	Grade Equivalent	Raw Score	Grade Equivalent
0–19	Below 1.0	27	1.6
20	1.0	28	1.6
21	1.1	29	1.7
22	1.2	30	1.7
23	1.3	31	1.8
24	1.3	32	1.8
25	1.4	33	1.9
26	1.5	34–100	2.0 and above
Grade Equivalent Display			

data are gathered, the publisher can regroup and produce various tables representating various demographics or groups.

Grade-Level and Age-Level Equivalent Scores

Grade-level equivalent scores are derived from the average raw scores of the children in the norming group who took the test in a particular month of school. The school year is divided into ten months. When first-graders participated in the norming of The Marion and Asher Reading Test, they were identified as being in the first (1.1) month of first grade (September), or in the second (1.2) month of first grade (October), or in the third (1.3) month of first grade (November), and so on, when they took the test. When the raw data were received and scored by the publisher, the raw scores for all first graders in the first month of school (1.1) who took the test were grouped, totaled, and averaged to identify an average raw score for the first grade, first month of school (1.1). That average raw score (or **mean**) becomes one of the scores to which children in your class could be compared. (See the grade equivalent display, [Box 2–2], for an example.)

As you can see, when the scores of the six hundred children in the first grade, first month who took The Marion and Asher Reading Test were averaged (the total of all the raw scores divided by six hundred), we find the average raw score to be twenty-one. This number will be displayed and charted by the publisher as the score associated with the 1.1 grade-equivalent reading level. (Notice that in Figure 2–1, relatively few students, just thirty-one out of the six hundred who took the test, actually had that score.) It should also be pointed out that this derived score, just like all the others described in this section, is only as valid as the comparison (norm) group from which it was derived is a valid comparison group for a child in your class, and then only valid for the particular test for which it was normed. Theoretically, the publisher uses the same totaling and averaging method to derive a norm-referenced grade-equivalent score for 1.2, 1.3, 1.4, and so on, as well as for 2.1, 3.1, 4.1, 5.1, 6.1, and so on, or the publisher might simply extrapolate some of them.

When the children in your class—let's say it's the third grade—take The Marion and Asher Reading Test, their individual raw scores could be compared to the table of grade equivalents produced by the publisher who normed the test. For instance, a third grader (we'll call her Robin) who gets a relatively low score could be designated as getting the same raw score as the average raw score of the norming group whose members were in first grade, first month (1.1) when they took the test. Does that mean that Robin is reading at a first-grade, first-month level? One would hope that no one would interpret it as such. Robin may have gotten the same raw score as the average raw score of the members of the norming group who took The Marion and Asher Reading Test when they were in the first month of first grade, but that is all you can say. Robin is not reading at 1.1 level. Actually, nothing about grade-equivalent scores can give you any real indication of a child's so-called "reading level." In fact, because grade-equivalent scores were so often misused and incorrectly interpreted by teachers, administrators, parents, policymakers, and the general public, the International Reading Association issued a statement in 1981 regarding their misuse and urged schools, teachers, and publishers not to use them. Unfortunately, these scores continue to be misused and incorrectly interpreted. (See Box 2–3.)

Age-level equivalent scores are derived and used very much like grade-equivalent scores. The main difference is that the norm group's raw data is regrouped and displayed by the age (in years and months) of the children in the norm group, as opposed to the grade and month of school. For example, the raw scores of all children who were six years and one month old when they took The Marion and Asher Reading Test would be grouped together, the scores totaled, and the total score averaged (divided by the number of children who were six years and one month old). That score would be reported on a table as the average of the raw scores of all children in the norm group who were six years and one month old when they took The Marion and Asher Reading Test. The raw scores of children in your classroom could be compared to these tables. If the raw score of Rachel, in your third-grade class, was the same as the average raw score of children who were twelve years and three months old when they took the test, Rachel would appear to be a very good reader as compared to the norm group on that particular test. Once again, these interpretations, if seen as "Rachel, a third grader, can read the same material as children who are twelve years and three months old," can be just as dangerous, inaccurate, and damaging as interpretations based on the grade-equivalent scores previously discussed. Publishers can easily produce tables of age-equivalent data gathered from their norm-group data. Also, just as with all the other derived norm-referenced scores, the data can be displayed for the total norm-group population, or for the suburban, middle-income group population, or for any other demographics the publisher wishes to extrapolate and publish.

Box 2–3	International Reading Association position statement on the misuse of grade equivalent scores

WHEREAS, standardized, norm-referenced tests can provide information useful to teachers, students, and parents, if the results of such tests are used properly, and

WHEREAS, proper use of any standardized test depends on a thorough understanding of the test's purpose, the way it was developed, and any limitations it has, and

WHEREAS, failure to fully understand these factors can lead to serious misuse of test results, and

WHEREAS, one of the most serious misuses of tests is the reliance on a grade equivalent as an indicator of absolute performance, when a grade equivalent should be interpreted as an indicator of a test-taker's performance in relation to the performance of other test-takers used to norm the test, and

WHEREAS, in reading education, the misuse of grade equivalents has led to such mistaken assumptions as: (1) a grade equivalent of 5.0 on a reading test means that the test-taker will be able to read fifth grade material, and (2) a grade equivalent of 10.0 by a fourth grade student means that student reads like a tenth grader even though the test may include only sixth grade material as its top level of difficulty, and

WHEREAS, the misuse of grade equivalents promotes misunderstanding of a student's reading ability and leads to underreliance on other norm-referenced scores which are much less susceptible to misinterpretation and misunderstanding, be it

RESOLVED, that the International Reading Association strongly advocates that those who administer standardized reading tests abandon the practice of using grade equivalents to report performance of either individuals or groups of test-takers and be it further

RESOLVED, that the president or executive director of the Association write to test publishers urging them to eliminate grade equivalents from their tests.

Stanine Scores

Stanine scores are a type of standard score developed by dividing the norming group's scores into nine fairly equal groupings, ranging from a low of stanine 1 through a high of stanine 9. The 5th stanine, or middle grouping of scores, is located in the center of the distribution curve. It includes all the raw scores that fall within one-fourth of a standard deviation on either side of the mean. Each grouping unit, in the stanines below and above 5, is approximately equal, so that the difference between the raw scores in stanines 4 and 5 is very similar to the difference between the raw scores in stanines 5 and 6. Because of this, stanine scores are a useful range for comparing children's progress from one test

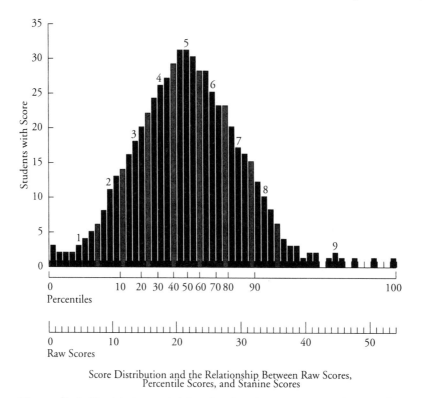

Score Distribution and the Relationship Between Raw Scores,
Percentile Scores, and Stanine Scores

Figure 2–1 The Marion and Asher Reading Test: Score Distributions for
First Graders in First Month of School

administration to the next and for reporting children's reading test performance. A difference of 2 stanines is considered to be significant. Usually, scores in stanines 4 through 6 are considered to be within an average range, scores in stanines 1 through 3 within a below-average range, and scores in stanines 7 through 9 within an above-average range.

Figure 2–1 illustrates the score distribution and the relationship between the raw scores, percentile rank scores, and the stanine scores of the norming group that took The Marion and Asher Reading Test in the first month of first grade. When a large number of students are in the norm group, the score distribution usually resembles a **normal distribution curve** (the classic bell-shaped curve, which indicates that test scores are distributed symmetrically around the mean).

Understanding the Problems with Standardized Tests and Scores

Based on the information presented regarding standardized tests, their development, and the quantitative scores derived from these tests, many problems and drawbacks may already be obvious. In the next sections, some of these are highlighted. The problems selected are the ones most often cited by the International Reading Association (1991) and by reading educators and researchers who have called for changes in the assessment of reading and related literacy tasks (Harman, 1992; IRA & NCTE, 1994; Johnston, 1992; Squire, 1987; Valencia, Hiebert, & Afflerbach, 1994; Valencia & Pearson, 1987; Walp & Walmsley, 1995). Additionally, readers wanting more information regarding analyzing and understanding reading tests and their scores may want to refer to Farr and Carey (1986).

Appropriateness of Tests

Appropriateness of the tests is a big issue closely related to concerns regarding measures of product versus process; selection of the norming groups; development of test questions to assess isolated and often questionable reading skills; decisions regarding cut-off (pass/fail) scores; problems of content validity, relevance, and authenticity; and arguments involving passage dependency versus passage independency. Many teachers and researchers believe that most of the current standardized and other commercial tests (including the criterion-referenced tests) are not complete or appropriate measures of students' real reading abilities and strategies.

Reading educators argue that these tests fail to assess students' strategy use, including the linguistic and cognitive strategies discussed in Chapter 1, because most of the norm-referenced and criterion-referenced tests focus on the product (getting the answer correct) rather than on the process (how the student attempts to get the answer). Many believe that assessing this process is far more important than assessing a product. They also believe that many of the test questions in these product-oriented measures inappropriately focus on isolated and sometimes questionable reading skills and include sometimes fairly arbitrary decisions about the score required to pass the test. They argue that the reading and skills sampled by these tests are not like real, authentic reading and literacy-related tasks. Instead, the tests seem to sample bits and pieces that have little relevance to the reading required in school and in life, for work and for pleasure. Finally, they argue that these tests not only fail to assess the linguistic and cognitive processes, but they also fail to assess the students' use of prior knowledge and the affective, cultural, and sociocultural influences of the students' real lives and situations. If teachers must use these tests in their classrooms, they also must recognize the problems and severe limitations of these measures. (See previously cited sources as calling for changes in the assessment of reading, and also see IRA [1991] and Winograd, Paris, & Bridge [1991] for more details concerning these arguments and the call for more authentic assessments. "The aim of **authentic assessment** is to assess many different kinds of literacy abilities in contexts that closely resemble the actual situations in which those abilities are used" [Valencia et al., 1994, p. 9].)

Many researchers and teachers believe that assessments should be done with authentic reading materials and assignments that are relevant to what the classroom teacher is actually teaching or planning within his classroom program. No standardized or commercial test could possibly have this high degree of content validity and relevance. Likewise, no norm-referenced group or composite norm-referenced group could possibly be just like your class. Nevertheless, because teachers still have to give standardized tests, it is a good idea to have some guidelines to evaluate their appropriateness. Therefore, a list of questions follows that teachers could ask themselves in order to review the appropriateness of a particular standardized test for their students. Also, in Chapters 3 and 4, alternative informal teacher-developed, process-oriented assessment approaches are discussed and described.

Questions to Consider When Reviewing Standardized Tests for Classroom Use

1. Does this test appear to assess skills and strategies that I believe are important to my classroom literacy goals?
2. Do the questions this test poses, and the structure of those questions, appear to be representative of how I believe these questions should be asked?
3. To what extent does this test measure what it purports to measure?
4. To what extent does this test measure what I believe is involved in reading?
5. Are there questions on this test that would assist me in determining what strategies my students are using to recognize and make sense of words within the context of sentences/paragraphs?
6. Are there questions on this test that would assist me in determining what strategies my students are using to comprehend reading materials?
7. When was this test normed? Who is in the norm group? To what extent does this norm group match the students in my class?
8. In addition to the skills and strategies and processes that I believe are important to reading in my classroom, what else is this test measuring? How much of the test (what percentage of the overall test questions) is measuring this other stuff?
9. Would students in my classroom do well on this test? Yes? No? Why or why not?
10. Other observations about this test:

Misuse of Test Results

Many problems for teachers, children, and their parents can develop when the derived norm-referenced or criterion-referenced test results are inappropriately used by schools. Although there probably are many other misuses of these test results, the most damaging seems to be when the derived norm-referenced scores, or the pass/fail results of the criterion-referenced standardized tests, are used for grouping children by ability; for matching children to materials designated to a grade level; for passing, failing, or assigning to remedial classes, or otherwise holding children back; and for making assumptions about children's reading abilities and instructional needs. Here is a look at each of these problems.

1. There is a tendency to use standardized test results to ability-group children for reading instruction. This is one reason why the IRA (1981) had cautioned publishers and school systems not to use, calculate, or make use of grade-equivalent scores. However, the use of these norm-referenced or criterion-referenced scores to ability-group children is probably just as harmful. The research and literature tend to suggest that the ability grouping of children for reading can do more harm than good (e.g., Allington, 1980, 1983; Hallinan, 1984; Good & Marshall, 1984; Indrisano & Paratore, 1991; Hiebert, 1983; Rosenbaum, 1980; Shannon, 1985; Weinstein, 1976). Allington (1995) indicates that "Grouping all the lowest achievers together is simply deadly for those children" (p. 7). Children designated as being in the "low group" often are treated differently from children in the "high groups"; they tend to be given more drill work as opposed to higher quality reading instruction, tend to remain in the low group, tend to develop negative self-concepts, and tend to dislike reading. Likewise, children in the "middle group" tend to be treated as mediocre and experience many of the same problems as the children designated to be in the low group. On the other hand, high-group children are treated with more respect, are allowed to do more independent reading, and usually are given a higher quality of reading instruction or reading assignments; not surprisingly, they tend to like reading more. Even so, Slavin's research and analysis (1987, 1991) indicate that children assigned to "high groups" (or even gifted programs) would do just as well if they were not ability-grouped or tracked at all. Slavin (1991) states that "these students [high achievers] will do well wherever they are" (p. 70). (Many researchers have reported or summarized the results or impacts of ability grouping. These include the work of those previously cited and Barr, 1989; Flood, Lapp, Flood, & Nagel, 1992; Harp, 1989; Paratore, Fountas, Jenkins, Ouellette, & Sheehan, 1991. Additionally, others— for examples see Cunningham, Hall, & Defee, 1998; Fountas & Pinnell, 1996; Lloyd, 1999; Opitz, 1998; and Wilkinson & Townsend, 2000—have suggested grouping and curriculum delivery alternatives that combine the more redeeming features of ability grouping with features of more positive options. Readers interested in the specific findings of these studies, or in learning more about the effects of ability and other instructional groupings, are referred to these works.)

2. There is a tendency to use standardized test results to match children to grade-level materials. Once again, the admonishment by the IRA regarding the use of grade-equivalents applies (1981). Remember the description of how grade-level equivalent scores are derived from norm-referenced test results? All of the children in the norm-referenced group, in a particular grade and month of school, had their raw scores totaled and then divided by the number of children in the group. That score became the designation for how a particular grade level in the norm group scored on a particular test.

If the overall norm group scored high, then the grade-equivalent score would tend to be higher than if the overall norm group did poorly. So, of course, these scores are tremendously affected by who is in the norm group. However, even if you believe that the norm group is an appropriate match to your class, it would still be inaccurate to say that a fourth-grade child in your class with a grade-equivalent score of 1.2 is reading at a first-grade, second-month level. Likewise, it would be inappropriate to try to match your fourth-grade student to material designed for children in first grade. Material designed for children in first grade usually is designated as such because publishers believe, among other things, that it would appeal to the interests and schemata of most first graders. Although reading authorities do not all agree regarding the designation of reading materials into grade levels, most agree that it is inaccurate to believe that a child in fourth grade should be put into first-grade materials based on a grade-equivalent score. Likewise, most also would agree it is inappropriate to put a first-grader into a book designated for sixth-grade use just because the first-grader got a grade-equivalent score of 6.5 on a norm-referenced reading test. Once again, the materials designed for use with sixth-graders usually are written to appeal to the interests, schemata, and sophistication of most sixth-graders, as opposed to those of a six-year-old, first-grade child. (In Chapter 6 see the section on leveling books, which presents suggestions for helping both teachers and children select appropriate books based on interest, motivation, knowledge of the literature and the child, self-monitoring, and other qualitative considerations.)

3. The pass/fail criteria from some basal, state-developed, and other high-stakes tests have been used to promote or retain children. They also have been used to recommend children for summer school or for remedial reading classes. In some schools where basals or competency-based instruction is used, the pass/fail criteria from these tests have been used to hold children back, not allowing them to advance to the next book, skill, or level. The rationale has been that if the criterion-scored test has not been passed, children must repeat the book or skill until the test can be passed. Obviously, this is a blatant misuse of test results and is unfair to children. This rationale also assumes that children must master one reading skill at a time, that there is an accepted scope and sequence of reading skills, and that mastering a particular book is more important than the child's development and pleasure in reading. Most reading authorities today would argue against this rationale.

4. There has been a tendency to make assumptions about children's reading abilities and their instructional needs based on the results of one isolated measure—a norm-referenced or a criterion-referenced test. This is inappropriate even if the test is excellent. Decisions about a child's reading abilities and instructional needs should never be made as a result of just one assessment. It is particularly inappropriate when you realize that many teachers might consider the content validity and relevance to authentic reading and literacy-related tasks to be highly questionable for many of the standardized tests they must give in school. Keep in mind that most of these tests are product-oriented and do not assess children's strategy use. Therefore, teachers, who believe that helping children

develop and enhance their reading, study, and other literacy-related strategies should be the basis for their classroom instructional program, can find little in most standardized test results that helps them plan instructional opportunities. (In Chapters 3 and 4 many informal reading and literacy-related assessments are presented to assist teachers in finding out necessary information concerning students' reading levels, strategies, skills, interests, and motivations. It is suggested that these assessments provide information that is appropriate for use in planning instruction and in evaluating literacy strengths and needs.)

Additionally, even though some believe it is justifiable, useful, and informative to use standardized tests to measure groups of students—as well as for **large-scale testing** (testing of children in an entire school, district, or state) and other **high-stakes assessment** purposes (when one test or assessment is used to make important decisions about students, teachers, and their schools)—unfair comparisons of groups and public disclosures (such as reporting scores in the newspapers) have become more and more problematic over the years. This misinterpretation and misuse of test scores has often been driven by politics. (See Farr & Carey, 1986, for more discussion regarding problems, issues, and trends surrounding the use of reading tests, and Wixson, Valencia, & Lipson's, 1994, argument for a redefinition of accountability—a redefinition that doesn't assume that standardized tests provide significant information about children's reading and writing. Concern over the misuse, misinterpretation, unfairness, and inappropriateness of large-scale, high-stakes test results is also evident in the IRA and NCTE publication, 1994, and position statements by the IRA, 1999, and the American Educational Research Association [AERA] [see AERA, 2001], as well as in the writings of other educators—for instance, Allington, 1994; Kohn, 2000; Shepard, 2000; Wilde, 2002.)

Consider and React 2–3

What is your experience with these previously cited problems and issues?

Loss of Valuable Information

When test results, no matter how good the test, are analyzed only for quantitative data (the number right, or the ranking of a student as compared to the norm group, or pass/fail information), valuable information can be lost. Test results must be qualitatively analyzed as well, in order to get as much information as possible from the results. The following scenario illustrates this idea.

Jose, a fourth-grade student, and Kiesha, another fourth-grade student in the same class, both take a standardized reading comprehension test with 120 multiple-choice questions. The children have two hours to complete the test; both get the exact same number of questions correct for a raw score of 60. Consequently, when the raw score was compared to the norm tables, both children were ranked at the same percentile rank and were given the same grade-equivalent and stanine scores. (If this were a criterion-referenced test and they got the same score, both would have been given the same pass/fail result.) Based on the quantitative data, both children seem to be identical in reading ability and skills. Mr. Frazier, in the next room, advised Mrs. Fox, a fourth-grade teacher, to put both children in the middle reading group based on these results. Mrs. Fox, however, wisely decided to examine each child's test results qualitatively. She looked at other things besides quantitative information.

Here's what she noted: Jose answered the first sixty comprehension questions on the test correctly. Mrs. Fox could tell, however, that he never attempted the last sixty questions. The questions he got correct dealt with the full spectrum of comprehension skills tested by the test: main idea, details, cause and effect, making inferences, drawing conclusions, and vocabulary in context. He did equally well on each of these types of questions.

Kiesha, on the other hand, seemed to have attempted most of the test questions, but she was successful with only about half of those attempted. Kiesha seemed to have the biggest problem with questions designed to measure cause and effect, making inferences, and drawing conclusions. When she did get questions correct, they were most often main idea, detail, and vocabulary-in-context questions. Even though she did better with those types of questions, she still answered some incorrectly.

Consider and React 2–4

Consider how each child did on the test. How would you analyze their results? See how your analysis compares to Mrs. Fox's.

Here is how Mrs. Fox qualitatively analyzed this information: Both children do not have the same reading abilities or skills. In fact, they are very different. Jose seems to be an excellent reader, or, at least, did very well with all the questions he attempted on the first half of the test. He seems equally successful at answering all of the traditional types of reading comprehension questions asked. If anything could be perceived as possible weaknesses, and Mrs. Fox doesn't agree that they are, Jose could be considered by some to be a slow but deliberate reader, or to be a poor test taker. Instead, Mrs. Fox believes, Jose worked slowly because the syntax of the test questions and paragraphs is somewhat difficult for him, since English is his second language.

On the other hand, Kiesha is not as strong a reader as Jose, at least as measured by this test. She is just as often inaccurate as she is accurate when she answers comprehension questions. She seems to have a particularly difficult time with questions designed to measure cause and effect, making inferences, and drawing conclusions. She does better with main idea, detail, and vocabulary-in-context questions, although even with these she has some difficulty. Mrs. Fox decides that she will informally assess Kiesha using some of the assessment ideas found in Chapters 3 and 4 before she makes any unfair or inaccurate decisions about Kiesha's reading abilities and instructional needs. Kiesha might just have had a bad day or might have been frustrated by the length and intensity of the standardized test. At any rate, Mrs. Fox believes that this test is not measuring all of the important components of reading and wants to assess Kiesha with authentic and relevant reading materials and assignments. She wants to find out how she can help Kiesha with her strategy development, rather than just labeling her a middle-group reader.

How to Discuss Test Results with Children's Families

Each individual family and child situation is different and should be treated as such. Even so, it is probably useful to anticipate possible questions or concerns that parents or other family members might have regarding their children's reading test results. Therefore, a few scenarios have been contrived to illustrate how you might discuss criterion-referenced and norm-referenced test results with children's parents and families. Keep in mind that the family members involved in these discussions may not be familiar with the testing and reading terminology you will use. For that reason, it is important that you first go over these terms with parents and perhaps even provide them with a list of pertinent definitions. (Readers could develop this list by lifting relevant terms and brief definitions from the glossary at the end of this book.)

Criterion-Referenced Scenario

Charlie, now a second grader, failed the criterion-referenced reading test for the basal program used in his first-grade classroom. Mrs. Galvez, his teacher, is meeting with Charlie's mother at the end of the first twelve-week grading period to discuss his progress in school. During this meeting, Mrs. Hetzel asks: "My son failed the reading test given at the end of first grade. I've been very worried that he is a poor reader and that he may not catch up in reading. What do you think?"

Consider and React 2–5

How would you answer Mrs. Hetzel's question? If you would like help, review the part of the chapter dealing with criterion-referenced scores. Then answer Mrs. Hetzel's question, and compare your answer to Mrs. Galvez's.

Mrs. Galvez's answer: "Yes, it is true that Charlie did not get a passing score on last year's reading test, but I'd like to explain what that means and what that doesn't mean. First of all, the test that was given tested only **discrete reading skills** (separate reading skills, sometimes presented in isolation on many norm-referenced and criterion-referenced tests) and selected vocabulary words that were supposed to be covered in Charlie's first-grade reading book. In order to pass that test, Charlie was supposed to get at least eighteen questions correct out of a total of twenty. I looked at Charlie's score, and he got fourteen questions correct, only four less than required to pass. So he really didn't do badly. However, because it was a criterion-referenced test, and Charlie's score didn't match the cut-off score of eighteen, he didn't pass. All that means is that Charlie couldn't correctly answer questions on all the discrete skills and vocabulary tested. I am not concerned because I went back and looked at the questions and Charlie's answers. This is what I found: Charlie knew how to answer questions on quite a few of the skills tested. He knows all his beginning and ending consonant sounds. He was able to successfully pick out important details. He recognized quite a few of the vocabulary words introduced in the first-grade book. There were a few vocabulary words he didn't recognize. Also, he was not able to correctly answer one question on main idea. However, I thought the answer he gave for that question could make sense to a first grader who had limited experience with the topic of the test passage. Overall, although he didn't pass the test, I don't consider him a failure or a poor reader in any way. In my classroom, I'm more interested in observing the processes and strategies children use to read. Based on my observations, Charlie has good phoneme-grapheme skills. He makes good use of his semantic and syntax strategies. He enjoys reading books he selects. He has a very good reading vocabulary for a second-grade child. Please don't consider Charlie a poor reader. I don't. I do not think he is behind, and I believe that Charlie will do fine in reading this school year because he has good reading strategies and I will encourage him to use them."

Norm-Referenced Scenario: One

Remember Robin, the third grader who got a fairly low score on the norm-referenced test? Her grade equivalent score was a 1.1 on the test. Because this is a test required systemwide, score reports were mailed to all families in the district. Robin's parents come to school to discuss Robin's test results with you. They ask: "How could this be possible? Robin has done well in school. Why is she only reading at the first-grade level? She's two years behind in reading!"

Consider and React 2–6

How would you respond to Robin's parents? If you would like help, review the part of the chapter dealing with grade-level equivalent scores. Consider what you might say. Then see if you would answer as suggested.

Suggested answer: "Robin is doing well in school. She isn't reading at the first-grade level, and she isn't two years behind in reading. Because parents, schools, and teachers too, often don't interpret grade-equivalent scores accurately, the International Reading Association strongly suggested that they not be used. (Show them the IRA's position statement, 1981, in this chapter.) All a score of 1.1 means is that Robin got the same raw score on this particular test as the average of the raw scores of the norm group who took the test when its members were in the first month of first grade. This is not the same thing at all as saying that Robin is reading at first-grade level. Once again, that is why the IRA warned against using those scores. In fact, most first graders do not have the reading strategies, schemata, and interests that Robin has. She is probably much further developed in her reading strategy use than the average first grader. Let me assure you that I do not feel that those test results indicate anything more than that Robin didn't do as well on that particular test as the norm group did. Also, because that test is testing only isolated reading skills, it didn't measure the processes Robin uses to read. I consider Robin's use of reading strategies much more important than her ability to answer questions measuring discrete and isolated skills. Because I anticipated your concerns, I'd like to show you what I found out about Robin's reading strategies when I informally assessed her. I think you will be pleased by her strengths."

Norm-Referenced Scenario: Two

Rachel is the third-grade student who got an age-equivalent score of twelve years and three months on the norm-referenced reading test. (Note that the grade-equivalent score was reported as 6.8.) When Rachel's grandmother saw her test results, she assumed that Rachel was reading like a twelve-year-old (or like a child in sixth grade). Later, at a parent conference, Rachel's grandmother asks: "How is Rachel doing in school? I bet she must be doing very well since I know she reads books on the sixth-grade level, the same as most twelve-year-olds. I'm so proud of her!"

Consider and React 2–7

How would you respond to Rachel's grandmother? If you would like help, review the part of the chapter dealing with age-level equivalent scores. Consider what you might say. Then see if you would answer as suggested.

Suggested answer: "Yes, Rachel is doing very well in school. She works hard and loves reading. It is also true that she did very well on the norm-referenced test that the school system gave this fall. However, it is not exactly accurate to say that she is reading on the sixth-grade level, or that she reads the same as most twelve-year-olds. It would be unfair to Rachel if we expected that. The age-equivalent score of twelve years and three months means that Rachel got the same raw score on that test as the average of the raw scores of the norming group members who took the test when they were twelve years and three months old. Of course, this does mean that Rachel got a lot of answers correct on the test, but because she is only eight years old, it isn't likely that her reading strategies will be as developed as most children who are one and one-half times her age. Also, of course, Rachel will have different interests and different experiences than most twelve-year-olds. That is why it might be unfair to assume that she would want to read, or would be comfortable reading, books that most twelve-year-olds are interested in. However, I do want to assure you that I feel Rachel is a very good reader, too. I've been assessing her reading strategies and she has excellent strategy use. I agree with you that she should do very well in school and, in fact, she is."

Summary

This chapter has presented an overview of standardized, formal, commercially prepared reading tests. The emphasis has been on understanding and interpreting tests that yield norm-referenced and criterion-referenced scores. Classroom teachers are often in the position of having to administer such tests to children. Additionally, classroom teachers must ultimately decide how to, or if they should, use the results of these tests, and how to explain the results to family members. Teachers who understand how these tests are developed, the test jargon, and the issues and problems associated with them are in a better position to make decisions and counsel parents based on test results. It is hoped that once classroom teachers understand the test development, the limitations, and the problems with these types of measures, they will seek other means of assessing children's reading abilities. In the chapters that follow, many informal assessment procedures are described. These assessments emphasize observing processes, rather than products, and doing assessments with real, authentic reading for the purpose of observing children's use of strategies.

Questions for Reflection and Response

1. What are standardized tests, and how are they different from more naturalistic assessment?

2. What are some of the different types and purposes of standardized and other commercial tests?

3. What are some of the important considerations teachers should be aware of regarding the use of standardized tests? Why are these important?

4. How are norm-referenced scores derived? How can you use this information to enhance your interpretation of the students' scores in your classroom?

5. What are some of the problems with using standardized tests and their scores?

6. How can you explain a child's failure on a criterion-referenced test to her parents/family? Develop and share your own scenario for this situation.

7. How can you explain a child's low score on a norm-referenced test to his parents/family? Develop and share your own scenario for this situation.

8. What about a child who scored high on a norm-referenced test—is he reading above grade level? What would you say to the parents/family? Design a scenario depicting this situation.

CHAPTER 3

ASSESSING AFFECTIVE, LINGUISTIC, AND OTHER QUALITATIVE INFORMATION

Focus and Goals of the Chapter

+ To provide a comprehensive overview of many assessment ideas and procedures for observing emergent literacy, affective areas, linguistic experience, and other qualitative information

- To provide information about the emergent literacy perspective and a specific technique for assessing its application to storybook reading

- To describe how observations, interviews, samples, and portfolios can be valuable tools and provide sources of qualitative data

- To provide specific assessments for determining children's interests, attitudes, motivations, and feelings concerning reading

- To describe and illustrate various procedures for sampling children's oral readings (informal reading inventories, miscue analysis, and running records)

- To provide, demonstrate, and discuss a modified technique for specifically analyzing children's phoneme-grapheme, syntax, and semantic cue systems use

- To provide examples, analysis, and in-depth discussion on specific children's linguistic strategies, showing how they use them to make sense of text and to create text

ASSESSING AFFECTIVE, LINGUISTIC, AND OTHER QUALITATIVE INFORMATION

- To facilitate an interest in looking at children's writing and invented spelling as a means of providing more information about their linguistic experience
- To provide ideas for collecting and using information from students' records, other teachers, parents/families, and the children themselves as part of the qualitative data on each child
- To reinforce the idea that both the children and their parents/families have a stake in children's assessment and should be actively involved.

Introduction

This chapter discusses and describes a variety of informal observational and sampling assessment procedures that would be useful to a classroom teacher. These assessment procedures can be done by the teacher within the regular school day without interrupting or forsaking other classroom activities and necessary instruction. In fact, several of these procedures should serve as springboards to instruction, while others are designed to be done as part of instruction. The information gathered through these informal assessments and others (described in the next chapter) will be analyzed in a "qualitative" way by the teacher. This **qualitative emphasis** involves the teacher observing many samples of students' motivations, work, and strategies to get a more complete view of each student in order to decide the most useful ways of helping the student develop effective reading strategies.

The informal assessments discussed and described in this chapter include:

1. Classification scheme for emergent reading
2. Observations, interviews, and samples/portfolios
3. Interest, attitude, motivation, and "feelings" assessments
4. Informal Reading Inventories (IRI)
5. Miscue or error analysis (Reading Miscue Inventories [RMI], and running records)
6. Qualitative analysis of oral reading using modified miscue analysis techniques.

Additionally, this chapter includes a detailed discussion, with examples, of assessing the **linguistic cueing systems** mentioned in Chapter 1. These cue systems include the phoneme-grapheme, syntax, and semantic systems. (**Cue** is used as a synonym for clue.) A discussion of information from children's other language processes—including writing and invented spelling—is presented. Finally, the chapter suggests and discusses the use of other available information for the classroom teacher, such as information the teacher can gather from students' records, other teachers, parents and family members, and the children themselves.

Emergent Literacy and Assessment

Teachers with more experience in preschool and the early childhood grades probably noticed the shift over the years from the term *readiness* to the term *emergent literacy*. This shift is in more than just educational jargon; it represents a shift in the philosophy and assumptions we make about children's literacy development. In many ways, the shift toward an emergent literacy philosophy (moving away from a readiness emphasis) paralleled the shift toward the inclusion of more authentic assessments of literacy (moving away from an earlier skills-based emphasis) as we assess and instruct children.

Rationale and Assumptions

We have become more aware of how much children know about language and literacy before they even enter school. As described in Chapter 1, children, from birth on, develop linguistic and cognitive experiences and strategies that are shaped by contacts with parents, family, friends, community, and the experiences each child has during these interactions (the child's sociocultural and cultural influences). This awareness has made us realize that a child's literacy development is much more complex than what can be measured by traditional readiness tests.

Readiness tests assumed a group of isolated, but related, sequential skills—skills that were deemed essential *before* a child could begin to learn to read. While this is no longer the dominant thinking in the field of literacy education, and the thinking or philosophy has moved instead toward the **emergent literacy** point of view (Teale & Sulzby, 1986), several research reports have called new attention to the importance of phonemic awareness and alphabetic concepts (e.g., Adams, 1990; Snow, Burns, & Griffin, 1998). These concepts are explained in the next section.

Proponents of emergent literacy are not antiskills (Strickland & Morrow, 1989a); however, they tend to believe that because of the complexity of each child's literacy development, it is more productive to observe children's understandings about reading and writing by viewing the strategies they use to go about real reading and writing tasks. Of course, these strategies involve the use of many skills. Teachers do need to know which skills underlie certain strategies, but the best way to know what skills children have or have not acquired is by observing their strategies in action (Strickland & Morrow, 1989a).

This view of children's literacy development, emergent literacy, has been stimulated by earlier theories regarding children's learning (i.e., Piaget, 1959; Vygotsky, 1962, 1978; and their followers) and is based on certain research assumptions and conclusions.

1. Language is best learned through use rather than through practice exercises on how to use language (Harste, 1990; Sulzby, 1992).

2. Children become literate long before they are formally reading from print, and this emergent literacy can be observed through their everyday explorations with print (Sulzby, 1985, 1992; Sulzby & Teale, 1987).

3. Emergent literacy is based on social interactions with people (Chapman, 1996; Harste, 1990), such as parents and teachers, and with the literacy products of people, such as storybooks (Sulzby, 1985, 1991; Sulzby & Teale, 1987) and informational books (Robinson, Ross, & Neal, 2000), and is further shaped by the parental/family beliefs and values concerning literacy (Anderson, 1994; Spiegel, Fitzgerald, & Cunningham, 1993).

4. Children are simultaneously acquiring both oral and written language and are constantly figuring out the oral and written language relationships used in their particular culture (Sulzby, 1992; Sulzby & Teale, 1987).

5. Children gradually acquire conventional literacy and eventually organize various aspects of it into a system that enables them to figure out print independently (Sulzby, 1991, 1992; Sulzby & Teale, 1987); however, this conventional literacy requires that children can eventually switch, as necessary, from using and understanding oral language to using and understanding written language (Cox, Fang, & Otto, 1997; Robinson et al., 2000).

Phonemic Awareness and Alphabetic Concepts

Phonemic awareness is an awareness or understanding that spoken words are made up of a sequence of individual sounds. Phonemic awareness can be observed when children pick out and manipulate sounds in spoken words. These sounds are called **phonemes**— phonemes are the individual speech sounds that make up words. Phonemic awareness activities are oral in nature and are not the same thing as phonics. (**Phonics** instead is letter-sound correspondence in written language, and it involves learning sound and spelling relationships in printed words.) Adams (1990) suggested several phonemic awareness tasks. These could be used by teachers as a guide to both assess and further develop young children's understanding of phonemic awareness. The examples that follow have been derived from the work of Blevins (1997).

1. *Hearing and identifying rhyming words;* for example, when listening to nursery rhymes, the child could be asked to tell or repeat the rhyming words.
2. *Hearing and picking out the different word sounds;* for example, when hearing a series of words (*silly, Sam, said, boy*), ask which one begins with a different sound (*boy*).
3. *Orally blending words and split syllables;* for example, the teacher says the sound /s/, and then adds the rest of the word—*it*—asking, "What is the word?" (*sit*)
4. *Orally segmenting words and counting sounds;* for example, the teacher asks, "What sounds do you hear in the word *sit*?" (/s/ /i/ /t/)
5. *Manipulating and playing with phonemes in spoken words;* for example, replacing the first sound in a word (*sit*) with another one (/f/) to make a new word. (*fit*)

Opitz (2000) emphasizes that phonological awareness is not the same thing as phonemic awareness. **Phonological awareness** refers to an awareness of *many* aspects of spoken language including words within sentences, syllables within words, and phonemes within syllables and words. This awareness is developmental: first young children tend to be aware that language is composed of words; next they tend to become aware that words are made up of word parts; eventually they become aware that words and word parts are made up of individual speech sounds. This last aspect is the most advanced and difficult stage, and it is what we refer to as phonemic awareness

(Cunningham, 2000). As you can surmise, phonemic awareness is part of the larger concept, phonological awareness.

Children eventually develop this phonemic awareness as a result of the oral and written language they have been exposed to. Reading nursery rhymes and books to young children and playing with rhyme words and language facilitate this development (see Opitz, 2000 for book ideas). Additionally, children who are allowed and encouraged to use their own spellings (invented spellings) further promote the development of their phonemic awareness. While literacy researchers generally agree that the development of phonological and then phonemic awareness is an important foundation of literacy development, they are generally not in agreement on the necessity for, amount of, and specific kinds of instruction needed to ensure this development (Richgels, 2001). Some believe that phonemic awareness must be taught for extensive periods of time and must be an emphasis of early childhood classrooms. Others believe that it should be taught only as one part of a more inclusive, comprehensive literacy program. And still others believe that many children have already developed a foundation of phonemic awareness by the time they come to school and do not need this instruction; or that if they do need it, they will continue their development as they have more and more opportunities to explore language through storytimes, invented spellings, and other rich literacy activities.

Adams (1990) and Snow et al. (1998) have asserted that to become successful readers, children need to acquire both phonemic awareness and insight into the alphabetic principle. Basically, the **alphabetic principle** can be defined as the concept that spoken words are represented by written spellings (or symbols). In order to demonstrate this understanding, children should be able to recognize letters and also distinguish the features of the various letters. Eventually, children should be encouraged to know and assessed to see if they know the names of the letters of the alphabet. Recognizing and knowing the features of individual letters, as well as phonemic awareness, are important to both reading and writing development: children's awareness of the relationships between the sounds they use to say words and the letters they use in reading and writing words are, of course, what this is all about.

In addition to the sources already cited in this section, many others are available and recommended to teachers for ideas to further develop and assess phonemic awareness and alphabetic concepts. Readers might want to consult Castle (1999); Ericson and Juliebö (1998); Fox (2000); Johns, Lenski, and Elish-Piper (1999); Rasinski and Padak (2001); Savage (2001); Strickland (1998); and Yopp (1995).

Classification Scheme for Emergent Reading of Favorite Storybooks
Even though many proponents of emergent literacy are opposed to skills-based readiness tests, they strongly acknowledge the need to continually assess young children's literacy development. As already indicated, they believe that this assessment can best be accomplished as a day-to-day, natural part of classroom work. Based on her extensive research,

Sulzby developed a storybook classification scheme designed to be used by preschool and early childhood teachers to assist them in observing and evaluating young children's literacy development. This procedure, along with other observations of children at work on literacy-related tasks, could be used to replace or supplement traditional reading readiness tests (Sulzby, 1991).

The steps for using this procedure are the following:

1. Allow the child ample opportunity to select a favorite storybook. It is important to use a known book the child has heard over and over again. This comfortably familiar book will give the child maximum opportunity to demonstrate her emergent literacy.

2. Find a quiet, comfortable spot and ask the child to read her book to you. (You could even eavesdrop while the child reads her book to another child.) If the child doesn't read immediately, or says, "I can't read," the teacher uses prompts such as "It doesn't have to be like grown-up reading; you can do it your own way." If the child still hesitates, the teacher can suggest they read the book together and allow the child to complete sentences or phrases as she reads with the teacher. After a little more of this, the teacher can encourage the child to finish the book on her own by saying, "It's your turn. Please finish reading it to me."

3. As the child reads independently, the teacher observes. (Allow the child to hold the book and turn the pages.) Using the storybook classification scheme, the teacher notes to what extent the child attends to pictures or to print. The scheme gives the teacher the "language" to use to describe the child's performance each time the child is assessed. Records of the child's performance over time can be kept in the child's portfolio. These records consist of the teacher's notations and can be as short or as detailed as desired.

My adaptation of the simplified version of the classification scheme and an assessment of emergent reading appears in Box 3–1. In this adaptation, the highest indication of literacy development is category VI (attending to print and beginning to read "conventionally"), indicating that the child is following and "really" reading the text of the storybook. On the other hand, a child assessed as reading in category I is primarily attending to pictures; whereas characteristics such as identifying the pictures, commenting on them, and following the action of the story are indications of the child's further development. Clearly, the child's strategies for reading in category I are not as fully developed as the child who has progressed to the stage where she is completely attending to print and can independently read a known storybook, as in category VI. E. Sulzby (personal communication, April 9, 2002) cautions that a simplified version can be misleading because it does not show movement at more refined levels; however, it may provide guidance and summarize things a classroom teacher can look for. Additionally, careful observations and notations can document finer development points.

In this chapter and in the next, many other ideas for qualitatively assessing children's literacy development and reading strategies are discussed and sampled. Although you may not see the term emergent literacy cited with these various assessment ideas, it

Box 3–1	A classification scheme and assessment for emergent reading		
Description of Storybook Reading Categories	Characteristics of Development	Check and Date All That Are Observed	Teacher's Notes for Clarification
I. Child is attentive to the pictures in the story.	• Looks at the pictures as the pages of the storybook are turned. • Identifies or labels the pictures. • Comments on the individual pictures. • Seems to be following the action of the story through the pictures.		
II. Child is attentive to the pictures in the story *and tells* an oral narration of the story as he/she looks at the pictures.	• Looks at the pictures as the pages of the storybook are turned. • Tells a story about the pictures, actually weaving the story from picture to picture.		
III. Child is attentive to the pictures in the story and *combines* storytelling with "reading" as he/she attends to the pictures.	• Looks at the pictures as the pages of the storybook are turned. • *Tells the story* when looking at the pictures *and* just as often seems to *read the story* while intoning like "someone who is reading" rather than "someone who is telling."		
IV. Child is attentive to the pictures in the story and "seems to be reading" the story as he/she attends to the pictures.	• Looks at the pictures as the pages of the storybook are turned. • Intonation and wording sound more like conventional reading. • The rendition of the story is similar to the actual story. • The rendition of the story is verbatim—like the actual story.		

Box 3–1	(*Continued*)		
Description of Storybook Reading Categories	Characteristics of Development	Check and Date All That Are Observed	Teacher's Notes for Clarification
V. Child has become attentive to the print in the story.	• Attends to the print on the pages as the pages of the storybook are turned, but...		
	• Reading skills and strategies seem to be still emerging. For instance, the child may refuse to attempt a word and indicates "I don't know that word."		
	• Reading skills and strategies seem to be still developing. For instance, the child focuses on one aspect of the word, ignoring other aspects.		
	• Reading skills and strategies seem imbalanced or awkward.		
VI. Child *is* attentive to the print in the story.	• Attends to the print on the pages as the pages of the storybook are turned and has begun to read "conventionally" or engages in what most would refer to as "real reading."		

Source: "A Classification Scheme and Assessment for Emergent Reading" is adapted from "Assessment of Emergent Literacy: Storybook Reading" by Elizabeth Sulzby in *The Reading Teacher,* 44(7). Copyright © 1991 by the International Reading Association. All rights reserved. Reprinted by permission.

is important to understand that the concept of emergent literacy includes all the early development and ongoing literacy development of the child. Therefore, when we observe and sample children's reading and other literacy-related activities, we are constantly gathering information about their emerging literacy development. Later, we will see how this information can be qualitatively analyzed and used by the classroom teacher to inform instruction.

Consider and React 3–1

What does the term *emergent literacy* mean to you? Have you seen evidence of emerging literacy in the children with whom you have worked?

Observations, Interviews, and Samples/Portfolios

Observing children in the regular classroom setting as they do their work, assignments, and other activities, in a natural, authentic manner, can give the classroom teacher valuable information regarding students' current and developing interests, motivations, strategies, and work habits. Talking to individual students about their work, assignments, and strategies provides additional information for the teacher. Additionally, selecting samples with students of different types and aspects of their work and other assignments for individual **portfolios** provides the teacher and child with material to reflect on, discuss, and monitor. Each of these informal procedures for gathering important qualitative data within the natural classroom, from authentic assignments and other real school work, is delineated in the sections that follow.

Observations

There are numerous opportunities during the school day for the teacher to observe how individual children do their work and reading assignments. The teacher must carefully choose from these opportunities. For example, if the teacher wants to see how individual children use their daily "free reading" time, the teacher can select one or two children per day and focus on observing those children, one at a time, during the free time. Or, if the teacher wants to see how students approach a textbook reading assignment, she can select one child at a time to carefully observe as the child pursues the assignment. The keys to observational assessment are

1. Deciding the purposes for the observation(s)
2. Deciding which times or assignments during the school day would provide the best or most useful opportunities to observe
3. Choosing one or two children to observe (individually) during each opportunity
4. Keeping careful notes on what you observe based on your purposes
5. Being open-minded enough to notice anything else you might incidentally observe (outside of your purpose[s]) that would be helpful to your understanding of the child and the child's development, strategy use, motivations, and so on.

Once you decide the purposes for a given observation, you can take **anecdotal notes**. These are notes, both general and specific, about what you observe or what the child is doing as it relates to your purpose for observing the child. Rhodes and Nathenson-Mejia (1992) indicate that anecdotal records are a powerful tool for collecting information on an ongoing basis during reading and writing and for evaluating the products of instruction. Prior to the observation, you can develop a list of behaviors to be observed or questions to be answered as a result of the observation. Here is a sample of what one such set of behaviors and questions might look like.

Sample of Observation for Assessing a Child's Use of Time During "Free Reading"

1. Does the child appear to be eager for the "free reading" time?
   NOTES

2. Does the child have a "free reading" book at his desk, or does he go looking for one?
   NOTES

3. How long does it take for the child to settle down and begin reading?
   NOTES

4. Is she easily distracted or does she seem to stay absorbed with the reading?
   NOTES

5. When "free reading" time is over, does the child seem to want to continue?
   NOTES

6. Notes regarding any other observations made by the teacher.
   NOTES

Interviews

Individual interviews with children can be especially enlightening. Once again, there are numerous times during the school day for the teacher to talk to a particular child (or to interview the child) as he does his work or works through a particular assignment. As when planning an observation, the teacher must first make some decisions regarding

1. The purpose(s) of the interview
2. When or during what activities/assignment the interview should take place
3. The child or children to individually interview
4. What to ask the child (in keeping with the teacher's assessment purposes).

The teacher again has a choice of taking anecdotal notes as she informally talks to the child. Here the teacher would need to keep her purpose clearly in mind and ask questions of the child as he works or after he has completed the assignment. Or, the teacher can develop a set of specific interview questions, in advance, and ask the child these questions at appropriate times during the interview procedure. Below is a sample of what one such set of questions might look like.

Sample of Interview Questions for Assessing a Child's Approach to a Textbook Reading Assignment

1. How do you know how to "start" the assignment?
   NOTES

  2. What do you do or read first?
  NOTES

  3. Then what?
  NOTES

  4. What is the hardest part of doing this assignment? Why?
  NOTES

  5. What is the easiest part of doing this assignment? Why?
  NOTES

  6. If you were the teacher, how would you change the assignment?
  NOTES

The "Reading Interview" (Goodman, Watson, & Burke, 1987, pp. 219–220) is a good tool to help you learn about your students' beliefs about reading and to speculate on the ways in which their reading proficiency has been influenced by reading instruction. (See Box 3–2.) Goodman et al. assert that what students believe about reading and reading instruction affects decisions they make about strategies to use during reading. Answers given by your students should provide valuable insight for you.

Box 3–2	Reading interview

Name _____ Age _____ Date _____

1. When you are reading and come to something you don't know, what do you do? Do you ever do anything else?
2. Who is a good reader you know?
3. What makes _____ a good reader?
4. Do you think _____ ever comes to something she/he doesn't know?
5. "Yes." When _____ does come to something she/he doesn't know, what do you think he/she does?
   "No." Suppose _____ comes to something she/he doesn't know. What do you think she/he would do?
6. If you knew someone was having trouble reading, how would you help that person?
7. What would a/your teacher do to help that person?
8. How did you learn to read?
9. What would you like to do better as a reader?
10. Do you think you are a good reader? Why?

Source: "Reading Interview" from *Reading Miscue Inventory: Alternative Procedures* by Y. M. Goodman, D. J. Watson, and C. L. Burke. Copyright © 1987. Richard C. Owen Publishers, Inc., Katonah, NY. Reprinted with permission.

Samples and Portfolios

Collections from a child's work can provide valuable assessment data for both the teacher and the child. This selective sampling can often show how a child begins work, how she develops the work, and how she revises or refines the work. It can provide information about a child's work habits, interests, writing skills, strategies, style, and motivation. In a similar fashion to the other informal assessment procedures described in this section, the teacher must decide

1. The purpose(s) for the sampling
2. The best or most informative work to sample to meet the purpose(s)
3. When to sample the work
4. What notations the teacher or child should make in order to label the sampling correctly.

Glazer (1994) indicates that when we use samples and selections of children's work for assessment, we are really "reviewing" their work, looking back and going over the samples, and reflecting on how children are progressing and what strategies they are using. No matter what we call it, a selection or collection, a portfolio, or a folder of samples, we can use it for authentically assessing children. We must think of it as an opportunity to review actual work the children have done.

Valencia and Place (1994) stress that the use of portfolios by students and teachers has a different emphasis than the student work folders of the past. Although the definitions and structures of portfolios may vary, they indicate that, in general, all involve the idea of aligning curriculum, instruction, and assessment; students' involvement in their own learning and evaluation; and students' growth over time. By engaging in self-reflection and self-evaluation with students, teachers can use this information to make instructional decisions. Likewise, students are encouraged as they accept more responsibility for their own learning. Additionally, the development and use of **rubrics,** which are the specific criteria or standards that will be used to score and evaluate students' performance, work, or skills, help both the students and teacher determine to what extent students have met the goals of a particular assignment, project, or task.

Samples for portfolios can be collected for each child in a classroom. These samples can be chosen by the children to represent their best work, most improved work, worst work, most creative work, or any other work the children wish to select and identify. The collection can also include some pieces identified by the teacher as representing different stages of development and progress, or pieces that show progress toward certain **benchmarks,** such as those provided, for instance, by a state department of education or a school district. These benchmarks usually describe or provide examples of student behavior, growth, or performance that may be useful in judging various stages of development. Likewise, parents and peers can be invited to identify special work.

A portfolio, folder, or box organizing and containing these samples should be kept for each child in the classroom. Many teachers find that the major responsibility for taking care of these portfolios is best given to the children themselves. In addition to serving as an excellent assessment tool, over time, the portfolios can also serve as a helpful addition to individual student conferences, report card assessments, conferences with other teachers with whom a child works, and parent/family conferences. Some teachers and students may even choose to send the portfolio to the next-year teacher to give that teacher a better idea of the child's progress. At the end of the year, the child, teacher, and parents or other family members can meet to see what should be forwarded to the new teacher and what should go home for the child's and family's collection.

Gahagan (1994, pp. 194–195) suggests self-reflection questions you could ask yourself as you consider using portfolios as part of your assessments.

1. What is my purpose for using portfolios in my classroom? What do I want to accomplish?
2. What do I want students to learn from the process of developing their own portfolios?
3. What do I want to communicate to parents/families and others through use of portfolios?
4. Who will own the portfolios?
5. What will be included in the portfolios, and how are the contents selected and organized? How often? Who is responsible?
6. What standards or criteria will be used for selecting the contents?
7. How will the portfolios be evaluated?

Some of these important questions will be answered in Chapter 5, and a suggestion for using portfolios or other collections of student-selected samples for conferences is provided in Chapter 6. Additionally, many sample forms included in the appendix illustrate how portfolios or other collections of student work, as well as rubrics, can be used for self- and teacher-assessment and to inform the teacher's instruction.

Tierney, Carter, and Desai (1991) stress there is no formula for doing portfolio assessment. It can be done in different ways by different teachers in different classrooms. The important elements are the spirit of ownership and the empowerment that is conveyed to all concerned. Finally, the IRA/NCTE (1994) task force publication reminds us that the most important agent in assessment is the teacher, and the most powerful assessments for students are likely to be those that occur in the daily activity of the classroom.

Teachers just getting into portfolio development do not have to do it all at once; in fact, they are cautioned (Paris, 1991) to move slowly. Trying to get it all together too quickly could be an overwhelming task. Instead, teachers can move into portfolio collection a little at a time so that they, and the children, feel comfortable with the process. Do as much, or as little, as you feel comfortable with; do what fits your beliefs and teaching situation. (Readers seeking more information on portfolio development, samples, and use of rubrics should refer to Farr, 1992; Farr & Tone, 1998; Fiderer, 1998, 1999; Graves & Sunstein, 1992; Paris, Calfee, Filby, Hiebert, Pearson, Valencia, & Wolf, 1992; Rickards & Cheek, 1999; Skillings & Ferrell, 2000; Valencia, 1990, 1998; Valencia, Hiebert, & Afflerbach, 1994; as well as those previously cited. Readers particularly interested in developing writing portfolios and using them to assess and evaluate students' writing should see Jenkins, 1996; Koch & Schwartz-Petterson, 2000. Additionally, for readers interested in the debates about alternative assessments, including portfolios, refer to Smith, 1991. Those interested in the research findings pertinent to portfolio practices and who want to learn about some of the unresolved issues should see Calfee & Perfumo, 1993.)

Consider and React 3–2

What experiences have you had using portfolios, other samples of students' work, and rubrics for assessment purposes? What about observations and interviews? Consider your experiences and what you have read, then react to this statement: "Observations, interviews, and samples/portfolios provide opportunities for assessment and monitoring of students' literacy use and strategies."

Interest, Attitude, and Motivation Assessments

Most literacy and other education researchers would agree that children who are motivated tend to have positive attitudes about reading and learning, and children who are encouraged and allowed to pursue their interests in school tend to do well in school-related work. In fact, almost everyone would argue that children's interests, attitudes, motivations, and feelings must be considered an integral part of instructional planning (e.g., Elley, 1992; Flippo, 1999, 2001a; Gambrell, 2001; McKenna, Kear, & Ellsworth, 1995). Therefore, it is relevant and important to assess what these interests, attitudes, motivations, and feelings about reading are for each child in your classroom.

The research related to children's interests, motivations, and feelings about reading indicate that

1. Interest stimulates deeper comprehension, leads to greater use of imagery, and stimulates more personal and relevant associations that further enhance children's learning (Tobias, 1994).

2. The purposes, experiences, and perceptions of children should be the primary focus in the classroom, and they should be the indicators that teachers use to

understand the conditions that support each child's desire to learn (Oldfather & Dahl, 1994).

3. Engagement in reading is the desired outcome, and this engagement can come about when teachers promote opportunities for personal significance, children's interests and choices, social interaction and sharing of literature, and strategies that help students find and understand books that meet their needs (Guthrie, 1996; Sweet and Guthrie, 1996).

Assessing areas relevant to children's interests, attitudes, motivations, and feelings can be an easy and natural task for the classroom teacher. Some information can be learned through the observations, interviews, and samplings already discussed. Valuable information can also be gleaned from discussions with parents or other family members, as well as with the children. Additionally, teachers can design their own interest, attitude, and motivation questions and procedures to assess aspects they believe are important. In the sections that follow, some samples are provided. It is important to note, however, that the best questions and procedures usually are those developed by classroom teachers to assess the needs, age groups, and special characteristics of the children they work with.

Interest Assessments

There is no limit to the variety of questions—and approaches to questions that you can take—in your interest assessments. For example, you might ask specific questions about the child's interests or the titles of favorite books. Or you might want to be more subtle and ask questions about how the child uses his free time. You can ask short-answer questions, discussion questions, fill-in-the-blank questions, true/false questions, "happy face" or "sad face" questions, or use any questioning format that seems most appropriate to you. Once again, the individual teacher is in the best position to make these decisions and design the questions.

Here is one example of a set of questions that provides information relevant to students' interests. Many of these questions were designed for the National Assessment of Educational Progress (NAEP) to show the frequency and variety of self-selected reading materials and students' reading purposes (see Applebee, Langer, & Mullis, 1988). Other questions (numbers 18–20) were taken (with minor editing) from a special one-on-one interview supplement to NAEP data (see Campbell, Kapinus, & Beatty, 1995).

1. How often do you read a story or parts of a story?
2. How often do you read a novel or parts of a novel?
3. How often do you read a magazine or parts of a magazine?
4. How often do you read biographies?
5. How often do you read sports books?
6. How often do you read hobby books?

7. How often do you read travel books?

8. How often do you read comic books?

9. How often do you look for information, in which you are interested, in an encyclopedia?

10. How often do you read a book about other times or places?

11. How often do you read a book after you see a TV show or movie that was based on the book?

12. How often do you read more than one book by a favorite author?

13. How often do you read just for fun?

14. How often do you read to learn something new because you want to?

15. How often do you read to talk with friends about it?

16. How often do you read to imagine yourself in the story?

17. How often do you read to relax?

18. What are the names of books you have read, on your own, because you wanted to?

19. What is the name of the book you most recently read, on your own, because you wanted to?

20. Where do you get the books you read on your own?

As you probably noticed, most NAEP questions were designed to quantify each response, which is understandable because of the large numbers of students involved. However, since you will be interested in finding out as much as possible about each student in your classroom, you might want to follow up each response with questions regarding what kind of stories, novels, magazines, biographies, sports books, and so on, each child particularly enjoys.

A review of various interest surveys and suggestions that appear in reading textbooks indicates a trend toward teachers using open-ended questions and designing their own probing questions. Teachers must also decide whether it is appropriate for children to write answers to each question (if so, allow ample room for each response), or if it is more appropriate to ask questions orally, with teachers taking notes as children voice their responses.

Here is another example of an interest assessment. As you can see, this one asks the child to draw pictures. The teacher can read the questions to younger children, or let children read the questions to themselves.

My Favorite Things Inventory   Directions: Draw a picture or pictures of your "favorite things." The heading sentence will give you an idea of what kinds of favorite things you might draw. (Teachers should leave ample space after each sentence so that children will have room to respond.)

1. When school is out each day, this is (or these are) my favorite thing(s) to do:
2. When I am on school vacation, this is (or these are) my favorite thing(s) to do:
3. If I could do anything in the whole wide world, this is what I would do:
4. When I am in school, this is (or these are) my favorite thing(s) to do:
5. If I could read about anything I wanted to read about, this is (or these are) what I would read:
6. My favorite hobby(ies) and/or favorite animal(s) are:

Once the responses are complete, the teacher can ask children to label each picture or write a sentence next to each picture to identify it. Or, the teacher can use this as an opportunity for language experience or for taking dictation from the child. The child can be asked to tell about the picture as the teacher records what the child says. This will usually yield more valuable data, as many children tend to tell more when they are not required to write, and the teacher will also have the opportunity to note the child's enthusiasm.

Assessments of Attitude, Motivation, and "Feelings"

In a way similar to ascertaining interests, the teacher can ascertain children's attitudes and motivations, as well as their feelings and self-esteem regarding their literacy. Many of the questions asked in the interest assessment can give the teacher information about children's attitudes and motivations. Often a teacher will devise additional questions that can be added to the interest assessment to yield specific and sometimes situational information about attitudes and motivations. In fact, adding these questions is recommended. Some examples of attitude and motivation questions are listed. Once again, the teacher can use any format for the questioning. It can be administered in oral or written form, depending on the child. Here are some sample questions:

1. On a scale of 1–10 (1 being the lowest and 10 being the highest), reading a book is a _____.
2. The thing I like best about going to the library is:
3. The thing I like least about going to the library is:
4. If I could pick three things I like best in school, and I could do them all day, here is what I would pick (list them in order, starting with your favorite):
5. I like to do my school work the most when the teacher . . .
6. I like to do my school work the most when the other students . . .
7. I like to do my school work the most when I . . .
8. I like to read the most when I . . .
9. I would do my school work best if . . .
10. Here is a picture of me reading. I feel . . .

Additionally, teachers can use other questions to ascertain more information about how children feel about their reading and writing abilities. Here is a sample of a sentence completion questionnaire asking children to describe, and then draw themselves, as readers and writers. This type of assessment can be done orally if the teacher believes it is best. Also, questions like these could be combined with other questions to ascertain interests and motivations.

"Feelings: Literacy-Related Survey"   Directions: Complete the sentences. Feel free to write as much as you like. Then draw the pictures. (Teachers should leave ample space so that children will have room for a full response.)

1. When I read, I feel _____
    _____.

2. When I write, I feel _____
    _____.

3. Sometimes I don't like to read because _____
    _____.

4. Sometimes I don't like to write because _____
    _____.

5. Here is a picture of how I feel about myself as a reader. I feel good/bad!

6. Here is a picture of how I feel about myself as a writer. I feel good/bad!

In summary, information about children's interests, attitudes, motivations, and feelings about themselves as readers is important and should be assessed. This information can be gathered through various questioning and observation methods. The teacher should use this extremely personal information to plan instruction and reading assignments that would appeal to each child and cause children to be motivated about their schoolwork and related reading. (Gambrell, Palmer, Codling, & Mazzoni, 1996; Henk & Melnick, 1995; and McKenna & Kear, 1990, summarize pertinent literature and provide additional assessments that can be used. Readers interested in research and more information are also encouraged to read Gambrell, 2001; Guthrie, 1996; McKenna, Kear, & Ellsworth, 1995; Oldfather & Dahl, 1994; Tobias, 1994; and to see Cramer & Castle, 1994; Guthrie, Schafer, Wang, & Afflerbach, 1995; Guthrie & Wigfield, 1997.)

Oral Reading Samples

Oral reading samples provide opportunities for the teacher to "view" a child's reading strategies. The teacher can observe these strategies in use during actual reading by carefully attending to certain signals made by the child. Additionally, follow-up questioning techniques can provide additional insight into the child's comprehension and use of strategies. Various informal and oral reading observation procedures have been used by reading researchers and classroom teachers for many years. In the sections that follow, the most widely accepted of these will be described and discussed.

> **Consider and React 3–3**
>
> As you read each of these procedures for sampling children's oral reading, consider and react to these questions: What can you learn from each? What advantages and disadvantages do you see in each?

Informal Reading Inventories (IRI)

Informal Reading Inventories, commonly referred to as IRIs, can be traced back to use in the 1920s (Johnson, Kress, & Pikulski, 1987). Administering these informal assessment instruments involves having children read from graded word lists and passages, and then answer comprehension questions to determine their reading levels. Although there are differences between each of the commercially prepared IRIs, and differences between how individual teachers might prepare their own IRIs, there are some general characteristics that describe the construction, administration, and use of most traditional IRIs:

1. IRIs are usually constructed so that the teacher administers them in several steps.

    a. First, the child reads **graded word lists** orally. (These word lists are constructed from groups of words that have been ranked by grade-level designations. They are used to help the teacher determine which passage to start the child on.)

    b. Second, the child reads **graded passages** (reading materials that have been identified as written at certain grade-level designations) orally as the teacher marks the **miscues** (the deviations from the actual wording of the text a child makes when reading orally) on a copy of each passage. These marked miscues help the teacher observe for word recognition strategies, strengths, and weaknesses. (Recording the child's oral reading on tape or some other medium, which can later be listened to as often as necessary, is one way of assuring that miscues will not be overlooked.)

    c. Third, following the oral reading, the teacher asks the child **coded comprehension questions** for each passage. (Each question is designated by the kind of question, for example, recalling of details, making an inference, drawing conclusions, and so on. These coded questions help the teacher evaluate the child's comprehension skills and strategies, strengths and weaknesses.)

    Additionally, many commercial as well as teacher-made IRIs today suggest that, before asking the predetermined comprehension questions, the teacher ask the child to **retell the passage**, telling everything he can remember. (This helps the teacher evaluate overall comprehension. Many suggest that if the retelling is complete, there is no need for the coded questions.)

2. IRIs can be used for several purposes (Johnson et al., 1987).

    a. IRIs can be used to estimate reading levels. (These include the **independent level**, at which the child is able to function independently in reading; the **instructional level**, at which the child can profit from teacher-directed reading instruction; and the **frustration level**, at which the child reaches complete frustration.)

    b. IRIs can be used to determine a child's specific reading strengths and weaknesses. (This includes aspects of word recognition and comprehension.)

    c. IRIs can be used to help a teacher understand more fully why a child is experiencing difficulty with some aspects of reading.

    d. IRIs can be used to help learners become more aware of their achievements as well as their specific strengths and weaknesses in reading.

    e. IRIs can be used to evaluate progress. (This is done by the teacher giving an inventory periodically to note changes in the child's reading and in the development of specific skills and strategies.)

Commercially Prepared IRIs   There are numerous commercially prepared IRIs available today from education publishing companies. Each has its own strengths and weaknesses; each has aspects that might be more or less appealing to different users. The only way to decide which IRI you might like best is to examine each of them. And since preferences vary, as do most people's theories and philosophies regarding reading assessment, it would not make sense to recommend any particular commercially prepared IRI for readers of this book. The best way to find an IRI that *you* like and that fits most closely with *your* particular views is to examine as many of them as possible. If you are reading this book as part of a literacy assessment course, no doubt your instructor will have his or her own preferences. No matter which IRI is selected, you will learn that it is only as good as the user is at administering it and at making evaluations from it. The IRI is a professional instrument—it does not yield black-and-white results or data. Instead it is an instrument designed to be used by the professional teacher. Use of an IRI and evaluation from an administered IRI involves knowledge, understanding, practice, and the ability to analyze.

Although no particular commercial IRI is being recommended, an article on IRIs by Pikulski (1990a) compared the features of four IRIs that have continued to be published for many editions. Examination of these features (as cited by Pikulski) shows differences that might be helpful to readers as they examine and compare available material. The four IRIs reviewed by Pikulski are cited in their most current editions and Box 3–3 provides a comparison chart from the Pikulski article.

Box 3–3	Informal Reading Inventories: Comparison chart			
Inventory	Grade Levels	Forms of Inventory	Length of Passages	Source of Passages
Analytical Reading Inventory (ARI)	Primer to 9th; 1st–9th for science and social studies	3 equivalent narrative forms; 1 social studies and 1 science form	Varies: 50–352	Written for inventory. Some science and social studies passages from textbooks
Basic Reading Inventory (BRI)	Preprimer to 8th	3 forms; A for oral, B for silent, C as needed	50 words at preprimer; 100 words primer to 8th grade	Revised from earlier editions; original source not stated
Classroom Reading Inventory (CRI)	Preprimer to 8th	4 forms in all; A & B for students in grades 1–6; C for junior high students; D for high school and adults	Varies; 24 words to 157 words	Written for inventory based on readability
Informal Reading Inventory by Burns & Roe (IRI-BR)	Preprimer to 12th	4 forms; all interchangeable	Varies; 60 words to 220 words	Primarily from graded materials in basal readers & literature books

Source: "Informal Reading Inventories" from "Assessment: Informal Reading Inventories" by J. J. Pikulski in *The Reading Teacher,* 43 (7). Copyright © 1990 by the International Reading Association. Reprinted with permission of John J. Pikulski and the International Reading Association. All rights reserved.

    Analytical Reading Inventory, 7th Edition
    Authors: Mary Lynn Woods and Alden Moe
    Publication date: 2003
    Publisher: Merrill/Prentice Hall, Upper Saddle River, NJ

    Basic Reading Inventory, 8th Edition
    Author: Jerry Johns
    Publication date: 2001
    Publisher: Kendall/Hunt, Dubuque, IA

    Classroom Reading Inventory, 9th Edition
    Author: Nicholas Silvaroli and Warren Wheelock

Box 3–3	(*Continued*)				
Use of Pictures	Use of Purpose Setting Questions	Number of Comprehension Questions per Passage	Types of Comprehension Questions	Criteria for Instructional Level	Time Needed for Admin- istration
No	Discourages discussion before reading, but allows examiner discretion	6 for levels primer–2nd; 8 for levels 3rd–9th	main idea factual terminology cause and effect inferential conclusion	95% for word recognition; 75% comprehension	not stated
No	Uses prediction from titles	10 for all levels	main idea fact inference evaluation vocabulary	95% for word recognition (only "significant" miscues counted); 75% comprehension	not stated
Yes	Yes	5 for all levels	factual inferential vocabulary	95% for word recognition; 75% comprehension	12 minutes
No	Yes	8 for all levels	main idea detail inference sequence cause and effect vocabulary	85% word recognition for Grades 1 & 2; 95% word recognition for Grades 3 & above; 75% comprehension	40–50 minutes

Publication date: 2001
Publisher: McGraw-Hill, Boston, MA

Informal Reading Inventory, 6th Edition
Authors: Paul Burns and Betty Roe
Publication date: 2002
Publisher: Houghton Mifflin, Boston, MA

In order to illustrate what some of the different parts of an IRI might look like, please note the sampled and identified teacher's copy of graded word lists, a graded passage, and a student record summary sheet reprinted or adapted from the *Analytical*

Reading Inventory (ARI, 1995). (See Boxes 3–4 through 3–6.) Those wanting to see a full IRI should examine one or more of the available commercial instruments.

Innovative alternatives to the more traditional IRls have been published. One, the *Qualitative Reading Inventory–3* (QRI) by Leslie and Caldwell (2001), is noted here because of its particular attention to prior knowledge, text structure, and mode of comprehension. The QRI assesses the reader's familiarity with the topic of each selection (prior knowledge), and also considers the type of text read (narrative or expository text structure) and the way comprehension is assessed (orally or silently) to interpret and qualify each reader's scores. (Prior knowledge, narrative and expository text structure, and comprehension are discussed in Chapter 4.) Another IRI, the *English-Español Reading Inventory for the Classroom* (Flynt & Cooter, 1999), has been specifically developed for teachers working in bilingual and English as a Second Language (ESL) classroom settings and is intended for determining reading levels from pre-primer through grade twelve.

Box 3–4	Graded word lists (teacher's copy)	
(Primer)	**(1)**	**(2)**
1. not	1. kind	1. mile
2. funny	2. rocket	2. fair
3. book	3. behind	3. ago
4. thank	4. our	4. need
5. good	5. men	5. fourth
6. into	6. met	6. lazy
7. know	7. wish	7. field
8. your	8. told	8. taken
9. come	9. after	9. everything
10. help	10. ready	10. part
11. man	11. barn	11. save
12. now	12. next	12. hide
13. show	13. cat	13. instead
14. want	14. hold	14. bad
15. did	15. story	15. love
16. have	16. turtle	16. breakfast
17. little	17. give	17. reach
18. cake	18. cry	18. song
19. home	19. fight	19. cupcake
20. soon	20. please	20. trunk

Source: "Graded Word Lists" from *Analytical Reading Inventory, 5th Edition* by M. L. Woods and A. J. Moe. Copyright © 1995. Adapted by permission of Pearson Education, Inc., Upper Saddle River, NJ.

Box 3–5	A graded passage, narrative material (teacher's copy)

Level 2, Form A (118 words, 13 sentences)   Form A /Teacher Record/Graded Passages

Examiner's Introduction (Student Booklet, page 66):

Imagine how you would feel if you were up to bat and this was your team's last chance to win the game! Please read this story.

   Whiz! The baseball went right by me, and I struck at the air!

   "Strike one," called the man. I could feel my legs begin to shake!

   Whiz! The ball went by me again, and I began to feel bad. "Strike two," screamed the man.

   I held the bat back because this time I would kill the ball! I would hit it right out of the park! I was so scared that I bit down on my lip. My knees shook and my hands grew wet.

   Swish! The ball came right over the plate. Crack! I hit it a good one! Then I ran like the wind. Everyone was yelling for me because I was now a baseball star!

Retelling:

TOTALS

Number of miscues =

Number of self-corrections =

O___ I___ S___ A___ REP___ REV___

Comprehension Questions and Possible Answers:

(mi) 1. What is this story about?
      (a baseball game, someone who gets two strikes and finally gets a hit, etc.)

(f)   2. After the second strike, what did the batter plan to do?
      (hit the ball right out of the park)

(t)   3. In this story, what was meant when the batter said, "I would kill the ball"?
      (hit it very hard)

(ce) 4. Why was the last pitch a good one?
      (because it went right over the plate)

(ce) 5. What did the batter do after the last pitch?
      (The batter hit it a good one and ran like the wind.)

(con) 6. What makes you think that the batter became confident?
      (held the bat back, decided to kill the ball or to hit it hard)

Story Elements	All	Some	None
Main character(s)			
Character(s) described			
Time of story			
Place			
Problem			
Plot details in sequence (includes turning point and resolution)			
Summary			
Examiner's Comments:			

Word Recognition	Comprehension
IND = 1	IND = 0
INST = 6	INST = 1–2
FRUST = 12+	FRUST = 3+
Examiner's Comments:	

Oral Reading Examiner's Comments:
- Made a meaningful prediction:
- Read fluently or word by word:
- Ignored end-of-sentence and/or intrasentence punctuation:
- Miscues caused or didn't cause significant change in meaning of passage:
- Emotional status:

Source: "A Graded Passage, Narrative Material" from *Analytical Reading Inventory, 5th Edition* by M. L. Woods and A. J. Moe. Copyright © 1995. Adapted by permission of Pearson Education, Inc., Upper Saddle River, NJ.

| Box 3–6 | Student record summary sheet |

Student _____ Grade _____ Sex _____ Age _____
                                                                    yrs. mos.
School _____ Administered by _____ Date _____

Grade	Word Lists	Graded Passages			Estimated Levels	
	% of words correct	WR Form __	Comp. Form __	Listen. Form __	Narrative	
						Grade
Primer					Independent	_____
1					Instructional	_____
2					Frustration	_____
3					Listening	_____
4					Expository at Grade Level	
5						
6					Science	Social Studies
7					WR Comp.	WR Comp
8						
9						

Checklist of Reading Strengths and Difficulties
(+ = strength, 0 = difficulty)

Oral Reading	Word Recognition	Retelling	Comp. Ques.
_ self corrections	_ single consonants	Narrative	_ main idea
_ word by word	_ consonant clusters	_ main characters	_ factual
_ sentence punctuation	_ long vowels	_ time	_ terminology
	_ short vowels	_ place	_ cause/effect
_ omissions	_ vowel digraphs	_ plot sequence	_ inferential
_ insertions	_ diphthongs	_ summary	_ conclusions
_ substitutions	_ use of context	Expository	
_ aided words	_ basic sight	_ enumeration	
_ repetitions	_ grade-level sight	_ time order	
_ reversals		_ compare/contrast	
		_ cause/effect	
		_ problem/solution	
		_ summary	

Source: "Student Record Summary Sheet" from *Analytical Reading Inventory, 5th Edition* by M. L. Woods and A. J. Moe. Copyright © 1995. Adapted by permission of Pearson Education, Inc., Upper Saddle River, NJ.

For more information about these and other IRIs, readers should examine the available instruments and evaluate each based on their own philosophies and needs.

Teacher-Made IRIs   Teachers can develop their own IRI assessment instruments. Although searching for appropriate passages can be time-consuming and, although technically, teacher-made IRls may not be as well constructed as commercially prepared ones, many think the benefits of the teacher selecting the specific materials to be used for the assessments are worth the time and possibilities of technical imprecision (Johnson et al., 1987). A teacher-made IRI is usually constructed with the same or similar components as the commercially prepared IRI. The steps for assembling an IRI are listed and explained.

1. Select a set of graded word lists or word-recognition tests from one of the published IRIs and randomly choose twenty words from each grade level. Or, to make it a "good fit" for your reading program, you could randomly select twenty words from each level of the basal program you are using in your classroom. Basals often contain a vocabulary list of words introduced at that level, usually printed in the back of the basal books. Also, some other published materials could be useful, such as Fry (2001); Johnson and Moe (1983); or Slosson (1981).

IRIs usually begin at the pre-primer or primer level and often continue through the seventh, eighth, or ninth grade. Some IRls now go through twelfth grade. If you develop your own, you will need to determine the span of grade levels you want your IRI to include. (The *ARI*, for instance, which has been sampled to illustrate what each section of an IRI might look like, spans though ninth grade.)

2. Select a series of graded passages (from approximately fifty to two hundred words) for each grade level you want to include in your IRI. You might decide to select passages from the basal reader program you are using, or from other graded classroom or library materials. (These are materials for which **readability levels** have been predetermined and/or materials that have been designated as appropriate for the interests, schemata, and vocabularies of most children at specified grade levels.) Usually, passages for the lower-grade levels tend to be shorter (i.e., fifty words), while passages for higher-grade levels tend to be longer (i.e., two hundred words or more). Additionally, many teachers prefer selecting passages from the content reading materials/textbooks used in their classrooms and school, such as an assortment of passages from science and social studies expository texts, as well as from narrative stories, such as those found in most of the basals. Whatever passages are selected, it is important to keep length, interest, schemata, and applicability in mind when making selections.

3. Write a set of comprehension questions for each selected passage. Usually from five to ten questions per passage is appropriate. These questions should encompass literal, inferential, and critical aspects of comprehension and should include questions requesting sequence of events, details, cause and effect relationships, comparison/contrast, word meaning in context, and other comprehension questions appropriate to the specific passage(s). Develop an answer or answers for each.

4. Write a retelling response to go with each passage. The retelling information should be in a checklist type of format, listing all the important information and ideas you would expect a child to remember from each passage if his or her comprehension was complete.

5. Develop an evaluation sheet that would allow you to record, analyze, and later evaluate each miscue and any **self-corrections.** (Self-corrections are the miscues that a child notices and fixes or self-corrects on his own.) Also, leave room for any summary notes you would want to make regarding the retelling and comprehension questions, as well as the child's use of syntax, semantic, and phoneme-grapheme cues.

Two printed versions of the teacher-made IRI must be prepared. One version is the student set. This would contain the word lists and the passages from which children will be asked to read. This version can be used over and over, as administration of the IRI does not require children to write any responses. The other version is the teacher set. Multiple copies of each of the word lists and passages should be made part of this set, since the teacher will need to mark any miscued words on a copy from each word list and passage read. This set also should contain multiple copies of the comprehension questions/answers for each passage, the retelling checklist for each passage, and evaluation sheets for each student.

Criteria for Determining IRI Levels   Criteria for determining the child's independent, instructional, and frustration levels; counting his or her miscues (deviations from text); and the system for marking miscues can be extracted from any commercially prepared IRI. Each is slightly different depending on the authors' orientation. See Figure 3–1, adapted from the previously sampled *ARI* (1995), depicting their system for marking and counting miscues.

Even though the criteria for determining reading levels varies, here are some "generic" definitions of the reading levels as used in most IRls, along with one set of reading level criteria. This criterion is almost identical to the original criterion that Betts (1946) established and is still used by the majority of commercially published IRls. Note that Johnson et al. (1987) indicate that the quantitative criteria for both oral reading accuracy and comprehension accuracy must be met for the indicated Independent Level and Instructional Level designations (pp. 21–23).

The *Independent Level* is the level at which readers function on their own with almost perfect oral reading and excellent comprehension.

Oral reading accuracy, 99 percent or more correct; comprehension accuracy, 90 percent or more correct.

The *Instructional Level* is the level at which readers profit the most from teacher-directed instruction in reading.

Oral reading accuracy, 95–98 percent correct; comprehension accuracy, 75–89 percent correct.

Miscue and How to Code	Example
Omission: Circle the word.	James Cornish lay (wounded) on the saloon floor.
Insertion: Write the inserted word or words.	It was a hot and $\overset{very}{\wedge}$humid day in Chicago in 1893.
Substitution: Write the substituted word.	The $\overset{house}{horse}$ trotted along the road.
Aided Word: Draw a line through the word pronounced for the student. An examiner should aid words for a student as little as possible.	The pony's ~~condition~~ was growing worse as his breathing grew louder and harder.
Repetitions: Underline the repeated words. Record only if two or more words are repeated.	<u>All the kids thought</u> this was a <u>great idea</u> and quickly invited Jack to belong.
Reversal: Use a curved line to indicate words or letters that have been reversed.	"Oh, no!" I shouted.

The following miscues are to be marked; but not added into the final count.

Self-correction: Record as **SC**. If a reader consistently self-corrects, the examiner knows that he or she is monitoring the meaning.	An old $\overset{boy\ SC}{beaver}$ dam from upsteam broke. No one could enter $\overset{SC}{(the\ tunnel.)}$
Hesitation: If a student hesitates after words or at the ends of lines, it should be recorded as a hesitation (/). Hesitations cause word-by-word or nonfluent reading.	I found a/lost/baby turtle./I took him home so he/could/live in my house.
Ignores Punctuation: If a student ignores end-of-sentence punctuation, record it by using a ⌣ between the two sentences. Sometimes when a reader ignores punctuation, he or she is not monitoring the meaning. If commas, apostrophes, or other intrasentence punctuation is ignored, place an **X** near them.	"I'm knocking a thousand times!" he shouted⌣ "I don't know the secret word," he declares⌣"but I have something important to tell everyone! I'm the new boy," he explained.

Figure 3–1 Examples for Marking of Miscues

Source: "Examples and Coding of Miscues" from *Analytical Reading Inventory, 5th Edition* by M. L. Woods and A. J. Moe. Copyright © 1995. Adapted by permission of Pearson Education, Inc., Upper Saddle River, NJ.

The *Frustration Level* is the level at which reading materials become so difficult that children cannot successfully respond to them.

Oral reading accuracy, 90 percent or less correct; comprehension accuracy, 50 percent or less correct.

Whichever marking system and criteria you use, consistency is most important. As long as the teacher recognizes his own marking system, and can make sense of his own criteria and method of counting miscues, the children assessed will be well served. After all, the classroom teacher's use of an IRI is only for his own instructional decision-making and evaluation purposes. As the teacher becomes more comfortable and skillful at using this assessment tool, more and more valuable information can be learned about children's strategies, strengths, and areas of needed instruction.

Miscue or Error Analysis

Miscue analysis (or, as some researchers refer to it, **error analysis**) is an excellent way of evaluating students' use of strategies, as well as of monitoring their reading strengths and areas of needed word recognition instruction. Researchers (Clay, 1968; Goodman, 1969; Weber, 1968, 1970) who studied children's oral reading errors (miscues) found that these errors allowed them to learn a great deal about children's reading strategies. The art of miscue analysis as an assessment tool and as a type of informal reading inventory was later depicted, explained, and published in 1972 by Goodman and Burke; more recently, an updated inventory has been published (Goodman, Watson, & Burke, 1987), and **retrospective miscue analysis** has been suggested as an instructional strategy that involves readers reflecting on their own miscues (Goodman & Marek, 1996).

Reading Miscue Inventory   The Reading Miscue Inventory (RMI) procedure(s) (1987) is an assessment tool designed to help teachers use and understand miscue analysis. It includes questions that are asked about each miscue and about patterns of miscues. The questions are concerned with

1. *Syntactic acceptability.* Does the miscue occur in a structure that is syntactically acceptable? (Is it grammatically correct? Are the words in the appropriate English order?)
2. *Semantic acceptability.* Does the miscue occur in a structure that is semantically acceptable? (Does it make sense in the context of the story or text?)
3. *Meaning change.* Does the miscue result in a change of meaning? (Does this meaning change involve "minor" facts/concepts or "major" facts/concepts?)
4. *Correction.* Is the miscue self-corrected by the reader?
5. *Graphic similarity.* How much do the two words (word in text and miscue) look alike?
6. *Sound similarity.* How much do the two words (word in text and miscue) sound alike?

Goodman et al. (1987) indicate that syntactic and semantic acceptability are the two most important questions in miscue analysis because they center on the major purpose of the reading process—to produce a meaningful and understandable text that sounds like language.

Administering an RMI procedure is similar in many ways to administering an IRI. RMI assessments are always teacher-made. That is, the teacher must select and prepare text material to be sampled. It is best, as with an IRI, to select material that the student has not yet read, in other words, unfamiliar material. However, even though the reading selection is new, students' concepts, schemata, and interests should be considered, as with the selection of the IRI passages.

The material should also be difficult enough to challenge the reader(s), as the teacher needs to hear a large number of miscues (twenty-five at least) in order to do an in-depth analysis. Rather than selecting fairly short passages (of approximately fifty to two hundred words) as in the IRI, the teacher should instead select an entire, cohesive text (a full story, article, chapter) on which to do an RMI. Although the actual length of the material will vary depending on the age of the reader and the type of material, the teacher should select material of at least five hundred words in length. Additionally, the teacher may want to collect a file of diverse material (diverse in difficulty, interests, and purposes) for assessing the many different readers in his classroom.

Two sets or copies of material is again necessary (as when doing an IRI)—one for the students to read, and one for the teacher to mark miscues on for each student. Here is a summary of the steps for administering an RMI.

1. Have the student read aloud for an extended period of time, marking the miscues on the teacher's copy. (Once again, record the oral reading on tape or some other medium for later use during the analysis.)

2. After the reading, have the student do a retelling. If portions of information from the text are missing, ask probing questions to see whether the student comprehended the entire selection.

3. Analyze the miscues and code them on an RMI coding sheet or on any paper you design to record this information. (See Figure 3–2 for a sample coding sheet provided to illustrate how this is done.) The coding involves asking the six questions, previously listed and explained, about each of the miscues (deviations from text).

4. After analyzing the miscues for their acceptability and their effect on comprehension, plan appropriate instruction based on the student's needs, as determined by the miscues that seriously affected overall meaning.

    A key to the RMI coding sheet symbols follows:

    Y (Yes) possible answer to questions in columns 1–4

    P (Partial) possible answer to questions in columns 1–4

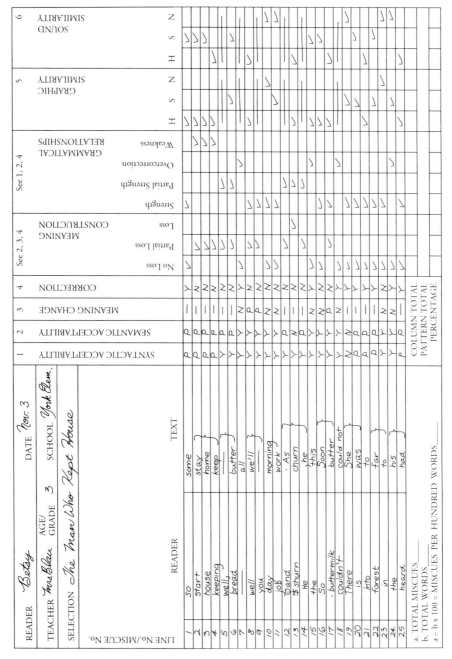

Figure 3–2 Miscue Analysis Coding Form

Source: "Miscue Analysis Coding Form" from *Reading Miscue Inventory: Alternative Procedures* by Y. M. Goodman, D. J. Watson, and C. L. Burke, Copyright © 1987. Richard C. Owen Publishers, Inc., Katonah, NY. Reprinted with permission.

N (No) possible answer to questions in columns 1–4

H (High) (for questions 5 and 6)—A high degree of similarity exists between the miscue and text.

S (Some) (for questions 5 and 6)—Some degree of similarity exists between the miscue and text.

N (None) (for questions 5 and 6)—No degree of similarity exists between the miscue and text.

Those wishing more details, examples, and procedures for using and analyzing the RMI should consult Goodman et al. (1987). However, most classroom teachers will find that asking the six questions concerning each miscue in a reading selection, whether for an RMI or adapted to use with the miscues revealed on IRI passages or other oral readings, is most enlightening. Even if exact RMI procedures/forms are not used, teachers asking these questions about each miscue will learn what strategies their students are using, how successful they are with these strategies, and in what areas teacher intervention/instruction seems necessary and prudent. It should be noted that, unlike IRIs, the RMI does not designate the students' reading levels. (Teachers who prefer not to quantify reading levels when using IRls can omit that aspect of IRI scoring and instead focus on the quality of the miscues and comprehension as inherent in the RMI procedures.)

Running Records   Another procedure for assessing students' oral reading is known as **running records**. Running records are fully described with examples in Clay's work (i.e., 1993a, 2000b), as well as in the bilingual, English and Spanish, version of the 1993 publication (Escamilla, Andrade, Basurto, & Ruiz, 1996). This procedure, like miscue analysis, is based on noting and analyzing samples of individual students' reading errors during their oral readings. However, in the RMI, these errors are called miscues. The teacher listens to the child's oral reading, keeping a running record of each word read correctly by use of a check mark ($\checkmark$)—or, as Clay calls them, "ticks"—and notes reading errors (substitutions, insertions, omissions and repetitions) by use of a symbol or by noting the substituted/inserted/omitted word. Examine the sample text and running record examples in Figure 3–3 to see what a running record might look like for a perfect oral reading, as well as for an oral reading with errors.

As noted on the teacher's running record for the first child, he read all of the words correctly; the teacher used a check mark to symbolize this for each word the child (Henry) read. The running record for the second child indicates that Jack omitted the word "little," substituted the word "money" for the word "monkey," substituted the word "throw" for the word "through," omitted the word "following," substituted the word "close" for the word "closely," repeated the word "behind," inserted the word "it," and repeated the word "his."

Sample Text (Read orally by Henry):

The little monkey swung through the trees, following closely behind his mother.

Running record for above oral reading (Recorded by the teacher on lined notebook paper):

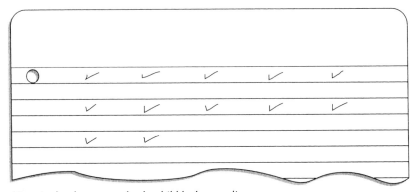

Note, in the above example, the child had no reading errors.

Running record for the same sample text (Recorded by the teacher based on oral reading by another child, Jack):

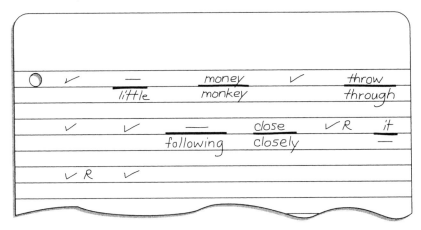

Figure 3–3 Sample Text with Running Record Examples

Clay provides much more elaborate conventions for marking and recording errors than are presented here; however, for the sake of brevity, the markings illustrated in Figure 3–3 present the basic idea. Once the teacher does a running record on a child, she records the information and analyzes the errors and self-corrections to see whether the reader used or neglected to use meaning, structure/syntax, or visual information. The teacher also checks for directional movement during the reading (left to right or right to left), calculates an error rate and self-correction rate for the reading, and uses this information to suggest books for the child.

Clay suggests that teachers make a record of each child reading three little books or book selections of different levels of difficulty. Each sample reading should be about one hundred to two hundred words, except for when assessing first readers. In that instance Clay says shorter text is fine. Clay further indicates that teachers should select a book the child has already read and has been successful with for the "easy" level text (95 to 100% correct), a book that has already been introduced to the child and that he is somewhat familiar with for the "instructional" level text (90 to 94% correct), and an unseen, unfamiliar text for the "hard" level text (80 to 89% correct). Clay uses these same percentages when calculating a child's error rate from his running records to determine the suggested reading level.

Modifying/Mixing Procedures and Keeping Oral Reading Records

The procedures so far described for informally assessing students, including notations about the quality of their oral reading and comprehension, can obviously be intermixed or combined in any way that makes sense to you, the classroom teacher. There are no hard and fast rules for doing informal assessments. In fact, that is the beauty of them. Informal assessments should be selected, modified, and mixed by each classroom teacher as he sees fit in order to precisely find out what he wants to learn about a child's literacy development and strategies. Many experienced teachers then pick and choose from the various procedures described throughout this chapter and in Chapter 4 in order to come up with their own informal assessment packages.

Consider and React 3–4

As you continue to read this chapter, begin thinking about a "mix" that fits your philosophy and the areas/strategies you wish to assess. You might also want to refer to any notes you made concerning the oral reading sampling procedures.

Whatever procedures you do select, modify, or mix, you will most likely want to sample students' oral reading in some way and then keep a qualitative analysis or record of each student's strategies and growth in her, or your, portfolio or other collection of the student's literacy work. Your analyses and records of your students' reading strategies can be updated or expanded as often as you like. These records will provide you with the qualitative data you need to assess students' achievement, plan for each student's instruction and individual work, conference students, provide information you can refer to for your evaluations of students, and report to parents/families. Whether you call it a running record, a set of dated oral readings and comprehension checkups, portfolio samples, or qualitative analyses is not important. What is important is that you are consistently and systematically assessing and instructing students based on their individual strategies and needs.

In the next sections, my modification or mix of procedures for analyzing the linguistic systems is presented. The oral reading assessment procedures I have developed over the years, which I refer to as doing **qualitative analysis,** use what I like best from miscue analysis. I borrow from the work of Goodman (1969), Goodman and Burke (1972), and Goodman, Watson, and Burke (1987), but I modify their procedures to shorten miscue analysis and make it easier for the classroom teacher to informally assess and analyze. Very much like Clay's running record assessment procedure, my modified miscue analysis techniques are not complicated and can be done with minimal paperwork for the classroom teacher. However, I do not quantify students' reading levels with my techniques, nor do I refer to miscues as errors. As far as I am concerned, error implies a wrongdoing and is negative; children's miscues, or deviations from text, I believe, are instead often very positive, indicating real strengths. Not all miscues are equal, so I examine them, looking for the strategies each indicates. I am able to learn a lot about a child's reading strategies and use of the linguistic cue systems by observing his reading attempts in this way.

Modified Miscue Analysis

The word recognition process involves use of the three cue systems: phoneme-grapheme (or, sound and sight cues); syntax (or, grammar and sentence structure cues); and semantic (or, meaning-related cues). Good readers use all three of these cue systems, with information from one or two systems enabling the reader to pick up information from the other cue system(s) and "guess" unknown or unfamiliar words. Through use of these cue systems, as students recognize or guess words in context, they are able to gain meaning from the passages containing these words. The use of these systems happens so quickly and automatically for good readers that they usually are not aware of the functions or assistance of each cue system. However, for the reader who is less proficient or less sophisticated, these systems do not necessarily go "on automatic." The classroom teacher should be adept at observing children's use, misuse, or nonuse of these cue systems in order to assist students with more effective use of each.

As noted in a previous section, the RMI and the RMI procedures were developed to carefully observe each of the cue systems and strategies used during oral reading. Use of RMI procedures is highly recommended to teachers interested in assessing their students' use of the three cue systems. Additionally, teachers can adapt these procedures

Box 3–7	Qualitative analysis of linguistic systems summary sheet			

Student: _____   Date: _____

		Cue System Usage		
Miscue in Full Sentence	Meaning Change*	Phoneme-Grapheme	Syntax	Semantic

*Was this a change of author's intended meaning?

to use with an IRI (especially if they also wish to determine independent, instructional, and frustration reading levels) or any selected passages/texts.

As each student reads orally from unread or unfamiliar selected passages or text, the teacher marks all miscues on a photocopy of the passage/text. Teachers can use any marking system to mark these miscues, as long as the teacher knows what his symbols mean. For ease in following this book, I use the same marking system used in the *ARI*. (See Figure 3–1.) After oral reading, the teacher can analyze the marked miscues to ascertain which cue systems were used, and to what extent. I have developed a Qualitative Analysis of Linguistic Systems Summary Sheet (see Box 3–7 and page A-361) for this purpose; however, teachers can record the same information on an ordinary piece of notebook paper.

Doing this type of analysis for a child on several types of texts over a period of time can give the teacher information about cue system usage and strengths, as well as weaknesses. If a lack of cue system usage is causing a loss of meaning, the teacher would intervene and provide instruction and modeling to encourage the use and development of the weaker cue system(s) to help recognize words and gain meaning from surrounding context.

Some might view this assessment and analysis of a child's phoneme-grapheme, syntax, and semantic strategies as a study of his decoding skills and strategies. Harris and Hodges (1995, p. 55) suggest that **decoding** starts with symbols and involves getting the intended meaning of words by identifying and analyzing symbols of familiar language. Others might view this assessment and analysis as a study of a child's encoding strategies. Harris and Hodges's definition (1995, p. 70) implies that **encoding** starts with an idea or with meaning and involves bringing meaning to the symbols to arrive at the message. Whether you use the term "decoding" or "encoding" will depend on your beliefs and philosophy; however, the important considerations are how the child uses these strategies, and to what extent he is successful at understanding what he reads using them. Your study of the child's encoding or decoding strategies (which are his word recognition and analysis strategies) will enable you to understand how he goes about reading, what strategies he uses, what needs he may have, and what instruction is prudent if he is having difficulty and is not understanding what he reads.

In the next sections, each cue system will be described, followed by short examples of marked passages utilizing modified miscue analysis and doing qualitative analyses to observe each use of the cue systems. Analyzing oral readings for cue system use in this way is not a cut-and-dried process. Instead, it involves qualitative analyses—the teacher must carefully assess, evaluate, and weigh each situation. It is important to understand that guessing is to be encouraged. By analyzing these guesses the teacher makes evaluations of cue system use. By guessing, the reader practices use of the cue systems. Additionally, it is important to note and analyze all of a student's self-corrections. Because we are looking for indications of strategy use (strengths), self-corrections (SC) are excellent indicators of those strengths. When we note which cue system a student uses to make his self-correction, we are noting the strength of that cue system. The emphasis is on what readers can do, and what strategies they are using.

Phoneme-Grapheme Cue System

This cue system involves use of the sound and sight of the word and includes a child's use of **phonics** (letter-sound correspondence in written language), word parts, **configuration** (shape of words), and **sight words** (words recognized by sight without analysis) to figure out or recognize words. Teachers should also keep in mind that considerations such as dialect differences, variations in fonts, capitalization, and handwritten text can all affect the way words might sound or look to readers. Indications that a child is successfully attempting to use his phoneme-grapheme system generally include when the child guesses an unknown word in text that

1. Sounds similar to the unknown word (phoneme), and/or has the same number of syllables
2. Looks similar to the unknown word (grapheme). Similar "looks" include such features as similar length, shape, beginning letters, ending letters, and/or middle letters.

Teachers I have worked with have found my "9 Ways" Checklist for Observing Phoneme-Grapheme Strategy Use helpful for systematically noting students' strengths. (See Box 3–8.)

Box 3–8	"9 Ways" checklist for observing phoneme-grapheme strategy use

Does the student read or guess a word that has the same _____ as the miscued word in the text?

	Yes	No	Clarifications
beginning letter(s) beginning sound ending letter(s) ending sound medial letter(s) medial sound shape (configuration) word length number of syllables			

Consider and React 3–5

Consider the passages in Figure 3–4, noting the miscues that two students make and see if you can ascertain whether they indicate strength in the phoneme-grapheme cue system. Make notations to back up your analysis and react to the questions that follow.

What do you think? Did you note some miscues that showed Mitchell's strengths in the phoneme-grapheme cue system? Why do you think they showed strengths? (Note that teachers usually would use much longer pieces, preferably whole stories or whole sections of text, to sample students' miscues.) For support of your assessment/qualitative analyses, see the indications of strengths in Box 3–8 of this section.

Now study the miscues marked on the next passage read by Caryl. Do you think they show strengths in the phoneme-grapheme system? Why? How did you make those decisions? (At the end of this chapter you will find sections marked "Oral Reading by Mitchell: Qualitative Analysis for Phoneme-Grapheme Cue System" and "Oral Reading by Caryl: Qualitative Analysis for Phoneme-Grapheme Cue System." You might want to compare your analysis of each reader's use of the phoneme-grapheme system with these sections.)

You have probably found it isn't that easy to say, "Yes, Mitchell was clearly using the phoneme-grapheme system," or, "No, Caryl was clearly not using it." That is because in real life, nothing is that black or white. Readers often partially use and partially do not use the system. For instance, I said that Mitchell's miscue "telegraph" for "telephone" showed strength in the phoneme-grapheme system. I said that because the words sound similar, have the same number of syllables, and they also look similar in length, shape,

Oral Reading by Mitchell

telegraph   *reaching*   *hill*
The telephone was ringing off the hook. Bill's
sister   *there with, its*
secretary was almost at her wits ^end. She
grasped   *SC*
yellow
grabbed the phone and yelled "yes" into the

receiver. Just then, I came in to give her some
help   *minute*   *last*
assistance. "Not a moment too soon," she later

told me.

Oral Reading by Caryl

seem   *home*
The little kitten seemed to be homeless. She
was , working   *silly*
wasn't wearing a collar and was very skinny.
seem   *new*   *purples*
She also seemed very nervous around people,
was ,   *because*
like she wasn't around them much before. We
pillows
gave her a bowl of milk with some small pieces

of bread soaking in it. She began eating and
puffing   *ball*
purring ×both at the same time.

Figure 3–4 Samples of Oral Readings

and beginning letters. However, they look different in the middle and at the end. Although Mitchell had not used every phoneme-grapheme cue available, when he guessed "telegraph" for "telephone," he used enough to help me make the qualitative evaluation that he showed strength in the phoneme-grapheme cue system in the oral reading of that passage. If we later find that Mitchell has problems with other cue systems that affect his comprehension of the passage, we will see whether the few partial weaknesses we spotted in the phoneme-grapheme cue system are contributing and worth specific instructional attention. But for now, let us go on and look at how this same reader (Mitchell) and our other reader (Caryl) do with their use of the syntax cue system.

Syntax Cue System

This cue system involves the use of grammar and sentence structure patterns to figure out or recognize words and to attempt to make sense from the text. Indications that a child is successfully attempting to use his syntax system include when the child guesses an unknown word in text that is the same part of speech, or serves the same function in the sentence, as the unknown word.

From birth on, children are exposed to the syntax of their language. At first, this exposure comes from only hearing language spoken in their home and surroundings. Later, children see syntax used in various written communications (e.g., notes from family members, greeting cards, posters, advertisements, and, of course, newspapers, books, and magazines around the house). Because of this early and constant exposure to syntax, children have a sense of "what combinations of words sound and look right, and what wording combinations do not sound or look right" even before formal reading and writing instruction begins in school. Many classroom teachers find that this developed sense of syntax is a tremendous asset.

Consider and React 3–6

Consider and examine the miscues in the passages that Mitchell and Caryl read (refer to Figure 3–4). This time, look to see to what extent the miscues are syntactically correct. In other words, examine each miscue to see if it is the same part of speech or if it serves the same function in the sentence as the actual word in the text. Make notations to support your analysis and react to the questions that follow.

First, go back to the miscues marked in the passage read by Mitchell. Keep in mind that you are looking now only for use of syntax. Even if the substituted word does not make sense, if it is the same part of speech or serves the same function as the word in the text, it can be correct syntactically.

Well, what did you decide? After your qualitative analysis of Mitchell's miscues for syntax, do you think he has a well-developed syntax system? Were there any exceptions? (Look at the end of this chapter in the section marked "Oral Reading by Mitchell: Qualitative Analysis for Syntax Cue System" for my qualitative analysis and compare it with your own.)

Now review Caryl's miscues in the marked passage to ascertain to what extent she uses her syntax system. What is your qualitative analysis of Caryl's miscues as they relate to her use of syntax? Do you think she has a well-developed syntax system? Were there any exceptions? (Look at the end of this chapter in the section marked "Oral Reading by Caryl: Qualitative Analysis for Syntax Cue System" and compare it with your own.)

As we have seen thus far, the phoneme-grapheme system and the syntax system each provide certain clues (or cues, same thing) to an unknown word. These cues are based on the way the unknown word sounds/looks (phoneme-grapheme) and the place of the unknown word/grammar of the unknown word (syntax) in the sentence. But what about meaning? Is it not important that the reader selects a word that makes sense in the sentence and paragraph? Yes, it is; that is the function of our third cue system, the semantic system.

Semantic Cue System

This cue system involves use of meaning to recognize words and to attempt to make sense from the text. It includes a child's use of vocabulary in context and other meaning clues to figure out or recognize words. Indications that a child is successfully attempting to use his semantic system include when the child guesses an unknown word in text that

1. Makes sense in the immediate sentence
2. Makes sense in the paragraph
3. Makes sense in the larger context of the story or text
4. Makes sense when you consider the meaning clues given elsewhere in the paragraph, story, or text. (For example, the story mentions "candles," "cake," "presents," and "balloons," and the child guesses "birthday" party. This guess makes use of the meaning clues ["candles," "cake," "presents," and "balloons"] embedded in the story. If the child had guessed "Halloween" party, he would not have made full use of all the clues ["cake," "balloons," and maybe "candles" would fit; but "presents" are unusual at a Halloween party].)

As you again analyze the marked passages read by Mitchell, and then by Caryl, look at each miscue to see whether it makes sense in each instance. (First, does it make sense in the sentence it is in? Then, does it make sense in the paragraph it is in? [We cannot determine from the one-paragraph samples we have whether the miscue would make sense at the next level, in the larger context of the story/text, or not. However, when you actually sample children's oral reading from their books, you will be using a lengthier piece, preferably a whole story or chapter—then you can check for this level of semantic system use.] Finally, are there any meaning clues in the paragraph [or larger context] that Mitchell or Caryl used to guess the miscued word? Are there any meaning clues that he or she missed that would have helped?)

Consider and React 3–7

Look again at Mitchell's passage, followed by Caryl's (see Figure 3–4). Try answering the questions just posed, considering each child's use of the semantic cue system. What other evidence do you see of their usage? Make notations to support your analysis.

After you do a qualitative analysis of each for use of the semantic cue system, compare your analysis to mine at the end of this chapter in the sections marked "Oral Reading by Mitchell: Qualitative Analysis for Semantic Cue System" and "Oral Reading by Caryl: Qualitative Analysis for Semantic Cue System."

We have seen how two readers use the three cue systems in one short sample of their reading. We have noted that each has his or her own cue system strengths and areas that are not as strong. (But we must keep in mind that we made these observations from only one isolated, short sample. In order to make a more accurate assessment of each child, we should assess his/her readings of several selections and on longer and different types of selections, over time.) We have also seen that, while each cue system serves a different function during the reading process, cues from each system usually are necessary for readers to guess or figure out the unknown word. When one system is not functioning as well as the others, it is still often possible for the reader to make good guesses and make sense of what he or she is reading. In that case, no instruction to develop strategies for the weaker area may be necessary. However, when the reader cannot make good guesses and cannot make sense of his reading (in other words, when there is an obvious loss of comprehension) then the teacher should provide direct instruction to help the child develop strategies for the specific area of need. (In Figures 3–5 and 3–6, note how Mitchell's and Caryl's miscues are recorded on a Qualitative Analysis of Linguistic Systems Summary Sheet. You can use copies of this sheet [see page A-361] or an adaptation to analyze the miscues of your own students.)

Consider and React 3–8

Consider once more the analyses of Mitchell's and Caryl's miscues on the sample we have for each. What do you think? Does either show a possible need for instruction or development in a specific word recognition or analysis area in order to comprehend what he or she read? What would you suggest? Why?

Remember, the emphasis should be on what strategies readers use. If they can get meaning from text with those strategies, that is fine. If not, the teacher should ascertain what strategy development would help them get meaning. (Compare your analyses of instructional needs with the ones at the end of the chapter, marked "Mitchell: Suggested Instructional Needs" and "Caryl: Suggested Instructional Needs.")

Finally, it should be pointed out that the syntax and semantic system strategies are closely tied and are not completely independent of each other (Harste, Woodward, & Burke, 1984). This is because both syntax and semantic cues are so dependent on the **context** (reading situation, surrounding text) of the material being read. They both involve the reader asking himself, "Does this fit in this sentence?" For syntactic analysis, the emphasis is, "Does it sound right here?" For semantic analysis, the emphasis is, "Does it make sense here?" Use of punctuation cues is one example of types of cues that involve

Student: *Mitchell*   Date: *September 26*

Miscue in Full Sentence	Meaning change*	Cue System Usage		
		Phoneme-Grapheme	Syntax	Semantic
telegraph The telephone was	(yes)	phoneme-grapheme cues were mostly used	syntax cues used	semantic cues used
reaching ringing off	(yes)	phoneme-grapheme cues were partially to mostly used	syntax cues used	semantic cues used
hill the hook.	(yes)	phoneme-grapheme cues were partially to mostly used	syntax cues used	semantic cues used
sister Bill's secretary was	yes – but not significant	phoneme-grapheme cues were partially used	syntax cues used	semantic cues used
there with its almost at her wits' end.	(yes)	phoneme-grapheme cues were partially used	syntax cues were partially to mostly used	semantic cues used
grasped She grabbed the phone and	no	phoneme-grapheme cues were mostly used	syntax cues used	semantic cues used
SC *yellow* yelled "yes" into the receiver.	at first yes, but SC	at first guess used phoneme-grapheme cues only	at first guess didn't use syntax, but used syntax for self-correction	at first guess didn't use semantic, but used semantic cues for self-correction
Just then, I came in to *help* give her some assistance.	no	phoneme-grapheme cues were not used	syntax cues used	semantic cues used
minute "Not a moment too soon,"	yes but only a slight change of meaning – not significant at all	phoneme-grapheme cues were mostly used	syntax cues used	semantic cues used
last she later told me.	no	phoneme-grapheme cues were partially to mostly used	syntax cues used	semantic cues used

*Was this a change of author's intended meaning?

Figure 3–5 Qualitative Analysis of Linguistic Systems Summary Sheet for Mitchell

both the syntax and the semantic systems. Students' sense of sentence structure and word order (syntax) involves punctuation cues, like knowing a sentence or phrase has ended (by observing a period or comma to separate the sentences/phrases). Students' sense of meaning involves punctuation cues too, like knowing a thought has ended (by observing that a period ends the idea). When a student uses punctuation to help himself get meaning from the text, he is using both syntax and semantic cues.

Student: _Caryl_   Date: _September 30_
                                                          (page 1)

Miscue in Full Sentence	Meaning change*	Cue System Usage		
		Phoneme-Grapheme	Syntax	Semantic
seem The little kitten seemed	yes – but not significant	phoneme-grapheme cues were mostly used	syntax cues were partially used	semantic cues were partially used
home to be homeless	(yes)	phoneme-grapheme cues were partially used	syntax cues used	semantic cues were partially used
was She wasn't	(yes)	phoneme-grapheme cues were partially used	syntax cues used	semantic cues were partially used
working wearing a collar	(yes)	phoneme-grapheme cues were mostly used	syntax cues used	semantic cues were not used
silly and was very skinny	(yes)	phoneme-grapheme cues were partially to mostly used	syntax cues used	semantic cues were partially used
seem She also seemed	yes – but not significant	phoneme-grapheme cues were mostly used	syntax cues were partially used	semantic cues were partially used
new very nervous	(yes)	phoneme-grapheme cues were partially used	syntax cues used	semantic cues used
purples around people,	(yes)	phoneme-grapheme cues were mostly used	syntax cues used	semantic cues were not used
was like she wasn't around	(yes)	phoneme-grapheme cues were partially used	syntax cues used	semantic cues were partially used
because them much before.	(yes)	phoneme-grapheme cues were partially used	syntax cues possibly(?) used (Later–see if Caryl thought an explanation might follow)	semantic cues possibly(?) used

*Was this a change of author's intended meaning?

Figure 3–6 Qualitative Analysis of Linguistic Systems Summary Sheet for Caryl

Classroom teachers are encouraged to do qualitative analyses of each child's oral reading throughout the school year. This will provide an authentic and rich source of information about the child's linguistic strategy use and development. This assessment information will be invaluable for instructional planning, conferences, and sharing progress with everyone concerned.

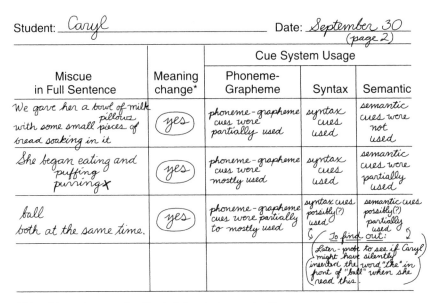

Student: _Caryl_   Date: _September 30_
                                                           (page 2)

Miscue in Full Sentence	Meaning change*	Cue System Usage		
		Phoneme-Grapheme	Syntax	Semantic
We gave her a bowl of milk with some small pieces of bread soaking in it ~~pillows~~	yes	phoneme-grapheme cues were partially used	syntax cues used	semantic cues were not used
She began eating and puffing ~~purring✗~~	yes	phoneme-grapheme cues were mostly used	syntax cues used	semantic cues were partially used
ball both at the same time.	yes	phoneme-grapheme cues were partially to mostly used	syntax cues possibly(?) used ¿ To find out: ?	semantic cues possibly(?) partially used (Later—probe to see if Caryl might have silently inserted the word "the" in front of "ball" when she read this.)

*Was this a change of author's intended meaning?

Figure 3–6 *Continued*

Fluency Considerations

Fluency in oral reading involves the ability to read both smoothly and accurately. Many have endorsed the importance of children developing their reading fluency (e.g., Allington, 2001; Johns & Berglund, 2002a; National Reading Panel, 2000; Pinnell, Pikulski, Wixson, Campbell, Gough, & Beatty, 1995; Snow et al., 1998; Zutell & Rasinski, 1991; and many more). Frequent opportunities to practice identifying and figuring out words through meaningful reading and writing experiences help readers achieve automatic word identification, also known as **automaticity,** which is closely related to fluency. While some have stressed that the rate of reading is a sign of fluency, others have emphasized that children's intonation and phrasing are equally important.

Clearly, it is not enough for students to just develop their proficiency in word recognition. As we have learned from monitoring their linguistic strategies, they need to read with the meaning of the text in mind. When students read *with* meaning, they are demonstrating some level of reading fluency. Fluent reading is accurate, quick, expressive, and most of all, meaningful. Rasinski and Padak (2001) stress that fluency is an important bridge between word recognition and comprehension. Many other researchers agree that fluent reading is highly correlated with measures of reading comprehension, and likewise, as automaticity and fluency develop, readers are able to read more quickly and focus more attention on the meaning of what is read (Chall, 1979; LaBerge & Samuels, 1974). Blachowicz, Sullivan, and Cieply (2001) have summarized that fluency requires good decoding skills, the strategies to orchestrate these when reading real text, and the comprehension to monitor what is being read, making sure that it sounds like real language (p. 97).

Even though most of the discussion and emphasis on developing and monitoring fluency has involved oral reading, it is important for teachers to realize that reading with fluency should extend beyond the primary grades to successful, independent, silent reading and comprehension as well (Worthy & Broaddus, 2001/2002).

We also know from the research of those already cited that readers who struggle with word recognition and oral reading are not fluent readers. This should come as no surprise. As we have seen from our assessments of linguistic strategies, students who lack cue system usage struggle over reading—focusing on one word at a time without regard to meaning—and students who make many miscues that are not semantically appropriate are not reading fluently. How can we help? How can we provide a reading environment that fosters fluency *and* comprehension? These questions will be answered in the chapters that follow, but for now it is important to understand that by assessing and continuing to monitor students' oral reading strategies and by developing instructional plans for them based on their strategy needs, you will be assessing and promoting their fluency.

You will be noting such things as

- the child's intonation, phrasing, inflection, and expression
- if the child's fluency and understanding are affected by inattention to punctuation and/or hesitations
- if the child's fluency and understanding are affected by the type of literature he is reading
- if the child is reading *with* meaning
- if the child knows he should be reading *for* meaning
- if the child's miscues are affecting his understanding of the meaning
- how quickly the child self-corrects his miscues
- if a lack of certain strategies is affecting the child's fluency, and if so, which strategies in particular?

Your qualitative analysis of the child's reading strategies is thus in effect a tool for also assessing his fluency. As you monitor his oral reading strategies over time, you can keep notes on improvements in the areas bulleted above to track and document his fluency development and to ascertain what and how much support he may need to become a more fluent and automatic reader. If you are also using IRIs to determine his reading levels, you will find that most of the major IRIs (e.g., see those listed earlier in this chapter) provide information relevant to fluency and rate of reading. As students mature and move from the early childhood into elementary and upper grades, it is suggested that teachers continue to observe and monitor their success with fluency by noting their reading rates as well. (**Reading rate** can be fairly easy to estimate by counting the number of words per minute read with comprehension in several different types of reading selections at students' independent reading levels. When rate is calculated using oral reading, the teacher should subtract any meaning loss miscues from the total number of words read per minute. When rate is calculated using silent reading, which becomes more and more appropriate for older youngsters and readers, the teacher should follow up the reading with comprehension probes to ascertain the students' understanding. Several means of assessing comprehension are provided in Chapter 4.)

Information from Children's Writing and Invented Spelling

Children's use of oral language and written language (writing, spelling, and reading) all involve language processes and development. When children speak, write, spell, and read they are telling us or showing us some of what they know. Juel (1988) indicates that in children's writing we see information about the rules they understand that appear in oral language. Research in children's language development is extremely important because it relates directly to the linguistic and cognitive demands of the classroom (Galda, Cullinan, & Strickland, 1997). Harste et al. (1984) explain that children operate from a linguistic data pool into which they put what they learn from each language encounter and draw out what they need for future encounters. Because of this, it is important to look at children's use of linguistic, as well as cognitive, strategies across language processes. Some have been doing this (e.g., Brown & Cambourne, 1991; Harste et al. 1984; Johnston, 1992; Sulzby, 1992; Templeton, 1997; and many others). Even though there is still much to be learned and more research to be done, we are continually learning from this research and the work and writings of others. This section will highlight some of that work.

Johnston (1992) indicates that when children are given opportunities to write, their hypotheses about language are reflected in their writings. Johnston also empha-sizes that writing, like reading, is a complex process, and he lists and discusses many of the concepts and complexities of writing that children must eventually work out (pp. 199–212). Clay devised a test she calls Concepts About Print to help evaluate some of these concepts and complexities. She describes the administration and scoring of this procedure in Clay (1993a, 2000a), and a bilingual (English and Spanish) version of her 1993 material can be found in Escamilla et al. (1996). Templeton (1997) discusses, with examples, the reciprocal development of reading and writing, yielding further insights about how children's literacy knowledge can be observed from both (pp. 157–181).

The research summaries on emergent literacy (i.e., Sulzby, 1992) provides evi-dence that "writing development always includes reading development" (p. 291), and that "the three aspects of reading—letter-sound knowledge, concept of word, and comprehension—have each been developing for the child across many literacy contexts, including writing" (p. 295). Sulzby says children are writing conventionally when they write "a text that another conventionally literate person can read from conventionally" and when they can also read their own written text conventionally (p. 295).

Harste et al. (1984) indicate that written language is learned from the inside out in a supportive and conducive environment. Reading supports writing, just as speech and experience support these processes by permitting learners to take alternative perspectives and stances on their knowing. Harste et al. studied the surface features of children's writing and organization from a variety of **graphophonic** (phoneme-grapheme), syntactic, and semantic perspectives. They concluded that although many complex processes are involved, it seems clear that children learn about language use from using language in all its forms, oral as well as written. They emphasize that different constraints and conventions apply to different forms of language, but that the decisions children make in reading and writing are based on their language learnings, as well as on their personal and social learnings, and are worth studying.

Brown and Cambourne (1991) and Curtis (1991) show how children's proofreading is a window into the learner's decision making and current working model of **conventions** (spelling, punctuation, capitalization, presentation, layout, style, structure, and coherence). Tompkins (2002) indicates that proofreading is a kind of reading that writers use when they review their writing. Tompkins compares the knowledge and actions of readers and writers and sees similarities in the knowledge and activities involved (p. 132). Yetta Goodman (1978) talks about "kidwatching" to describe observations and evaluations of children's language development that classroom teachers can make. Revie (1991) identifies major **markers** (or signs of a child's growth—similar to the term *benchmarks* which represents the same idea) in an Australian research project and uses them for evaluation. Some of these markers include the following: uses cueing systems and strategies in flexible ways to gain meaning from print; represents most sounds in writing; shows recall of visual patterns in spelling; and shows evidence in spelling of self-generated rules for vowel sounds.

Even though there are many relationships between oral and written language, and the other language processes, care must be taken when evaluating them. For instance, Ken Goodman (1984) points out that oral language and written language involve different media and have different constraints. Wilde's (1992) work with spelling, punctuation, invented spelling, and developmental punctuation provides some excellent examples of these differences, as well as some insights.

Invented Spelling and Developmental Punctuation

The term **invented spelling,** which refers to writers' own spellings, is recognized as being based on their individual knowledge of language. Wilde (1992) indicates that the term *invented spelling* first came into usage in the writings of Chomsky (1971) and Read (1971) and that it involves the writer's attempt to recreate written language, rather than any implication of errors. Since English spelling is not completely regular, writers may have a hard time applying their knowledge of learning to some words. Likewise, Ken Goodman (1982) indicates that he prefers using the term *invented spelling,* rather than *spelling error* or *misspelling,* just as he has used the term *miscue* in oral reading analysis, as opposed to the term *error.* The connotation of error or misspelling is one of mistake or failure, while the connotation of miscue or invented spelling is one that credits the reader/writer as developing strategies toward achieving the accepted conventions. Self-corrections from proofreading are important indications of development and strengths. Furthermore, research indicates that inventive spellers are especially prepared for the use of phonetic knowledge that word reading requires (Richgels, 1995, p. 108).

Wilde also states that the term **developmental punctuation** parallels invented spelling and involves children's use of punctuation based on their evolving knowledge of how written language works. Capitalization is usually included as an aspect of punctuation. She summarizes punctuation studies and indicates that they suggest that various types of punctuation gradually emerge in children's writing, reflecting a developing knowledge of syntactic and other linguistic structures.

For Wilde (1992), one of the most important understandings coming out of the studies of children's spelling and punctuation is that teachers can learn a great deal from looking at children's writing. She provides many examples of observations teachers can make about children's thought processes as children write and teachers watch them and listen to their reasoning. Wilde sees obvious relationships between spelling and reading, but points out that the connections are not simple and there are many differences. For instance, the relationships between sounds and letters aren't necessarily reversible. She cites that the letter k is usually pronounced /k/, but the sound /k/ could be spelled with c, k, or q. She also points out that spelling requires more attention to all the letters of a word, where reading does not. The main implication, she says, is that although spelling and reading are related, they are not mirror images of each other. Another example shows Wilde's point: Children can write many words that are in their oral language vocabularies that they do not yet recognize in print, but this doesn't mean they can spell them correctly. However, as children mature and approach adulthood, their oral, writing, reading, and spelling vocabularies eventually tend to grow more equal.

When we examine children's language, we need to be careful that we examine both the processes they use and the products of their language use. If we study just their writing and spelling to see whether they are using appropriate conventions, we can lose sight of the strategies and processes children are using to construct their thoughts and record them. Likewise, if we study just their reading to see whether they can decode and understand what they read, we can lose sight of the strategies they are using and how they go about using them (process). Although we need to be careful, we should not be afraid to look at oral language, writing, spelling, and reading to note what we are able to observe. In fact, researchers such as Harste et al. (1984) encourage us to take risks and look carefully at children's language processes. Wilde (1992) encourages looking at children's writing, spelling, and punctuation to learn what they are showing us. Wilde

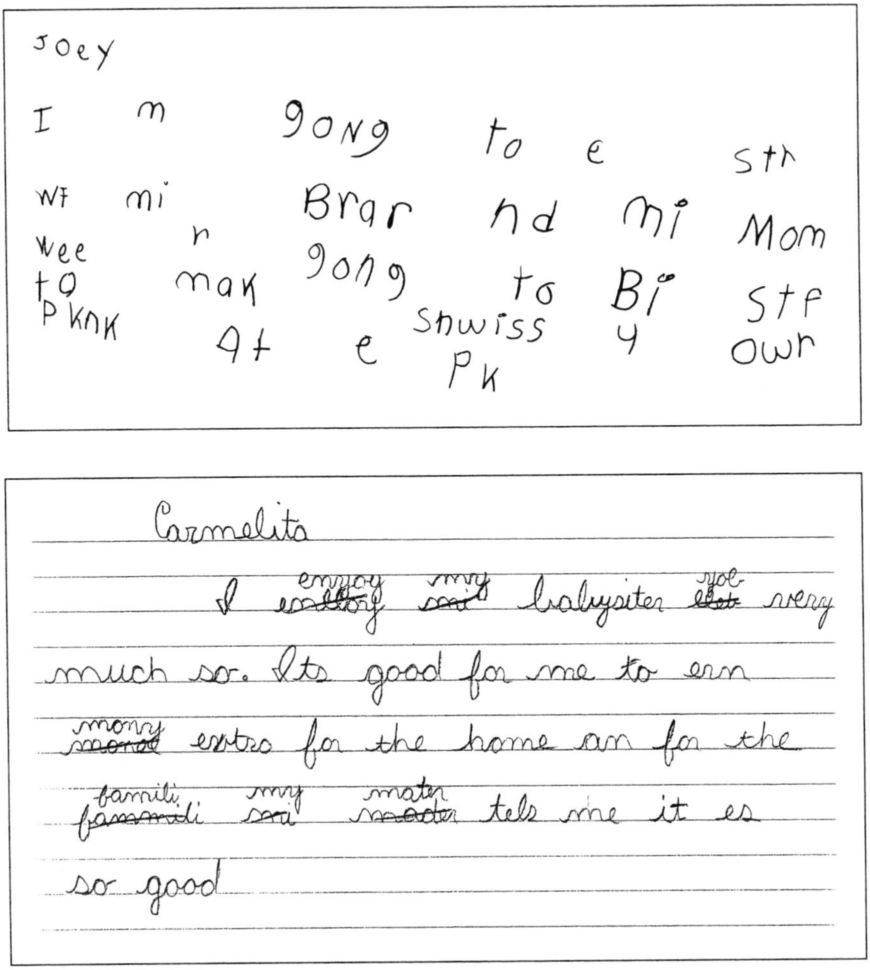

Figure 3–7 Samples of Children's Writing

(1997) also provides a number of common patterns of invented spellings and discusses what they each mean, indicating that "children are powerful informants once we have the linguistic background to interpret what they are doing" (p. 83).

In this spirit, Templeton (1995) shows how, when invented spellings occur, "they can be an excellent indicator of the degree of a child's phonemic awareness." He provides the following example: "The child who writes ILKDGSNKTS ('I like dogs and cats') is able to attend primarily to individual consonant sounds within a syllable" (p. 117). Templeton emphasizes to teachers that "children's invented spellings will give you invaluable clues as to what they know about words and what you can help them attend to" (p. 212).

In Figure 3–7 you will see two short samples of children's writing. The first is from Joey, a first grader. The second is from Carmelita, a fifth-grade bilingual student.

Although the process of analyzing children's invented spelling and developing punctuation is very complex and involves many aspects, variables, and complexities beyond the scope of this book, looking at these children's writings—even if we are admittedly only looking at one sample from each student and these samples are very limited—can give us some information about their linguistic understandings, as supported by the ideas of the researchers of language development and invented spelling cited in this section.

Consider and React 3–9

Consider these samples and see what observations you can make by looking at some of the invented spelling, developmental punctuation, and other obvious surface features. Note your observations, then compare them to mine. How did you do? How did I do?

Joey wrote his story to go with a picture he drew of two children and a female adult approaching a building. In the background there were trees and flowers. Here is a translation of the story that Joey read aloud to me as he pointed to each word: "I am going to the store with my Brother and my Mom. We are going to buy stuff to make sandwiches for our Picnic at the Park."

Did you note that Joey has formed a word, often using invented spelling, for each word that he read? Did you see that even though his spelling is mostly invented, he is spelling words using many logical approximations for beginning, ending, and some medial sounds? For instance, he spells "Park" as "PK." Joey is from eastern Massachusetts, where many people don't pronounce the "r" in "park." His invented spelling seems logical for the beginning /p/ and ending /k/ sounds he hears when he says "Park." He also seems to be somewhat aware of syllables. Note, "Bra-r" (bro/ther), "go-ng" (go/ing), "sn-wis-s" (sand/wich/es), and "PK-nK" (pic/nic). The length and shape of many of his invented spelling words seem appropriate for the length and shape of the words they represent, and he seems to have a good sense of word boundaries.

Additionally, he shows recall of visual patterns ("e" for "the," "mi" for my," "gong" for "going"), and uses symbols and some correct spelling to accurately represent words ("I," "m," "to," Mom, "r," "4" "at"). Joey did not use any punctuation in his writing, but when he read his story to me, he did hesitate after reading "Mom" and "Park," so I put in the punctuation I heard when I wrote Joey's translation. Because of this I believe he is developing a sense of sentence boundaries; even though he is not writing punctuation yet, he read punctuation as evidenced by his intonation. (His voice went down at the end of each sentence, and he paused slightly between the reading of the first and second sentences.) Each of his sentences makes sense, and the sentence structure seems appropriate. The story told by the writing matches the information in Joey's picture. Joey uses appropriate words and capitalization to fit the message he wants to convey. He indicates an understanding of who the key characters are and the other key vocabulary in his descriptive story by capitalizing all the names ("I," "Brar" [Brother], and "Mom") and by capitalizing "Pknk" (picnic) and "PK" (park).

In Figure 3–7, let's look at a writing sample done by Carmelita, a fifth-grade bilingual student. English is Carmelita's second language, Spanish her first. Carmelita was asked to write about ways she considers herself to be a contributor to her family and/or the greater community in which she lives. After writing it, she read her piece, and I wrote the translation and put in the punctuation I heard: "I enjoy my babysitting job very much so. It's good for me to earn money extra for the home and for the family. My mother tells me it is so good."

Carmelita's self-corrections show her struggle with English spelling conventions, but she obviously is using phonetic approximations as she works on this piece. Her approximations are logical for the way the words sound to her. Carmelita's spelling and grammar are influenced by her first language (Spanish), which is to be expected. Although her grammar, sentence structure, and punctuation are not perfect, she successfully structures her message to make sense. There is meaningful continuity from one sentence to the next, and the paragraph fits the topic she was to write about. She indents for the paragraph, uses punctuation at the end of the first sentence, and capitalizes the first and second sentence. Her vocabulary seems adequate to meet this writing task and convey her ideas. She is probably limited by her obvious difficulty with spelling English words. However, the more opportunities she has to write, the more opportunities she will have to proofread and self-correct, which seem to strengthen her spelling and should give her opportunities to attend to the other conventions.

You will undoubtedly want to read other sources, as well as those cited in this section, to better understand and use the research and thinking regarding spelling development and early writing (e.g., Clay, 1987; Cramer, 2001; Dahl & Farnan, 1998; Dombey, Moustafa, & others, 1998; Fresch & Wheaton, 2002; Gentry, 1997; Gentry & Gillet, 1993; Jenkins, 1996; McGee & Richgels, 2000; Temple, Nathan, Temple, & Burris, 1993) and other modes of written language to effectively observe and analyze your students' writing. I hope you will continue to look at your students' writing as another source of information about their literacy development.

Other Available Information

Teachers can also gather important information about their students from student records, other teachers, parents and family members, and students themselves. These observations, samples, and interviews should be used as part of the assessment process. The information gathered should be evaluated in light of the other assessments you have done. Obviously, biases can exist, and others (particularly other teachers, and parents/family members) may have a different philosophy or knowledge about reading assessment and the reading process than you have. This different philosophy could lead to someone regarding a child as a "poor reader" because he does not have perfect oral reading skills, even though his comprehension is excellent. Therefore, it is important that you keep these potential differences in mind as you review and evaluate the various sources of other available information on your students.

Even though different philosophies about assessment and reading can lead to different evaluations concerning a particular child's reading abilities, there is still good reason to seek out these other sources as part of your assessment and analysis of each child. In the sections that follow, some of the benefits from these information sources will be cited. Additionally, ideas for questions you could ask, and a suggestion for organizing the information, will be provided.

Information from Student Records

A child's student record should be viewed as a brief history, as reported by past teachers, of the child's school experience to date. History can sometimes be inaccurate or stilted, but it still reveals some events that have transpired. These events often concern family history (parents' education, divorces, marriages, deaths, etc.); medical history (problems, medications); test scores and grades (often affecting self-concept and teacher/family attitudes); and teachers' comments.

As you review this history, you may learn a lot about the child's sociocultural background, family life situation, and school successes and failures. This information should help you better understand the child's self-concept, the parents' and family's beliefs and concerns, and, perhaps, some of the advantages and disadvantages you will be dealing with as you work with this child.

Information from Other Teachers

Interviews with teachers the child had the previous year, and before, can be revealing. You can learn how the child's reading abilities were previously assessed and diagnosed and what specific type of reading instruction was provided. You can also use this opportunity to make inquiries concerning something you have observed and have questions about, something you noted in the school records, or something the parents or child have said.

As noted, different philosophies concerning reading assessment and the reading process may lead to very different evaluations of the same child. However, information about how the child was previously assessed and taught reading will be valuable to your qualitative analysis. For example, if you have noted that the student relies almost totally on the phoneme-grapheme cue system for word recognition and refuses to make syntactic or semantic guesses, you might learn (from previous teachers) that the child was taught reading by an emphasis on phonics and that past teachers insisted on correct word-by-word pronunciation during oral reading. This information could shed light on the child's over-reliance on the phoneme-grapheme system and his under-reliance on the other systems. You might evaluate that the child has not been given instruction or opportunity to use the other two cue systems. Here are some ideas for the kinds of questions you could ask other teachers. Feel free to develop your own questions or add to this list.

Questions You Could Ask Other Teachers

1. How would you describe this child's reading?
2. How were his/her reading abilities assessed?
3. What type of reading instruction was provided?
4. How would you describe this child's oral language, self-expression, and writing abilities?
5. How did you assess these?
6. What kind of language and writing activities were provided?
7. What are this child's strengths?
8. What are this child's needs?
9. How does this child learn best?
10. Is there anything else you could tell me that would help me work with this child?

This information, along with other information you have gathered from student records, can be recorded on the Sources and Information form you will find in Box 3–9. This form is just one suggestion for organizing these data; you may want to devise your own form or your own way of recording this valuable information.

Box 3–9	Sources and information

Child's Name _____

Sources:	**Teacher's Notations About:**
From Student Records	Family history:
_____	Medical history:
date(s)	Child's strengths:
	Child's needs:
	Past teacher's comments:
	Special programs attended:
	Past schools:

Box 3–9	*(Continued)*

Past test results:
Anything else:

From Other Teachers

_____
teacher's name

_____
date

Reading abilities:
How reading was assessed:
Type of reading instruction provided:
Language and writing abilities:
How language/writing were assessed:
Type of language/writing activities provided:
How child learns best:
Child's strengths:
Child's needs:
Anything else:

From Parents/Family

_____
name/relationship

_____
date

Child as a reader:
Child as a writer:
Family involvement in writing:
Child's strengths:
Child's needs:
Child's joys, interests, aspirations:
Learns best by:
Concerns:
How family would like to be involved:
Anything else:

From the Child

_____
date

Child as a reader:
Child as a writer:
Family involvement in reading:
Family involvement in writing:
Child's strengths:
Child's needs:
Child's joys, interests, aspirations:
Learns best by:
Concerns:
What he/she would like to do in classroom:
Anything else:

Information from Parents/Family

Interviews with parents/family serve two important purposes. First, of course, they provide you opportunities to learn more about the child's sociocultural background, family history, medical history, and emergent literacy background (including the families' values and beliefs about literacy). This information will fill in many blanks left from perusal of the student's record, update that information for you, and give you an opportunity to make your own comments/evaluations regarding this information (rather than just relying on records and past teachers' comments). You can also ask questions about specific areas you have noted or observed, or about comments made by the child or by other teachers. Additionally, parents/family usually have valuable insights into their child's needs. They can be very helpful and they should be allowed to participate in their child's assessment and education.

The second, and equally important, purpose of the parent/family interview is to gain their confidence, support, and assistance with the kinds of instructional activities you will be encouraging and doing with their child. The studies and reviews by Anderson (1994); Spiegel (1994a); Spiegel et al. (1993); and Taylor, Pressley and Pearson (2000), support the importance of establishing partnerships with parents and families. This importance is emphasized by IRA (2002) in their position statement. Parent/family as well as teacher perceptions, confidence, support, and help are vital to the child's self-concept, development, and literacy growth.

Parents and family members are a big part of the child's life, literacy, and culture, and they can contribute much to your information about the child. After all, they have been involved with their child's emergent literacy from the beginning. The IRA/NCTE (1994) task force on assessment publication stresses that all "stakeholders" must participate in assessment. The study of **family literacy** can provide critical information. The IRA's Family Literacy Committee actively studies and reports the ways that parents, children, and extended family members use literacy at home and in their communities. Readers interested in finding out more about family literacy can contact the IRA and read Hoffman (1995); Morrow (1995); Morrow, Paratore, Gaber, Harrison, and Tracey (1993); Purcell-Gates, L'Allier, and Smith (1995); Shanahan, Mulhern, and Rodriguez-Brown (1995); Taylor (1997, 1998); Thomas, Fazio, and Stiefelmeyer (1999a & b); Wasik et al. (2000); and the studies about parents' perceptions and beliefs previously cited.

Some ideas for the kinds of questions you could ask parents/family members are listed. You will note that most of these questions can also be asked of the child. When the question has been rephrased for use with the child, it is indicated in parentheses. This important information from the family, as well as the answers you get from the child, can later be recorded on the Sources and Information form.

Questions You Could Ask Parents/Family Members and the Child

1. Tell me about your child. (Tell me about yourself.)
2. How do you think your child learned to read? (How did you learn to read?)
3. How do you view your child as a reader? (How do you view yourself as a reader?)
4. How do you view your child as a writer? (How do you view yourself as a writer?)
5. How is reading used in your family?
6. How is writing used in your family?
7. Do you use notes or letters to exchange information?
8. Do you have family records such as baby books, family histories, medical records, etc., in your home? Do you look at these together?
9. Do you use lists in your home for grocery shopping, jobs to do, etc.?
10. Do you do activities together, like putting something together by reading directions or baking cookies and cakes by reading recipes?
11. Do you do storybook reading or storytelling in your home?
12. Do you share ideas and talk about things at home?
13. Do family members help each other with homework or writing reports?
14. What are your child's greatest strengths? (What are your greatest strengths?)
15. What needs do you think your child might have? (What needs do you have?)
16. What are your child's greatest joys, interests, and aspirations? (What are your greatest joys, interests, and aspirations?)
17. How does your child learn best? (How do you learn best?)
18. How would you like to be involved in your child's literacy and learning at school? (What would you like to do as a reader and writer in our classroom?)
19. Do you have any worries or concerns?
20. Is there anything else you'd like to tell me?

Consider and React 3–10

Review and consider the questions suggested for other teachers and those suggested for parents/family members and the child. Are there questions you would add to these lists? What are they and why?

Information from the Child

Throughout the assessment and instruction process, the child will be your most important source of information. Never discount or forget this source. Only the child can provide you with specific information about what he likes and doesn't like, how he reads and doesn't read, and how he wants to pursue particular learning and reading tasks and strategies. Classroom teachers should talk and conference with their individual students as often as possible. These times can be used to evaluate strategies, model strategies, discuss problems and successes, and plan with the child, as well as add to or reevaluate his portfolio of sample work. As the child develops his reading interests, confidence, and strategies, you will be able to monitor and evaluate these best during your individual conference times. Additionally, you might want to ask the child some of the questions that have been previously listed and record the information on the form provided (see Box 3–9). Any extensive notes you have from the various interviews can be dated and attached to this form for future reference. (Those interested in gaining an indepth view of how children perceive their own reading should see Martens, 1996; Michel, 1994. Also, for a discussion of children's explanations and perceptions of their reading, see Hinchman & Michel, 1999.)

Summary

This chapter has described a variety of informal observational and sampling assessment procedures that can be done by the classroom teacher during the regular school day. Use of these assessments should provide the teacher with a qualitative approach to sampling and analyzing the collected information on an ongoing basis. This information, relevant to individual children's emergent literacy development, includes their interests, attitudes, motivations, and feelings, as well as their word recognition and analysis strategies, which include the phoneme-grapheme, syntax, and semantic strategy systems. Other sources (records, other teachers, parents/families, and the child) are noted to provide important additional information for teachers.

The reading assessment procedures, as detailed in this chapter (especially from IRI, RMI, running records, and modified miscue analysis) have focused more, but not entirely, on the oral reading and word recognition and analysis aspects of these assessments. In the next chapter, the focus will be on sampling and analyzing several silent reading procedures, as well as on emphasizing the cognitive (comprehension, schemata, metacognition, and study strategies) aspects of various assessments of content and narrative readings.

Questions for Reflection and Response

1. What is the emergent literacy perspective, and how can it be useful to the classroom teacher?
2. What are some qualitative assessment tools that the classroom teacher can use? Which do you like best? Why?

3. If you are interested in using portfolios as part of your assessments, try using Gahagan's (1994) questions. What were your findings? How can you make use of them?

4. What affective areas do you believe are most important to assess? Why? How would you assess them?

5. What can teachers learn from assessing children's oral reading? What procedure(s) or "mix" seems to be the "right fit" for you, and why are you most comfortable with it?

6. What can you learn from observing children's writing, invented spelling, and developmental punctuation? Try observing some students. What have you gleaned?

7. How can you gather information about the child from student records, other teachers, parents/family, and the child? What makes this information valuable?

8. How can you involve the children and their parents/families in assessment, and how can you indicate to them that their involvement is valued and important?

9. Using the modified miscue analysis technique described in this chapter (or using the oral reading sampling "mix" you prefer), assess the oral reading of one (or more) student(s). What have you learned about his or her phoneme-grapheme, syntax, and semantic strategies? What else do you want to know about this student? Do you see any specific instructional needs at this time?

Qualitative Analysis Discussion of Mitchell's and Caryl's Oral Readings

In the sections that follow are my analysis with explanations of Mitchell's and then Caryl's oral readings and instructional needs. See how your analysis compares.

Oral Reading by Mitchell: Qualitative Analysis for Phoneme-Grapheme Cue System

The following miscues show Mitchell's use of the phoneme-grapheme cue system and are also an indication of his strength in this system.

"telegraph" for "telephone"

"reaching" for "ringing"

"hill" for "hook"

"sister" for "secretary"

"there" for "her"

"with" for "wits"

"grasped" for "grabbed"

"yellow" for "yelled"

"minute" for "moment"

"last" for "later"

For example, with the miscue "telegraph" for "telephone," Mitchell used the phoneme-grapheme cue system because "telegraph" sounds a lot like "telephone"; both words are about the same length, both words have a similar shape, the beginnings of both words are identical, both words have the same number of syllables (three), and both even have a "ph" in the last syllable.

The only real difference is that the last part of each of the words does sound, and mostly look, different.

Oral Reading by Caryl: Qualitative Analysis for Phoneme-Grapheme Cue System

The following miscues show Caryl's use of the phoneme-grapheme cue system and are also an indication of some strengths in this system.

"seem" for "seemed"

"home" for "homeless"

"was" for "wasn't"

"working" for "wearing"

"silly" for "skinny"

"new" for "nervous"

"purples" for "people"

"because" for "before"

"pillows" for "pieces"

"puffing" for "purring"

"ball" for "both"

For example, with the miscue "purples" for "people," Caryl used the phoneme-grapheme cue system because "purples" looks and sounds fairly similar to "people," both words are about the same length, both words have a similar shape, the beginning consonant and consonant sound of these words are identical, both words have the same number of syllables (three), and both even have a "ple" in the second syllable.

The only real differences are that "purples" ends in an "s" and "people" doesn't and that the vowel sound and blend in the first syllable of "purples" /ûr/ is very different from the vowel sound in "people" /e/.

Caryl does use the phoneme-grapheme system, but often only partially. For instance, she often leaves out word endings ("seem" for "seemed," "home" for "homeless," and "was" for "wasn't") and, even though she always miscues with words with the identical first letter(s), she often ignores the rest of the word ("because" for "before," "pillows" for "pieces," "new" for "nervous," and "ball" for "both"). And, although she is often accurate with both the beginning and end of a word, she sometimes ignores the middle ("working" for "wearing," "silly" for "skinny," and "puffing" for "purring").

Oral Reading by Mitchell: Qualitative Analysis for Syntax Cue System
The following miscues show Mitchell's use of the syntax cue system and are also an indication of strength in this system. They are syntactically correct.

"telegraph" for "telephone"

"reaching" for "ringing"

"hill" for "hook"

"sister" for "secretary"

"grasped" for "grabbed"

"help" for "assistance"

"minute" for "moment"

"last" for "later"

The only exceptions to a perfect use of syntax was when Mitchell substituted "there" for "her," and then, in an attempt to make the sentence sound right and make sense, he substituted "with" for "wits'" and inserted "its." Although "there with its end" is not how the author had structured the sentence, it shows Mitchell's strong attempt to make his new sentence syntactically correct. Mitchell was using his excellent sense of syntax to try to fix the flow (syntax) of the sentence after he miscued the word "there."

Additionally, "yellow" for "yelled" was incorrect syntactically, but then Mitchell self-corrected because he knew it didn't sound right (syntactically) or make sense in the sentence (we will address this when we discuss Mitchell's semantic system). Remember that self-corrections are important indications of a child's strategy strengths.

Oral Reading by Caryl: Qualitative Analysis for Syntax Cue System

The following miscues show Caryl's use of the syntax cue system and are also an indication that most of the time Caryl does use her syntax system. They are syntactically correct.

"home" for "homeless"

"was" for "wasn't"

"working" for "wearing"

"silly" for "skinny"

"new" for "nervous"

"purples" for "people"

"pillows" for "pieces"

"puffing" for "purring"

Additionally, Caryl twice miscued "seem" for "seemed." Although "seem" for "seemed" is not completely correct syntactically—the sentence doesn't completely flow or sound right grammatically, and, in fact, isn't grammatically correct ("seems" would have been grammatically correct)—the miscue "seem" does not indicate a complete lack of syntax usage. These miscues seem more like poor grammar usage than a complete lack of syntax.

However, the miscues "because" for "before" and "ball" for "both" are syntactically incorrect as is. These miscues indicate that Caryl might not always use her syntax system. In both cases, the substituted word cannot be used the same way in the sentence as the word in the text. When Caryl miscued and substituted "because," and later "ball," she made those sentences structurally incorrect. However, it should be pointed out that if Caryl believed an explanation would follow, then "because" does seem plausible syntactically. Likewise, if Caryl silently inserted the word "the" before "ball" when she read, "ball" would be syntactically correct. Overall, Caryl seems to mostly use her syntax system, but does not always make miscues that are syntactically correct.

Oral Reading by Mitchell: Qualitative Analysis for Semantic Cue System

The following miscues indicate that Mitchell always attempts to use the semantic cue system and is always either partially or fully successful.

1. "Telegraph" for "telephone," "reaching" for "ringing," and "hill" for "hook" all make sense in the sentence when you read this sentence as Mitchell did, with these miscues. Also, when you look at the following sentence, you again see that Mitchell was trying to make it all make sense by the miscues he makes. However, the miscues do not hold up and make sense as he continues to read the rest of the paragraph, and then, when he realizes this, Mitchell uses the meaning clues and his strong semantic system (and his strong syntactic system) to self-correct (yellow SC), and he continues reading with comprehension.

2. "Sister" for "secretary" makes sense in the sentence and in the paragraph. There aren't any real meaning clues that Mitchell doesn't use.

3. "There with its end" instead of "her wits' end" (an expression he was not familiar with) is a little awkward, but it makes sense when you have read the first sentence the way Mitchell did. Again, although it makes sense in that sentence and with the previous sentence, the meaning breaks down as Mitchell continues to read the rest of the paragraph. However, when this happens, as already pointed out, Mitchell uses the semantic clues and continues with obvious comprehension.

4. "Grasped" for "grabbed" makes sense in the sentence and in the paragraph, and there aren't any meaning clues that Mitchell doesn't use.

5. "Yellow" for "yelled" did not make sense at all at the sentence or paragraph levels, and there were meaning clues. Mitchell used those clues *immediately* to self-correct. (I believe the word "phone" was more familiar and recognizable to Mitchell than "telephone." When he realized that he'd been reading about a telephone, rather than a telegraph, the meaning all came together for him.) This self-correction showed Mitchell's strength in using his semantic cue system and is a positive sign of his fluency.

6. "Help" for "assistance," "minute" for "moment," and "last" for "later" all make sense in the sentences and in the paragraph. They indicate, once again, Mitchell's strong use of his semantic cue system.

Oral Reading by Caryl: Qualitative Analysis for Semantic Cue System

The following miscues indicate that in some places Caryl did use the semantic cue system.

1. The miscues "seem" for "seemed," "home" for "homeless," and "was" for "wasn't" all make sense at the sentence level. But each does not make sense in the overall paragraph, and Caryl does miss out on meaning clues.

2. Likewise, later the miscues "silly" for "skinny" and "puffing" for "purring" make sense at the sentence level, but in the overall paragraph they do not make as much sense. Once again, Caryl doesn't pick up on meaning clues.

3. However, the miscue "new" for "nervous" does make sense at the sentence level and at the paragraph level if Caryl had realized that the kitten was homeless and wasn't

around people much. Here it seems that Caryl could have been picking up on meaning clues.

4. Finally, there is a possibility that "because" for "before" could make some sense if the reader believed that an explanation would follow. Likewise, "ball" for "both" could possibly make sense when you consider the miscue "puffing" in front of it. One would be more likely to puff at a ball than at "both." Since Caryl is ignoring the punctuation (comma between "puffing" and "ball"), she doesn't realize that she should hesitate after "puffing" and start a new phrase with the next word "ball." (Attention to punctuation is a function of both syntax [structure] and semantic [meaning] awareness strategies.)

The other miscues that Caryl made indicate that she wasn't using the semantic cue system. They don't make sense at the sentence level and, of course, also don't make sense in the rest of the paragraph. Here again, Caryl didn't use meaning clues.

"working" for "wearing"
"purples" for "people"
"pillows" for "pieces"

Mitchell: Suggested Instructional Needs

No real need for direct instruction on any of the three cue systems has been demonstrated in this one short, oral reading sample. Overall, Mitchell seems to use adequate strategies in the phoneme-grapheme area. As combined with his strong use of the syntax and semantic systems, Mitchell's word recognition abilities seem fine. He seems to be a fluent oral reader. However, further assessment of his comprehension of this paragraph and other oral reading samples on longer pieces with more familiar language and schemata would assure this analysis. (He did make partial phoneme-grapheme miscues in the first two sentences that strongly affected and changed the meaning of the passage. If, when his comprehension is assessed, it is determined that Mitchell understood the paragraph, as written by the author, then there is no need for concern.)

Author's Note About Mitchell's Comprehension   Later, when asked to retell, Mitchell was able to give a complete retelling and seemed to fully comprehend what he had read. And when metacognitively probed concerning his initial miscues, he provided good rationales for and awareness of his first guesses. Additional oral reading and comprehension assessments done with Mitchell on other types of and longer text selections, within his schemata, supported his cue systems' strengths and overall good comprehension and fluency.

Caryl: Suggested Instructional Needs

Analysis of this one short oral reading sample has indicated that Caryl has fair usage of the phoneme-grapheme cue system and fair-to-good usage of the syntax system. However, she seems weak in her semantic cue system. More assessments of Caryl's oral reading strategies on longer pieces and on different types of texts, over time, as well as assessments of her comprehension, are necessary. However, based on this one sample, it is suggested that Caryl might benefit from instruction to

1. Develop semantic strategies, particularly at the paragraph level, making use of overall meaning clues and the specific meaning of words embedded in the paragraph

2. Develop more use of her stronger syntax strategies to check to see whether her semantic guesses "fit" and "sound right" in the text

3. Pay attention to more than just the first letter and/or ending of each word, and then guess words that "fit" based on phoneme-grapheme considerations, and syntax, as well as words that will make sense in the paragraph.

Author's Note About Caryl's Comprehension   Later, when asked to retell, Caryl could not give a complete retelling. (See Chapter 4 for a description of what a complete retelling involves.) When asked comprehension questions, she was able to answer several, but not all, correctly. Caryl had trouble telling how she arrived at her answers, even when probed a lot. Although Caryl had some comprehension of the paragraph, it was not good enough to indicate complete understanding. Caryl's miscues did cause a loss of overall comprehension. When probed about what she was thinking when she made several of her miscues, Caryl could not explain. Additional oral reading samples and comprehension checks done with Caryl on other types of, and longer, text selections supported the same instructional need decisions.

CHAPTER 4

ASSESSING COMPREHENSION, COMPREHENDING STRATEGIES, AND OTHER COGNITIVE INFORMATION

Focus and Goals of the Chapter

- To provide a comprehensive overview of many assessment ideas and procedures for observing comprehension, comprehending strategies, and other cognitive and qualitative information

- To provide information about the different demands of narrative and expository text

- To describe and illustrate how retellings of text, use of questions, metacognitive probing, content reading samples, and writing samples can each provide more qualitative information about a student's comprehension and strategies

- To demonstrate how teachers can do metacognitive probing as an extension of other comprehension assessment and as a part of regular classroom instruction

- To provide specific techniques for assessing students' comprehension, prior knowledge and schemata, study skills and strategies, and metacognition

- To provide sample applications of various cognitive assessment ideas that class-room teachers have developed and tried with students

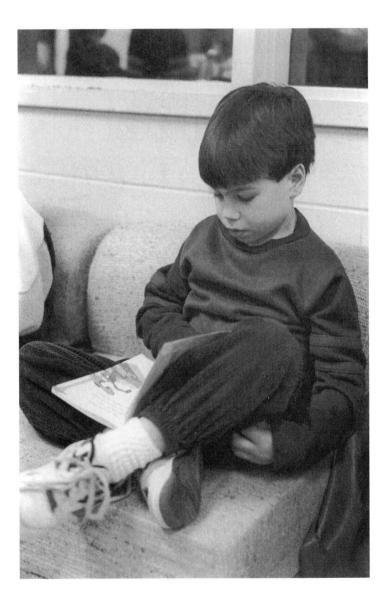

Introduction

This chapter focuses on descriptions of assessment procedures that can be particularly useful when sampling strategic reading and other cognitive strategies. These procedures include ideas developed to assess comprehension, schemata and prior knowledge, study skills and strategies, and metacognitive strategy use. Most of these assessment procedures can be used with expository text (content and informational material) as well as with narrative text (story-type material). In Chapter 3, assessments included sampling students' linguistic strategies by assessing their oral reading strategies and fluency, and by observing other written language development through their writing. The assessments described in this chapter will focus on assessing students' cognitive strategies by sampling their comprehension and other strategic reading and study processes. Individual teachers will probably prefer some cognitive and strategy assessments over others and are each encouraged to select the procedures that are most appropriate to their own beliefs and teaching styles, and to what they wish to find out.

Comprehension and Comprehending Strategies' Assessments

Comprehension is the heart of reading. It is both the process and the product of reading. In other words, **comprehension** is the process by which we read and get information and/or meaning from text; it is also the result (product) of our reading of text. Therefore, nothing can be more crucial to assessment and instruction in reading than the observation and development of children's comprehension and comprehending strategies. In the sections that follow, text structures and various techniques for assessing comprehension and comprehending strategies will be discussed. These include use of narrative and expository texts, and use of retellings, questions, metacognitive assessments, think-aloud verbalizations, some content reading procedures (content reading inventories, cloze assessments, and retellings of content text), and writing samples.

Using Narrative and Expository Texts

The type of text you select to assess comprehension and other cognitive strategies will make certain text demands on the reader. It is important for teachers to realize that the features and structures of different types of reading materials will make some materials more difficult to comprehend. The most common labels for text types are narrative text and expository text.

Narrative text usually includes most story-type materials. Narratives tell stories about characters, events, and actions. Even though there are many kinds of narrative texts (fairy tales, mystery stories, novels, etc.), most narratives include common structure and text features. For example, narratives are organized into a sequential pattern and usually have a beginning, a middle, and an end; narratives have one or more characters, settings, plots, problems, and actions; and narratives usually have resolutions to the problems presented.

Narrative texts are generally acknowledged to be easier for students to read and understand than expository texts. This is because even young children are able to recognize and use the story structure found in most narrative materials. The research indicates that children build an internal sense of story structure as they listen to and read stories. Once familiar with story structure, different aspects of the story can be anticipated because of the common text structure and features found in most narratives.

Expository text includes most content and informational-type texts. These types of materials are most usually found in informational books, textbooks, and informational magazines and newspapers. Even though there are many kinds, content, and purposes of expository materials, certain frequently used text structures are found in most expository texts. These are (1) description—which presents information about the topic; (2) collection—which presents a number of ideas or descriptions in a related grouping, such as a sequence or listing of things; (3) causation—which presents ideas in a cause and effect relationship; (4) response—which presents a problem or question followed by a solution or answer; and (5) comparison—which presents the likenesses and differences between two or more things or ideas (Meyer & Freedle, 1984). Within any expository material, several of these text structures may be present. Children unfamiliar with reading these text structures can have difficulty constructing meaning from expository texts.

Children generally have much more limited experiences with expository text than with narratives. Expository text is less predictable, less familiar, and contains many more text structures than narrative text. Lipson and Wixson (1997) cite studies by Elliott (1980) and Taylor and Samuels (1983) indicating that even middle-grade students are often unaware of or unable to use expository text structure to aid their comprehension, and Craig and Yore's (1995) more recent study and Goldman and Rakestraw's (2000) review show similar findings. Additionally, Alvermann and Phelps (2002), Duffelmeyer (1994), and Vacca and Vacca (2002) suggest that expository text is generally more difficult to comprehend because of the complexity and density of the concepts presented, but that comprehension can be enhanced by students' awareness of text structures and structure cues. Nevertheless, insights gained from studies with young children, for instance, Pappas' (1991, 1993) work, suggest that kindergarteners can and do enjoy, and often even prefer, reading informational books dealing with things they are interested in learning about. In fact, Pappas indicates that many children are able to understand these informational books as well as they can understand story-type materials. Based on their review of the research on comprehension, Robinson et al. (2000) indicate that this research supports the importance of reading both narrative and expository books to children, and that this experience builds reading comprehension, including vocabulary development. Even so, in a Center for the Improvement of Early Reading Achievement (CIERA) study, Duke (1999) found a scarcity of informational texts in first grade classrooms, and disparity in the availability of these informational texts between low socioeconomic status (SES) and schools with high SES populations. Duke indicated that even though researchers have urged schools to use more informational texts in their early-grade classrooms, schools are generally not doing so, and when they are, the texts appear more often in high SES situations.

More use of nonfiction literature, beginning in early grades, would allow children to become more familiar with various structures of expository materials. Doiron (1994) suggests that we present more of a balance between the use of fiction and nonfiction literature forms for children, and Pappas, Kiefer, and Levskik (1999) make a similar suggestion, urging teachers to use many different genres and registers with their students. Additionally, the Expert Study findings (see Flippo, 1998, 1999, 2001a) and the report of the Committee on the Prevention of Reading Difficulties in Young Children (Snow, Burns & Griffin, 1998) support the importance of using a wide variety of genres with children. Sanacore (1991, p. 214) also indicates and lists the benefits of using a variety of texts with young children. Benefits include the following: ease and facility in reading for information are nurtured with early exposure to expository text; the increased use of expository text balances exposure to various discourse types used in reading; frequent use of expository text helps children develop the idea that all types of texts can be functional, enjoyable, and challenging; and exposure to a variety of texts allows children to develop flexibility in their reading. Finally, Yopp and Yopp (2000) echo their agreement and share ways to incorporate informational texts into primary-grade classrooms.

Consider and React 4–1

What is your reaction? How can teachers facilitate a balance between the use of fiction and nonfiction literature in their classrooms?

Overall, children's comprehension of text, both narrative and expository, is of the utmost importance. Teachers must be able to use appropriate methods for assessing children's comprehension and their strategies for reading these varied materials. One way is to use retellings. Retellings of text can provide useful insights into what children understand from their classroom reading assignments and the materials they select to read on their own.

Retellings of Texts

Retellings were mentioned in Chapter 3 as a means of assessing students' comprehension following the oral reading of any passages or reading selections. Teachers listen to the retellings, noting the details, ideas, and other information as students recall and verbalize what they have read. Students who verbalize excellent recall of the passage/selection are evaluated as having high comprehension of the material. Students who have difficulty retelling the passage/selection are "probed" by the teacher (asked probing questions) in order to instigate students' recall of the material. The teacher then assesses whether the retelling was complete. A complete retelling is when the student has recalled and retold all of the information in the passage(s) that the teacher is looking for. (When administering most commercially prepared IRIs, teachers are directed to ask the comprehension questions at the end of each passage if the student was not able to give a complete retelling during the free recall and probing. However, if the retelling was complete, the teacher can consider the child's comprehension score to be 100 percent for that selection.)

In addition to its use as part of oral reading sampling, retellings are used extensively by teachers and researchers for assessment purposes in various situations and with various materials, read orally or silently. When students give free recall of what they remember, or can highlight or paraphrase aspects of a story or other information they have read, we can take a look at what each student sees as important without "setting up" the information for the student. (When we construct specific questions to go with a passage or selection, we are actually "setting up" the information we see as important, rather than waiting to see what the student sees as important. When we do this, we are losing an opportunity to fully observe a student's comprehension and ideas.)

Classroom teachers are encouraged to use retellings as another valuable tool for informal reading assessment in their classrooms. Brown and Cambourne (1987) indicate that use of learners' retellings is a natural way of collecting developmental data on children. These retellings reflect how well the child reads, comprehends, and can retranslate the material. The retellings can provide the teacher with information regarding the control that the child has over reading and writing (the child can be asked to write his/her retelling). Additionally, retellings provide information about the child's knowledge and use of vocabulary, knowledge of genre and form, ability to paraphrase and sequence information or events, and so on.

Morrow (1988) points out that retelling not only can be used as a diagnostic tool for assessing comprehension of text and stories, sense of story structure, and language complexity, but it also can be used as an instructional strategy. Research (Gambrell, Koskinen, & Kapinus, 1991) has indicated that practice in retelling results in improvements in the quality of the retellings, supporting the idea that by doing retellings, readers learn about organizing and remembering the information they have read. Cambourne's (1988) work emphasizes that observation, assessment, and instruction in the classroom are what the teacher does all day, and that assessment should not be viewed as something separate from instruction. This book also endorses that philosophy.

Consider and React 4–2

What do you think? Do you view observation, assessment, and instruction as integrated activities that the classroom teacher does all day? Do you believe that current research and thinking regarding comprehension and comprehending strategies support this idea? As you read this chapter, look for this support in the cited literature.

Directions for using retelling as an assessment tool are provided (Morrow, 1988). Teachers can alter these procedures to fit their purposes and needs.

1. Students should be told before reading or listening to a story or text that they will be asked to retell it. (Further information should be provided if the intent is to test or teach a specific aspect of comprehension—for instance, sequence. In that case, the child should be told to concentrate on what happened first, second, third, etc.)

Purpose

2. The student's retellings should be recorded on tape or some other medium for further reference.

3. Ask the child to retell the story or text by saying, "A little while ago, you read the story (name the story). Would you retell the story as if you were telling it to a friend who has never heard it before?" or some similar opening.

4. Use prompts only when necessary. For instance, if the child has difficulty beginning the story, you could say, "Once there was . . ." or "The story was about . . ." If the child stops retelling before the end of the story, you could ask, "What comes next?" or, "What happened next?" If the child stops retelling and cannot continue with the prompts offered, you can ask a question about the story that is relevant at the particular point at which the child stopped. For instance, "What was the girl's problem in the story?"

5. When the child is unable to retell the story, or if the retelling lacks detail or necessary information, prompt the retelling by asking probing questions step by step. For example:

"Who was the story about?"

"When did the story happen?"

"Where did the story happen?"

"What was the main character's problem in the story?"

"How did she go about solving it?"

"How did the story end?"

Obviously, many areas of students' abilities and strategies in comprehension and language can be assessed during the retelling procedure. Mitchell and Irwin (2002) developed the Retelling Profile, which could be used as is or modified by classroom teachers to keep records of students' retellings. (See Box 4–1.) Classroom teachers also can, more informally, reflect on aspects of students' retellings as they assess and instruct using the retelling procedure.

Box 4–1	Retelling profile

Directions: Indicate with a check (✓) the degree to which the reader's retelling reflects the reader's comprehension in terms of the following criteria:

TEXT-BASED COMPREHENSION

	None	Low Degree	Moderately Low	Moderately High	High Degree
1. Retelling includes information directly stated in text.					
2. Retelling includes information inferred directly or indirectly from text.					
3. Retelling includes what is important to remember from the text.					
4. Retelling provides relevant content, concepts, and context.					

READER RESPONSE

5. Retelling indicates reader's attempts to connect background knowledge with text information.					
6. Retelling indicates reader's attempts to make summary statements or generalizations based on the text and apply them to the real world.					
7. Retelling indicates reader's highly individualistic and creative impressions of or reactions to the text.					
8. Retelling indicates reader's affective involvement with the text.					

LANGUAGE USE

9. Retelling demonstrates reader's language fluency (use of vocabulary, sentence structure, language conventions, etc.).					
10. Retelling indicates reader's organization or composition abilities.					
11. Retelling demonstrates reader's sense of audience or purpose.					
12. Retelling indicates reader's control of the mechanics of speaking or writing.					

Interpretation: Items 1–4 indicate reader's text-based comprehension of information;
Items 5–8 indicate reader's response and reactions to text;
Items 9–12 indicate reader's language use.

Source: "Retelling Profile" by Judy N. Mitchell and Pi A. Irwin. Printed by permission of the authors.

Questioning and Questions

Questioning is probably the most common and basic method of assessing and promoting comprehension (Heilman, Blair, & Rupley, 2002). It can be used to assess all types of reading materials, and it can be combined with most types of reading assessments. The most critical decisions regarding questioning involve "What type of questions do I ask?" and "How do I ask them?" The questions that teachers ask children and the response mode teachers provide will influence the answers children give and the process children use to answer the questions. Because of this, it is extremely important that teachers are aware of the demands, constraints, and influences of any questions that they use to evaluate children's understanding. Both the focus and form of questions should be carefully considered before conclusions about students' abilities to answer are made (Lipson & Wixson, 1997).

Structured questions (systematic questions focused by the teacher's purpose) can be used to assess comprehension and can be a valuable assessment tool. However, structured questions can impose someone else's view of what is most important in the reading. Therefore, teachers must take care in selecting and developing these questions. If, for instance, your questions focus on details in the reading selection, students will be led to believe that the details are the most important aspects of the material. On the other hand, if your questions focus on the ideas and concepts discussed in the reading, then students will be led to believe that the ideas and concepts are the most important aspects. Teachers should use questions that fit the material being read, the kind of information sought, and the kind of message they want to give readers about what is important about a particular reading.

Pearson and Johnson (1978) indicate that questions must be considered in relation to the probable source of the answer if we are to know what is required for the reader to respond. They describe three types of questions and the conditions required to answer them.

1. **Text-explicit** questions are those that can be answered by finding the information that is explicitly stated in the text or story (Raphael, 1986, calls this *Right There QAR* [Question-Answer Relationships]—meaning the answer is right there in the text or story. Other reading experts call these literal questions.)

2. **Text-implicit** questions are those that involve inferring information from the text or story; the information is not explicitly stated. (Raphael calls this *Think and Search QAR*—meaning the answer can be inferred from the text or story, but you need to pull the information together by looking for it in different parts of the text. Other reading experts call these inferential questions.)

3. **Scriptally implicit** questions are those that involve the reader using his background knowledge and schema to answer the questions; the information is not stated or implied in the text or story. (Raphael calls this *In My Head QAR*—meaning the answer isn't in the story or text, but if you think about what you already know from your own

experience, and use what was in the story or text, you can answer this question. You can sometimes even answer the question without the story by using your own experience entirely.)

Questioning can serve as an important instructional, and assessment, tool. **Open-ended questions,** ones that do not have one "correct answer," can be used for both assessment and instruction. Questions like these solicit students' opinions and personal responses to their readings. These types of questions can give you information regarding students' impressions, rationales, and other important cognitive as well as affective information. They can also encourage students to reflect on their readings and assess their own understandings. An example of an open-ended question is, "In your opinion, what can be learned from this story?"

Teacher-posed questions can be asked before, during, and after a reading, depending on what type of information the teacher is wanting to observe and what type of information the teacher wants to call attention to and enhance or develop. For example, questions asked before a reading can help set a purpose for the reading and can help readers make predictions based on the questions asked, as well as make use of their own backgrounds and schemata to anticipate the reading. The teacher can use students' responses to these questions to assess their abilities to make predictions and also to assess their schemata and vocabulary knowledge relevant to the reading. Questions asked during a reading help students make important connections and can help the teacher assess students' abilities to assimilate and use relevant information in the reading. Finally, questions asked at the end of a reading can assess students' recognition and recall of important information and ideas and also help students summarize and explain their rationales.

These are but a few examples of how questions can be directed, asked, and placed to assess and develop comprehension. Many teaching strategies have been developed over the years that integrate questioning with instruction and encourage students' responses, conversations, and active thinking about and engagement with what they read. Teachers interested in reviewing these procedures might consult the compilations of strategies by Buehl (2001); Johns and Berglund (2002b); Readence, Moore, and Rickelman (2000); Stephens and Brown (2000); Tierney and Readence (2000); Wiesendanger (2001), and Yopp and Yopp (2001). Also, Beck, McKeown, Hamilton, and Kucan (1997) is recommended for examples of a teaching and questioning approach that encourages students' engagement with the text and should further develop their comprehension. And in the sections that follow, note how questions are used to enhance the other comprehension assessments and comprehending strategies described in this chapter.

Consider and React 4–3

Consider how you, and teachers you've had over the years, have used questions to assess and enhance comprehension and to encourage the comprehending strategies of students. What examples could you give?

Metacognitive Awareness Assessments

"Knowing how one knows something" or "knowing how one arrived at one's answer to a question," and "knowing when you know" or "knowing when you don't know" are phrases that describe the advanced cognitive process known as **metacognitive awareness.** When a student can describe how he came up with the answer to the question you have asked him regarding material he has read, he has shown metacognitive awareness. When a student simply answers a question about material he has read, he has demonstrated only comprehension of the material. All too often, teachers ask comprehension questions without going one step further by asking the student, "How did you come up with that answer?" Many researchers today believe that knowing the answer (showing comprehension of the material read) is not enough. Teachers should be encouraged to assess and develop their students' metacognitive awareness strategies in order to assess and further cultivate the students' comprehension, thinking, and reasoning strategies.

As with other informal assessment procedures, it is difficult to separate metacognitive awareness assessment from metacognitive awareness instruction. When you ask students probing questions regarding their reading in order to assess their metacognitive awareness, you are also simultaneously probing them, asking for relationships, and modeling to help develop metacognitive awareness. The classroom teacher's role is one of guidance—guiding students (individually) to monitor their thought and reasoning processes, asking probing questions along the way to keep students on task, and assisting them in their awareness of these cognitive processes. The teacher "assessor" and the teacher "instructor" do the same work. As the student describes how he knows, the teacher assessor observes the strategies. As the student describes how he knows, the teacher instructor guides the student toward being aware of the strategies he (the student) is using. When the student runs into trouble, the teacher assessor and the teacher instructor ask probing questions to get him back on track. If the student gets "stuck" and probes do not work, the teacher instructor can model how she (the teacher) might come up with the answer.

Researchers monitor metacognitive awareness in order to learn more about students' cognitive development, use of strategies, reading, writing, and thinking. However, metacognitive assessment procedures have not been widely used by classroom teachers. One reason is that the term *metacognition* may be intimidating, and metacognitive assessment may seem more complex or daunting than it actually is. Another reason could be that there are not yet many models or assessment samples available to demonstrate how it can be done. In this chapter, several metacognitive assessment procedures and techniques are described and examples provided. Once teachers are comfortable with how to probe and monitor students toward metacognitive awareness, they will find that it is easy to design their own assessment and instruction procedures for metacognition, whether for assessment, for instruction, or for both. (Also, refer to Chapter 8 for teaching ideas that enhance use of metacognitive strategies.)

Metacognitive Probing as a Follow-Up to Questions or Retellings   **Metacognitive probing** is part of metacognitive assessment and instruction and can be done as a follow-up to any comprehension monitoring you do with students, whether you do it following a set of prescribed comprehension questions or after a free-recall or retelling of any reading material. For example, one way for classroom teachers to do metacognitive assessment is by "probing" students about how they arrived at their answers to prescribed comprehension questions, such as those found after each IRI passage. First the teacher asks comprehension questions, then she goes back to selected questions and probes the student.

Consider and React 4–4

In the sample that follows, note the dialogue and the probing technique Ms. Cohen uses as she assesses and then instructs her third-grade student, Tyler, following his oral reading. What do you observe about Tyler's metacognition? Does he use information in the story to support his answers?

Ms. Cohen: When I asked what this story was about, you said, "It was about a boy who got into trouble when he forgot to do his chores around the house." How did you come up with that answer?

Tyler: Because it said so in the story.

Ms. Cohen: Can you show me where it says so?

Tyler: Right here it says, "Mark was so excited about going swimming with his friends that he forgot to do his chores."

Ms. Cohen: OK, but it doesn't say that Mark got into trouble. How did you know that?

Tyler: Because, down here in the last part it says that his mom punished him because the kitchen wasn't swept and the dishes weren't done.

Ms. Cohen: Good, but how did you know that sweeping and doing the dishes were Mark's chores?

Tyler: Because in the beginning of the story it said so.

Ms. Cohen: Can you read me that part?

Tyler: Sure. It says, "Mark's job this week was cleaning the kitchen. He was supposed to clean the floor and wash the dishes every day."

Ms. Cohen: Very good, Tyler. It seems like you put information together from three different parts of the story to answer the question. Is that right?

Tyler: Yes, that is how I did it.

Ms. Cohen: Good, now let's see how you were able to figure out the answer to this next one.

Metacognitive probing can be done following any reading selections (after RMIs or running records, or from storybooks, basal or other stories, content textbooks, and all types of varied literature). Just as modeled by the previous Ms. Cohen and Tyler dialogue, teachers can do metacognitive probing as a follow-up to most comprehension questions or retellings from all sorts of literature and texts. The selections and comprehension questions do not have to be from an oral reading assessment. Metacognitive assessment can be done following most silent reading selections.

Consider and React 4–5

Here is another dialogue between Ms. Cohen and Tyler. This time, Ms. Cohen has decided to probe Tyler after he silently read part of his social studies chapter on transportation. What do you observe about Tyler's metacognition? Does he use information in the text, as well as his own experience and prior knowledge, to support his answers?

> Ms. Cohen: Tyler, what would you say is the most important thing you read so far in this chapter? (Note, Ms. Cohen has just "set up" a critical comprehension question for Tyler to answer. She has not yet probed for metacognition.)
>
> Tyler: I think the part about how without transportation people wouldn't be able to get food.
>
> Ms. Cohen: Can you tell me why you think that is the most important idea? (Note, now Ms. Cohen has metacognitively probed.)
>
> Tyler: Because it says in the book that people would starve to death.
>
> Ms. Cohen: OK, where does it say that?
>
> Tyler: Here it says that, "without the supplies the settlers couldn't survive."
>
> Ms. Cohen: And you take that to mean that the people would die?
>
> Tyler: Yes.
>
> Ms. Cohen: Is there anything else that you read so far in the chapter to support your answer?
>
> Tyler: It said in the beginning that transportation, like trains and trucks, and in the old days, wagons, were the way most food grown by farmers was transported to stores. If people couldn't buy food in stores, where would they get it?
>
> Ms. Cohen: Very good, it seems that you used information you found in at least two places in the chapter and your own personal experience and knowledge (that most people relied on stores for their food) to determine that the most important idea in this chapter, so far, is that "without transportation people wouldn't be able to get food." Is that right?
>
> Tyler: Yes. I know that my mom buys all our food at the grocery store. If we couldn't buy it at the store, we'd probably starve, too.

Recipe for Metacognitive Assessments

Teachers can design all sorts of reading situations that can be used as "set ups" for metacognitive probing. Once again, the basic ingredients need only include

1   Selection, passage, story, or text for students to read (orally or silently, depending on what the teacher wants to monitor)
1   Teacher
1   Student (teacher works with one student at a time)
1   Or more comprehension questions (for "set-up" question)
1   Initial metacognitive probe ("Why did you answer that way?" or, "How did you know that?" etc.)

Several follow-up probes (according to need or "taste")

Teacher-Designed Exercises for Assessing Metacognition   Here are several teacher-designed exercises for assessing and reinforcing metacognition designed by classroom teacher Polly Gibson (see Gibson & Flippo, 1996). Teachers can come up with literally hundreds of such exercises on their own. These will get you started and give you some ideas. Develop your own creative spin-offs or use the "Recipe for Metacognitive Assessments" to design situations more suited to your needs, students, purposes, and materials.

I Know It Because I Read It   This metacognitive awareness assessment and exercise reinforces the notion that much of our knowledge comes from reading. Through teacher questioning, the learner focuses on retelling certain information about the passage and realizes that the ability to answer the questions comes from having just encountered the answers during the reading process.

DIRECTIONS: Read the following passages. Then answer the questions. After you have answered the questions, explain how you knew the answers.

Acting with Readers' Theatre   Have you and your classmates ever tried to act out one of your favorite stories? It is a simple and fun activity. First read the story several times so that you and your classmates are familiar with it. Next, choose your characters. You'll need one child for each character in the story, plus a narrator to retell the story. A good way of choosing is to draw the names from a hat. The rest of the class will be the audience.

The narrator is the only person with a speaking part in a Readers' Theatre pantomime. He or she retells the story in order, making sure to include all of the characters. As the characters are introduced, they act out their parts using only expressions and gestures. This type of acting is called "pantomime."

When the retelling is finished, the audience will offer feedback about the performance by judging the retelling for accuracy and how well the actors represented their parts. Once you have done this, repeat the entire activity, using new actors. Then compare the two performances. Take turns telling about the things that you liked best about each performance.

1. What are the advantages to drawing the actors' names from a hat? How did you know the answer?

2. What is the narrator's job? How did you know the answer?

3. What role does the audience play in this activity? How did you know the answer?

4. What is pantomime? How did you know the answer?

5. How does this activity help you with reading comprehension? Why? Did something you read in the previous paragraphs help you arrive at this answer? What?

I Know It Because I Have Experienced It   While the first exercise involves students' recalling and retelling details gleaned from the reading process, this exercise encourages students to draw upon their experiential backgrounds in order to formulate answers to questions. Cognitive experience plays a significant role in our ability to assimilate and accommodate new information. The student who understands how he knows can use that information to strengthen his ability to add to or build new experiences.

DIRECTIONS: Read each sentence and answer the questions. Be able to tell how you knew the answers.

1. Fido has fleas. Who or what is "Fido"?

2. The entire family helped decorate the tree. What time of year was it?

3. Tom made a wish and quickly blew out the candles. What day was it?

4. We sat down to eat just as the sun was rising. What meal did we eat?

5. He shouted, "Stop! You're under arrest!" What was his job?

6. The voice bellowed, "Strike three and you're out!" What were they doing?

7. When we saw the Golden Arches, Mom said, "Let's eat!" Where were we?

8. Golden leaves covered the ground. What season was it?

9. The Fourth of July fireworks were beautiful. What country would this probably be in?

10. Eggs everywhere! But no hens! What day was it?

Something's Missing   Successful readers rely on three cueing systems to assist them during the reading process. The phoneme-grapheme cueing system provides readers with cues based on the way that words sound or look. The semantic cueing system allows readers to make word approximations based on the meaning of surrounding words and text, and the syntactic cueing system allows readers to make word approximations based on their knowledge or awareness of the structure of language.

The following exercise provides the reader with two reading scenarios that use different materials written with distinct differences in difficulty (a science experiment; and a short passage adapted from a children's story book, *The Little Engine That Could,* Piper,

1990). All capitalization and punctuation have been deleted. This exercise illustrates (to the reader) the importance of various punctuation and other grapheme cues to the utilization of semantic and syntax cues in order to gain comprehension. The more difficult the material, the more essential various grapheme cues can become. In addition, this exercise assesses (for both the teacher and the student) the strategies that the child is using as he or she attempts to achieve comprehension without the aid of some of the grapheme cues.

DIRECTIONS: Read both paragraphs and answer the questions:

Paragraph One you will learn how a water drop magnifier works the materials that you will need are an eyedropper some water index cards a piece of clear plastic wrap clear tape and scissors first cut a round hole in the center of the index card about the size of a quarter place a piece of the plastic wrap over the hole and tape it into place next fold all four of the edges of the index card in about 1 cm then put one drop of water onto the plastic your magnifier is complete place it on top of a page of your favorite book to see what happens to the letters

1. Was this paragraph difficult to read? Why or why not?
2. If you found reading this paragraph difficult, what are some things that you could do to make it easier to read? Do them.
3. Reread the paragraph. Did your changes help make the reading easier? Why or why not?
4. What is the paragraph about? Where might you expect to find this paragraph? Why do you think that?

Paragraph Two huff and puff huff and puff huff and puff the little train chugged happily along the tracks she couldn't wait to get to the station where many excited children were waiting to receive one of the toys the happy little train was carrying

1. Was this paragraph difficult to read? Why or why not?
2. Was reading this paragraph easier than reading the first paragraph? Why or why not?
3. If you found reading this paragraph difficult, what are some things you could do to make it easier to read? Do them.
4. Reread the paragraph. Did your changes help make the reading easier? Why or why not?
5. What is the paragraph about? Where might you expect to find this paragraph? Why do you think that?

I Can See It in the Numbers   It is important that students and teachers use metacognitive strategies across all content-reading areas. This next exercise exemplifies the types of strategies that a student is using when he or she reads an English sentence and then translates that sentence into a mathematical sentence. Comprehension in this case depends upon whether the student is aware of the language cues that are necessary for an appropriate mathematical translation. (Heddons & Speer, 2001 were used as a resource for the National Council of Teachers of Mathematics standards and for these specific story problems.)

DIRECTIONS: Read the following story problems. Underline the words that will help you translate the problems into mathematical sentences. Then translate each story problem into a mathematical sentence. Solve each problem. Then write your mathematical answer in a word sentence. Finally, explain how you were able to do this.

1. Seth has three baseball cards. Morgan gave him four baseball cards. How many baseball cards does Seth have in all?

2. There are thirty-six boots lined up in the classroom. There are four equal rows of boots. How many boots are in each row? How many pairs of boots are in each row?

3. Hillary had five dolls. She gave three dolls to Kate. How many dolls does Hillary have left?

4. Sam's father gave him twelve cherries. If Sam shares the cherries equally with two other friends, how many cherries will each of the three children have?

5. Carl is planning his sixth annual Halloween party. He is ten years old. Last year he invited seven friends. This year he plans to invite eight friends. Of course, he will want to invite and include his three younger sisters, his mother, and his father. Carl would like to give each child three small pumpkins for the face-designing contest. The children will play games at the party. Two equal teams will bob for apples, and four equal teams will play pin the nose on the pumpkin. Help Carl plan his party by answering the following questions.

Remember to underline the words that will help you write a mathematical sentence for each example, write a complete sentence to answer each question, and tell how you knew the answer.

   a. If all of those invited to the Halloween party attend, how many will be at the party?

   b. How many children will be at the party?

   c. How many pumpkins will Carl need?

   d. How many children will be on each apple-bobbing team?

   e. How many children will be on each nose-pinning team?

   f. How many years did Carl not have a Halloween party?

   g. How many people will wear identical costumes at Carl's party?

   h. How many boys will be at the Halloween party?

Consider and React 4–6

Earlier in this chapter, I suggested that teachers need concrete examples of how metacognitive assessment can be done. What do you think? Do you feel you have enough examples to try it out on your own? The next section will provide you with one more procedure for your consideration.

Think-Aloud Reading Protocols   **Think-aloud reading protocols** are verbalizations of a reader's thoughts before, during, and after reading. To assess comprehension and metacognition in process, readers are usually asked to read a portion of text and then to voice their thoughts. These voiced thoughts, at the beginning of reading, during reading, and at the end of a reading selection, should reveal some of the thinking (metacognitive processes) used in comprehending text. Teachers could take notes or record these verbalizations, and then go back over them with the student to detect and follow his metacognitive strategies (to probe the student further about what he may have been thinking, and to reflect, hypothesize, and reiterate with the student regarding his metacognitive awareness and strategies during various parts of the reading).

Think-alouds give the teacher an opportunity to get a picture of what is going on in the heads of children as they construct meaning from text. Passages should be selected or written so that readers cannot know for sure what the outcome or topic is until they have read the last segment of text. In this way, readers must anticipate and hypothesize about the text's meaning during their think-alouds based on the clues they pick up on in each part of the text. The teacher asks readers to think aloud about the meaning of a passage after reading each text segment (Wade, 1990).

Teachers interested in fully assessing children's reading strategies will probably want to ask children to explain how they arrived at their particular hypotheses concerning the meaning of the text at various stages of the think-aloud verbalizations. Development of strategic readers involves teachers and students monitoring and discussing reading, thinking, and reasoning processes (Davey, 1983; Duffy, Roehler, & Herrmann, 1988; Herrmann, 1992; Schmitt, 1990; Palincsar & Brown, 1984). Readers must be given a full opportunity to play an active role throughout the process of monitoring and assessing their own comprehension strategies. For more indepth discussion about and examples of think-aloud strategies, readers should see Wilhelm (2001).

Content Reading Samples

Over the years, reading specialists and researchers have developed procedures for informally assessing students' comprehension of content materials. Probably the two best known of these are the "content reading inventory" and the "cloze procedure." Both of these procedures, along with some ideas for variations, will be detailed in the sections that follow. Readers will also be reminded of the usefulness of retellings, and ideas will be given on how to apply retellings to assess content reading comprehension.

Content Reading Inventories **Content reading inventories** are also sometimes called **group reading inventories.** They are based on silent reading and can be given to groups of students, or even to a whole class, in one sitting. This distinguishes them from the previously described (in Chapter 3) Informal Reading Inventories (IRIs), which are designed to be administered to one child at a time as the child reads orally. However, these content reading inventories, or group reading inventories, can also be administered silently to one child at a time.

Content reading inventories are similar to IRIs except that they specifically focus on the silent reading and comprehension of textbook materials. Teachers usually design these inventories themselves to assess students' potential comprehension of various textbooks they will use in class. Just like the IRIs, there are some commercially available content reading (or group reading) inventories. However, if a teacher wants to know how well a student, or a group of students, can read and understand a particular textbook, it makes most sense for the teacher to make the inventory himself. These inventories can be fairly easy to make. Here are some generic directions (teachers can modify these based on the specific content textbook and reading selected).

Directions for Making a Content Reading Inventory

1. Choose a content textbook that will be required reading for students in your class (a social studies text, science text, etc.).

2. Select a section from a chapter that students have not already read. This section should be lengthy enough to represent a total concept, idea, or area. Length can be anywhere from three to five pages of text.

3. Develop a set of questions to evaluate your students' understanding of the vocabulary as well as the explicit and implicit comprehension of the selection. Approximately ten questions are recommended. Use three or four of the questions to measure vocabulary knowledge in context. Use another three or four questions to measure text-explicit understanding, and three or four other questions to measure text-implicit understanding.

4. Develop a set of possible answers to match your questions. Try to develop possible answers that are inclusive of all the possibilities you'd consider as "acceptable" for your students.

5. Optional: Develop a second set of questions to evaluate how well students can "handle" the particular textbook—questions to determine whether students know how to use the table of contents of the book, the index, the glossary, the answer keys, and so on. Once again, the exact nature of these questions will depend on the particular text and on how you plan to use the text in your classroom. If you decide to do this, about ten questions should be enough. As before, develop a set of all-inclusive possible answers for this second set of questions.

Directions for Giving a Content Reading Inventory

1. Explain to the students that you are interested in seeing how well they do with a textbook that you are planning to use this school year.

2. Give out copies of the book and the questions you developed.

3. Ask students to turn to the selection you've chosen and read it silently. Have them write answers to the questions you developed, or if you are giving the inventory to just one child or to a small group of children, you can have the child tell you his or her answers. Keep in mind that your purpose is to find out whether a child, or the group, can successfully handle a particular textbook.

Obviously, these directions can be modified as you see fit. Many teachers like the idea of developing a content reading inventory for every book they hope to use in a school year. Teachers often use the inventory as a way of deciding how, or if, they will assign the book or assignments in the book to their students. Of course, scoring these inventories should be done qualitatively, as teachers are concerned with what textbook reading strategies their students seem to have, rather than with a score or number right or wrong. Poor performance by students can also be an indication of poor questions developed by the teacher, a poorly written text, and/or a lack of schemata for the content read, as well as many other factors.

Cloze Assessments

Cloze assessment is usually accepted by most reading researchers as a quick but fairly accurate method of determining individual students' abilities to read specific textual materials. The cloze can be _____ with expository material (content _____) or with narrative material (___ type material), and it ___ be given to one _____ at a time, or ___ the whole group or _____ in one sitting. In _____ to illustrate what the ___ looks like and how ___ might feel to take ___, this part of your ___ has been developed into ___ traditional cloze assessment. After ___ silently read this cloze _____ through once, go back ___ try to pencil in ___ many of the missing ___ as you can. Then ___ at the text as ___ was written without deletions _____ score yourself on this _____ test.

The cloze is _____ made and can be _____ for any text or ___ excerpt from expository or _____ material that the teacher _____ to use. Developing a ___ involves a systematic deletion ___ words from the selection. ___ blank is left in ___ of the deleted word ___ the student must fill ___ the blank with a ___ that makes sense within ___ surrounding text. The traditional ___ test involves deletion of ___ fifth word, with the ___ sentence and the last ___ of the material left ___. Additionally, the traditional cloze ___ requires students to fill ___ the blank with the ___ deleted word in order ___ the replacement to be _____ as correct. The rationale ___ that students would have ___ understand the text in ___ to provide the deleted ___. The procedure provides a _____ quick estimate of the relative difficulty of a particular text for a particular student. Scoring guides for the cloze vary, and there is disagreement in the field regarding the usefulness, merits, and scoring of this procedure; however, Bormuth's (1968) guide to scoring is one that is frequently used:

Cloze assessment is usually accepted by most reading researchers as a quick but fairly accurate method of determining individual students' abilities to read specific textual materials. The cloze can be used with expository material (content material) or with narrative material (story type material), and it can be given to one child at a time, or to the whole group or class in one sitting. In order to illustrate what the cloze looks like and how it might feel to take one, this part of your text has been developed into a traditional cloze assessment. After you silently read this cloze material through once, go back and try to pencil in as many of the missing words as you can. Then look at the text as it was written without deletions and score yourself on this cloze test.

The cloze is teacher made and can be developed for any text or any excerpt from expository or narrative material that the teacher desires to use. Developing a cloze involves a systematic deletion of words from the selection. A blank is left in place of the deleted word and the student must fill in the blank with a word that makes sense within the surrounding text. The traditional cloze test involves deletion of every fifth word, with the first sentence and the last sentence of the material left intact. Additionally, the traditional cloze test requires students to fill in the blank with the actual deleted word in order for the replacement to be counted as correct. The rationale is that students would have to understand the text in order to provide the deleted word. The procedure provides a fairly quick estimate of the relative difficulty of a particular text for a particular student. Scoring guides for the cloze vary, and there is disagreement in the field regarding the usefulness, merits, and scoring of this procedure; however, Bormuth's (1968) guide to scoring is one that is frequently used:

> 58–100% Independent Level (Interpretation: material may be too easy for the student; material can be handled independently, with ease, by the student.)
>
> 44–57% Instructional Level (Interpretation: material can be used by the student with the teacher's guidance/instruction.)
>
> 0–43% Frustration Level (Interpretation: material is too difficult for the student to use, even with teacher's guidance/instruction.)

Your score and approximate comprehension level on this material can be calculated by dividing the number of blanks into one hundred (there were fifty blanks in this cloze), and then multiplying by the number of exact words you were able to fill in the blanks. That will give you a comprehension score for this excerpt using a traditional cloze scoring procedure.

Consider and React 4–7

How did you do on the cloze? Please calculate your score and comprehension level on this exercise. Then read the arguments cited regarding scoring the cloze and the suggestions for using a modified cloze. What is your reaction?

Over the years, there has been controversy regarding scoring procedures for the cloze. Some believe that the Bormuth criterion is too high. Because of this, other criteria have been established to accept lower scores. For example, Pikulski and Tobin (1982) indicate that correct replacement of 50 percent or more of the deleted words should be the independent level, scoring between 30 and 50 percent should be the instructional level, and scoring less than 30 percent should be the frustration level. Some have argued that synonyms should be acceptable in place of the deleted word, but the research indicates that even though students' scores are slightly higher when synonyms are accepted, exact word replacement yields approximately the same results (McKenna, 1980). Other researchers indicate that accepting synonyms lowers the reliability of the procedure (e.g., Henk & Selders, 1984). They and others argue that accepting synonyms is not worth the time or effort involved (Pikulski & Tobin, 1982).

A Modified Cloze　You may be feeling frustrated because several of the fill-ins you had to count as incorrect seem to make sense in the passage. This is understandable. It is one reason that many teachers use a **modified cloze.** When you accept synonyms, phrases, or other words inserted in the cloze that still make sense and do not change the overall meaning of the passage(s), you are doing a modified cloze. Other modifications might include

1. Deleting every sixth, seventh, eighth, ninth, or tenth word, instead of the traditional deletion of every fifth.
2. Deleting certain types of words, such as adjectives, verbs, or selected vocabulary words. Obviously, the teacher would have a diagnostic or instructional purpose for deleting some types of words and not others.
3. Using deletion blanks that are representative of the exact length of the deleted word, instead of making all the blanks the same length. This could give students a grapheme clue to the missing word.
4. Using other variations of deletions or missing text. For example, deleting punctuation, deleting whole lines, or deleting the bottom half or even middle part of lines of text, as in using mutilated text. (**Mutilated text** is text that has been mutilated or altered so that part of the lines of text are missing, blurred, or smudged. Therefore, students would need to use a combination of phoneme-grapheme, syntax, and semantic cues, as well as their comprehension of the mutilated piece, to guess the mutilated parts and make sense of the text.)

As you might imagine, by modifying the cloze in one of the ways indicated, the traditional scoring system would no longer be considered valid. However, many teachers who advocate informal assessments and who see the advantages of combining assessment with instruction would argue that the gains in insight about the learners' use of strategies and development of strategies far outweigh the loss of the quantitative data created by the more standardized cloze scoring procedures. Additionally, many teachers who advocate the use of more authentic text would also advocate the use of longer passages, even whole stories or chapters, instead of doing a cloze on a relatively short piece. Overall, most agree that a modified cloze can be an excellent assessment/instruction tool and can help teachers gain insights into students' reading strategies when used by teachers who know what they are looking for.

Directions for Making and Giving a Cloze   Here are the directions for developing and giving a traditional cloze test. Keep in mind that if you wish to develop and give a modified cloze, that is perfectly acceptable. Just modify any of the steps, as suggested in the previous section, to fit your students' needs and your assessment and instruction decisions.

1. Select a 250–300 word passage, or consecutive passages, of text you have not previously assigned to students.

2. Retype or photocopy the passage(s), leaving at least the first and last sentences intact. Beginning with the second sentence, delete every fifth word, replacing the word with a line to show where the word has been deleted. The line should be exactly the same length for each deletion, giving no hint as to the length of the missing word. (You can also choose to white-out the deleted words on a photocopy of the passage(s) and then insert a line for each deletion. Once this is done, you can make enough photocopies for each student you plan to assess.) Do not make more than fifty deletions in all. Once you have made fifty deletions, leave the rest of the passage intact.

3. Give students a photocopy of the cloze and tell them to read it once.

4. After students have read the deleted passage(s), instruct them to fill in as many of the blanks as possible with words that make sense in the passage(s). Encourage them to guess what the missing words could be, so as not to leave blanks.

5. Score the students' responses, or have them score their own, using the Bormuth (1968) or Pikulski and Tobin (1982) scoring procedures, or any other evaluation procedures that you prefer, if you choose to use a modified version.

Retellings of Content Text   In this chapter, retellings have been discussed as a means of assessing students' comprehension following any reading selection. Directions were given for using retelling as an assessment tool with examples for prompting children after reading a story. Retellings are being included again in this portion of the chapter as a reminder to teachers that retellings are appropriate assessments of comprehension following expository, as well as narrative, text. In this section, directions for doing a retelling will be reiterated, with an emphasis on doing the retelling following the silent reading of content material.

Using a Retelling for Assessing Silent Reading Comprehension of Content Material

1. Select textual material to be used for your retelling. Prepare for the retelling by listing the important information, facts, or ideas covered by the content text within the selected material. You can do this informally on a photocopy of the

textual material, or, if you prefer, you can prepare a more formalized listing or outline to use as a checklist as the child "retells" the content read. See the sample of what this might look like (Box 4–2).

2. Tell the child, before she begins silently reading the material, that you will ask her to retell what she read when she is finished. Have the child read silently at her own pace.

3. Following the silent reading, ask the child to retell what the selection covered, or what it was about, by saying something like, "Toby, could you tell me what those pages were about?" Or, "Toby, could you retell what you just read?" As the child retells, use your checklist to ascertain how much she could remember without any prompts from you.

4. If the child leaves out important points or information, you can begin to prompt by saying something like, "Is there anything else you can remember, Toby?" Check any additional information against your checklist.

5. If the child still has left out important information, concepts, or ideas, you should prompt further to see how much she might remember with some aid from you. Make notes of your findings. Feel free to use the remaining time to help the child locate other important information she might have missed. There is no reason to make your assessment separate from instructional opportunities. In fact, it would make the most sense to do the retelling assessment with content materials or text that children do need to read and understand as part of your social studies, science, or other curricula program. Here are a few sample prompts to help the child remember or retell more.

    "Toby, can you remember what the text said about _____ ?"

    "What do you think was the most important idea, or thing, discussed on those pages?"

    "Toby, if you had to list the events that led up to _____, which ones would you list?"

    "You told me that _____, but you haven't mentioned _____ yet; could you tell me what you remember reading about it?"

    After the retelling is complete, you can review the child's responses and decide to what extent she understood the textual material and the points made. This information should be made part of your student's portfolio or folder—whatever record-keeping procedure you choose to use for children in your class. Keep in mind that, like all other assessments discussed in this text, a retelling is only one sample and should be analyzed only in combination with findings from other informal assessments and samples, including other retellings. It is unwise, unfair, and inaccurate to make decisions about children's abilities and strategies based on isolated data.

Box 4–2	Sample checklist for content retelling

Child's Name _____   Date _____
Content Sampled _____

Retelling Information Pre-Listed by Teacher	Child Retold With: Free Recall Aided Recall (Check Appropriate Column)		Additional Information Given by Child During Retelling

Notes/Observations Made by Teacher

_____
_____
_____
_____
_____
_____

Writing Samples

Students' writing provides an excellent opportunity to further assess their comprehension of material that they have read, both narrative and expository. This writing sampling can give us information about the child's overall understanding, grasp of ideas and important concepts, vocabulary knowledge, and a myriad of related reading comprehension strategies and skills (e.g., sequence of events, recall of details, cause-and-effect relationships, etc.). Fallon and Allen (1994) show how even young kindergarteners' writing can provide valuable insights into their content learning. Teachers can learn about children's misconceptions, as well as their insights, by reading and discussing their writings with them. Writing samples can be another way of doing a retelling of narrative or expository text. Following the written retelling, teachers can ask probing questions to better understand the child's ideas and to see what comprehending strategies the child might have used to make sense of the reading and then record his understandings.

> Robert P.
> It is bloody. It is waistfull. It is exspensiv. It is bad. It is good for our countys busness, We have to cleside If it is more bad than it is good. I think it is more bad and should be stoped.

Figure 4–1 Writing Sample for Robert, age 10

The sample of Robert's writing (see Figure 4–1) illustrates the usefulness of using children's writing to assess comprehension. Robert, age ten, is in a multigrade classroom of nine-, ten-, and eleven-year-olds. Robert was asked to write a description of the "perils of war" based on a reading assignment for social studies.

Consider and React 4–8

Consider Robert's comprehension as you review his writing (Figure 4–1) and note the follow-up dialogue between Robert and his teacher, Mr. Garcia. What did you learn about Robert's comprehension of his social studies reading assignment? See if you agree with Mr. Garcia's analysis.

> **MR. GARCIA:** Thank you for letting me read your paper, Robert. You make many interesting points. Can I ask you a few questions about what you've written?
>
> **ROBERT:** Sure! Go ahead.
>
> **MR. GARCIA:** You say that war is bloody, wasteful, and expensive. What drew you to those conclusions?
>
> **ROBERT:** Well, in the article you gave us to read, it said that thousands and thousands of people were killed or badly hurt.
>
> **MR. GARCIA:** That is true. Is that what you mean when you say "bloody"?
>
> **ROBERT:** Yes.
>
> **MR. GARCIA:** What about your conclusion that war is wasteful and expensive? Can you elaborate about that?
>
> **ROBERT:** Okay. Well, isn't it wasteful for people to die and get hurt?
>
> **MR. GARCIA:** Oh yes! I agree! What about the expensive part?
>
> **ROBERT:** The article said that the war cost the United States many millions of dollars. I'd say that is expensive! Wouldn't you?

MR. GARCIA: I think so, too, Robert. What about your judgment that war is bad? How did you arrive at that conclusion?

ROBERT: Well, after all I just said, don't you think it is bad?

MR. GARCIA: I do, Robert, but I'm more interested in what you think and why. I like to read and hear your ideas. What about it?

ROBERT: So many people die or get maimed and it costs so much money, too. It said that even though all of these bad things happen, big businesses in the United States make lots of money from war. It said it is good for the U.S. economy. Even so, I think it's bad, and I don't think we should let wars happen.

MR. GARCIA: I couldn't agree with you more, Robert. I'm glad to see you got so much out of that article. Thanks for discussing it with me.

As can be seen, Robert showed strong understanding of the article he read. Additionally, Mr. Garcia noted that Robert grasped and could use key ideas and vocabulary from the piece, and that he demonstrated an ability to compare, contrast, and evaluate the important ideas presented.

Sometimes teachers might want to provide more structure or organization to children's writing in order to get more specific information about their comprehension. For example, Au, Scheu, Kawakami, and Herman (1990) illustrate use of a **story frame** to solicit children's written responses to literature. The frame might look something like this:

The problem in the story is _____

_____.

The problem is solved when _____

_____.

At the end of the story _____

_____.

The author's message is _____

_____.

The message makes me think _____

_____.

Did you like this story? Tell why or why not: _____

_____.

The story frame gives the teacher information concerning students' understanding of and response to characters, setting, problems, events, solutions, theme, and application, as well as their personal response. In many ways this may resemble a book report format or outline.

Cudd and Roberts (1989) suggest a similar idea: **paragraph frames** using a cloze approach with content material. Sentence starters, including specific signal words or phrases, are provided for the student. When these starters are completed by the student, a paragraph representing the child's understanding of the content she read is available for the teacher to observe the comprehension. Cudd and Roberts provide the following example.

Before a frog is grown, it goes through many changes. (1) First, the mother frog

_____

_____ .

(2) Next, _____

_____ . (3) Then, _____

_____ . (4) Finally _____

_____ .

(5) Now they _____

_____

I have presented only a few examples of how children's writing can be used to assess their comprehension of reading as well as some of their comprehending strategies. Using writing samples is one of the assessment techniques teachers have available. It is hoped that teachers will never restrict themselves to any one approach to assessment. (Readers who are interested in more examples of the use of writing for comprehension assessment are directed to the works of Heller [1995]; Irwin & Doyle [1992]; Jenkins [1996]; and Pappas, Kiefer, & Levstik [1999].)

Consider and React 4–9

Do you have experience with other ideas for using writing to assess comprehension? What could you suggest?

Prior Knowledge and Schemata Assessments

In Chapter 1, schema (schemata, plural) was referred to as the mental picture and mental organization of information relative to a given idea, topic, concept, event, person, or thing. It is also the knowledge or information a person stores in his or her memory about something and is based on that person's cognitive and other prior knowledge and experience. In Chapter 1 we sampled an example of difficulties with comprehension due to a lack of cognitive experience (the cricket example). Without some cognitive experience with a topic, it is difficult to comprehend reading material written about it. In other words, if a child or adult lacks a schema for a given topic, it would be difficult to read with understanding something about that topic. Therefore, before assigning readings in social studies, science, and other textbooks and literature containing difficult, complex, unusual, or sensitive vocabulary/ideas/topics/concepts, or even before starting a new unit, a classroom teacher would be wise to assess students' prior knowledge and schemata relative to those ideas/topics/concepts in the unit.

The Role of Prior Knowledge

Prior knowledge is closely tied to schemata, as it involves the knowledge (vocabulary and other background knowledge) that students bring to the text before reading it. It is important that teachers know how to assess students' vocabulary and background knowledge in order to know more about the prior knowledge they bring to their reading and study assignments. Moe (1989) indicates that by the time children enter school they have extensive speaking and listening vocabularies. This is also supported by the emergent literacy research. By grade one, Moe estimates, their speaking vocabulary can easily exceed four thousand words and their listening and understanding vocabulary can range from ten thousand to twenty thousand words. This richness of vocabulary experience can be tapped by classroom teachers interested in assessing students' prior knowledge.

Holmes and Roser (1987) identify and discuss five techniques for observing vocabulary and prior knowledge.

1. *Free recall* The teacher asks students to tell everything they know about _____ and records their responses. This technique provides the most information in the shortest possible time, but can be problematic for very young readers or for readers who have retrieval problems and/or have problems organizing their thoughts and information.

2. *Word association* The teacher selects several key words and asks children what comes to mind when they hear each word. This technique is fast to prepare and administer, usually yielding more information than free recall.

3. *Structured questions* The teacher prepares specific questions and asks them to find out what students know prior to reading. This technique is effective and yields the most information, but it is time-consuming to prepare the questions.

4. *Recognition* The teacher prepares several statements and key terms and has students select the words, phrases, or sentences they believe are related to the key terms or would be found in a reading related to the key terms. This technique is effective and efficient, and is helpful to children who have trouble retrieving information.

5. *Unstructured discussion* Students freely generate their own ideas about a word or topic without any focusing from the teacher. This technique is the least effective and efficient procedure of the five.

Richards and Gipe (1992) describe other techniques for assessing children's background knowledge, and they indicate that readers who connect what they read with what they already know are more likely to make appropriate inferences for text ideas that are not explicitly stated. One technique they call "Yes/No . . . Why?" involves the reader indicating "yes" when she knows about or understands an idea in the text or story and "no" when she disputes or doesn't understand an idea. Following the "yes" or "no," the reader must supply a reason for her response. Another technique, "It Reminds Me Of . . .", requires the reader, after reading paragraphs in the text or story, to relate what she reads to her own background experience. Both techniques give teachers an opportunity to observe children's prior knowledge. Readers interested in more details about these techniques should see the Richards and Gipe article.

Nagy (1988) indicates that two important learnings come from studying schemata that are relevant to vocabulary knowledge (and prior knowledge) and comprehension: (1) knowledge is structured and consists not of lists of independent facts, but of sets of relationships; and (2) we understand new information by relating it to what we already know. In the sections that follow, ways of assessing schemata, which encompass prior knowledge and vocabulary knowledge, are discussed and demonstrated.

Consider and React 4–10

Schemata assessment could be another intimidating idea for some classroom teachers, particularly if they lack examples and specific suggestions about how to proceed. What do you think? These next two sections provide many ideas that classroom teachers can use. See if there are some that you particularly like and would find useful in your classroom? Which ones and why?

Ways of Assessing Schemata

How can schemata be assessed? Teachers can informally assess their students' schemata, or stored knowledge, on a topic in a variety of ways. Several general ways will be suggested. Following those, two teachers' examples of creative assessments and adaptations will also be provided. Teachers can be as creative as they like in assessing schemata and other prior knowledge. These assessments can also serve as an introduction to a unit or topic of study and for instruction within the unit.

1. One way of assessing schemata would be to ask students to draw a picture about what they know about a topic or idea. By reviewing children's pictures, and asking probing questions when you need additional information, you can often glean what children know about the topic.

2. Another way to do this is to ask children to diagram what they know about a topic. Children should be encouraged to label different parts of their diagrams. Once again, the teacher might need to ask some probing questions to fully understand what an individual child means. When analyzed, diagrams can provide valuable information about the child's knowledge, depth, and organization of information relative to the topic under consideration. Drawing diagrams might be more effective for older students, while drawing pictures might be more suitable for children in the lower grades.

3. A third possibility includes using small-group discussion as a means of assessing schemata. For example, a teacher could divide his class into small groups and generate a discussion about the topic. By eavesdropping and actively listening, the teacher can informally assess what youngsters in the group know about the topic. Also, the teacher can choose to talk individually with children about the topic and ask probing questions to see what each one knows. Of course, discussion could take place in a large group or the whole class as well; however, the teacher would not necessarily find out about each child's schemata in this way.

4. Similar to using small-group discussion, but more fun for many students, the use of drama can be a tool for assessing schemata. Several very creative teachers I have worked with (Trisia Spinney, Mary Hess, and Marie Saball) have suggested using dramatizations twofold: first to determine how much students might already know about a topic, concept, or event; and second, as a means of assessing their understanding following the study of or reading on the particular topic, concept, or event.

5. The fifth, more general, suggestion involves writing. Teachers can ask children to write something about the topic and use that as a means of assessing schemata. However, teachers are cautioned to not rely on this method alone, as some children are intimidated by writing and might not share everything they know about a topic. Likewise, teachers are cautioned that other children might be intimidated by having to draw, diagram, engage in open discussion, or act. Therefore, it is best, as with all other types of assessments, to use more than one assessment technique or example to try to determine a child's schema on a particular topic or idea.

Teachers and children can keep dated samples of a child's schema on a given topic in the child's portfolio. These dated assessments can provide valuable evidence of the child's growth in content-area learning, including vocabulary development and breadth of understanding. Below are some simple directions for getting a dated sample.

1. Ask the child to talk about the concept or topic in order to share with you all he knows about it.

2. Ask the child to diagram or draw a picture or semantic map to illustrate the information.

3. With the child, date and label the diagram or semantic map.

4. Later, with the child, analyze the diagram/semantic map and look for (a) the accuracy of details; (b) the logical flow of ideas relative to the concept/topic; (c) the knowledge of key vocabulary related to the topic; and (d) the child's overall knowledge concerning the concept/topic.

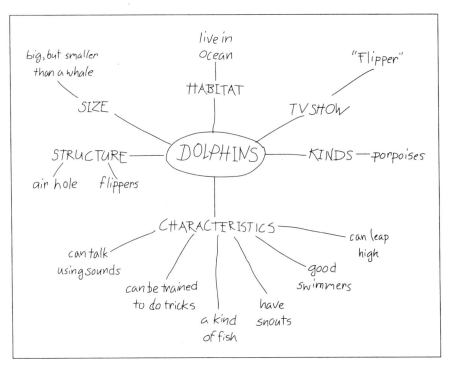

Figure 4–2 (Part I) "Before Studying" About Dolphins

Source: Figures adapted by permission from *Semantic Mapping: Classroom Applications* by J. E. Heimlich and S. D. Pittelman. Copyright © 1986 by the International Reading Association. All rights reserved. Reprinted by permission.

5. After a unit of study or after reading about the topic or concept in your classroom, you would solicit another diagram or semantic map from the child. This diagram or map should be reviewed to assess the child's growth in the topic or content area under study.

Figure 4–2, adapted from samples in Heimlich and Pittelman (1986), illustrates the potential to measure growth in content area learning. In Part I of the diagram we see a student's "before studying" knowledge (schema) for dolphins. In Part II, the semantic map represents the student's acquired knowledge and vocabulary relative to dolphins "after studying" about dolphins.

Teacher-Developed Assessments and Procedures

As mentioned, teachers can be creative and design interesting methods of assessing and enhancing children's schemata for different topics. What follows are original ideas and adaptations developed by classroom teachers with whom I have worked.

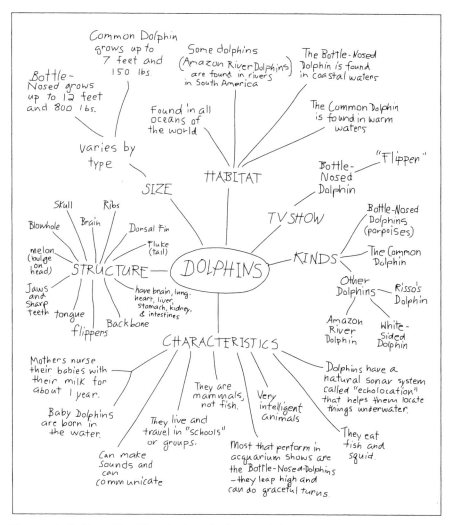

Figure 4–2 (Part II) "After Studying" About Dolphins

Assessing Schemata for "Native Americans and Their Contributions"
By Catherine Calise

Focus of Assessment   The focus of this assessment is to determine the students' schemata for Native Americans in preparation for a study unit on this topic. Students will be reading and researching, using both narrative and expository text during this unit, to learn about various Native American cultures and appreciate their contributions to society and life in North America. Another goal of this unit is to encourage an understanding that contemporary Native Americans are really as diverse a group as everyone else (in order to avoid any tendencies of stereotyping these cultures).

Directions for the Teacher   Students will be asked to reflect on their knowledge of Native American cultures and life and then to record information that they know on an "inquiry sheet." The sheet provides categories that students are asked to consider, and each student writes words or phrases in the appropriate columns to detail information about Native Americans. It looks like this:

Tribes/Names	Where They Live(d)	Contributions to Society	Other Information
_____	_____	_____	_____
_____	_____	_____	_____
_____	_____	_____	_____
_____	_____	_____	_____

After individual students have completed the sheets, everyone will participate in this group activity:

1. Categories are written on the board.
2. Students volunteer to contribute one piece of information for the category of their choice.
3. When information is listed, students check it off their inquiry sheets (leaving the word/phrase visible).
4. Other students contribute until all information is recorded.
5. Students and teachers review each piece of recorded information and determine if it should be designated with an "M" (myth), "R" (reality), or "UQ" (uncertain/query needed) coding.
6. This chart, with all recorded, coded information, is copied onto poster board for teacher/class reference and for research purposes. (If something is miscoded, or otherwise inaccurate, after individuals/groups study and research, the coding should be corrected by student researchers.)

The process of elimination is designed to encourage depth of thought. It is hoped that interest in making further contributions will stimulate the students to think and generate more ideas. The coding of listed student-generated information as myth (M), reality (R), or uncertain/query needed (UQ) helps note and clarify information as accurate, inaccurate, or possibly inaccurate.

The teacher may decide to use a follow-up assessment procedure, encouraging the group to reflect on their responses and then list "what they would like to know" about Native American cultures (see Ogle, 1986, for details regarding her K-W-L strategy).

Finally, the papers will be collected for the teacher's reference. These, along with the students' contributions and discussion, will give the teacher specific information on students' schemata for this topic.

What to Look For   The teacher will look at the quantity and quality of students' knowledge—specifically, their accurate understanding of Native American cultures, of how they live today, and of their contributions (as opposed to stereotypical representations that may provide false or misleading information). Also, questions or things that students list as wanting to know more about can be indications of knowledge. (It is difficult to formulate pertinent questions or lists about a topic unless you already know something about it.) After examining the clarity, organization, and depth of student responses, the teacher will be able to use this activity to assess the group's schemata and specific needs and interests for reading, research, and further discussion. It also should be useful in providing directions for instruction and learning for individuals and the entire class.

Special Necessary Materials   Inquiry Sheet
Suggested additional reading: Ogle, D. M. (1986). K-W-L: A teaching model that develops active reading of expository text. *The Reading Teacher, 39* (6), pp. 564–570.

Assessing Schemata for "Household Items" Using "Box Talk"
By Terese Heslin

Focus of Assessment   Using this "hands-on" approach, the teacher of younger children can stimulate and encourage verbal interaction that should provide information about each child's prior knowledge and schema for the selected topic or concept. This technique also can help develop or further develop each child's schema for the concept or topic under study. I call the technique "Box Talk," and I've developed this sample assessment/teaching strategy around the topic "household items." Using a box containing manipulatives, items, and pictures related to the topic, the teacher begins.

Directions for the Teacher   Interacting with a small group of three or four children allows for frequent participation opportunities for each child. Too small a group may hinder the interaction. The teacher asks the children for their ideas, listens carefully, guides the learners into discussions and activities to assess and enlarge their schemata, offers a variety of related experiences to allow opportunities to assess and use the schemata, and generally observes and assesses the use of children's schemata for the topic/concept in as many situations as possible.

Questions that could be used to initiate the sharing of ideas for assessment purposes include:

When holding up an item

Tell me something you know about this.

Describe/tell me about any parts of this.

Does this look like anything you have seen at home? At school?

How/When could we use this?

When holding up a picture

Tell me what you think is happening in this picture?

Where might this be?

Have you ever been to a place like this?

You can also have a child hold up an item or picture and have him question the group. (Note: First model the questioning about items/pictures as just described.)

Write the children's responses to the questioning on large chart paper. Read them to the group. Key words such as the names of items or the function they perform may reoccur. This is to be expected. Call attention to this common information.

The teacher could facilitate the compiling of a word list from the "Box Talk" topic/concept. The words could then be categorized by function or product, or any relevant heading, crossing out or checking off words as they are used in specific categories.

What to Look For   Look for common factors, words, functions, or key points. Listen to the descriptions, reasons, or attitudes that accompany the responses. You are looking for evidence of each child's understanding regarding the concept or topic. You will determine this by the children's answers to the questions you pose, and also by the questions they pose as you (or they) select items from the box.

The teacher also could arrange for opportunities or experiences that would allow the children to demonstrate their existing schemata. Observe and assess the use of the schemata and any generalizations or applications made by the children. Experiences could include dramatic play, storybook reading, shared-reading poem, and tell-a-story pictures (record the child's story by writing down what the child says or by recording it on tape or some other medium).

Look for children referring to the chart or word list to include "Box Talk" words in their writings. When they come across a "Box Talk" word in a book, they could chart it, citing the title of the book. By observing the use of the "Box Talk" words in each child's writing/reading, you will learn a lot about the child's understanding and schema for the topic/concept under study.

Special Necessary Materials   "Box Talk" box and pictures, manipulatives, items related to concept; chart paper; cassette recorder; materials for activities/experiences related to the schemata being assessed (dramatic play props, puppets, etc.); books related to the concept; shared-reading poem.

Study Skills and Strategy Assessments

Children are given a wide variety of assignments in school. Some are done under the close supervision of the classroom teacher; others are given with the expectation that students will do them independently in school or at home. Typical school-related assignments can include using the dictionary, using the encyclopedia, doing library research, outlining a chapter, taking notes from a reading assignment, doing a research paper, studying a chapter, studying for a test, and so on. These assignments and the independent work that students must do to accomplish them are important elements in the development of independent and self-reliant learners. The only problem is that students often do not know how to go about doing these school-related assignments.

It is important for the classroom teacher to realize that all children may not know how to proceed, what to do, or what is involved and expected relative to a given assignment. If a teacher does not realize this, it is possible that a child could be given a bad grade in a subject area, not because he didn't understand the subject (for example, the content of the chapter in the social studies book), but because he didn't know how to go about doing the assignment (outlining the social studies chapter assigned as homework). Teachers can do some informal assessments, including observations of students in their classrooms, to see whether they have the study skills, or know the study strategies, necessary to get assignments done. In the sections that follow, suggestions for determining what study skills and strategies to assess are provided. Additionally, samples of possible assessment techniques and procedures are provided to give classroom teachers some ideas.

Selection of Appropriate Skills and Strategies

Here are several steps teachers can take in selecting and making decisions about informal assessment of study skills and study strategies.

1. First, consider the assignment(s) you plan to give your students. Figure out what study skills and strategies they would need in order to successfully complete each assignment. For example, if you plan to have students look up the definitions of new or unknown words they encounter in their textbooks, and then want them to write an appropriate contextual definition for each one, it is important to see whether they know how to use the dictionary efficiently and also if they understand that a word might have several meanings.

2. Once you have determined the necessary skills and strategies for doing an assignment, think about different ways you can assess your students' use of these skills/strategies. For example, if you are interested in assessing the efficient use of the dictionary, one way you can assess this is by observing each child as he attempts to find a word in the dictionary.

3. As with other assessments, snap judgments are not a good idea. Allow opportunities to observe/assess children's use of necessary skills and strategies in different situations or with different materials. Also allow for different approaches and styles. Often a youngster might approach an assignment differently from how you might approach it. However, if the youngster's approach works for him and the results are appropriate to the assignment, you probably should not intervene.

4. If you learn that a child does not have the necessary study skills or appropriate strategies for doing a particular assignment, plan some direct teaching time and appropriate learning activities. Work with the child before expecting him to do the assignment. Chapter 8 contains some instructional possibilities for study skills and strategies. These can be used as examples for your planning and for your use. You might also want to develop your own teaching strategies, which could be more appropriate to the child and to your particular assignment needs.

Teacher-Developed Assessments and Procedures

Each teacher and classroom situation is unique. In this section, examples of possible assessment and study strategy enhancement techniques, ideas, and procedures are provided. Classroom teachers are encouraged to use these possibilities to generate their own ideas for assessing students in various skills and strategies. Assessments should be used only when they fit the unique aspects of a teacher's assignments and students. The following original ideas were developed by teachers to fit their unique classroom assessment and instruction needs.

Assessing Note Taking and Studying Strategies from Expository Text
By Sabrina A. Provencher

Focus of Assessment   The focus of this assessment is to find out how children go about taking notes and studying for a chapter test in one of their textbooks, and to find out how successful they are with the strategies they use.

Directions for the Teacher   The teacher will ask children to take notes from and study the next, but so-far unread, chapter (or section of a chapter) in their science or social studies book, or in any content-area material that the children have a purpose for reading. The children will be told that they will be given time to take notes and study the material in the chapter. They also should be told that, after they study, they will be given an essay test on this new material, but, because it is new and because you (the teacher) are most interested in seeing how they study and learn, it will be an open-book and open-note test. That way, they don't have to memorize anything. Even though the entire class may participate in this activity, the teacher will focus most of her observation, attention, and time on a few students in order to thoroughly observe their individual strategies. The teacher will then instruct the children to go ahead and read the chapter and take whatever notes they think are important.

What to Look For   The teacher will carefully observe the children to see what study strategies each uses to take notes and prepare for the test. For instance, the teacher might want to observe the rate at which the material is read. Since the children are aware that they will be tested on the material, they may read more slowly or deliberately than if they were not preparing for a test.

The teacher might observe to see whether the children skim the chapter or read the headings first before beginning the text.

While the children are reading and studying, the teacher should record her observations of what the individual children seem to do to aid their understanding. Do children make notations? Do they refer to pictures or graphs in the text? The teacher should look to see whether children go back to reread some material, trying to ensure their understanding of the text. Do students use the glossary for help with unknown vocabulary?

When the children appear ready for the test (be sure you have given them ample time based on the length and difficulty of the content material), the teacher will remind the children that they can use their notes and the textbook. Ask if there are any questions and carefully note what questions they ask. This could help the teacher observe the level of understanding and could provide more information about individual children's strategies. Because the quality of the question often reflects the depth of understanding, children's questions are just as important as their answers.

The teacher will then give the students an open-book and open-note test to check their understanding of the content of the reading. A good test question might be:

"What is the most important idea or thing you read in this chapter or reading, and why?"

After the children complete their test, the teacher and children can check the children's test answers and study notes to see whether important material was included and whether headings and other boldface information (including new vocabulary) can be found in the notes.

Finally, after the test, individual children can be asked questions such as, "What was the hardest part of reading and studying for you? How do you decide what to take notes on? How did you study this material? Why did you study it in that way? Would you do it the same way next time?" (The teacher should be prepared to ask as many probing questions as necessary in order to stimulate children's self-reflection and to find out as much as possible about the strategies children use.)

Special Necessary Materials Textbook chapter or excerpt, plenty of notebook paper, and a pencil for taking notes. Open-ended essay question for the follow-up test.

Assessing Strategies for Reading a Bar Graph
By Demetri Orlando

Focus of Assessment   This idea was developed to assess children's abilities to gather, read, and integrate information presented in graph form. It examines children's use of information presented on the graph and how they relate it to what they already know. (This assessment presupposes that children know the days of the week and have basic mathematical knowledge, necessary for reading the bar graph. See Figure 4–3.)

Directions for the Teacher   This activity may be done with individual children or in small groups while the teacher takes notes regarding the children's strategies and abilities. (The graph used in this assessment was developed by a small group from the class and is from its members' own observations and measurements of the rainfall during one week of the previous month. The students being assessed would not have taken part in the making of the graph.)

Give children copies of a bar graph and ask them to look at it. Observe how long it takes them to orient it properly (with the horizontal axis down). Ask these questions:

1.   What does this bar graph tell us? How do you know?
2.   On which days did it rain? How do you know?

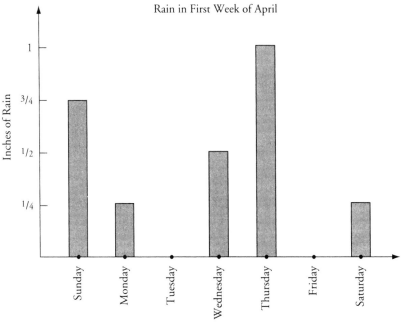

Figure 4–3 Bar Graph for Sample Assessment

3. What do you know about the weather on Tuesday and Friday? How do you know?

4. What kind of things would you do on a day like Thursday? Why?

Observe how the students use the bar graph to answer the questions. Do they use the appropriate part of the graph for the question they are answering? Can they answer questions accurately? Can they explain their answers, and do the explanations indicate an understanding of how to read a graph?

What to Look For The teacher should observe to see whether the child provides accurate answers to the questions based on the information in the assessment graph and whether she can support those answers by referring back to the graph. For example, in question 1, the child is asked to tell what information the graph provides. Does she use the title or the information on the axis to support understanding? Does she use the graphical information to draw a conclusion concerning what the graph presents? For example, a child who answers "The first week in April is very rainy" may have a better grasp of the purpose of this graph than one who just answers "April" or "rain."

Question 2 asks the child to list the days that were rainy. Does the student include all five days it rained, regardless of the amount of rain? Does the student list them in chronological order, or by quantity of rain? Can the student explain how she arrived at her answer by referring to appropriate parts of the graph?

The third question asks the child to tell what she knows about the weather on Tuesday and Friday. How does she support her answer?

The fourth question asks about Thursday, when it was most rainy. Does the child give a response appropriate to a day of pouring rain? Can she support her answer by referring to the graph?

Special Necessary Materials Bar graph and questions to be answered. (Note: Different groups of children can develop and generate graphs on a computer, like the one in this sample assessment, to display information they have researched. The teacher can later use these to assess others on graph reading.)

Assessing Map Reading Skills
By Sherry Latham and Cristina Acevedo

Focus of Assessment   The focus of these assessment ideas is to observe children's knowledge of maps and their ability to read them. Map reading, along with reading other graphic texts, is important to the understanding of many content materials. Learning to read maps also facilitates understanding of abstract symbols, finding locations and routes, and knowing one's relationship to the world.

Directions for the Teacher   Map reading knowledge and skill/strategies can be assessed in a variety of ways. Several are suggested. The teacher can select from these—use several or modify these ideas to assess young or older children—to gain insight into their more specialized map reading skills.

The checklist for qualitative assessment of map reading skills is used in this first assessment idea. As the teacher tries other suggested assessment possibilities, she can continue to record notations about the child's responses on this checklist. (See Box 4–3.)

Box 4–3	Checklist for qualitative assessment of map reading skills						
Student Name _____ Grade _____ Teacher _____ Date _____							
Instructional strategies: _____	Uses a Variety of Strategies	Draws Conclusions	Understands Basic Vocabulary	Recognizes Essential Details	Can Work Independently	Will follow guided inquiry to solve problems and extend understanding	
Student is able to identify symbols on map key							
Student shows knowledge of compass directions							
Student can locate cities, states, towns, countries							
Student can identify land and water forms							
Comments: _____							

Informally discuss the purpose and parts of a map with the child and ask open-ended, probing questions to discern the child's understanding, strategies, abilities, and skills with map reading. The teacher will note the quality of the child's skills on the checklist.

Showing Maps   Ask questions and elicit responses from the child about the uses of maps in daily life and in the classroom. (Displayed close by in the classroom, within the child's reach, should be a folding travel map, wall map, relief map, atlas, and globe. These maps should include all the samples [i.e., state, country, etc.] that the teacher will need for her assessment purposes.)

Possible questions include the following: "I visited the city of _____ on my vacation (point to location). Where did you go on your vacation? Can you show me on any of these maps?" Also: "How can people use maps when they are traveling? Here are many different kinds of maps; what do you think could be the uses of each map? What other ways could these maps be used?"

Symbols of Map Key   Point out the map key (legend) to the child and allow her to share her knowledge about map keys and their symbols. Show the child a map of the state or province in which she lives and ask: "Because symbols are pictures that represent something else, find the symbol for a road and explain it to me. Now compare the road symbol to the river symbol and find examples on the map. Do you see any lakes? Tell me how you knew they were lakes." Question the child until you have covered all symbols in the map key.

Locating Places on Maps Using Compass Directions   Show the child the compass rose on the map of the country and ask what she knows about it. "What do the letters and arrows mean?" Ask the child to locate places (states and cities) using the compass directions.

Directions game: Teacher and child take turns saying, "I'm thinking of a city (state, province) that is north of _____." Student answers and then asks her own question, "Which state/province is south of _____?" Game continues as teacher records child's responses and strengths.

Puzzle   Cut a map apart and ask the child to reconstruct it, explaining her strategies in doing so. This could give the teacher more information about the child's map reading and compass direction skills.

Invented Map Game   Teacher and child can play an invented map game to further assess map reading skills. By taking turns picking game cards and following instructions, the child and teacher can be led on a trip using compass directions and map key symbols. The teacher and child can invent rules, game card instructions, and a game board.

What to Look For   Using all or some of these assessment ideas, the teacher can observe the child's knowledge, skills, and strategies in reading and using maps to get information. Some assessment observations may include the following: (1) Does the student draw reasonable conclusions? To what extent? (2) Does the student recognize essential details? To what extent? (3) Does the student understand basic vocabulary? To what extent? (4) Can the student find and use information independently? To what extent? This information should be noted on the checklist to help the teacher plan instruction and learning activities.

Special Necessary Materials   A checklist, a variety of maps, map puzzle, invented map board game.

Comprehension and Metacognitive Strategy Assessments

Ideas and procedures, with examples, for sampling and probing into students' comprehension, comprehending strategies, metacognition, and other strategic reading processes have been presented throughout this chapter. Although it has been pointed out that these ideas and procedures are best when they have been designed by the classroom teacher to fit the unique curriculum, materials, and students in his particular classroom, it is sometimes helpful to see samples of assessments that other teachers have devised. Here are three such examples of strategic reading assessments and applications to stimulate your own creative ideas.

Teacher-Developed Assessments and Procedures

These samples show how teachers teaching in primary grade classrooms, and others teaching in upper elementary/middle-school classrooms, assess children for comprehension and metacognitive strategies. These teachers regularly have large populations of second-language and other diverse learners in their classrooms. The samples show how these teachers have creatively blended assessment and instruction of various strategic reading and learning areas into their regular classroom curriculum and workday.

Assessing and Enhancing Comprehension of Expository Text Using Paragraph Frames and Writing
By Nellie Anne Kwasny Langlois

Focus of Assessment The twofold purpose of this assessment is to provide the teacher with information about what the student has learned from the expository reading, as well as to help the student organize information read in order to improve comprehension. (Several diverse learners in this class particularly need structure and support in order to recall information from text.)

Directions for the Teacher This example shows application of this procedure for our primary grade classroom unit "Insects and Their Worlds." Among the topics studied is bees. During the course of this unit, all students read *Bees and Beelines* by Judy Hawes, and, after reading it, complete the teacher-prepared expository paragraph frame. (Possible answers appear at the end of this example.)

I have learned many interesting things about bees, such as how they get from their homes to flowers and find their way back again. (1) First, I learned that _____

_____.
(2) Next, I learned that to do this, they, like me, _____ where they have lessons in _____. (3) Then I learned that they fly _____.
(4) I then learned that a bee has five _____ so that he can see _____
_____. (5) I learned that bees use familiar _____, _____,
and _____ to help them and they use the _____, too. (6) If a bee finds flowers ripe with nectar, he gets help from other bees in the hive by _____
_____. (7) They do this to tell _____.
(8) The most interesting or important thing I have learned about bees from this reading is

_____

_____

_____.

(9) I think it is the most interesting or important thing because _____

_____

_____

_____.

Students should be provided with as much space as possible to write their answers to the final two questions. These answers should provide insight into students' overall comprehension of the material, along with their abilities to think, reflect, and reason (metacognition) about the material read. Possible answers to the first seven blanks are as follows:

(1) bees can fly more than a mile from home to get nectar and then fly home in a nearly straight line called a beeline.

(2)   go to school . . . flying home

(3)   backwards

(4)   eyes . . . in all directions at once

(5)   buildings, trees, and hills . . . sun

(6)   dancing

(7)   how to get to the flowers

What to Look For   The teacher conducts this assessment in order to evaluate each student's comprehension of the topic under study. To what extent has the printed page provided the reader with information? The teacher uses the completed expository paragraph frame to assess new knowledge and its accuracy.

The two responses at the end of the paragraph frame should help the teacher assess what each student has learned and the personal significance the text has for him. It is an opportunity for the student to reflect on overall understanding of the reading and for the teacher to assess the value each student places on the reading along with the student's interest in the area of study. Additionally, the teacher can examine the last response to note a student's ability to justify his answer. If the teacher doesn't understand a student's response to any item, it is important to give him an opportunity to explain it. You might say, "This is an interesting answer. Can you tell me more about what you mean?" Moreover, students who write particularly interesting or divergent answers could be probed to explain their reasonings and rationales.

Special Necessary Materials   Teacher-prepared paragraph frame based on a reading selection; for this example, Hawes, J. (1964). *Bees and beelines*. New York: Thomas Y. Crowell.

Suggested additional readings include:

Cudd, E. T., & Roberts, L. (1989). Using writing to enhance content area learning in the primary grades. *The Reading Teacher, 42* (6), pp. 392–404.

Olson, M. W., & Gee, T. C. (1991). Content reading instruction in the primary grades: Perceptions and strategies. *The Reading Teacher, 45* (4), pp. 298–306.

Assessing Comprehension and Metacognitive Strategies of First Graders Using the Basal Reader
By June Rappaccioli, Carmen Kennett, and Isabel Moraga

Focus of Assessment   This sample assessment application has been developed for use with our reading program, which is used as the basis for reading instruction for first graders in our school. Using stories from the basal, we assess and teach comprehending and metacognitive strategies. This sample application, done with Francesca, one of our first-grade ESL students (Francesca's first language is Spanish, but she is fluent in English) demonstrates a typical assessment and instruction dialogue.

Directions for the Teacher   (1) The teacher helps the child establish a purpose for reading. (2) The teacher asks the child to monitor her own reading. (3) The teacher asks the child to read the story silently. (4) The teacher formulates one initial comprehension question, such as, "What problem does Hippo have?" (5) Based on the child's answer, the teacher formulates as many additional comprehension questions as necessary to solicit the requested information, then follows up with metacognitive probing. Here are excerpts of dialogue between Mrs. Kennett and Francesca as Mrs. Kennett assesses Francesca's strategies.

(Questions and probing from the beginning of the story.)

MRS. KENNETT: What problem does Hippo have?

FRANCESCA: He cannot think what to wish for.

MRS. KENNETT: How do you know that?

FRANCESCA: Because it is in the reading.

MRS. KENNETT: Where in the reading did you find that?

FRANCESCA: (Going back to the reading.) Here it says, "But he could not think what to wish for."

MRS. KENNETT: Does that mean that Hippo didn't solve his problem?

FRANCESCA: Yes, that is true.

MRS. KENNETT: Why do you say that?

FRANCESCA: Because he went to see Snake for help.

(Questions and probing from the ending of the story.)

MRS. KENNETT: What is Hippo wishing for when he closes his eyes at the end of the story?

FRANCESCA: I don't remember.

MRS. KENNETT: How can you find the answer?

FRANCESCA: Looking in the book.

MRS. KENNETT: Why didn't he wish to be like any of his animal friends?

FRANCESCA: Because he didn't like the way he looked.

MRS. KENNETT: What did he wish for?

FRANCESCA: He wished to be himself.

MRS. KENNETT: Why did he wish to stay as he was?

FRANCESCA: Because he realized he looked better just the way he was.

MRS. KENNETT: Did Hippo get his wish?

FRANCESCA: Yes.

MRS. KENNETT: How do you know?

FRANCESCA: Here it says, "Your wish has come true."

What to Look For (1) What follow-up procedures did the child use and need to reach comprehension? (2) To what extent is the child metacognitively aware? (3) Is the child able to give reasons to support her answers? (4) Is the child able to go back and find information when she realizes she lost some understanding or doesn't know? (5) What strategies does she use to regain her understanding?

Teacher's Notations: Francesca did a fairly good retelling of the story. When I asked her comprehension questions, she was able to answer them correctly. I believe that Francesca shows the development of some metacognitive awareness and has done very well for a first grader. Because of her age, she does get distracted at times; however, she was able to use the necessary strategies to gain comprehension of the overall story.

Among the strategies that Francesca used were referring back to the reading, giving a reason to support her answer, and searching the story and finding information when she lost her understanding or didn't know.

Special Necessary Materials An interesting story from your school's reading program ("Hippo Makes a Wish" by Mike Thaler from *Make a Wish* (1993), Needham, MA: Silver Burdett Ginn, pp. 136–146, was used in this particular assessment/instruction dialogue), and card or note paper for the teacher to record her findings and other notations based on the assessment dialogue.

Assessing Comprehending/Metacognitive Strategies of Sixth Graders Asked to Perceive Bias in Literature
By Ashley Pope, Marie Clark, Lorraine Thornton, and Anne McSweeney

Focus of Assessment   The focus of this assessment is to observe the comprehending and metacognitive strategies students use when asked to read a selection, and to see whether they can perceive the author's bias. The procedure involves first establishing the students' overall comprehension of the material, and then assessing the strategies used by the student to perceive and comprehend the author's bias.

This sample is part of a larger instructional unit for our sixth graders (most of them are ESL students, with Spanish as their first language) on the encounter between the Europeans and the indigenous peoples of the Americas. The unit includes study of the conditions and situation of the Spanish, as well as those of the indigenous of Latin America, and the impact of the encounter on each group. Before beginning the unit, we each assessed our students' schemata and interests related to these themes. Before this assessment was administered, students were introduced to the concept of bias as it relates to the study of historical events.

Directions for the Teacher   Ask the student to read the selection silently and indicate that, when she is finished reading, you will ask questions about what she has read and about the bias of the author. (For the purpose of assessing the student's perception of bias, do not divulge the source of the reading or the name of the author until you have completed the assessment.)

To check for overall comprehension ask, "What was this passage about?" or another leading question. If the student cannot answer, you may need to probe a little more to see whether she has comprehended the material. Keep notations on any questions you ask, indicating whether you think the student demonstrated overall comprehension, and other notes about the student's comprehension.

To check for detection of author bias, and the ability to support one's reasoning, ask, "What is the bias of this author?" Do this after the student has demonstrated overall comprehension of the passages. Additional questions or probes may be necessary for the student to fully answer the question. Make a note of these questions and probes. You are looking for the student's ability to recognize bias and support her own opinions from the reading, rather than on the opinion itself.

Next, to check for metacognitive awareness and strategies, ask, "Why do you think that?" The student may refer back to the reading to seek support for her answer. Additional metacognitive probes may be necessary to receive a full answer. For example: "What did you read that makes you answer that way?" "How did you come to that conclusion?" "What particular words or phrases make you think that was the author's bias?" Note any additional probes you use and your thoughts regarding the student's metacognition.

As the student answers each question, respond and clarify by modeling the answer back, asking other questions as necessary.

What to Look For   When assessing a student's comprehension, ability to perceive bias, and comprehending and metacognitive strategies, look for the following:

> To what extent does the student support her perspective using information from the passage?
>
> Does the student refer to general impressions gained from the text or does she refer to specific excerpts?
>
> Is the student attentive to the tone of the passage?
>
> Does the student refer to the connotations of particular words or terms?
>
> Does the student also use prior knowledge in support of her argument?
>
> Does the student relate the author's bias to the broader context of the unit?
>
> Does the student look at whether the author has substantiated his claims?
>
> To what extent are affective elements influencing the student's metacognitive awareness?

Ask the student to share her insights regarding her comprehension and comprehending strategies with you. Ask questions to stimulate this sharing: "Did you feel this was a difficult reading selection for you? Why?" "What did you do to try to understand it?" "What did you need to do in order to clarify your answers when I probed?" Make additional notations on the strategies the student shares. You also may wish to share your reflections with the student, affirming her strengths, and seeing whether she has any other strategy insights to share with you.

.See the sample dialogue between the teacher and one student, Rosa, who does comprehend the text but does not indicate strong metacognitive insights. Following this dialogue, see the teacher's notes regarding Rosa's strategies.

> TEACHER: What was this passage about?
>
> ROSA: The Spaniards and indigenous people fighting.
>
> TEACHER: Yes. They were fighting. Is that what they were doing at the beginning of the passage?
>
> ROSA (looking at reading): No, they were trading.
>
> TEACHER: That is right. What is the bias of this author?
>
> ROSA: The author likes the Spanish.
>
> TEACHER: Yes. Why do you think that?
>
> ROSA: He doesn't like the indigenous people, he likes the Spanish.

TEACHER: Yes, I agree. Can you tell me more about why the author likes the Spanish people and doesn't like the indigenous people?

ROSA: He says he doesn't like them.

TEACHER: Yes. The author does indicate that he doesn't like them. Can you show me where he says or shows he doesn't like them?

ROSA: He never comes out and says it. You just know.

TEACHER: Okay. Is there anything else in the reading that shows the author's bias?

ROSA: I don't think so.

Teacher's Notations: Rosa gave limited answers to comprehension questions. While I believe she generally understands the selection, she did not demonstrate strong use of metacognitive strategies. Her responses were based on impressions, and she was not able to substantiate these with quotations, specifics, or references from the text. Additionally, she showed lack of interest in the follow-up discussion regarding her strategy use. I wonder about her interest in this material and how much that has affected this assessment.

Next is a dialogue sample between the teacher and another sixth-grade student, Antonia. This dialogue, as well as the teacher's notations that follow, indicate Antonia's strong comprehension and metacognitive strategies.

TEACHER: What is this passage about?

ANTONIA: It is about the encounter of the Spanish and indigenous people on the Island of Española. They were involved in trade when the Spanish and the indigenous start fighting.

TEACHER: Yes. You understand the main ideas. Can you tell me what the bias of the author is?

ANTONIA: He believes Indians are warlike and aggressive.

TEACHER: Why do you think that?

ANTONIA: Because the author uses words like ferocious, daring, and courageous.

TEACHER: Yes. You are able to support your answer using the reading. Is there anything else?

ANTONIA: The story says the Indians went to get their weapons and tie up the Spanish.

TEACHER: Why does this show the author's bias?

ANTONIA: Well, because he is guessing that that is what they meant to do.

TEACHER: Where does the author say that?

ANTONIA: Right here where it says, "with the design of . . ."

TEACHER: Yes. You looked at whether the author substantiated claims. Can you show me another place where the author's bias comes through?

ANTONIA: He's on the side of the Spanish.

TEACHER: Why do you say that?

ANTONIA: Because of the words he uses to describe them.

TEACHER: What kinds of words?

ANTONIA: He refers to them as Christians, practicing restraint, and having spirit.

TEACHER: Yes. You used word connotations to perceive bias.

Teacher's Notations: Antonia showed excellent recall and comprehension. She used several metacognitive strategies to perceive bias. She is able to support her answers by using the text. Antonia noted whether the author substantiated his claims. She used the connotations of words in the text to support her responses. When we discussed her strategy use, she was very aware of her strategies and seemed to enjoy our discussion.

Special Necessary Materials   Note paper for the teacher's assessment notations; appropriate literature selections. (The reading used in this sample was from "How the First Skirmish Between the Indians and the Christians Took Place in Samaná Bay on the Island of Española" from Benjamin Keen, translator, *The Life of the Admiral Christopher Columbus by his Son Ferdinand* (Revised edition), New Brunswick, NJ: Rutgers University Press, 1992, pp. 88–90.)

Summary

This chapter has described informal assessment procedures, techniques, and ideas that can be implemented by the classroom teacher within the regular school day to sample, assess, and develop students' cognitive strategies. Use of these ideas should provide the classroom teacher with opportunities to observe students' comprehension, strategies for comprehending, schemata and other prior knowledge and experience, study skills and strategies as they apply to doing classroom assignments, and metacognitive strategy use. The focus has been on what readers do and what strategies they use to get meaning from text, rather than what they cannot do.

The emphasis of the descriptions and samples provided has been that classroom teachers are in the best position to devise their own assessment and instruction procedures for their own unique situations, students, and materials. However, samples have been provided so that teachers can use them to help conceptualize their own ideas or to provide an idea that can be adapted and modeled.

Questions for Reflection and Response

1. What are some of the differences between reading narrative and expository text? Why is it important for the classroom teacher to understand these differences?

2. What assessments of comprehension and comprehending strategies do you believe are most informative? Why? Try at least two or more of them with one or two students. Share, if possible, or describe your findings.

3. If you haven't already done so, try doing "a retelling" with the same students as in number two. Compare the information you glean from this with what you learned about the students' comprehension from the other assessments.

4. Why are prior knowledge and schemata so important to the reader? How can they be helpful to the classroom teacher? Try two or more of the assessments suggested in this chapter. Describe your results.

5. Why is assessment of students' study skills and strategies important to the classroom teacher? Which study skills and strategies are most important in your current classroom situation? Why? Try at least two of the assessment ideas suggested in this chapter and describe your results.

6. Why is assessment of students' metacognition so important? What does the teacher learn about the students' strategies from such assessment? Try two or more of the techniques suggested in this chapter with one or two students. What did you learn about their metacognition and the strategies they each use?

7. If you did not use the "Recipe for Metacognitive Assessments" in number six, try using it to design and develop your own "set up" for metacognitive probing. (Refer back to page 124 in this chapter for the "Recipe.")

8. How can the classroom teacher encourage comprehension and the students' use of many cognitive strategies in the classroom?

CHAPTER 5

ANALYZING INFORMATION QUALITATIVELY

Focus and Goals of the Chapter

- To demonstrate how to analyze and use gathered information qualitatively, pulling it all together for the classroom teacher
- To show how keeping a portfolio for each child helps to organize the available information
- To provide ideas of what to include in the portfolio and how rubrics can be developed and used to specify criteria and facilitate evaluation of performance
- To discuss the analysis and inclusion of both quantitative and qualitative data along with the development of an Analysis and Program of Instruction Report for situations where in-depth study seems prudent
- To provide an in-depth view of the Analysis and Program of Instruction Report for Emily, a second-grade student who shows weak linguistic strategies, a lack of fluency, very little comprehension of written text, and almost no concept of herself as a reader
- To provide an in-depth view of the Analysis and Program of Instruction Report for Freddy, a third-grade student who shows fairly strong linguistic strategies and a literal understanding of text, but who has difficulty with inferential un-derstandings, metacognition, and other higher-order comprehension strategies
- To provide information and questions that should help each classroom teacher develop his or her own instructional plans and monitor the progress of students.

Introduction

Once classroom teachers have observed children and their strategy use and have gathered other pertinent assessment information, they should be ready to organize and analyze this information in order to plan relevant instruction for their students. In this chapter, suggestions for organizing, analyzing, and using assessment information are made. Additionally, examples of in-depth assessment work-ups done on actual children are provided in order to illustrate how an analysis can be done. However, the examples in this chapter and elsewhere are not meant to provide you with exact guidelines or limit you to these examples; they are given only to illustrate a possible way to proceed. The best procedure will always be the one you devise to meet your preferences and your students' strengths and individual needs.

Organizing Available Data and Information

The first step to analyzing information qualitatively usually involves gathering and organizing assessment information for each child in your class. In this way, you will be putting "the pieces" together in order to gain a perspective on the whole child. Of course, in order for this to be meaningful, you would have assessed the child using appropriate and relevant assessment techniques during authentic reading and other literacy-related assignments and work. (Suggestions for these were discussed in Chapters 3 and 4.) When you believe you have observed the child enough to develop plans for his further instruction, as well as for his independent work, it is time to gather and organize your findings.

Keeping a Portfolio for Each Child

Some collection of each child's dated work and your dated assessment notes and samples should be kept in order to give you a perspective regarding the whole child and his or her development. Some teachers prefer keeping their own folder, checklist, samples, and notes on each child and have the child keep a separate portfolio with his own selected samples and reflections on his work. Other teachers keep one portfolio or folder on a child and share decisions with the child regarding its upkeep and what should be included in the portfolio and why. Still other teachers collaborate and share ideas with each child regarding the portfolio, but allow the child to really own, have the final say, and be responsible for his portfolio. The way you decide to manage portfolios will depend on your own philosophy, management style, and tolerance for a democratic environment.

If you keep the portfolio, you keep total control regarding what is to be included, noted, and saved. This also gives you optimum privacy regarding your notations and other assessment findings, although the child may not have as much opportunity to assess and self-reflect on his strategies and development. Even if the child keeps his own portfolio, and reflects on the work samples he has collected, he may not feel empowered if he believes that the separate folder you keep is somehow more important than his portfolio. Naturally, if the child jointly keeps the collection with you, you lose some control and privacy; however, you may instead gain many opportune conferencing and sharing meetings with the child. Additionally, portfolios provide an excellent venue for student engagement and motivation, allowing students to feel that they are are important members of a learning community (Clark, Chow-Hoy, Herter, & Moss, 2001).

Gahagan (1994) suggests the idea of three separate but related portfolios or collections. One could be the child's "working folder," where all his ongoing work is kept. One could be the teacher's collection of the child's assessment data and samples of the child's work selected by the teacher. One could be the student's "showcase portfolio," a collection of samples selected and showcased by the child. This showcase folder is completely selected and managed by the child. However you decide to do it, the key idea is that the child must believe that he has some degree of control, ownership, and decision-making opportunities regarding his portfolio or sampled work.

The more opportunities you give the child to own his work, be a part of the decision making, and be a real partner in the assessment of his work, the more you will foster the child's development as an independent, responsible, and reflective learner. Farr (1992) stresses that portfolios should belong to the student. The importance of this ownership is evident in all the literature regarding portfolio assessments.

Consider and React 5–1

What do you think? How much ownership should students have over their portfolios? Why?

Ideas Regarding What to Include in the Portfolio   Because decisions regarding what to include in a portfolio are personal, no data checklist can be provided. However, here are some possible items, samples, and data collections for consideration:

1. Dated samples of the child's original writing attempts, and any self-reflections the child wishes to include

2. Dated samples of the child's reading selections, and any self-reflections the child wishes to include

3. Dated samples of the child's oral readings with miscues, retellings, and metacognitive probing responses noted, and any comments, reflections, and evaluations that you or the child would like to make

4. Dated samples of the child's content reading, writing, and study assignment work, with relevant teacher and child notations, evaluations, or reflections

5. Dated self-reflections of the child's portfolio selections and content, and organization rationales

6. Dated self-reflections summarizing the portfolio samples, strengths, and ideas for changes

7. Dated peer reflections summarizing the portfolio samples, strengths, and ideas for changes

8. Dated notations or copies of any interest or attitudinal assessments or statements that you or the child think should be included

9. Dated notes from family, other relevant notations regarding the child's emergent literacy, or any sociocultural considerations you or the child think are important

10. Anything else you or the child consider significant to his or her literacy picture.

Glazer (1994) further suggests that the samples might include children's drawings, research projects, and other subject area work; recordings on tape (or on some other medium) of children's responses to reading and listening activities; and anecdotes describing children's interactions and activities in the classroom.

Valencia and Place (1994) suggest that teachers ask self-reflective questions as they review portfolios or the samples/collections of children's work:

1. What did I learn about this child?
2. What goals might be appropriate for this child?
3. What instructional strategies might be helpful in reaching these goals?
4. What other things would I like to see in this portfolio to help me better understand this child's literacy abilities?

Use of Rubrics and Anchor Papers Rubrics can be used effectively to help you set standards and establish the criteria for evaluation of each assignment or paper to be sampled or included in the students' portfolios. At first these rubrics are usually designed by the teacher, clearly specifying the criteria or evidence to substantiate a high, middle-of-the-road, and low evaluation for a particular piece of work. In this way, all of your students will know what is expected of them for a particular assignment and evaluation. Note that a teacher can divide the criterion designations into as many levels as she chooses; this can best be determined by the teacher according to the natural categories she conceives for the evaluation of a particular project or piece of work, or for a particular proficiency level.

Figure 5–1 is an example of a rubric that Mrs. Gonzalez developed to provide the criteria for how she will evaluate children's understanding of the fairy tale genre her class has been immersed in and studying, including the original fairy tales that they each draft. Note that Mrs. Gonzalez is very explicit as to the evidence she wants to see for each of the possible evaluations she envisions.

In order to illustrate for the children what papers or examples of work would look like for each of the scoring criteria, Mrs. Gonzalez also shares and displays **anchor papers,** or actual models or samples of student work to correspond to the scoring criteria for each performance level of the rubric. This makes clear to her third-grade students in advance how she will evaluate different levels of proficiency or performance. Mrs. Gonzalez carefully selects her models (anchors) from the work of her previous years' classes, and of course she will conceal actual students' names for purposes of anonymity.

Goal: The student will understand the fairy tale genre

Objectives/ Scoring Criteria	During a group or class discussion, the student will state, discuss and provide examples of the characteristics of fairy tales he/she has read during the fairy tale immersion period.	The student, verbally or in writing, will summarize the plot and events of specific fairy tales he/she has read.	The student will write a draft of an "original" fairy tale*—including some of the characteristics of fairy tales discussed in class. These have been listed by the teacher and displayed in the classroom for students' reference.
3	The student stated and discussed three or more characteristics of fairy tales, indicating examples for each from fairy tales he/she had read.	The student summarized the plot and events of three or more fairy tales (verbally or in writing).	The student wrote an "original" fairy tale* using at least three of the characteristics of fairy tales that were discussed in class and listed on chart paper by the teacher.
2	The student stated and/or discussed two characteristics of fairy tales, indicating examples for at least one of them; or the student stated and/or discussed one characteristic of fairy tales and cited examples for at least two of the characteristics stated by himself or by other students.	The student summarized the plot and events of two fairy tales (verbally or in writing).	The student wrote an "original" fairy tale* using two of the characteristics of fairy tales that were discussed in class and listed on chart paper by the teacher.

Figure 5–1 Fairy Tale Rubric

	The student stated and/or discussed one characteristic of fairy tales but did not indicate a name of a fairy tale containing the example; or student didn't state or discuss any characteristics but did support at least some of the characteristics someone else had stated by providing an example from a fairy tale he/she had read.	The student summarized the plot and events of one fairy tale (verbally or in writing).	The student wrote an "original" fairy tale* using one of the characteristics of fairy tales that were discussed in class and listed on chart paper by the teacher.
1			

Figure 5–1 (*Continued*)

*The original fairy tale may be very similar to the published ones, since the latter may be used as models.

Steps for Developing a Rubric

1. Carefully plan for your assignment and the skills, strategies, or understandings you want to assess.
2. Review and specify your overall goal and each of your objectives for the particular work or area of study.
3. Decide the number of performance or proficiency levels into which your objectives could naturally be grouped.
4. Describe the scoring criteria you will use for each of these levels, assigning a number to each (e.g., 3 for "best work," 2 for "satisfactory work," and 1 for "work that shows some knowledge" or "needs improvement").
5. Select or develop anchor papers and models that correspond to each of your scoring criteria.
6. Share and discuss the rubric and anchor examples with your students.

Once students understand how rubrics are used to evaluate specific or selected work, they can gradually take a more active part in the evaluation process. Skillings and Ferrell (2000) describe a classroom where students generate their own rubrics. In this way the students assume more control for developing the criteria for their performance on a variety of reading and writing tasks. Additionally, the actual development of rubrics enhances students' understanding of the concepts and skills that will be evaluated. As students become partners in the establishment of criteria and the evaluation of their own accomplishments, they can often verbalize what they would need to do or need to demonstrate in order to get higher performance evaluations.

In the appendix, many sample forms have been included to illustrate some of the ideas suggested in this chapter and elsewhere to facilitate using and organizing portfolios and rubrics as part of your ongoing assessment and planning with students. Teachers interested in more in-depth information and more samples on how to organize and manage portfolios and use them to inform instruction are referred to books by Farr and Tone (1998) and Tierney, Carter, and Desai (1991). Kuhs, Johnson, Agruso, and Monrad (2001) is suggested, as well as the sources indicated in Chapter 3, for more details about constructing rubrics. Those interested in learning about various schoolwide and larger-scale portfolio assessment projects would find the Murphy and Underwood (2000), and the Valencia, Hiebert, and Afflerbach (1994) books informative; those interested in reading scenarios by teachers of various age groups (elementary through college) describing their use of portfolios should see Graves and Sunstein (1992), and Sunstein and Lovell (2000); and, finally, those interested in using portfolios to collect and sample students' writing are referred to Jenkins (1996) and to Koch and Schwartz-Petterson (2000).

Developing an Analysis and Program of Instruction Report

Sometimes there is a need for an in-depth report analyzing a child's reading and reading-related strategies. Certainly, this will not be the case for every child in your classroom if you are a regular classroom teacher. But if you are teaching in a special program, if you want to refer a child to a special program, or if you perceive a special situation, it is possible that you might feel a need to develop an in-depth report on a child. Here, then, is an outline of some areas you might want to consider in such a report; as with other suggestions in this book, it is only one possibility, and you may change it in any way that better meets your purposes or the child's needs.

Analysis and Program of Instruction Report

I.   Personal information about a child, child's background, and family/sociocultural situation (as pertinent and available)

II. Summary of past evaluations and reported results (as reported by parents, the child, and past teacher(s); report cards and/or cumulative records)

III. Summary of current assessments and notes (discussion and examples, as pertinent), regarding

    A.   Child's interests/attitudes/motivations/feelings

    B.   Child's use of content reading and study strategies (in materials necessary for child's success in school)

    C.   Child's use of cue systems (syntax, semantic, and phoneme-grapheme) and notations concerning fluency

    D. Child's comprehension of narrative and expository materials

    E. Child's metacognitive awareness/strategies using narrative and expository materials

(Attach all marked pages, sheets, and excerpts, and copies of any writing and portfolio samples used for the above assessments, to this report.)

  IV. Recommended instructional plan

   V. Summary of and justification for recommended instructional emphases (overview and rationale)

Follow-up (if you provided direct instruction as per recommendations in part IV):

  VI. Summary notes and discussion regarding your observations and child's progress as a result of the recommended instructional plan

(Include any additional recommendations you might make at this time.)

Consider and React 5–2

Is there any other information or data that you would include to customize an in-depth report for your students?

Analyzing Available Information

It is recommended that classroom teachers **qualitatively analyze** all pertinent assessment data they collect. Sometimes the data is already based on qualitative assessment (assessment that focuses on the quality of the child's responses, strategies, or work). However, sometimes the data to be analyzed is based on a quantitative-type of assessment (an assessment that focuses on the number correct or the number incorrect, or on assessment instruments that report a score of some kind). In this case, the classroom teacher can still qualitatively analyze the data by looking for more information beyond the score, grade, or number correct. In the sections that follow, ways of analyzing both types of data will be illustrated and discussed.

Teacher-Developed Reports with Discussion

Chapter 1 describes quantitative data and differentiates it from qualitative data. Chapter 2 discusses standardized tests and other quantitative data, while Chapters 3 and 4 describe and discuss various qualitative assessments and data. That information will not be repeated here. In this section, the focus is on the application of previously discussed information. In order to illustrate how a teacher might analyze and use the available information in a qualitative way, rather than just accepting or rejecting the quantitative data and thereby possibly losing some relevant information, two sample in-depth analyses and program of instruction reports done by classroom teachers are provided. After you read the information, review the teachers' discussions of the findings and progress in the sections that follow.

Wish our paper did this.

Analysis and Program of Instruction Report: Emily
Developed by Nancy Gregg

I. Personal Information

Emily is a second grader. She is seven years old and appears to be a healthy child. She comes from a lower-middle-income family of European American ethnicity. Her father was formerly employed as a shipyard worker, but now he is on disability. Her mother has worked in a local factory. She is in the process of opening her own small store. Both parents have completed high school. Emily lives with her parents and two older brothers (ages sixteen and fourteen) in a semi-rural area. The children have all been raised here. Not much reading by the parents or brothers seems to occur in the home. Much of the family's leisure time is spent watching videos or playing computer games. However, Emily's family environment appears to be both stable and nurturing. Emily belongs to Campfire Girls and attends Sunday school at the family church.

II. Summary of Past Evaluations and Reported Results

Emily's mother related that the school had recommended that Emily spend a year in a transition class between kindergarten and first grade. Likewise, the school recommended that she repeat first grade. Her father was opposed to the idea each time. The mother is concerned and would like to do "the right thing" for Emily; however, she has been put in the middle, between her husband and the school, and really isn't sure what "the right thing" is. Emily was promoted to second grade. School records, report cards, and past teacher information indicate that Emily is a very poor reader and lacks fluency. Her first-grade teacher taught reading by using phonics worksheets and flashcards for sight words. No books seemed to have been used in the classroom, and opportunities for writing were limited to copying off the chalkboard. Emily's mother is well aware that Emily is having difficulty with reading.

III. Summary of Current Assessments and Notes

A. *Interests/attitudes/motivations/feelings* Emily is an alert, happy, and cooperative child. She was quick to answer all my questions about free time, friends, and activities. She likes playing outside, playing with Barbie dolls, and playing games with her family and friends. However, when it came to her feelings about school or reading, she had no ready responses. She was indifferent about school. Questions about her favorite book, choices of material, and ideas drew a blank. She had almost no concept of herself as a reader. My analysis is that Emily has not been exposed to a great deal of literature, or opportunities to read, and therefore does not have a well-developed schema about reading. She does, however, seem motivated by my interest in her, and by the one-on-one time I'm taking with her. She is outgoing and eager to please.

B. *Use of content reading and study strategies* I explained to Emily that we had some brand new books this school year. She and I looked over the new science book to get familiar with it. I read her the beginning part of one of the first chapters, about plants, to get her interested in the book. Then I explained that I wanted her to read the next section about plants to try it out and see how she liked the science book. Emily seemed willing to try, but she omitted many words without making any effort to "guess" any of them. She read word by word, without expression and without looking for meaning. Next, I repeated my explanation and this activity with the new second-grade social studies book. Once again, Emily was willing to try the book out for me. This time I asked her to guess when she came to an unknown word. She made several attempts to guess unknown words using her phoneme-grapheme cue system, primarily using phonics. However, she almost never tried to verify her guesses with semantic or syntactic strategies and became frustrated by her very unsuccessful solo phoneme-grapheme attempts. (These were all signs that she clearly does lack fluency.)

I plan that my students will be doing some independent work this year, and I think that some use of dictionaries and various books and textbooks will be involved. I decided to assess Emily's sense of alphabetical order, as well as use of a table of contents. First, I made a folder of "animal" pictures with the names clearly pasted on them. Each letter of the alphabet was represented only once. For example, there was a labeled picture of an anteater, a butterfly, and so on. I mixed them up and asked her to put them in alphabetical order, which she did.

She then looked up several of these "animals" in a children's dictionary. She was adept at finding the appropriate letter and then looking for a picture of the same animal. Later, when I thought she had the idea, I gave her some words without pictures to find. She was unable to locate words such as "sad," "bag," and "jump" that did not have corresponding pictures in the dictionary.

Emily did not know what a table of contents was or how to find a story or chapter using one in various children's books. However, once the term *table of contents* was explained, Emily was clearly able to use a simple one.

C. *Use of cue systems* The qualitative results from the sampled materials (several stories and other narrative materials, and two expository sections) strongly indicate that Emily does not often use her semantic and syntactic cue systems. Additionally, Emily's phoneme-grapheme cue system, which she totally relies on, is not very strong or reliable. For example, when I asked her to try to make a good guess at unknown words, she sounded out the following sounds for the words in parentheses: stri (special), stray (states), stray (stand), and feist (first). It should be noted that she always guesses or uses the correct beginning consonant sound or letter, but falters with most **blends** (combinations of letters that blend to make one sound, with minimal change to the sounds of the individual letters) and doesn't know or attempt **medial sounds** (sounds in the middle position of a word) or most ending sounds. However, it is clear that Emily does *attempt* to use phonics and is at least partially accurate with its use. Her writing samples also show that she is using logical phonetic approximations in her invented spellings. I believe that if Emily were encouraged and shown how to try to verify or guess using her other cue systems, she'd be more successful with her overall word recognition, including her phoneme-grapheme attempts, and could eventually, in time, achieve some fluency in her reading.

About one-third of Emily's miscues were **omissions,** instances where Emily would not attempt to guess and instead omitted the words.

D.   *Comprehension*   Emily had repeated difficulty with certain recurring words in both content readings. Emily repeatedly could not read the words "stand" and "states" in the social studies material or "stem" and "hold" in the science book. Because these words were important to the meaning of the passages and were repeated often, and Emily had no semantic strategies for guessing their meaning, she was without comprehension on most of the content reading selections.

A review of samples taken from her new science log and her portfolio yielded the same conclusions: Emily's writing, to date, does not indicate that she has comprehended the material that she was to read silently. Additionally, she could tell me very little pertinent information from the collage she was asked to make to report and accompany our current science unit readings. In both her writing and portfolio samples, she did not seem to be able to make any connections to the readings, and I realize now that she hasn't "gotten the idea" that she should be reading for meaning.

On the narrative materials, Emily could sometimes answer one or two comprehension questions about the stories when only factual answers were called for. However, she usually did not comprehend most of what she read. Certainly, she could not do a retelling or answer questions that involved inferences, drawing conclusions, or other higher-level questions.

On the other hand, when I gave her picture books to read, she was able to answer many comprehension and metacognitive questions with precision. I believe she was successful with picture books because she approached these books with a purpose and with confidence since she herself was verbalizing the stories. Emily showed ownership of these stories and was able to relate them to her own experiences by virtue of what she drew out of them. I think these things (reading with a purpose, ownership, and relating material and ideas to her cognitive experience) will be vital in structuring her instructional plan.

Emily has not really been exposed to literature in her home life or in her first-grade experiences and therefore is not yet comfortable with books or their purposes. It is difficult for a child to understand that she should read for meaning when she has not had any real practice with this idea.

Finally, I tried checking her comprehension again by reading familiar stories aloud. For example, when I read her *The Three Bears* (as retold by Paul Galdone, 1972), she enjoyed the story, almost bubbling with anticipation, obviously predicting in her mind the next page. She followed the story and was able to discuss it and answer numerous questions about it. Once again, I felt that Emily's comprehension has been limited by her past opportunities to read and share literature in her home and school.

E.   *Metacognitive awareness*   I tried metacognitively probing Emily about the content of everything I had her try to read. But even when she comprehended something, and knew an answer, she was not aware of how she knew it. For instance, Emily knew that a neighbor might be afraid of a mouse, but she had no idea how she knew that. Therefore, I decided to try to assess her metacognitive awareness with *The Surprise Picnic* (1977), a picture book by John Goodall. Perhaps if no "real" reading was involved, she could focus more on comprehending. Emily was able to give me a story line. Before she turned a page, I would ask her to predict what would happen. Emily made excellent guesses. I then would ask her, "How do you know that?" She was able to point out picture clues, such as facial expressions, clouds in the sky that looked like rain, and so on. She also responded well to such questions as "What is happening to the boat?" (It's floating away.) "How come?" (It's not tied up.)

IV. Recommended Instructional Plan
     Based on the information, assessments, samples, and observations discussed here, I recommend the following instructional plan for Emily:

1.   Develop instruction that includes many language-experience activities. Building upon Emily's interests, I believe we can incorporate many opportunities to discover and practice word recognition strategies for reading.

2. Include lessons to provide specific instruction and opportunities to practice using the three cueing systems to help make a "good guess."

3. Read to Emily as often as possible. She enjoys being read to and I hope that frequent story times, as well as reading expository material that she has a real interest in, will help her develop a love for literature and reading, and more of an interest and purpose in seeking meaning from what is read.

4. Gradually build Emily's sight vocabulary by working with her to develop a word bank of recognized words.

5. Use opportunities for repeated readings of stories that Emily already knows, giving her practice with successful oral reading, her known sight words, and reading with some intonation and expression. These repeated readings should help her learn what fluent reading "feels" like.

6. Help Emily develop more regard for herself as someone who can read and is in fact "a reader."

7. Develop instruction to help Emily understand basic vocabulary in specialized areas, such as science, social studies, and math, and to use necessary books, textbooks, and other learning tools, such as dictionaries. I hope we can begin to work in some of these areas.

8. Develop strategies for using context to infer the meaning of unknown "key" vocabulary words that are important to understanding content reading materials in our classroom.

V. Summary and Justification

It appears that Emily has a limited literature and experiential background. She is unaware of how she can help herself with attempts to figure out what she is reading. Both of these factors hinder Emily's progress in reading development. When taught how and then given the opportunity to demonstrate her understanding of how to put things in alphabetical order and how to use a table of contents, Emily succeeds admirably. It is clear that she is bright enough and can learn. Her phoneme-grapheme strategies are all that she relies on, but without use of the other two cue systems she's unsuccessful and has not achieved any semblance of fluency. She needs instruction and practice in using the other strategy systems. She needs frequent opportunities for repeated readings of stories she is successful with. Additionally, Emily should be given materials she is interested in and which she can relate to her present schema.

In conclusion, Emily is still at the beginning stages of learning to read. Taking all the assessment and other data into consideration, I believe that Emily should always understand the purpose of her reading; she should be given a variety of material to read that always takes into account her given schema of the subject; and she should be given many opportunities with language experience, personal word banks, writing, and the like in order to give her a feeling of success and ownership of her reading.

VI.   Summary Notes and Discussion Regarding Progress

It was readily apparent from Emily's assessment results that her reading attempts were usually limited to trying to decode individual words using limited phoneme-grapheme strategies, particularly phonics. Emily had not displayed an awareness that understanding what she read was important. For that reason, my primary goals during instructional sessions with her were that she realize she should be reading to get meaning and to gradually improve her image of herself as a reader.

I used several methods to help her develop this awareness. Because she was exerting so much time and energy unsuccessfully decoding words phonetically, I used a language experience technique with picture books in our first sessions. Emily would "read" a picture book and then retell the story in her own words. As she dictated, I wrote the story for her. Because the story was primarily made up of words familiar to her, Emily was able to read most of the story comfortably. The remaining words that she did not remember gave us the opportunity to discuss semantic clues that would help her make good guesses for words she did not know. Throughout all her instructional sessions I emphasized that it was important that she be aware of how she knew what she knew. In these language experience stories I specifically would ask her to tell me what clues in the sentence or story helped her guess an unfamiliar word.

Another method I used to help Emily get meaning from her reading was to activate any prior knowledge or schema she had for a topic or idea she was about to read. Early on we would always discuss any picture clues on the cover of the book or at the beginning of a selection that she could relate to previous experiences or knowledge. Later Emily could discuss what she knew about a topic merely from a title or table of contents.

The biggest emphasis of our instructional sessions was to make Emily aware of how semantic and syntactic cues could help her figure out words. (I decided against any additional phoneme-grapheme instruction because Emily had received that, to the exclusion of everything else, in first grade, and I believed that although her phoneme-grapheme cue system wasn't terribly strong, at least she knew how to use phonics. I wanted her to learn to use the other two cue systems along with it.) I began by using a slightly sticky tape to "blank" out words at random. Because Emily could not read the simplest of stories fluently, I would read a story and stop at the blanked-out word and have her make what we called a "good guess." We defined a good guess as any word that made sense in the sentence. The good guess did not have to be the same word the author wrote, merely an appropriate word in that particular sentence. Later in the instructional sessions, I required that the guess be almost an exact synonym for the missing word and that it make sense in the surrounding text as well. Of course, this technique of blanking out words required that we discuss specific ways of looking for syntactic and semantic clues. Very often I would have her pinpoint what clues "told her" how to make a good guess.

This method of blanking out words and having Emily make good guesses also enabled me to track particular words and types of words that caused her problems. Several follow-up lessons provided Emily the opportunity for repeated readings of these stories to practice reading these words in context and experience more fluent reading.

Incidental to what was just discussed, we had several opportunities to work in various children's dictionaries. Children's dictionaries often use a word in various sentences to show meaning, rather than defining it as in adult dictionaries. This gave Emily an opportunity to read, in context, words that had previously troubled her. Emily developed the strategy of inserting "blank" for the words she did not know and then moving forward in the text, looking for semantic clues. At times she would repeat "blank" several times and go forward in the text looking for clues. Now Emily also uses this strategy when she reads alone. She knows that doing this can keep her from "getting stuck" (trying to phonetically sound out a word she doesn't know).

We have been using a variety of materials for Emily's reading instruction. Aside from the dictionaries, she has read out of many picture books, easy story books, and several fiction and nonfiction books with few picture clues, and also a children's magazine that she selected. We have also done a lot of repeated readings of books she's been especially successful with, and of her language experience stories.

Progress Notations

11/1—Emily is showing strong use of her syntax cueing system with this story. She is also using the strategy of repeating a phrase or sentence to clarify syntactic and semantic clues. Note that several times she repeats, "A friend (blank)(SC) gave me his prize (best) rabbit." She repeats the sentence three times before self-correcting "friend" and choosing "best" as an appropriate substitution for "prize." Emily is not becoming frustrated and is showing patience with this method.

Emily continues to reverse words such as "saw" and "was."

Her retelling is incomplete. Again, she cannot retell or answer questions concerning the section she struggled with about the blackbird. Still, she basically understands the passage.

11/9—Again, Emily uses syntax clues well. I've noted that even when she miscues, the miscues are usually syntactically correct. Later she comes back and self-corrects using semantic and sometimes phoneme-grapheme (usually phonics) cues.

Repetitions are still serving Emily well. Many times they lead her to make appropriate guesses. Several of her miscues are appropriate syntactically and semantically ("you're getting" for "you'll get," "puppy" for "pup," "laying" for "lying"). In general, however, her syntax cueing system is stronger than her semantic cueing system. For the most part, she only partially uses phoneme-grapheme strategies.

Emily worked hard to get meaning from this passage. Despite many deviations from the text, she has a good sense of what this passage is about. Her incorrect answers to some of my comprehension questions are understandable. Emily said the child felt sad when she first saw the hurt pet. Emily had substituted "sad" for "scared" in the passage. The semantic clues that Emily could have picked up from the text were very subtle, if there at all. "Sad" was in fact a very appropriate guess within the context of this passage.

"Fight" was a word Emily could not decode by the use of phonics. Again, she tried to use her strategy of saying "blank" and repeating the sentence to search for syntax and semantic clues. However, "fight back the tears" is probably an expression she has not heard before.

11/15—Science textbook notes: Emily depended on the phonics and some grapheme cues to make better guesses in this content material ("listen" for "learn," "scent" for "salt," and "world" for "would"). She also continued to use her syntax and developing semantic strategies, at least partially ("listen" for "learn," "scent" for "salt," and "ocean" for "sea").

Emily answered some of the comprehension questions I posed fairly well. However, she could not summarize what the section was about, although her answers did show that she was aware of her previous knowledge about the senses.

11/20—Metacognitive awareness notes: During this session, she read *Little Bear's Friend* (1960), by Else Homelund Minarik. I used this opportunity to ask Emily some comprehension questions about the story. In turn, I asked her what made her answer a question in a certain way. For example, Emily knew by inference that Mother Bear was teasing Little Bear. I asked Emily how she knew that, and she was able to pinpoint the sections of the text that gave her clues. As her awareness of semantic clues has improved, Emily's metacognitive awareness in relation to her reading has improved.

12/2—My current qualitative analysis of Emily's reading is very different from my earlier analysis of her reading strategies. The most obvious difference is that she does not omit words and is willing to make "good guesses." We have not worked much on phoneme-grapheme strategies except as a way to verify some of her "good guesses."

Her inclination for reversing words—such as "was" for "saw"—is troublesome. I'm hoping, however, that as time goes on she will learn to recognize these words on sight and use **context clues** (syntax and semantic clues in the text) to verify. Emily's use of the syntax and semantic cueing systems is definitely improving. Perhaps this example will illustrate the improvement: Emily repeated a sentence three times before reading "A friend gave me his best (prize) rabbit." Emily substituted the word "blank" for both "friend" and "prize." She was able to find the syntax and semantic clues that enabled her to get the correct meaning from this sentence. When she substituted the word "best" for "prize" she showed enormous progress from when she read "Pat is be the tree" for "Pat sat by the tree" in one of her earlier oral readings.

My current qualitative analysis shows that Emily is willing to search the text at the sentence level and sometimes beyond in order to find semantic clues that will help her "get meaning" from text. Most often, syntax clues serve her best; very often, her first substitution will show use of syntax and at least partial semantic strategy use. Her self-corrections involve repeating the text and finding clues that she originally missed.

12/18—Notations and suggestions for continued instruction: In the relatively short time we have worked together, Emily has improved dramatically in her use of the syntax and semantic cueing systems. This instruction needs to be continued so that Emily will grow stronger in these cue systems and begin to see how the phoneme-grapheme system (particularly her use of phonics) can help her verify her "good guesses."

Emily understands how to look up a word in the dictionary using alphabetical order and can use this strategy for looking up unfamiliar words. This is a strategy that future instruction could expand upon.

It has been extremely helpful for Emily to realize that she already has a schema for many of the stories and the reading material she is exposed to. I know that as she continues to read, her experiential background will continue to broaden. Any future program for Emily should continue to build relationships between her schemata and her reading.

Emily is just beginning to think of herself as a reader. "Getting the meaning" from the text is positive feedback that Emily thrives on. If Emily continues to read a wide variety of material, it will open many doors for her as well as give her opportunities to strengthen her linguistic and cognitive strategies, and to continue to develop some fluency with reading.

Additionally, as we continue to work together, I plan to give Emily more and more opportunities to write her own text and respond to the materials we read together. Based on my experience as I used dictation with her, I believe that more emphasis on using writing to respond to the reading materials that she has comprehended will also help strengthen the reading strategies Emily is developing.

Consider and React 5–3

What do you think? What continued instruction would you suggest for Emily? Why?

Analysis and Program of Instruction Report: Freddy
Developed by John Trainor

I. Personal Information

Freddy is nine years old and in the third grade. He is of average size and weight for his age. Freddy occasionally suffers from mild asthma, but this has not interfered with his school performance. He had a slight lisp that he worked on with a specialist for about two years, ending after his first year in the first grade. There is no longer any noticeable speech problem, and Freddy does not consider himself to be speech-impaired.

Freddy is of bicultural parentage. His mother is third-generation Italian American, and his father is Puerto Rican. His father left when Freddy was one year old and now lives in another city and region. No contact is maintained. The family lives in subsidized housing and is completely dependent on social and economic resources provided by the state. Freddy has two siblings: A sister, age twelve, is in the sixth grade and is average academically, and a brother, age seven, in the first grade (for the second time), who has performed poorly in school but has shown recent improvement. His brother was diagnosed with Attention Deficit Hyperactive Disorder (ADHD), but has recently been taken off medication and is showing improvement.

Freddy's mother recently took the General Educational Development (GED) exam and earned her high school diploma. His father did not graduate from high school.

In spite of the less-than-ideal home and family situation, Freddy does have the benefit of a mother who appears to make every effort to provide a secure, safe environment. The mother says she keeps careful watch on her children and appears to be very protective. While this may keep the children from falling in with the "wrong crowd," it has limited Freddy's experiences. He indicates that he spends most of his time in the house watching television and videos. He often is not allowed outside to play.

The family is very close. There is no father in the home. Each of the three children was fathered by a different man and consequently has a different last name. At this time there does not seem to be any stigma indicated by Freddy regarding his social, economic, or family status. He is generally happy and well behaved.

Freddy is enrolled in a Big Brothers program. He has a Big Brother he sees once a week. His relationship with him seems to be successful.

There is little literature or writing exposure in Freddy's home. The only printed material I learned of is the *TV Guide* and whatever books and materials are provided from school. His mother indicated that she doesn't have time for personal reading or letter writing, and she does not have time to read to Freddy.

II. Summary of Past Evaluations and Reported Results

Freddy was retained once in the first grade. His mother said it was a result of his poor performance with reading. She also thought his speech impediment, now overcome, had an effect on his school work during kindergarten and the first year he was in first grade.

His previous teacher indicated that Freddy was an average student and reader. His difficulties in school stemmed mostly from behavior problems. He had some good days and some really bad days. She didn't have any specific ideas about what caused his mood swings, but judging from his background there are many possibilities. Like many kids in his situation, she said, he resolved many of his problems with classmates through fighting.

The extent of the mother's involvement with school work and reading has been limited to seeing that Freddy does his homework. She is pleased with his last year's report cards and is satisfied with that teacher's comments that Freddy was doing fine. No reports of standardized tests or other assessments are entered in his cumulative file.

III. Summary of Current Assessments and Results

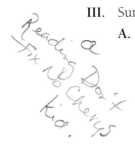

A. *Interests/attitudes/motivations/feelings* Freddy's interests are similar to those of other boys his age: sports, fishing, camping, airplanes, travel, and mountain climbing. He wants to be a pilot and a professional baseball player when he grows up. His favorite solitary activity at home is building with Legos. The theme that most often turns up in his favorite stories and videos is that of good conquering evil. This is evidenced by his interest in folk tales and the videos, TV shows, and cartoons he most enjoys. His explanation for why these were his favorites always included the good guys defeating the bad guys and justice being rendered in the end. In school, his favorite subject is science. When asked to design his own schedule in school, he chose to have science twice a day. He enjoys reading at school, particularly during the sustained silent reading times, but says that he does not enjoy reading at home. He enjoys writing when given the opportunity to write about things that interest him.

Freddy's attitude toward reading is relatively good but appears to be entirely based on in-school activities. He enjoyed reading in school last year, but would have liked to have more time to read silently each day. He was comfortable reading silently with his reading group but was uncomfortable reading aloud. He did not like answering questions at the end of a story, but enjoyed preparing "book selling" reports after reading a story or book. He found the books and stories the teacher assigned to be easy. He seldom reads at home because there is limited material. He has lost his library withdrawal privileges at school because he lost books. He has mixed feelings about libraries, partly because of behavioral problems that cause him to get into trouble in the library, and partly because he can't take any books home. He considers himself to be an "okay" reader; generally, he feels good about his reading ability, but he realizes that many of his classmates are better readers and that he has difficulty with some reading material.

B. *Use of content reading and study strategies*   Freddy did fairly well in his independent reading of a selection from his social studies textbook that I sampled. With the exception of two questions, he was able to answer the comprehension questions adequately. One of the questions that gave him some difficulty asked what a ghost town was. He replied that "all the people die, they are laying around, and the spirits come." He was obviously incorporating aspects of his existing schema for ghosts into this explanation. It should also be noted that ghost towns were mentioned early in the reading as more of an aside to the focus of the rest of the selection, which dealt with Arapaho Indians. Freddy also had some difficulty answering the question, "Who were the first people to live in the area where Denver is now?" He was unable to answer that question until Arapaho Indians were mentioned in another question. He had some difficulty with the word "Arapaho" when he was reading and had asked me to tell him what it was. Apparently, he just wasn't familiar with the names of the various Native American tribes, at least not "Arapaho Indians." I made similar observations as Freddy read a selection from our science textbook and later from a story about environmental issues in a children's magazine.

After talking with Freddy's past teacher, it was apparent that she placed limited emphasis on content materials, study strategies, and content reading skills. She considered basal reader stories and workbooks, and practice with more basic reading skills, like phonics and other word recognition skills, to be a greater priority with readers like Freddy. Textbooks were used as a reference source, but only for the best readers in the class. Dictionaries and other reference materials were not used. Maps were rarely used. The school library was used as a resource for classroom projects, but the librarian selected the books that the children would use and laid them out on a table. Knowing this previous background, I also decided to evaluate some of Freddy's study strategies and skills, since I'd like Freddy and other students to do more independent work this school year.

In terms of textbook usage, Freddy seems to be familiar with only the table of contents. He was unable to suggest the use of the index as a way to locate more information on Plains Indians—again, he had never heard of them. He also seemed unaware that his textbooks had a glossary in the back. He was able to find words in the dictionary and when I asked, he was able to differentiate between multiple meanings of several words. His library skills are generally good for a third grader with limited library experience. He basically understands how to use a library catalogue system and can use the title, author, or subject to locate materials (though he mistakenly assumed that he could find a book written by Jack London under "J" for "Jack"), and he understands the difference between fiction and nonfiction.

C. *Use of cue systems*   Freddy does show fairly strong usage of semantic and syntax strategies, as evidenced by the large number of self-corrections that he made. He demonstrated his syntactic strength two ways. First, when he read silently, he would often read softly aloud to himself. On several occasions, he would stop and self-correct because to him, "it didn't sound right." He wasn't referring to pronunciation, or even to meaning in most cases, but to grammatical structure and flow. This is further evidenced by many self-corrected miscues he made. For example, in the sentence, "It was wide and deep, so they would have to swim across," Freddy substituted the word "it" for the word "so." The resulting sentence makes semantic sense: "It was wide and deep, it they would have to swim across." (To Freddy, the substituted "it" referred to the creek mentioned earlier.) However, the use of "it" in this case was grammatically awkward, and on that basis, Freddy went back and quickly self-corrected. He seems naturally aware of the grammatical flow and structure of what he reads.

Freddy's strength with his semantic cueing system is evidenced by the large number of self-corrections made where he had used his phoneme-grapheme cueing system but had lost meaning as a result of stopping to sound out a word, and then went back to self-correct. There are many examples of this sort of reading behavior. This sentence contains two such examples: "From the creek (wreck), she received a 9-inch gas (gash) on her head." Both of these miscues were self-corrected. Both show strong use of phoneme-grapheme cues and syntax. However, they made no sense at even the sentence level (she could have received a gash from a creek, but not gas) and were self-corrected by Freddy when he came to the end of the sentence because he knew they didn't make sense semantically.

Freddy's use of his cueing systems is generally good. It appears that as long as he is reading within his existing conceptual and cognitive network, all three of his cueing systems contribute to his fluency, and he is definitely reading for meaning. The phoneme-grapheme system appears to be what he uses first, but if meaning is lost he is quite capable of self-correcting, using his fairly strong semantic and syntactic cueing systems.

When I observe his writing, Freddy's invented spellings also show some indication of this. I believe his phonetic awareness is very obvious in his writing and editing attempts. He tries to spell words phonetically, and most of his attempts resemble the length of the words and logical visual patterns for words he is trying to spell. His writings also show attempts to tell stories that make sense and convey his message.

D. *Comprehension*   Freddy seems to be capable of comprehending and answering main idea, factual, and terminology questions. His retellings usually contain the basic idea and flow of a story or selection, but are often a little short on detail. Additionally, Freddy often has difficulty answering questions that relate to cause and effect, inference, and drawing conclusions. In general, while he does seem to get the more text-explicit (literal) information out of his readings, text-implicit (inferential) and higher-order comprehension are not easy for him. His writing and portfolio samples basically confirm the same findings.

E. *Metacognitive awareness*   Freddy is generally unaware of how he knows what he knows or is unable to verbalize it. This was evident in all of his readings. Typically, when asked how he knew a particular answer was a good one, he replied, "Well . . . because." If probed deeper, he often would begin to reread the story or selection aloud. Even after being directed to look back in the material for supporting evidence, he would not do so unless reminded. When he did refer to the selection he usually just reread it, typically from the beginning. However, after continuous probing from me, he was often successful in locating the appropriate passage from the story or selection. Furthermore, with the exception of a story about a baseball player, he did not make any effort to use his background experience to justify his answers.

Frankly, I believe he is just not accustomed to being asked to explain his answers, make inferences, draw conclusions, or discuss his rationales. This inexperience with discussing, hypothesizing, and going beyond what is explicitly stated in a text or story is also evidenced, as previously indicated, in his general comprehension of reading materials. Freddy is currently a literal reader, but I believe that with teacher-modeling and probing, more exposure to concepts and things "new to him," and individual attention, he will develop his higher-order comprehension abilities and awareness.

IV.   Recommended Instructional Plan

1. *Comprehension*   Freddy would benefit from instruction designed to improve his reading comprehension. For the most part, he seems to have little

problem with the more literal, text-explicit type of questions: main idea, recalling facts, and explicit terminology with contextual definitions. However, Freddy seems to have some difficulty with higher-order, inferential, text-implicit comprehension and questions, such as determining cause and effect, making inferences, and drawing conclusions. He may benefit from an instructional plan that seeks to address this area, especially cause and effect and reading for more **implicit detail** (from information implied, but not explicitly stated, in the text), along with an emphasis on developing his metacognitive awareness.

2. *Metacognitive awareness*   Freddy should benefit from instruction designed to enhance his metacognitive awareness. He is generally unaware of how he arrives at his answers and is unable to pinpoint details to justify his answers. It may well be that Freddy is just unaccustomed to metacognitive probing and questioning and simply needs opportunities to do more of it. On the other hand, it may be that Freddy is not thinking about what he is reading, and/or his limited experience with discussing reading and literature makes it difficult for him to make many appropriate connections. Any instructional plan should aim at developing Freddy's metacognitive awareness, by teacher-modeling and probing after reading, and by scaffolding instruction during reading to help Freddy read with greater attention to the detail in the story or selection.

3. *Attitude, interest, and motivation*   Freddy generally has a fairly good attitude toward reading and himself as a reader. His biggest problem in this area seems to be that he is living in an environment that does not place great value on reading, discussion, and other intellectual pursuits; hence, he sees little need to read or to write other than what is required for school. Freddy may benefit from an instructional plan that seeks to address his affective behavior toward literacy. Some suggestions include renewing his privileges at the library so that he may take books home, setting aside a predictable and consistent block of time each week to visit the school library and get books, keeping a written record of books he has read, and talking with his mother about the ways she could support reading in the home by possibly setting aside twenty or thirty minutes each evening for reading only (no television). Freddy has mentioned that he likes to read when he goes to bed; his mother, of course, wants him to go to sleep. Maybe a compromise could be reached where Freddy goes to bed twenty or thirty minutes earlier and is allowed to read for that time.

V. Summary and Justification

Freddy is a capable but limited reader. He is able to decode the text in a meaningful manner and use his cue systems to recognize words. However, he does not read often enough, does not have a literary environment in his home, and generally does not comprehend what he reads beyond the more text-explicit information. One aspect of this instructional plan is to improve Freddy's literary environment. Freddy likes to read and enjoys good stories. He needs the opportunity to select and take home a variety of books of his own choosing from the library. He also needs time set aside specifically for reading and discussing what he has read. Part of our instructional time together will be spent in the school library and in sustained silent reading. Additionally, I will make a point of taking the necessary time to give Freddy a chance to talk about his readings with me. Likewise, I will model literary discussion for him by talking about books I'm currently reading with him. I will also strongly encourage his mother to support reading in the home, and I will give her some ideas on how she can do this, considering her time limitations.

The second aspect of this plan addresses Freddy's comprehension and metacognitive awareness development. Instruction for Freddy must be planned with an eye toward developing and enhancing these areas. One possible way would be by comparing and contrasting selected fairy and folk tales. Freddy is interested in these types of stories and, by constructing webs and charts to compare and contrast similarities and differences among stories, Freddy may improve his ability to read for greater detail, to comprehend using higher-order cognitive strategies, and to become more aware of how he knows what he knows. If this instruction is successful, perhaps we can later use the webs and charts as a basis for writing about fairy tales and folk tales. And maybe Freddy would like to write his own. I would also like to try using webs and flow charts with Freddy, and other students, to accompany some of our content reading. In any case, as the school year develops, I hope to branch out and focus on comparing and contrasting other types of literature that Freddy may suggest as he expands his literary horizons a little more.

VI. Summary Notes and Discussion Regarding Progress

My goals for instructional sessions with Freddy focused on two large areas. First, and the one receiving the most attention, was to improve his metacognitive awareness and comprehension by having him justify his answers to text-implicit comprehension questions that deal with cause and effect, inferences, and drawing conclusions.

I began this instruction by modeling how to think aloud and how a good reader goes about answering questions and justifying answers. In a fairly short period of time, Freddy became adept at verbalizing his thoughts as he read and was able to ask himself how he arrived at a particular answer. We continued to work on this during the fable lessons, as we worked on cause and effect relationships and making comparisons, and in our discussions following the reading of the folk tales, fables, and fairy tales. Later, we continued our think-alouds and our discussions during and after we read sections of *Charlotte's Web* (1952) by E.B. White together. After awhile, Freddy wouldn't even wait for me to ask him how he knew his answer was a good one; after answering a question, he would immediately explain why, using the text to back up his answer. As a result of his increased metacognitive awareness, Freddy generally answers comprehension questions with more confidence and less hesitation.

The second area of focus for our instructional time has been to improve Freddy's affective reading behaviors and the amount he reads. The idea was for him to value reading as an entertaining and meaningful activity. To this end, we spent as much time as possible in the school library. I wanted him to spend some time each week browsing for books and to take at least one interesting book home. I tried to work from books that he decided he wanted to read, such as fables, an animal encyclopedia, a baseball book, a book on airplanes, and *Charlotte's Web*. We spent a portion of time at the library looking for books, then a portion of time back in the classroom, with both of us reading our selections. I modeled reading behaviors for him and stopped reading only to help him with a difficult section of text. I'm unsure of the growth in this area. It seems to be more of a long-term goal. I spoke to his mother about Freddy's competency as a reader and how he needs to be encouraged to do more of it. I explained that Freddy had been granted his library borrowing privileges once again. Whether his mother supports his reading remains to be seen. The only really solid evidence I have that Freddy has come to value reading more than before is that as our "special" sessions together have progressed, Freddy now often comes to them with a book or subject in mind. It shows that he is thinking more about books and reading. I also think that his desire to read *Charlotte's Web* is an indication that he views himself as a good reader (this book is being read by some of the better readers in our class) and that he is willing to read a thick book with few illustrations, a behavior not in evidence before.

Freddy and I enjoy our reading sessions together. Freddy does not consider it to be regular "school work" and enthusiastically applies his energies to our activities. One of the most important aspects of our work, from Freddy's perspective, may be that he receives positive feedback on his reading abilities. I constantly tell him he is a good reader, and I think he is beginning to believe in himself.

Progress Notations

10/15   Comprehension: Freddy showed slight improvement in his reading comprehension. He seems able to read more difficult passages with greater understanding. But he still has comprehension difficulties with text-implicit questions dealing with cause and effect, inferences, and drawing conclusions. For instance, while he seems better able to identify the more obviously stated cause-and-effect relationships, he still has difficulty with the implicitly stated ones.

10/27   Metacognitive awareness: As our work together progresses, Freddy has begun to skim sections of his reading to arrive at the section of the text that he is looking for.

10/31   Metacognition: I have continued to model for Freddy how I arrive at answers to questions by pointing out sections or sentences to support my answers. Freddy has developed his own skimming strategy as he repeatedly is asked to explain his answers. Today Freddy was able to go directly to the section of the passage that he wanted to reference and did so with accuracy and confidence.

11/15   Attitude and interest: The most significant change observed in Freddy's attitude toward reading is that he appears to have an improved self-concept as a reader. Today he decided that he wanted to read *Charlotte's Web*. He was inspired to read the book because several of the better readers in our class are reading it. It is noteworthy that he wanted to associate himself with the "best" readers. It is also a change in his reading behavior because it is a long book with few illustrations, just the kind of book that Freddy avoided at the beginning of our work together.

11/20   Metacognitive awareness, comprehension, and attitude: Freddy really seems to be improving. I see real growth in the areas of metacognitive awareness and reading attitude. Even though we haven't been working on cue system development, I keep monitoring that through oral reading sampling. He still leads with his phoneme-grapheme system and uses his syntax and semantic strategies to self-correct. However, I believe his comprehension is developing, mostly due to his new metacognitive awareness and strategies, and the more we read together and discuss our readings, the more he seems to enjoy reading. He also seems much more confident of himself as a reader.

12/17   Notations and suggestions for continued instruction: Now, Freddy enjoys reading for pleasure. He also values reading for informational purposes, as in his selection of books on baseball and airplanes. He seems to need the motivation provided by another interested, literate individual to maintain any kind of real, lasting interest in reading. His strengths with the three cueing systems indicate that he can read independently for meaning when given appropriate materials. He is once again able to withdraw books from the library and is comfortable looking for books there, both with me and on his own. He is also proudly keeping a list of his favorite books in his portfolio, and he asked me if we can take the time to do a project to illustrate favorite parts of favorite books for the classroom. Additionally, Freddy wrote a paragraph for his portfolio on his favorite book of all, *Charlotte's Web*.

Freddy has the potential for continued growth as a reader if he is able to select materials he'd like to read, if he continues to learn to value reading through the example and encouragement of others, and if he has the opportunity to discuss what he has read with someone who is able to help him probe deeper into the reading material.

These three factors are also precisely those that put him at risk as a developing reader. If Freddy spends more quality time reading material he's interested in, he should continue to grow as a reader. Should Freddy be unable to spend time outside of school engaged in meaningful reading, I suspect he will not develop much beyond a purely functional-level reader. He will be literate, but he may have difficulty reading the kinds of materials required for middle or high school, or perhaps more advanced work.

I will continue to work one-on-one with Freddy as much as my teaching schedule and other students allow. However, I'm hoping that more literacy activity can start to take place in Freddy's home to keep his current momentum going.

Consider and React 5–4

What do you think? What continued instruction would you suggest for Freddy? Why?

Discussion of Reports on Emily and Freddy   The analysis and reports on Emily and Freddy provide helpful insights into each child's background, strategies, needs, and progress. These reports were selected for inclusion in this chapter because each provides an example of somewhat different instructional needs and emphases. However, there are also some similarities regarding each child's affective needs. I will briefly highlight the instructional needs that each teacher observed and analyzed, summarize how each of these teachers proceeded to deal with these needs, and then discuss each teacher's feelings and recommendations concerning the child's potential.

Consider and React 5–5

Before you read my comparison, try doing your own. Consider the two children's strategies and needs. How were they different? What were the similarities regarding their affective needs? Compare your analysis with mine. How did you do? How did I do?

Nancy Gregg analyzes that Emily needs word recognition instruction. She found that Emily does not have the necessary strategies to figure out words in context and will not guess because she is afraid of being wrong. Emily's main decoding strategy seems to be use of phonics (part of the phoneme-grapheme cue system), and, of course, she is not very successful at reading using phonics alone. Additionally, even though Emily's only real strategy is phonics, she is not particularly strong in the phoneme-grapheme area, probably because her phonics skills seem limited to beginning consonant sounds. Although Emily does know some words by sight, her sight words are few. Overall, she does not demonstrate signs of fluency.

Ms. Gregg also realizes that Emily's comprehension and metacognition of textual materials are poor, but notes that Emily can comprehend picture books, answering many comprehension and metacognition questions based on her own reading of the picture books. Ms. Gregg decides that even though Emily's comprehension is weak, she will concentrate her instructional efforts on developing Emily's word recognition strategies involving the semantic (including vocabulary development) and syntax systems in the hope that this will be the first step toward text comprehension. (Ms. Gregg does, in fact, emphasize metacognitive awareness of strategy use and comprehension as part of her word recognition instruction.)

Finally, Ms. Gregg analyzes that Emily needs to realize that one reads for a purpose and needs to develop a sense of ownership of whatever she reads. These needs, combined with the very strong need of relating the material read to Emily's cognitive experience, drive Ms. Gregg's instructional decisions. These instructional decisions include the use of **language experience activities** to build on Emily's interests and schemata, with the teacher taking dictation (from Emily) to write Emily's own stories and later have Emily read them back, as well as encouraging Emily to write her own stories; the development of a personal **word bank** for Emily from these activities and other writings and readings to build on Emily's memory of sight words; a focus on the three cue systems (particularly the semantic and syntax systems, which Emily seemed not to be using) to make good guesses when encountering unknown words; the use of repeated readings of stories that Emily has already been successful with, in order to help develop some experience with fluency; and the development of Emily's interest in and love for literature.

According to John Trainor's analysis, Freddy needs comprehension and metacognitive development instruction, as well as more opportunities to discuss material he has read with someone else who is interested and literate. He found that Freddy's word recognition strategies were good and that Freddy could successfully comprehend the explicitly stated information in textual materials. However, he also found Freddy to have problems with text-implicit questions and higher-order comprehension, particularly with cause-and-effect relationships, drawing conclusions, reading for more implicit detail, and metacognitive awareness.

Mr. Trainor also analyzes that it is most important to help Freddy develop an interest in reading and help him see the many reasons there are to read and to write. Additionally, he believes there is a need to encourage Freddy to read more and to view reading as a pleasurable activity that he can do at home as well as in school.

These needs cause Mr. Trainor to make instructional decisions that include a focus on higher-order comprehension, including cause and effect, drawing conclusions, reading for implicit details, and metacognitive awareness through use of teacher modeling and think-aloud procedures; a focus on library opportunities to develop interests and purposes for reading; and the development of more free reading opportunities and discussions about the readings for Freddy during the day, as well as the encouragement of pleasurable reading opportunities at home.

Both teachers feel very positive about their child's progress, yet each indicates it is important that these and other instructional efforts are continued. Nancy Gregg believes that Emily needs to continue her syntax and semantic development work (particularly semantic development) and further see how phonics can play a part in the verification of a guess. She also recommends more use of writing as a means of responding to reading and additional opportunities for a continuation of repeated readings, as well as a wider variety of reading. John Trainor thinks Freddy needs continued encouragement and opportunities to discuss what he has read with someone who is able to help him probe deeper into the materials. He also believes it is important that Freddy continues to have opportunities to read outside of school. Although Mr. Trainor feels positive about Freddy's progress, he cautions that without these opportunities, Freddy could have problems reading the more complex content materials necessary for middle and high school assignments. Both teachers believe their students are beginning to view themselves as "readers" and are more self-confident as a result of their qualitative assessment and instruction.

Developing Your Own Instructional Plans

The previous in-depth instructional plans, developed by elementary classroom teachers, were meant to give you an idea of some of the considerations that can go into planning for an individual child's literacy development needs. Of course, your own instructional plans will be determined by your decisions and the real needs and strengths of the individual children with whom you work. Your analysis and plans may not need to be so detailed. In fact, you might find that for most children you can pencil outline each child's instructional needs in front of her folder or portfolio (with or without consultation with the child—again, this depends on what type of portfolio you are using and how democratic your style is). The pencil outline can be changed any time you and the child think that her instructional needs have changed. The only real guidelines you will need to follow as you develop individual instructional plans are the guidelines you create for yourself. Here is a list of some questions you might wish to contemplate when developing your own instructional plans for children in your classroom:

1. Are my instructional plans based on my own observations and other assessments of this child during authentic, functional reading and other literacy activities? Is there enough information to support a need for instruction for this area?

2. Will this instruction, if successful, really help this child develop and use necessary reading and study strategies, leading him/her toward more fluency and independence as a learner?

3. Will this instruction have a negative effect in any way on this child's interest in reading and/or self-concept?

4. How can I integrate this instruction into the real school day in a meaningful, functional, and interesting way for this child?

5. Are there other children in my classroom who also need this instruction? (If so, grouping for instruction will be thoroughly explored in Chapter 6.)

Consider and React 5–6

Are there other questions you would consider as you develop your own instructional plans for students? What are they? Why are these questions important to consider?

Monitoring Progress

In the sample in-depth instructional plans, you probably noted each teacher's **progress notes,** or the notations each made regarding the child's progress. Once again, any method you select for doing ongoing assessment and recording of a child's progress is fine, but it is important that as you work with individual children, whether one-on-one or in small groups, you observe and assess the children each time. Your observations and assessments will usually be informal and be based on real classroom work (i.e., functional and authentic reading, writing, and study strategies). You can keep your notations in their folders or portfolios, on a separate "teacher's observations journal," or on an analysis sheet, rubric evaluation, or other page that you can attach to the child's dated work. It is also likely that you will want the child to participate in the monitoring of his own development. Children can record their reflections concerning their progress in their own journals or on their own analysis sheets or pages—or, as pointed out elsewhere, they can develop their own rubrics to evaluate their work. These also can be attached to their dated work and kept in their portfolios.

These ongoing notations, with examples, will be a valuable aid to both the teacher and the child. It will be useful for future instructional planning purposes, conferences with the child, conferences with the family, report card evaluations, and, most important, the child's development as an independent learner and reader.

Summary

This chapter has provided some ideas, guidance, examples, and discussion to assist the classroom teacher with the task of pulling together assessment information on a child and analyzing and using that information to develop an instructional plan for the child. The purpose of assessment should always be to inform instruction and to help teachers effectively plan instruction for children. It was the intention of this chapter to aid this purpose.

Part One of this book has focused on assessment and analysis in the classroom. Once initial decisions regarding the child's needed instruction have been made, classroom teachers will want to refer to Part Two for organization and classroom management ideas; a discussion regarding issues relevant to assessment, instruction, and learning; and criteria for and samples of strategy lessons to facilitate instruction and ongoing assessment. Classroom teachers are reminded that because assessment and analysis are ongoing, teachers must continue to observe and assess children's strategies and development as they work with them.

Questions for Reflection and Response

1. How can you use portfolios, or other sampling ideas, to collect, evaluate, and organize relevant and important samples and sources of information about students? What do you suggest?

2. When do you think it might be prudent to develop an in-depth report on a student, such as those sampled in this chapter? Why?

3. As you reviewed Emily's report, what assessment and instructional decisions did you agree with? Was there anything you would pursue differently? Why?

4. If you were Emily's teacher, what would you do next? How? Why?

5. As you reviewed Freddy's report, what assessment and instructional decisions did you agree with? Was there anything you would pursue differently? Why?

6. If you were Freddy's teacher, what would you do next? How? Why?

7. Using the in-depth report format presented in this chapter (and adding any other information you want to include), try gathering data over time on one particular student and develop your own report. Before you begin, review the questions on page 196–197 and be prepared to defend your assessment and instructional decisions. Then work with the selected student and summarize your results. What continued instruction do you recommend?

#1 - P/T conferences, drive instruction, show develop

PART TWO

ORGANIZATION AND INSTRUCTION IN THE CLASSROOM

CHAPTER 6

ORGANIZING FOR READING DEVELOPMENT AND INSTRUCTION

Focus and Goals of the Chapter

- ♦ To provide a comprehensive overview of ideas and procedures in order to facilitate grouping, organizing, and managing instruction in the classroom

- • To provide information to help teachers assess and create the environment, context of instruction, and classroom organization with which they feel most comfortable

- • To provide information, ideas, and examples to help teachers organize their available instructional time, space, materials, records, and plans

- • To illustrate that teachers can accommodate for individual learners' needs within the larger context of the classroom using various flexible grouping ideas

- • To demonstrate how many reading and study skill/strategy groups can be organized in the classroom

- • To demonstrate that various cooperative learning groups, such as special interest, literature circles, author preference, and student authoring groups, can be part of the classroom and can facilitate an individualized and student-centered program

- • To provide ideas to facilitate the assigning of students' individual instruction and the organizing of record keeping, including self-reflection journals

- • To provide specific ideas and examples to facilitate reciprocal conferencing and sharing with individual students and with students and their parents/families; for the purpose of assessment of progress, planning, and evaluation; and for development of equality of participation

- To provide many specific ideas and examples for reporting and sharing students' progress with parents/families, including letters, journals, report cards, and several self-evaluation and alternative procedures to keep students and parents/families actively involved

- To provide many classroom ideas for strategy development and literature exposure appropriate for whole class involvement, including sustained silent reading (SSR), genre immersion, content literature study, book authoring, field trips, and cross-age and other shared learning opportunities.

Introduction

The classroom teacher's role involves observing and studying the literacy strategies of her individual students. This aspect was discussed and detailed in Part One: "Assessment and Analysis in the Classroom." Once the classroom teacher has initially assessed and qualitatively analyzed the strategies and perceived needs of her students' instructional plans are made. Based on those plans, the teacher focuses more of her energy on qualitative instruction with continuous assessment. The chapters of Part Two: "Organization and Instruction in the Classroom" provide organization and classroom management ideas to facilitate the desired instructional program and atmosphere, as well as discussion regarding issues relevant to instruction, and some sample strategy lessons and procedures to facilitate specific reading and study strategy development.

Chapter 6 begins by helping you reflect on your beliefs, goals, needs, and the classroom environment and organization you want to develop. Next, ideas are presented for designing the environment for your program, including organizing time, space, materials, and record-keeping procedures. There are also suggestions for various flexible grouping arrangements to facilitate instruction. These include strategy and skill groups and various cooperative learning groups, such as interest and content groups, literature and author preference groups, and peer and authoring groups. Discussion is included regarding the use of guided reading, leveled texts and determining the appropriateness of texts, authentic materials and purposes, individual work and record keeping, conferencing and the monitoring of development, reciprocal parent/family sharing, alternative evaluation ideas, and whole class activities and involvement. Later, in the appendix, you will find sample portfolio and rubric forms, checklists, and other record-keeping and evaluation ideas to further illustrate how all of this might come together.

Although many possibilities and samples are provided, these are just ideas for how classrooms may be organized and managed. The actual planner, organizer, and implementer is always you, the classroom teacher. Your program will be successful only if you select and develop your own ideas based on your own beliefs, goals, style, and the needs you perceive in your own classroom.

Assessing the Environment and Organization You Want to Create

Your classroom environment and organization should match the beliefs you have about assessment and instruction and the expectations and goals you have for your classroom program, as well as meet the needs of the children in your classroom. Different teachers have different philosophies, preferences, and styles. It is important that you develop a classroom environment and management plan to provide the atmosphere needed to further the program you envision—a program that you believe will meet the needs of all the individuals in your class.

Consider and React 6–1

Do you agree? Why are your own beliefs and the goals you have for your program so important? Consider your own ideas, then read to see what the cited research indicates.

Lipson and Wixson (1997) provide extensive evaluation suggestions for examining the **context of instruction,** including teachers' beliefs and the classroom environment, classroom organization, grouping patterns, and classroom interactions. They make the important point that there is a growing body of research that indicates that the **instructional context** (setting and conditions of instruction) and how teachers organize for and carry out instruction can support learning or can actually contribute to disability. It is not enough to examine just students' strategies, motivations, and so on; we must also examine the context of instruction to see if we are providing a setting and conditions that will facilitate the learning of individual students. Some students may be negatively affected by factors that may not influence another student at all, or some students may be positively influenced by factors that cause problems for others.

Since we know that all students will not necessarily thrive in the same environment, this can present a problem for teachers. How can teachers create a classroom environment that will meet the needs of all their students? My suggestion is for teachers to first take a careful look at their own beliefs, instructional goals, and need for control to see how these might be designed into the context of their classrooms. Then teachers must look further at their plans to ensure the flexibility necessary to accommodate each and every learner in their classrooms. If teachers can develop programs that meet their own beliefs, goals, and needs, they are halfway there. If their programs allow for the needs, environments, groupings, interactions, and amounts of autonomy necessary for each child, then they have achieved classroom contexts that are conducive to learning.

Context of Instruction Reflection Guide

In order to begin to assess your own beliefs, goals, and needs, try answering the questions in this Context of Instruction Reflection Guide.

Reflections Regarding Beliefs and Classroom Environment

1. What are my beliefs about assessment and instruction? Why?
2. What are my goals for my students' learning? Why?
3. How can these be reflected in my classroom environment and organization?

Reflections Regarding Organization, Grouping, and Interactions

1. Do I have a preference for certain grouping arrangements in my classroom? Why?

2. What type of interactions between children and children, and children and teacher, do these groupings encourage? How?

3. Do these grouping arrangements and likely interactions match my stated beliefs about assessment and instruction and the goals I have for my students' learning? How?

4. What alternative grouping arrangements might help achieve my stated beliefs and goals?

Reflections Regarding Control Issues

1. To what extent am I comfortable with children having control regarding their assessment, learning, record keeping, and evaluation? Why?

2. To what extent am I comfortable with parents/families having a role in their children's assessment, learning, and evaluation? Why?

3. To what extent do I need control of assessment, learning, record keeping/ evaluation? Why?

4. What record-keeping, conferencing, monitoring, and evaluation ideas would meet my level of comfort, provide as much autonomy as possible for the children, and provide as much parent/family involvement as possible?

Consider and React 6–2

What did you learn about your beliefs and the context of instruction that you prefer? Are you surprised by any of your responses? Are there any other questions you would add? Why?

Use your reflections and findings to plan and organize for ongoing assessment, instruction, and learning. Your beliefs about teaching and learning are a very important part of the classroom context and will influence literacy learning in your classroom (Deford, 1986). Beach (1994) reviews the research on teachers' beliefs and indicates that more research needs to be done. Although beliefs and knowledge do affect the context of the classroom, she sees evidence to indicate that the context of the school and community also affect individual teachers' beliefs and knowledge (p. 194). For instance, Beach shows how teachers are influenced by the rules and expectations of their school administrators, and that this can mediate and affect individual teachers' beliefs and actions. In his review of the research on teaching, Fenstermacher (1994) indicates that while he sees a difference between teachers' beliefs and teachers' knowledge, teachers' beliefs and reasonings do affect their classroom teaching procedures. He summarizes that the most important thing learned from the study of teacher knowledge should be that teachers need to know what they know (p. 50) and, more important, "that they know that they know" (p. 51).

Accommodating for Individual Learners

Use the findings you have on the individual children in your classroom in order to plan the atmosphere and conditions you believe that each child needs for his or her development. Remember to continue to assess the children as you work with them in the context of the classroom. When assessment and instruction are interwoven, you are able to continually monitor strategies and development and make adjustments whenever you see a need. Hiebert, Valencia, and Afflerbach (1994) remind us that the aim of authentic assessment is to assess many kinds of strategies in contexts that closely resemble the situations in which those strategies are to be used (p. 9). Wolf (1993) indicates that assessment is "informed" rather than "informal" when it is carried out by a knowledgeable teacher who, over time, carefully observes and documents students' performance across different contexts in authentic learning tasks.

In order to illustrate how individual needs can be anticipated within the larger context of the classroom, let's look at what Emily's and Freddy's teachers (from Chapter 5) believe would be optimum contexts for their students' learning. Ms. Gregg assesses that Emily needs a very supportive environment and frequent interaction with the teacher. She needs word recognition strategy instruction that encourages guessing unknown words in context, using semantic and syntax strategies. She also recommends that Emily's instruction include vocabulary development, with emphasis on key words used in various classroom readings and work, sight word instruction using language experience activities, and opportunities for repeated readings of stories she's been successful with in order to develop fluency. Ms. Gregg believes that Emily would do well in small teacher-directed strategy groups for this instruction. She also thinks Emily would benefit from various interest, literature, and authoring groups. She indicates that Emily needs as much support as possible to encourage her to read a wider variety of literature, develop an interest in and love for literature, and develop, through writing, a sense of ownership for what she reads. She believes that Emily does best in a risk-free environment, but Emily does like the teacher to have a good deal of control in regard to monitoring, evaluating work, and record keeping. Emily can take part in this, but Emily wants the teacher to take the lead. Emily's mother wants to be involved, and Emily benefits from as much parent involvement (mother and father) as possible.

Mr. Trainor assesses that Freddy needs a very literate environment and frequent opportunities to read and discuss his reading. He also indicates that Freddy needs strategy instruction and continued support in several higher-order comprehension areas. Mr. Trainor believes that Freddy would do well in small strategy groups that meet regularly with the teacher to discuss and pursue literature with special attention to cause-and-effect relationships, making inferences, drawing conclusions, and metacognitive awareness. He believes that Freddy does best when he is given the autonomy to choose literature in areas of his own interest and is given plenty of free time to select books from the library and read on his own. Freddy would benefit from opportunities to read and work on projects with other students with similar interests, Mr. Trainor believes, and should be encouraged to develop additional reading interests. Mr. Trainor thinks Freddy would benefit the most from an environment that gives children some control over their learning, evaluation, and record keeping. He knows Freddy likes to work with him as a partner in learning, but with encouragement, Freddy can take even more responsibility for all aspects of his school work and evaluation. Freddy would also benefit from more parental involvement in conferences and evaluations, but his mother indicates she has no time; however, this involvement should still be encouraged.

This knowledge of your individual students' needs, combined with awareness of your own beliefs, goals, and needs, should help you recognize and develop classroom organization ideas and procedures that are appropriate and a good match for you and your students. Read the sections that follow with these needs, beliefs, and goals in mind, referring back to your reflections and findings as often as necessary as you consider various environment, grouping, record-keeping, conferencing, sharing, and other program decisions. (Readers interested in other assessment ideas concerning classroom contexts and environments should see Lipson & Wixson [1997], and Searfoss [1993].)

Consider and React 6–3

How can you integrate the information about your own beliefs, goals, and needs and your knowledge of individual students' needs and preferences in order to plan and organize your classroom?

Designing an Environment and Program for Individual Development

There is no recipe or outline that can tell you how to design your classroom time, space, materials, and record-keeping procedures to accommodate your instructional program. However, discussions and questions are provided to remind you of some areas to consider as you organize a program to fit the desired context of instruction for you and your students. (Additionally, Carr, 1999, and Morrow, 1997 are recommended to readers who would like more ideas, suggestions, and discussions regarding classroom organization for literacy instruction.)

Organizing Time

Time is something that most classroom teachers feel there is never enough of. Because of lunch, recess, announcements, housekeeping, and a multitude of other noninstructional interruptions and demands, as well as predetermined instructional times not in your control (e.g., library, art, music, special programs), this is very true. That is why it is important to carefully organize the instructional time that is left after all the other blocks of time have been removed. One way to do this is to actually "block out" a normal classroom week to see what instructional time is left after everything else has been accounted for. The instructional times schedule form in Figure 6–1 illustrates what might be involved. Once we see how much time is left to us for our work with children, we can plan accordingly. Whatever time we have must be divided among the opportunities for children to do their individual reading, writing, and other work and the **direct instructional activities** (activities involving planned and specific teacher-directed instruction) that we want to plan for individuals and groups of children each week. It should be kept in mind that

1. All children or groups do not necessarily have to meet with you each day or even each week.
2. Depending on their needs and the specific kinds of instruction planned, some children may meet with you more or less often than others.
3. Some children or groups of children can work independently or cooperatively within a group after a fairly short meeting with you, for direction and guidance, once a week, or once every two weeks, or even once a month.
4. Reading/study strategy instruction can take place during and as part of content instruction (science, social studies, math) and should be integrated with writing and other communication activities.
5. When ongoing assessment and instruction are integrated, so that both can happen at the same time, "time" need not be taken away from teaching and spent on testing. (Winograd, 1994, suggests that managing time for both assessment and instruction could otherwise be a critical problem for teachers, but the problem is solved when assessment is embedded in instruction.)

In the sections that follow, the discussions should be helpful to you in weighing your students' instructional needs (based on your assessments and instructional plans for each child) to make decisions about how you will allocate your time to individuals and small groups of children.

Organizing Space

Many of your decisions regarding the allocation of space for your classroom instructional activities—individual, small group, and whole class—will be determined by the size and shape of your classroom, the number of students you have, and the amount and type of

Weekly Schedule

Days	Pre-determined or Otherwise Scheduled Time Blocks	"The Leftovers" or your Available Instructional Time Blocks

Mondays
8:00 – 8:30 Announcements, attendance, lunch money, & Opening
12:00 – 12:45 Lunch & Recess
2:00 – 2:30 Music Teacher
3:00 – 3:15 Announcements, Clean-up, & Dismissal

8:30 – 12:00 (3½ hrs.)
12:45 – 2:00 (1¼ hrs.)
2:30 – 3:00 (½ hr.)

Tuesdays
8:00 – 8:30 Announcements, attendance, lunch money, & Opening
12:00 – 12:45 Lunch & Recess
2:00 – 3:00 Art Teacher
3:00 – 3:15 Announcements, Clean-up, & Dismissal

8:30 – 12:00 (3½ hrs.)
12:45 – 2:00 (1¼ hrs.)

Wednesdays
8:00 – 8:30 Announcements, attendance, lunch money, & Opening
12:00 – 12:45 Lunch & Recess
2:00 – 2:30 Library
3:00 – 3:15 Announcements, Clean-up, & Dismissal

8:30 – 12:00 (3½ hrs.)
12:45 – 2:00 (1¼ hrs.)
2:30 – 3:00 (½ hr.)

Thursdays
8:00 – 8:30 Announcements, attendance, lunch money, & Opening
12:00 – 12:45 Lunch & Recess
2:00 – 2:30 Computer Lab
2:30 – 3:00 Science Lab
3:00 – 3:15 Announcements, Clean-up, & Dismissal

8:30 – 12:00 (3½ hrs.)
12:45 – 2:00 (1¼ hrs.)

Fridays
8:00 – 8:30 Announcements, attendance, lunch money, & Opening
12:00 – 12:45 Lunch & Recess
2:00 – 2:30 P.E. Teacher
3:00 – 3:15 Announcements, Clean-up, & Dismissal

8:30 – 12:00 (3½ hrs.)
12:45 – 2:00 (1¼ hrs.)
2:30 – 3:00 (½ hr.)

Figure 6–1 Finding Available Instructional Times

furniture in the room. Whatever the limitations, planning and organizing for optimum use will help you make the most of the space you have.

Certain organizational questions and reflections may be useful. For instance:

1. Is there a place where I can work individually with a child that will ensure a certain level of quiet and privacy for assessments, conferencing, and strategy work?

2. How can I arrange the room in such a way as to allow enough space for one or more small instructional and/or cooperative learning groups? (I probably want at least one group to be able to meet with me, and I might want one or two others to be able to meet independently.)

3. Are there other special space allocations I will need to consider in order to carry out my grouping plans for the instruction of the children in my class?

4. How can I set up the room so that each child has personal work space, good light, and a view of the board and the part of the room from which I'm likely to conduct a whole-class lesson? *X/y*

5. How can I plan this use of space so that the children will be encouraged and comfortable as they engage in reading and other literacy-related activities?

Children need to feel safe and comfortable in order to do their best work. For most of us, it is important to have a work place we feel is ours—a place where we can leave our work, work tools, and personal things and know they will be there when we return. When deciding on classroom organization, keeping a balance that meets both your teaching needs and the children's learning needs is not easy. You might find the sample classroom diagrams shown in Figures 6–2 and 6–3 helpful as you plan and arrange furniture for the optimal use of space. (Readers are referred to Reutzel & Wolfersberger, 1996, for additional ideas.)

Organizing Materials

Much like the discussion in the previous section, the learning materials in your classroom and how they are organized will, in many ways, be determined by what materials your school gives you. However, teachers often spend their own resources and use their limited supply funds to purchase materials that otherwise would not be in their classrooms. For instance, many teachers develop a classroom library of good children's books and other literature that they and the children can use for assessing, teaching, learning, enjoying, and sharing. (None of these is meant to be mutually exclusive of the others; in fact, it is encouraged that they instead be inclusive and overlap.) Additionally, many resourceful teachers borrow many books from the school and public libraries on a weekly or biweekly basis to assure a literature-rich environment for the children.

When organizing books and other learning materials in your classroom, you could consider these questions: *mostly 9th + Journalism*

1. Who will use them? ╱
2. Who needs easy access to them?
3. Will books and other materials be "inviting" to students?
4. What can I do to organize the learning materials in a way that will best promote children's access to, use of, and interest in them?

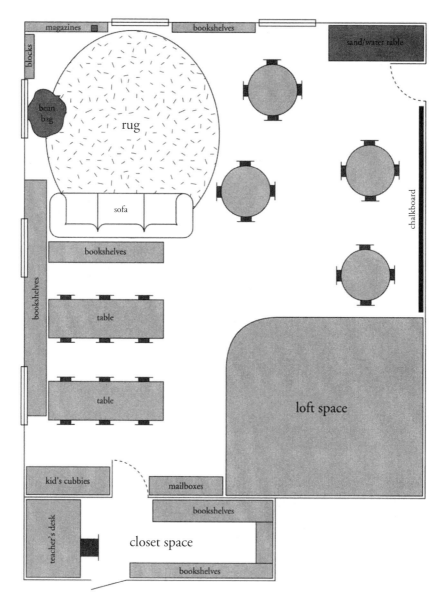

Figure 6–2 Sample Classroom Diagram

Before spending money or precious time to secure more learning materials for your classroom, you might also want to consider this question:

5. What additional books and materials do I need in my classroom in order to carry out the individual instructional plans for my students and to promote the reading, writing, and study strategies and interests I believe are most important?

(Routman, 2000, is suggested as another resource for organizing classroom libraries.)

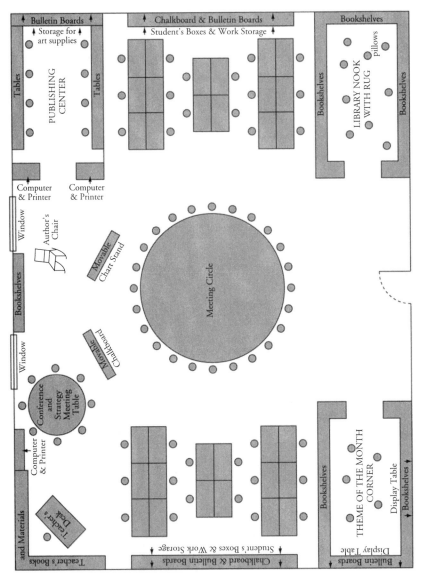

Figure 6–3 Sample Classroom Diagram

Organizing Records and Plans

Chapter 5 presented the development of two in-depth individual instructional plans, as well as the suggestion of using short pencil outlines when more in-depth plans are not necessary. As was emphasized, the classroom teacher uses all the pertinent information he has gathered to plan each child's literacy instruction. In this section, I will discuss how this information can be used to organize and plan for the instruction of the entire class.

When a teacher has thirty children in the classroom, it sometimes seems daunting or unrealistic to believe that he can actually develop instruction to meet the needs of each child. However, good organization and careful record keeping, based on the qualitative analysis of data gathered for each child, can facilitate the individualized qualitative instruction of each child, even in a classroom of thirty. The suggestions and ideas listed and illustrated below should make this clear.

1. Develop a summary list or summary record of all of the reading skills/strategies, study strategies, and any other literacy-related strategies or information you have been observing and assessing. For example, you can list the strategies/ information in pencil horizontally across a large paper or chart and then list the name of each child in your class vertically down the left side.

2. Go through each folder or portfolio to review the instructional plans noted for each child. If you indicated an instructional need or preference in any of the areas listed on your summary list, indicate in pencil on your chart that the child should receive instruction in that area. If your chart is large enough, you could also include any special notations regarding the kind of instruction you recommend or any other information that might help you later as you group and plan.

3. Use this summary list or summary record to plan your instructional groups for reading, study strategies, special interests, and other reading and literacy-related groupings.

Some children will be penciled into many instructional or special areas on your chart, while others, based on their skills/strategies and interests, will be noted in fewer places. Likewise, you might have indicated many children for a particular strategy area, while for another, only one child may be in need of instruction. This is a summary of some of the information from your assessments and analyses. It is the basis for **individualization** (the adjustment of teaching-learning activities to students' skills/strategies, interests, and needs). If you find that several children need particular instruction with syntax and/or semantic development, then it makes sense to work with those children in a small group on syntax and semantic development strategies to maximize the use of your direct instruction time and energy. However, if you find that only one child needs your intervention and support to develop his syntax strategies, you should plan accordingly to work with that child. Keep in mind that needs, interests, and skill/strategy areas are penciled in rather than inked in because needs and interests change, and therefore group membership changes, too. Also, new needs and new interests often surface, and new skill/strategy and interest groups can then surface, too. This flexibility, or what I call the "movability" and "exit-ability" of your groups, is one of the things that differentiate the groups suggested in this book from the more static, inflexible, and "lock-in" ability groupings of the past. **Flexible grouping,** then, can be defined as classroom groupings of students that are fluid and that are called together for a focus on particular skills, strategies, interests, motivations, literature, and other purposes, but *not* with a particular focus on ability levels.

Figure 6–4 provides an illustration of what a teacher's summary list or summary record for some suggested flexible groupings might look like. This one has been partially

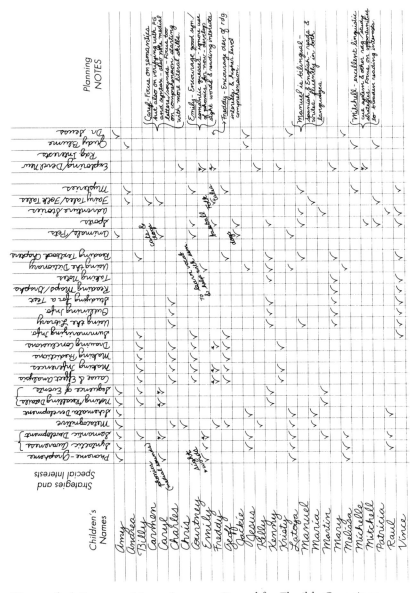

Figure 6–4 Summary List or Summary Record for Flexible Groupings

filled out, indicating the instruction, interest preferences, and planning notes for several children in the class. This is only a suggestion; your list may have additional or different skills, strategies, and interest areas listed. Or, you may develop a totally different whole class record-keeping system based on your program, philosophy, and creativity. You might also want to refer to the sample record-keeping list in the appendix for another idea of how this can be done.

Flexible Grouping and Planning Based on Analyses of Assessments

As indicated in the previous section, direct instruction based on qualitative assessments can result in a variety of flexible grouping situations. Some type of grouping is necessary to meet the needs and interests of individual children in your classroom (e.g., Flood et al., 1992; Fountas & Pinnell, 1996; Galda, Cullinan, & Strickland, 1997; Heilman, Blair, & Rupley, 2002; Hiebert, 1991; Opitz, 1998a; Opitz & Ford, 2001; Routman, 1996; Strickland, 1994/1995; Templeton, 1995). Teachers can literally have one or two dozen, or more, groupings. How can that be? How can that be managed?

Consider and React 6–4

What do you think? How can it be managed? How can a teacher organize, group, and develop instruction to meet the needs of each child? React to these questions, then read the next sections for more ideas.

Skill/Strategy Groups

If you refer to the sample Summary List in Figure 6–4, you will note that many reading and study skill/strategy concentrations are listed across the top of the chart. Students who show a real need for instruction in these areas based on their individual instruction plans have been checked in pencil on the teacher's summary list. (In order for you to read the planning and column notes on this condensed-size list, notes are provided for just a few children.) Using this information, the classroom teacher can plan his direct instruction skill and strategy groups. These groups will be very different from ability groups. The focus will be on developing reading and study skills/strategies in needed areas using real literature and real content assignments, using readers' existing strategies, and involving readers in reflecting on strategies they each use to solve problems. The teacher will meet with skill/strategy groups according to the weekly schedule and based on how often these groups need to work on their strategy development with the teacher. When a child no longer needs direct instruction in an area, he will be able to leave the group. Based on ongoing assessments of all children, if a child needs to be added to a group, she will be invited to join. Between direct instruction sessions, these children will focus on follow-up strategy assignments the teacher makes and their independent reading pursuits. Overall,

Writers workshops relate
Choice Lit circles

the goal of these groups will always be to foster fluency, comprehension, and the reading independence of all learners.

    Let's look at the skill/strategy groups, and the members of each, in this hypothetical combination class of second and third grades. The information in Figure 6–4 has been used to form the groups.

Phoneme-Grapheme	Amy Emily Latoya Melissa
	(for sight word and fluency development)
	Caryl (for phonics—noting medial letters and sounds)
Syntactic Awareness*	Amy Emily Jesus Latoya Melissa Raul
Semantic Development*	Amy Caryl Jesus Martin Raul
	Billy Emily Latoya Melissa

*(Note: Because of the interdependence of syntax and semantic strategies—they are both context strategies—it is often easiest and best to work with them together. Whenever possible, the teacher will do so. Children with stronger semantic strategies will be able to use those to support their syntax development. The focus in all three of the word-recognition development groups [phoneme-grapheme, syntactic awareness, and semantic development] will be to facilitate and further the fluency and independence of the readers in these groups.)

Metacognitive Development	Amy Charles Chris Freddy Geoff Latoya
	Kelly Maria
Schemata Development	Amy Jesus Latoya Maria Raul

(Note: These children were found to have very limited schemata for many concepts and words that most children in this age group seemed to have some schemata for. Therefore, this group may need more special attention when new content units/vocabulary are introduced in class. This group may meet on those occasions as a pre-meeting to the whole class introductory session on the new unit.)

Noting/Recalling Details   Amy   Billy   Caryl   Kenny   Martin
Sequence of Events
(Note: Most of the children in these groups had difficulty giving full retellings as well as difficulty with specified explicit/literal comprehension questions.)

Cause-and-Effect Analysis	Billy	Charles	Courtney	Freddy	Geoff	Kristy
Making Inferences	Billy	Charles	Courtney	Freddy	Geoff	Kristy
Making Predictions from Text	Billy	Charles	Courtney	Geoff		
Drawing Conclusions	Billy	Charles	Courtney	Freddy	Geoff	Kristy

Summarizing Information	Billy	Courtney	Geoff	Vince	
Using the Library	Charles	Manuel	Mary	Kenny	Vince
Outlining Information from Text	Charles	Kenny	Mary	Vince	
Studying for a Test	Charles	Kenny	Mary	Vince	
Reading Maps, Graphs, Graphic Aids in Text	Mary	Vince			
Taking Notes from Text	Kenny	Mary	Vince		
Using the Dictionary	Emily	Jesus	Kenny	Latoya	Melissa

(For Emily, focus on learning new vocabulary and checking the meaning of words to help with semantic strategy development.)

Reading Textbook Chapters　Billy　Geoff　Kenny　Manuel　Mary　Vince

You probably noticed that Emily is in the phoneme-grapheme strategy group, but only meets with that group when the focus is on sight-word development and fluency. (Emily's teacher recommended that Emily not focus on phonics, because she had been overrelying on phonics to the exclusion of all other word recognition and analysis strategies.) Emily is also in the syntactic awareness and the semantic development strategy groups. (Emily's teacher recommended that Emily receive direct instruction on the use of syntactic and semantic clues, which are context clues. She also recommended that Emily receive help developing new vocabulary, which is part of semantic development. Emily's teacher wants Emily to eventually use all of the cue system strategies to develop into a fluent and independent reader. She is just at the beginning stage of this.) In order to help Emily's vocabulary development and to assist her in verifying the meanings of words she encounters or uses in her readings and writings, she is also in the dictionary skills group.

Freddy is in strategy groups that focus on metacognitive awareness development, cause-and-effect analysis, making inferences, and drawing conclusions. (Freddy's teacher recommended that he receive direct instruction on these higher-order comprehension strategies.) When the same children are in more than one group, the teacher may want to combine the instructional focus sessions to include a broader range of skills and strategies.

It should be pointed out that even when the focus is on developing use of a particular skill or strategy, an equal emphasis is on reading, and understanding and enjoying the literature being read. The teacher uses the literature as an opportunity for modeling and discussing the use of the focus skill or strategy(ies). During all strategy instruction, the teacher encourages children to take advantage of their existing strategy strengths as they work on developing other strategies. The emphasis is on reflecting on the skills and strategies children use as opposed to drilling on isolated skills. So, for instance, one of Emily's strengths is that she knows that sounding out words (phonics) is a way to figure out words, and, in fact, she's been relying on only that. When she works in the syntax and semantic strategy groups, the teacher needs to let Emily use her strength in phonics as a means of self-checking that her new syntactic and semantic strategy guesses actually fit the way the word looks and sounds. Emily should also be given opportunities to reflect on how she figured out an unknown word using her existing and developing strategies. (See Chapter 8 for a strategy lesson that Ms. Gregg developed for Emily.)

Consider and React 6–5

What do you think? Can skill and strategy instruction be combined and balanced with real reading activity and enjoyment of literature? Can teachers help students develop certain strategies and use their existing strengths as resources?

Special Interest and Motivation Groups

Special interest and motivation groupings are based on assessing children's interests, attitudes, and motivations as they pertain to reading. Many children get hooked on reading because it gives them an opportunity to pursue a special interest. Sometimes immature readers are not sure what they are interested in reading; however, once children have an opportunity to meet with whatever special interest groups they would like, they often realize existing interests or discover new ones. As with all the other groups, these groups will change—in this case, as often as children indicate a lack of interest or a new interest. As with other classroom groups, some children will obviously be in more than one interest group. In order to keep the groups vital and interesting, the teacher needs to be sure that groups have access to a large and rich selection of narrative and expository books, magazines, and short stories on their interest topic. Group members can take some of the responsibility by finding books in the school and public library and sharing them in the group. (Teachers could consult such sources as the Children's Book Council's [CBC] and International Reading Association's [IRA]; Harris's, 1997, *Using Multiethnic Literature in the K-8 Classroom*; Post's 2000, *Celebrating Children's Choices*; and Stroll's, 1997, *Magazines for Kids and Teens* to help them locate books and materials that children will enjoy. Each year the IRA and the CBC also publish a Children's Choices list of favorite books. The annotated list for the year is published in October by the IRA in *The Reading Teacher* journal, and single-copy reprints can be ordered for a nominal postage/handling charge.)

Note the listing of special interest/motivation groups from the class represented in Figure 6–4.

Animals/Pets	Amy	Caryl (particularly cats and dogs)	Courtney	Jackie (particularly dogs)	Latoya			
Sports	Courtney	Freddy (mostly baseball)	Jackie	Kenny	Manuel	Mitchell	Patricia	Vince
Adventure Stories	Manuel	Martin	Raul	Vince				
Fairy Tales/ Folktales	Andrea	Carmen	Caryl	Freddy	Maria	Patricia		
Mysteries	Andrea	Courtney	Geoff	Manuel	Michelle	Vince		
Exploring New Reading Interests	Chris	Emily	Freddy	Kelly	Kristy	Mary	Michelle	Mitchell

(Note: The teacher thought that these children, in particular, would benefit from developing a greater interest in reading. This group will focus on finding literature to spark their interests.)

Note that Emily and Freddy are both in the group that will explore and develop new reading interests based on their teachers' recommendations. Also, because of Freddy's existing interests in baseball and folktales, he is in two other special interest groups. These groups—along with other groups such as the literature and author preference groups, peer and authoring groups, and the content study groups mentioned in the sections that follow—are examples of **cooperative learning groups.** Cohen (1994) defines cooperative learning as students working together in a group small enough that everyone can participate on a collective task that has been clearly assigned. Students are expected to carry out their task without the teacher's direct and immediate supervision. Cohen differentiates these groups from groups such as reading strategy groups, which are formed to aid teacher-directed instruction (p. 3).

Although there is clearly no one way to approach organizing and managing cooperative learning groups, my review of some of the suggestions made by others on cooperative learning (e.g., Cohen, 1994; Galda, Cullinan, & Strickland, 1997; Pappas, Kiefer, & Levstik, 1999; Templeton, 1995) has helped me devise the following recommendations.

1. Be sure your classroom organization will facilitate cooperative learning; arrange desks or tables into groupings that invite discussion, sharing, and working together. Leave ample space.

2. Keep the groups fairly small, with no more than about four or five children in each.

3. Give children a clear message regarding the goals to be accomplished.

4. Define group assignments and work to be completed.

5. Guide children as much as necessary as they decide who will do which tasks and who will take the role of group coordinator.

6. Set reasonable time limits to complete the work. *tough*

7. Use children's interests and other meaningful indicators to group children for a common purpose, but strive for groups that are heterogeneously mixed with regard to linguistic and cognitive strategies, academic achievement, and sociocultural considerations.

8. Be sure children know how they are to report their work and provide guide-lines to help them decide when it is complete.

9. Give children guidance, but try to give groups as much autonomy as possible.

10. Help children reflect on their individual contributions to the group goals, work, learning, and other accomplishments.

Consider and React 6–6

What is your experience with cooperative learning groups? Do you have any recommendations to add?

Literature Circles and Author Preference Groups

Literature circles and author preference groups are formed as the special interest groups are formed. In fact, some of the special interest groups just listed are also, literature preference groups and could be classified as either or both. However, some of the groups in this category focus on a particular author or genre of literature. For instance, students might choose to focus on short stories, comic books, plays, or biographies. Although there are many ways to organize literature circles and preference groups, Daniels (2002); Day, Spiegel, McLellan, and Brown (2002); and Hill, Noe, and Johnson (2001) present many ideas, strategies, suggestions, and forms that you may find useful.

In the Figure 6–4 sample, many children were not sophisticated enough to know the authors or type of books and literature they prefer. Some, however, had read or had heard read aloud Dr. Seuss or Judy Blume, and they were already hooked on these authors. Teachers should keep in mind that getting children hooked on a certain author can be very desirable. Eventually, children will exhaust the possibilities with one author and move on to another. The important thing is the experience of not wanting to put down a book, of learning that reading a book can equal or surpass the satisfaction one gets from a favorite television show or movie. Here are two author groups that would be initially formed from the sample in Figure 6–4.

Judy Blume Author Preference   Andrea   Jesus   Michelle   Patricia
Dr. Seuss Author Preference   Amy   Jesus   Latoya   Melissa

Peer and Authoring Groups

As the name implies, these groups are **peer groups,** or groups of children of the same age who meet to help each other with specific work, readings, or assignments. They will involve some teacher organization and direction, but not necessarily teacher-directed instruction. Teachers can form these groups based on any projects, interests, or observed needs. Leal (1993) and Wood, Roser, and Martinez (2001) show that when peer groups discuss books and other literature they are reading, major benefits and thought-provoking discussions emerge. Authoring groups are also a particularly helpful form of peer grouping. In these groups, children can perfect their ideas and writing as well as get editorial help from their peers. Many books have been published regarding the advantages and use of writing groups and could be consulted for their wealth of ideas (e.g., see Cramer, 2001; and Spandel, 2001).

Guided Reading Groups

What about "guided reading" groups? What are they, and what do they involve? The specific answers given will really depend on the philosophy and beliefs of who is answering these questions. However, we can define **guided reading groups** generically as flexible reading groups in which the teacher guides students through the reading of the text or story for a meaningful reading experience, and provides necessary support and modeling along the way. Using this generic definition, we can say that *all* of the teacher-directed flexible reading groups already described in this chapter involve a guided reading experience *and all* of the assessment and analysis ideas described and sampled in Chapters 3 through 5 of this book would support and provide important information to teachers using guided reading. Additionally, in Chapter 8 you will find many teacher-strategy lessons that fit this definition of guided reading and a list of criteria to help guide your instructional decisions.

There are, though, differing adaptations of guided reading, again depending on the teacher's philosophy and beliefs. The two dominant views are briefly depicted here with the main difference pointed out.

1. Guided reading using leveled texts is very popular and has wide support (see, for example, Fawson & Reutzel, 2000; Fountas & Pinnell, 1996, 1999; Peterson, 2001; Rog & Burton, 2001/2002; Weaver, 2000). This view contains all of the elements of the generic definition given for "guided reading" and *adds* the idea that the guided reading will be done using appropriate leveled books matched to the students' individual reading levels. (Note: *These* reading levels are *not* necessarily the "ability levels" discussed in Chapter 2. Reading levels can be determined in many ways.)

2. Guided reading using a variety of texts that have not necessarily been "leveled" (for example, see Opitz & Ford, 2001). This view contains all of the elements of

the generic definition given for "guided reading" *without* the need for grouping children based on leveled texts.

Optiz and Ford (2001, pp. 2–4) emphasize that guided reading is planned, intended, focused instruction, with the ultimate goal of fostering independent readers. They also emphasize the following principles of guided reading:

- All children have the ability to become literate.
- All children must be taught by skilled teachers.
- The goal of guided reading is to help children become independent readers.
- Guided reading is only one component of an effective reading program—students must also have opportunities to be read to by the teacher and to read independently.
- Reading for meaning is the primary goal.
- Children learn to read by reading.
- Children need to become metacognitive readers.
- To become independent, students need to develop self-monitoring reading strategies.
- All children need to be exposed to higher-level thinking activities.
- Children need to experience the joy and delight of reading.

Personally, I lean toward the second view of guided reading because it is a "better fit" with my own beliefs and the context of instruction with which I am most comfortable. However, I certainly acknowledge that the texts and books selected for the instruction of the various and diverse children in your classroom *are* important. (This has already been illustrated by the two sample analysis and program of instruction reports included in Chapter 5.) In the sections that follow, methods and sources for determining the appropriateness of texts and books are provided.

Leveled Texts   **Leveled texts** are books and texts that have been ordered according to their difficulty for readers. The texts are then usually "matched" to particular readers. As mentioned in the previous section, texts can be leveled and/or matched in many ways. There is no "just one way" to level and/or match texts and readers. Below are a few ways that are currently used:

1. Some publishers level texts and books to grade level designations. Often students are identified as reading at a certain grade level on a standardized test and then are "matched" to the publishers' designated materials. (See Chapter 2 for a discussion regarding this and the problems associated with ability grouping.)

2. Some teachers use informal reading inventories (IRIs) to determine students' independent, instructional, and frustration level, after considering their word recognition and their comprehension of sampled texts. This information is then often used to "match" students to publishers' designated materials. (See Chapter 3 for details on using an IRI.)

3. Some teachers are using the systems or levels designed by others (e.g., Clay, 1993a, 2000b; also see "Running Records" in Chapter 3) and Fountas and Pinnell (1999), or using other systems to level books according to levels that have been categorized by certain characteristics that support the reading of the text for young readers (for example, by the language structure of the text). This is *not* done by grade levels; however, levels are designated by the particular system in the order of difficulty.

While there are certainly advantages to using leveled texts, their use can cause problems too. One problem is in not understanding how various texts have been leveled and in so doing assuming that all leveled texts will fit your students' needs, your needs, and the context of instruction you believe in. Another problem is when use of leveled texts has been overdone and there is more focus on the texts than on the students. The students' needs, strengths, interests, and motivations should come first. Brabham and Villaume (2002) present a very good overview of the use of leveled texts, the good news and the bad. They point out that when teachers really understand the criteria involved in leveling texts and have themselves reviewed text features, they can build an understanding that will help them further support the literacy development of their students. It seems, then, that one of the main advantages to using leveled texts is in what teachers can themselves learn as they go through the leveling process.

Other Ways of Determining the Appropriateness of Texts   There are some suggested "other ways" of determining the appropriateness of books and texts for students. These can be used on their own or in combination with some of the others listed here or with one of those indicated in the "leveled text" section. Once again, your decision and mix will be based on your beliefs, the needs of your students, and the context of instruction you are comfortable with.

1. Evaluate the books and texts yourself in light of the skills, strategies, interests, motivations, schemata, and needs of your individual students, as well as the purposes of your strategy lesson (see Chapter 8 for many strategy lesson samples).

2. Evaluate the books you suggest for individual students in light of the
   • quality of the literature
   • text features

- organization of the book
- size of print
- density of the print
- difficulty of concepts presented
- density of concepts presented
- predictability of the plot
- helpfulness of the illustrations
- helpfulness of any graphic displays

and many other features of text suggested by many reading authorities. For instance, see other suggestions in the works of Opitz and Ford, 2001; Rasinski and Padak, 2001; and Routman, 2000. Also, the detailed categories of text characteristics developed by Fountas and Pinnell (1999, pp. 18–19) would be an excellent source to give you ideas concerning other features of text you might want to consider for a particular child.

3. Teach your students a method of self-monitoring the difficulty of a book for themselves. After all, the idea is to develop readers who are self-sufficient and independent; therefore, give your students a simple tool to self-assess whether a book is just right or comfortable for them.

    I have always suggested what I call "the five-finger method." Even kindergarteners can do this, and older students in elementary and middle school don't seem to mind it, either:

- Pick out a book that you would like to read.
- Begin reading the book to yourself.
- When you come to a word you don't know and can't figure out, put one of your fingers on the word.
- Keep reading and continue to put fingers on words you don't know.
- If you use up all of your fingers and your thumb, too, on a page, you've come across five words you don't know or can't figure out. Maybe this book is too hard for you right now. If you would like to try the next page, it is okay, or maybe you want to try another book that also looks good to you.
- If students continue to use up all five fingers on pages of a book, they should be able to self-determine how appropriate it is for them.

Other Possible Groups

There is really no limit to the number or kind of groups a classroom teacher or group of children might decide to form. As stressed throughout this book, the teacher is limited only by her own philosophy and creativity, and by the needs/interests of children in her class. Teachers are encouraged to develop any groups of whatever number for whatever purpose they see a need for. (After reviewing the research on grouping, Flood et al., 1992; Harp, 1989; Opitz & Ford, 2001; Paratore et al., 1991; and Radencich & McKay, 1995, support the idea of flexible skill/strategy instructional groups for reading, as one alternative to ability grouping. Furthermore, Flood et al., 1992, suggest interest and content groups similar to those suggested in this chapter. Keegan & Shrake, 1991, suggest literature study groups; Pardo & Raphael, 1991, suggest content study groups; Rogovin, 2001, suggests research inquiry groups; and Berghoff & Egawa, 1991, suggest other interesting grouping possibilities. Additionally, Monson & Monson, 1994, report that Jerry Harste suggests that inquiry on topics that kids are genuinely interested in pursuing can become the focus of conversation, collaboration, and the research of a group, permeating their reading and writing activities. Finally, those interested in a research review of small group learning might want to consult Cohen, 1994. Readers are referred to these authors, as well as to the appendix of this book, for more ideas regarding possible groupings and related arrangements including the use of computers.)

Consider and React 6–7

What are your ideas? Are there other types of cooperative learning groups you would suggest for enhancing reading and literacy development and interests?

Qualitative Teaching Using "Real" Reading Material and "Real" Purposes

The emphasis throughout this book has been on teacher assessment and teacher intruction based on **authentic reading materials** with **authentic purposes**. This section is a reminder that anything less than real reading materials and real reading and study purposes could put an inappropriate focus on your instruction. If we concentrate on skills instruction for the sake of learning skills, then we have put a dead-end focus on skills and drills. If we use purposeful and/or enjoyable reading opportunities to further develop reading and study strategies, then we have put the focus on reading for a purpose and enjoying reading, while at the same time enhancing an important skill or strategy. Children will either perceive that reading for understanding, for research purposes, and for pleasure is the most important thing, or they will perceive that learning skills is the most important thing. How we assess, what we choose to emphasize or to give importance, and the materials we choose for our teaching will give children a memorable message. Be sure you give the message you have intended.

Reutzel and Cooter (1991) review the research and point out how little time children actually spend reading independently in typical classrooms: only seven to eight minutes per day in the primary grades, fifteen minutes per day in the intermediate grades, and only 3 percent of the school day in the junior high grades. They indicate that a big concern seems to center on making sure students use their time wisely during their reading periods. But unfortunately, this has translated into managing reading through worksheets and workbooks, rather than organizing for effective reading instruction by allowing children opportunities to take ownership of their reading time, make choices (within reason) about what they read, and providing a classroom situation and routine that encourages reading as a primary activity. Teachers must also provide the opportunities for children to regularly use and demonstrate reading strategies, respond to books, and read authentic materials.

It isn't hard to use authentic materials, purposes, and assignments. In fact, it is far easier to teach with these than with the contrived alternatives. Although there is an abundance of the latter (worksheets, basal readers, workbooks, etc.), the reality is that using them takes lots of time. This valuable time could instead be used to do real reading, research, thinking, writing, and other study related to the content units we must teach and the areas and literature that children are genuinely interested in learning, reading, and researching. If children are given more time to pursue these assignments they will see that reading is a meaningful and purposeful activity and that reading can be used to learn new information, to clarify existing information, and for pleasure and personal pursuits. More time spent on these authentic pursuits, as opposed to the contrived alternatives, means that children will have more exposure to content learning in their classroom.

Teachers can help children manage these various assignments and individual pursuits. In the next section, some suggestions are made for managing work and assignments, and for individual record keeping.

Individual Work, Assignments, and Record Keeping

Although the classroom teacher may use group instruction a lot in order to manage limited time, it is of utmost importance to make the individual child and his work your priority. It is critical to help each child be aware of the importance of his individual work, manage his assignments and projects, and keep individual records. Deciding how to do this, like everything else, is up to the teacher. Some suggestions and illustrations are listed here. Additionally, see the sample portfolio, individual work, and record-keeping forms in the appendix for more examples.

1. Teachers can develop daily and/or weekly assignment sheets that can be put in each child's mailbox, folder, or cubby or given out each morning or each week. These assignment sheets could list the work the teacher suggests for individuals for the day or week, so that each child knows what is expected of him or her. Of course, the teacher uses his weekly schedule and the plans for strategy and interest group meetings in filling out the assignment sheets. Note that, even though the teacher may use a standard form of his own design, there should be plenty of room for the teacher to also write any other assignments or comments he may have for each child. (See Figure 6–5.)

Assignment Sheet for _____Caryl_____

Day/Date ___Tuesday_____

_____ ✰ Read your selected literature.
_____ ✰ Write your reflections/ideas in your journal.
       Participate in your group meeting for:
_____ ✰ *Noting and Recalling Details*_____
_____ ✰ *Fairy Tales / Folk Tales*_____
_____   _____

_____ ✰ Work on your weekly science/social studies project.
       Do math concepts work on:
_____ ✰ *Borrowing from ten's place practice*_____

       Plan for conference meeting with teacher scheduled for:
_____ ✰ *11:30 – 11:45 a.m. (Wed.) ← Caryl is this OK with you?*
       Someone else cancelled so I have this time open.

       Other things, work, assignments, comments, suggestions:
_____ ✰ *Caryl, if you have the time today, would you also*
_____   *try to meet with Emily and help her review her*
_____   *sight words? Thanks !!*
_____   _____

Figure 6–5 Individual Assignment Sheet Example

2. Teachers can also develop a more generic method of assigning individual work for the day or week. Almost the same information suggested for the individual assignment (daily or weekly) sheets could be listed on the board each morning, or on chart paper at the beginning of each week. Children check the board to note what is assigned for the day and then do whatever assignments apply to them. For instance, the teacher might list for Monday:

    Individual Reading

    Work on Your Weekly Science/Social Studies Project

    Journal Writing

    Math Concepts (Carrying Numbers) Practice

    Strategy and Interest Group Meetings:

        Semantic Development

        Outlining Information

        Making Inferences

        Judy Blume

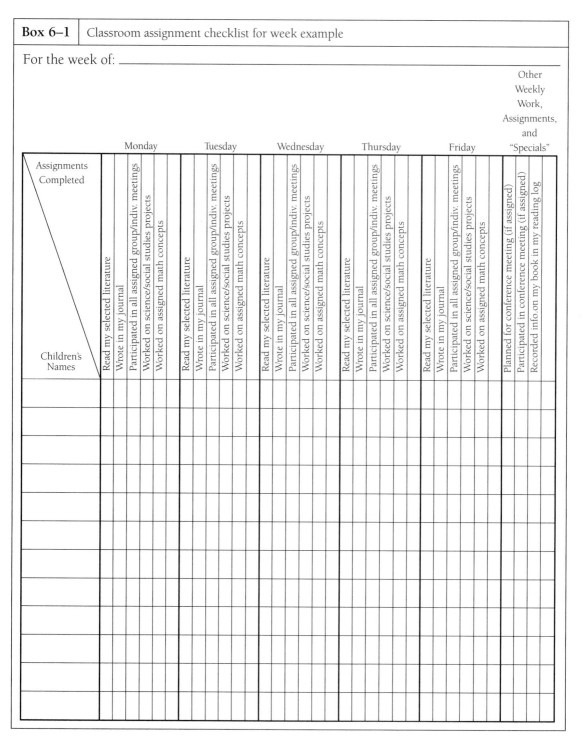

Box 6–1 | Classroom assignment checklist for week example

For the week of: _____

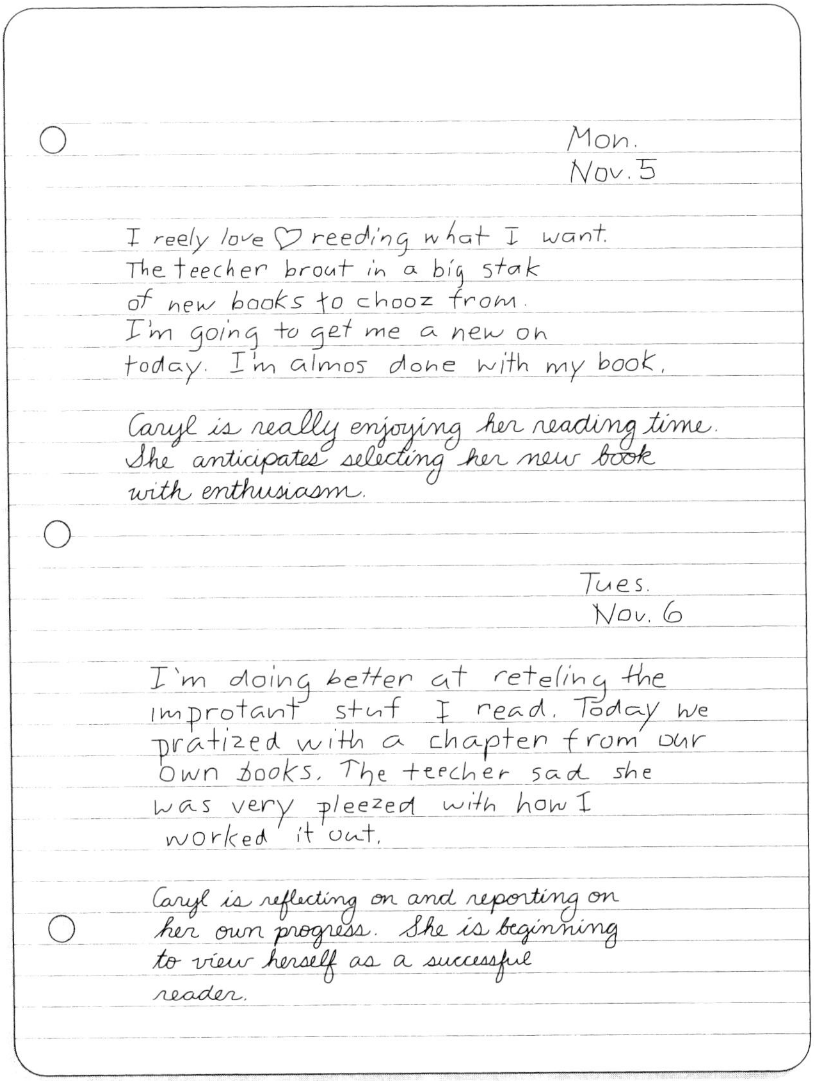
Mon.
Nov. 5

I reely love ♡ reeding what I want.
The teecher brout in a big stak
of new books to chooz from.
I'm going to get me a new on
today. I'm almos done with my book.

Caryl is really enjoying her reading time.
She anticipates selecting her new book
with enthusiasm.

Tues.
Nov. 6

I'm doing better at reteling the
improtant stuf I read. Today we
pratized with a chapter from our
own books. The teecher sad she
was very pleezed with how I
worked it out.

Caryl is reflecting on and reporting on
her own progress. She is beginning
to view herself as a successful
reader.

Figure 6–6 Sample Reflection Journal Entries

3. Teachers can also develop a classroom checklist for the day, week, or even month that children can use to check off work they have completed. In this way, both teacher and child monitor the completion of each day's work. This type of checklist can be used with or without the individual assignment sheets suggested in number 1. Additionally, these can also be developed for flexibility. Teachers can leave themselves room to add any special assignments for the day and for the week and still have a standard form from which to monitor work. (See Box 6–1.)

| **Box 6–2** | Possible reading log format example |

My Reading Log: _____

(name)

Title, Author, Publisher, Publishing Date	Type of Book (Fiction, Nonfiction, etc.)	My Thoughts/Comments About This Book:	My Recommendations About, or for, This Book:

4. Children can be given even more responsibility for their individual record keeping by keeping reflection journals of their daily work and accomplishments, by keeping a reading log of books they've finished and their evaluations of these books, and by adding especially well done pieces or examples of their work to their portfolios. Teachers can make reflection writing/self-evaluations part of the daily and/or weekly classroom routine. Likewise, the teacher can provide a format for the reading log, which children can keep in their folders or portfolios. Children can make entries whenever they are finished with a book. Teachers can encourage self-reflection and careful selection of representative work for the portfolios at all times. In the next section this will be emphasized as we discuss conferencing and monitoring development. See Figure 6–6 for an example of entries in a child's reflection journal. Also see Box 6–2 for one format of a reading log.

Conferencing, Sharing, and Monitoring Development

Even though we may have many workable classroom organization management charts and ideas, we must also schedule opportunities to meet and talk with individual children. A personal touch and individual discussions and sharing are vital to consistently monitor children's development in all aspects of their and your literacy goals. As with everything else, you will need to plan individual conferencing visits in your weekly schedule. It is optimum to have a conference with each child at least every week or two. If you plan for fifteen minutes per child, you could have a conference with each child every two weeks by setting aside about four hours each week (if you have a class of thirty children). Additionally, it is important to make the rounds each day, chatting with each child and letting the children share their work with you. These chats are best conducted as you circulate throughout the room, stopping to visit with children as they work on their various literacy projects and readings. By touching base at least once per day with each child as you move about the classroom, and by meeting with each child at least every two weeks for a fifteen-minute private conference/discussion, you will have continuous opportunities to monitor the child's development and to reevaluate instructional strategies and interests.

Searfoss (1993) recommends scheduling conferences when children are ready by establishing procedures for signing up for conference appointments. He suggests a weekly or monthly calendar posted for this purpose. The teacher can indicate the times she is available for conferences, and children can select the times and days they prefer. This gives children shared control in planning. Also, Robb (1998) is recommended for many ideas for managing reading and writing conferences for upper elementary and middle-school students.

Conferencing and Sharing

A quiet, comfortable, and private place should be found for individual conferencing. The child should bring his portfolio or folder and any reading, writing, or work he would like to share with you. You should bring anything you would like to share with the child: a book you think he might like, a piece of writing you would like to discuss with the child, and the like.

The purpose of this conference is for you and the child to take the time to reflect on his work and accomplishments over the past one or two weeks. It is a time when the teacher can praise and admire a child's efforts and work, give constructive and positive assistance, read the child's reflection journal and other writings, reevaluate the child's reading strategies by listening to his oral readings and discussing the readings together, and help the child choose pieces or examples for his portfolio or for sharing with his parents/family.

It is also a time when the child can get personal feedback from his teacher, share his thoughts and ideas, get additional help from the teacher, let the teacher know if he is interested in joining new groups or dropping others, and reassess his own strategies, accomplishments, and literacy goals. For both the teacher and the child, the conference sharing and discussions are extremely valuable. Each will come to the meeting with his own purposes. Opportunities must be created for both teacher and child to get something he or she wants out of the meeting.

Before the conference, Siu-Runyan (1994, p. 162) suggests that each student is asked to

1. Select samples of your best work and arrange them in your portfolio or folder in whatever way that makes sense to you.

2. Think about why you selected the pieces that you did and what you want to say about them.

3. Look at all the pieces you selected and think about yourself as a reader and writer.

4. After you have thought about your development as a reader and writer, reflect on the ambitions you have for yourself and share those at our conference.

Consider and React 6–8

What is your experience with student conferencing? Do you have any suggestions you would add to Siu-Runyan's list?

Note the sample conferencing sheet (Box 6–3), which provides space for both the teacher and the child to record what each gained from the meeting, as well as some things they would like to accomplish at the next conference.

Monitoring Development and Revisiting Instructional Plans

Making the rounds, chatting, conferencing, and sharing provide excellent opportunities to monitor children's strategy development and provide new assessment information for continually rethinking instructional plans. Strategy and interest group instructional sessions are also constant sources for new assessment data. Teachers should view these opportunities as part of their ongoing assessment of individual children. While we teach

Box 6–3	A sample conferencing sheet		
Conference Sheet _____			
(date)			
(Child's Name) What I Feel Was Gained or Accomplished:	Comments My Hopes/Goals for the Next Meeting:	(Teacher's Name) What I Feel Was Gained or Accomplished:	Comments My Hopes/Goals for the Next Meeting:

children, and while we visit and conference with them, we also are assessing their development. Careful notations are important in order to document these ongoing assessments. These notations can be kept in the folders or portfolios we keep on each child. Remember the "progress notations" that Nancy Gregg and John Trainor made in their student reports (Chapter 5)? Something like this is necessary in order to monitor each child's progress. With large classes of children and numerous things going on all the time, it is not safe to rely solely on memory. The dated progress notations you write and keep in each child's folder, together with initial assessment data and instructional plans, conferencing sheets, and portfolio samples, will serve you well. It will be part of the information you and the child use to make decisions to pencil a child in or out of instruction groups; write meaningful and professional report card comments and evaluations; and have meaningful and professional conferences with the child, her family, and other professionals who are interested in the child.

Reporting to Parents/Family Members

Parents and other family members play a key role in a child's emerging literacy and continuing development, as well as in your assessment of the child. In Chapter 3 it was suggested that parents/family members are important sources of information about the child and that their beliefs about literacy shape much of the child's literacy experience. Their continuing understanding of the child's work, strategies, goals, and needs, and of your assessment and evaluation system, are very important to your success and the child's. Family involvement is so critical that the U.S. Congress and the Department of Education have continued to promote partnerships with parents and information for parents to increase their participation in their children's education (e.g., see U.S. Department of Education, *Community Update*, 2001a), and as pointed out earlier in this book, the IRA (2002) has continued to emphasize the importance of family and school partnerships as well. Paris (1991) indicates that teachers need to develop a system of record keeping and of sharing the information with students and parents as part of using portfolios and authentic assessments in the classroom. This is equally important no matter what sampling and data collection methods you are using. This section, therefore, is devoted to discussion and ideas related to conferencing and sharing with parents/family members; to communications to and from the family regarding the child's work, report card comments, and grading; and to using some alternative reporting methods and evaluations when reporting to parents/families.

Reciprocal Conferencing and Sharing with Parents/Family

Most parents/families want to be involved, informed, and have a say in their child's education—particularly their child's reading, study, and other literacy development. Often they do not know how to get involved or what they can do (Flippo & Branch, 1985;

Rasinski, 1994; Unwin, 1995); but parents, "no matter what their social or economic standing, have the potential for making an educational difference in their children's lives when offered sincere opportunities for becoming an important member of the education team" (Come & Fredericks, 1995). Classroom teachers can provide a means for this involvement and sharing to take place. Edwards, McMillon, Turner, and Laier (2001) point out the report by Taylor, Pressley, and Pearson (2000) and their own studies of the effectiveness of networking with parents to show that marshalling parents and teachers together around the common goal of their children's literacy development works. The reciprocal conferencing and sharing suggested here should further the child's development, the parents' involvement, and the teacher's continual assessment of the child's progress, needs, and strategies. **Reciprocal conferencing and sharing** is a process that involves the sharing of information and perceptions between two or more mutually interested individuals for the purpose of benefiting the child and empowering the family, child, and teacher. Here are some suggestions for using reciprocal conferencing and sharing in your classroom.

1. Plan to involve parents/family members in mutually monitoring, along with you and the child, the child's reading, and other skill and strategy development. You can do this by having the child write to her family, inviting them to a reciprocal conference and sharing time. (When and how often you schedule conferences will depend on your schedule and other planning considerations.)

2. Decide with the child what might be important to share with her family. In what ways can she show her family her developing strategies and her reading and study development? Let the child suggest selections from her portfolio and explain why these items would be beneficial to share with her family.

3. As part of your planning with the child, develop an agenda or plan of what you and she would like to share with the family. You and the child can write the agenda together.

4. Allow the child to be an equal participant in the conference. The child can show and explain her portfolio items, and explain evidence of her developing skills and strategies and existing strengths according to the agenda you and she developed. The child can also share her and your literacy goals and what you are both working on according to her instructional plan. The teacher can make suggestions to the child during the conference in order to help her report her development and not forget an agenda item; for example, "Mary, don't forget to show your grandmother the report you researched in the library, the one you did that so well displays your very fine developing library research skills. Why don't you review that with her now?"

    Of course, during the reciprocal conference and sharing the teacher should be an equal partner. The teacher can answer family questions, supplement something the child has shown or discussed, and summarize the child's progress. Likewise, family members are equal participants. Family members can ask questions of the child or teacher, discuss things that they have observed about the child's work and progress, and suggest ways they can become more involved or help with their child's literacy development. The teacher can facilitate this process by ensuring that everyone has equal time and an equal opportunity to share, and by asking leading questions to keep everyone focused. (Tierney et al., 1991, emphasize that a spirit of ownership and empowerment should be conveyed to everyone concerned with the child: the parents/family members, the teacher, and, of course, the child.)

5. As a conclusion to the reciprocal conference and sharing, the child, family, and teacher can fill out an evaluation sheet in order to express their thoughts regarding the merits and accomplishments of the sharing. It is also desirable for the teacher to list any outcomes or plans made as a result of the conference. The sheet should be dated, and photocopies or carbon copies of the evaluation sheet should be given to the child and to the family. One copy should be retained by the teacher and kept in the child's portfolio or folder. See the sample Reciprocal Conferencing and Sharing Evaluation Sheet (Box 6–4).

Letters, Journals, and Other Home Communications

In addition to the suggested reciprocal conferencing and sharing, there are other ways of keeping in touch with and involving parents. Several are listed. You certainly will be able to think of others, or you can combine these suggestions with ideas gleaned from this book or from your own experiences in the classroom.

1. Teachers and children can plan a family meeting at the beginning, middle, and end of the year. At the beginning of the year, the focus of the meeting may be on soliciting parents' help, informing parents of your classroom organization, explaining your philosophy, and explaining how you will assess and work with children throughout the school year. The midyear meeting could focus on soliciting parents' input, updating parents on changes and developments in the classroom, and continuing to solicit family help and active involvement. Year-end meetings might focus on how families can aid their child's development over the summer.

2. Children can develop and write a periodically published class newspaper informing their parents/families of what is going on in the classroom.

3. Teachers can develop and write their own periodically published newsletter for parents or have a column in the children's newspaper where the teacher can report his news to parents.

4. Teachers can share special literature developed for parents by providing copies of it or by summarizing the information and letting parents know how to

Box 6–4	Reciprocal conferencing and sharing evaluation sheet

_____
date

My Thoughts Regarding the Accomplishments of the Sharing	My/Our Thoughts Regarding the Accomplishments of the Sharing	My Thoughts Regarding the Accomplishments of the Sharing
_____ : (Child's Name)	_____ : (Family Member's Name)	_____ : (Teacher's Name)

Plans/outcomes decided as a result of this sharing conference:

_____

_____

_____

_____

_____

_____

_____

order it or where to find it in libraries, bookstores, and so on. For example, International Reading Association's (IRA) publication, *Reading Today*, free to IRA members, has a "Parents and Reading" section in every issue. IRA also publishes free brochures and other materials for parents. Many are available in Spanish (send a self-addressed postage-paid envelope for single copies of the brochures). The association also has a parent series with booklets available at a small cost. All of these materials can be ordered by writing to International Reading Association, 800 Barksdale Road, P.O. Box 8139, Newark, DE 19714, USA (or on-line, at *www.bookstore.reading.org*). IRA and the Children's Book Council also publish yearly lists of carefully selected trade books that children enjoy. These lists are recommended for teachers and parents and, like many of the IRA publications for parents, single copies are free with just a nominal charge for postage/handling; bulk copies can also be ordered at a reasonable price.

The ERIC Clearinghouse on Reading, English, and Communication has published a book designed to help Spanish-speaking parents get involved in the education of their children. *Let's Read! 101 Ideas to Help Your Child Learn to Read and Write* by Behm and Behm (1993) is available in a bilingual edition that has English and Spanish versions on facing pages. Likewise, many other books are available to provide information to parents of babies (Butler, 1998, *Babies Need Books*), young children (Butler & Clay, 1987 a, b; Campbell, 1998), and older school-age youngsters (Power, 1999) to promote literacy development. (Power's book contains both English and Spanish reproducibles.)

5. Children, parents, and teachers can use journals to share their thoughts and to reflect on each other's responses. These can be used in many ways. For instance, Fuhler (1994) reports the use of literature response journals by her students and their families. Parents and children read the same book, each reflecting on the reading, and then write their ideas in a mutual journal. These journals not only inform and involve families in their children's learning, but provide valuable assessment information for all concerned. Shockley (1994) reports the use of home-school journals, too. She uses them to stay in touch with parents/families, to invite sharing of family stories, and to solicit family reflection on the child's literacy and reading of books.

6. Finally, teachers and children can write notes and letters to families informing them of special events, special study units, special assignments, special accomplishments, or special needs. Flippo and Smith (1990) developed a Home Letter Example and discussion to illustrate how home letters can foster family involvement as well as update families regarding their children's class activities, study units, and assignment needs. (See the example in Box 6–5.)

good example

Box 6–5	Home letter example

Dear Parents:

Our class theme for the coming month will be "The Universe." Classroom lessons and activities will relate to this theme. During the month, students will be learning about the planets in our solar system and many aspects relating to our universe.

This is a large topic. We will be focusing on it in all areas of learning and communication. Your child will be reading and writing about our universe, as well as talking about and listening to information on this topic.

This unit will be educational, interesting, and timely as we will touch upon such things as the earth's ozone layer, the importance of the spacing between planets, and the recent discoveries made possible by missions of the shuttle spacecrafts.

As you can see from the following objectives, we have a full and exciting month ahead of us.

1. Students will learn the names, locations, and physical makeup of the planets in our solar system.
2. Students will learn to calculate distances between planets.
3. Students will become aware of the earth's atmosphere and the importance of environmental concerns.
4. Students will further develop their research and oral presentation skills by completing a research project and presenting it.
5. Students will listen to and talk with experts who deal with various aspects of our universe.

In order for us to accomplish these objectives, your child and I need your help. Your child will bring home a weekly activity sheet. The activities on these sheets will require minimal time on your part, but they will prove invaluable to your child's growth during the month's study of the universe.

With this in mind, the first home activity is described below. This home activity involves watching the shuttle landing which will occur on April 1. Please assist your child in recording the time of the landing, the length of the flight, and any information you can help your youngster discover regarding the purpose of the mission. Remember that this does not need to be an extensive project, but instead an enjoyable excursion into the realm of space with your child. The information you record will enable your child to be an active and informed participant in our classroom activities.

I appreciate your help and time spent on these home activities. In future weeks, I will be sending you additional home activity sheets for this unit. I hope you will enjoy participating in your child's education as much as your child will enjoy your involvement.

Sincerely,
Mrs. Smith

Source: "Home Letter Example" adapted from "Encouraging Parent Involvement Through Home Letters" by R. F. Flippo and J. A. Smith in *The Reading Teacher,* 44 (4). Copyright © 1990 by the International Reading Association. All rights reserved. Reprinted by permission.

Obviously, as in other communications with parents/families, letters should be purposeful but also considerate, positive, respectful, and encouraging. Even when there is a serious problem, positive solutions and ideas can best be fostered when the problem is approached in a positive way. For additional ideas concerning communications with families and other positive home and school connections, books by Power (1999); Rasinski (1995); Rockwell, Andre, and Hawley (1996); and Shockley, Michalove, and Allen (1995) are suggested. And, an article by Youngs (2002) provides more suggestions for involving and communicating with parents. Report cards also can be used as a positive communication tool. In the section that follows, report cards are discussed and applications and communications with parents/families are suggested.

Report Card Comments and Grading

Many classroom teachers feel trapped by the report card format and grading requirements of their school systems. Using letter grades or percentage grades, or even using rating scales such as 1–5, often cause teachers to spend many painful, soul-searching hours trying to come up with and justify a grade that will be fair to the child, maintain the child's self-confidence, and yet conform to the school requirements. It is unfortunate that in so many school systems we are locked into this type of reporting procedure, one that de-emphasizes the strategies and accomplishments of the child and instead seeks to quantify what cannot be fairly and accurately quantified. However, if you must use traditional report cards and grading systems, then do your best to supplement this with other ways of reporting progress and sharing goals and development with the child and family, such as those suggested in the previous sections, and the self-evaluations and alternative evaluation ideas suggested in the next section.

Consider and React 6–9

What is your experience with report card grading problems? Do you feel "trapped" by the format or grading requirements? What solutions have you found? Read the ideas that follow and see what you might add.

When preparing report cards, make good use of the teacher's comment section by using the space to show each child's skill and strategy strengths and to emphasize that grades do not tell the entire progress story. You can indicate that you are attaching a letter or some other evaluations to supplement the report card and to highlight the child's specific strategy use, development, accomplishments, and needs. In this way, you can emphasize your qualitative analyses and instructional planning for the child, and de-emphasize some of the quantitative information in the report card, which, when provided alone, can often be misleading. The additional evaluations you include should fit your individual philosophy, program emphases, and the perceived needs of your students.

On a more positive note, even though traditional report cards are still predominant, many more progressive schools are using different types of reporting and evaluation procedures with their students. Some involve the teacher writing more lengthy evaluations of the child's development, along with the elimination of letter and number grades. In the section that follows, more ideas for reporting children's progress are listed and some are sampled; these self-evaluations and other alternative evaluation ideas can also be used to supplement the traditional report card when a traditional report card is required. (Readers might also be interested in reading Jongsma, 1991, who discusses problems associated with grading and gives some suggestions for change, and Azwell & Schmar, 1995, who present many alternative ideas. Additionally, Falk, 2000, and Trumbull and Farr, 2000, each present in-depth views and discussions of grading and reporting students' progress using standards.)

Self-Evaluations and Alternative Evaluation Ideas

Several alternative evaluation ideas are suggested here. Each can be modified or can be combined with each other and with any other evaluation procedures you may want to use.

1. Journals and the students' written reflections and evaluations of their own work can be summarized and reported to parents/families. Children can write these summaries with some help from the teacher. The summaries, along with samples from children's portfolios or folders, can provide convincing documentation of skill/strategy use and accomplishments. Additionally, children who work with various strategy and interest groups could also do peer evaluations to support the child's accomplishments. (Hansen, 1992, 1998, describes use of students' evaluations of their reading and writing, and could be consulted for more ideas.)

2. Hill (1991) suggests goal-based assessments as a viable option. Children can develop lists of what they specifically wish to improve, setting literacy goals for themselves. The teacher also develops a list of what she wants children to accomplish, setting additional goals for children in the class. Later, children develop a list of what they can now do, assessing to what extent they have met their own and the teacher's goals. The list of the child's literacy achievements can be continually updated.

3. Self-evaluation report cards can be developed by the children. Each child can either design and develop his own unique report card, highlighting and commenting on the kinds of work and strategies he wishes to emphasize and report, or children can follow the same report card format used at their school, grading themselves and making comments regarding their own progress. Diana

Report for: Melanie
Term 2　　　　　Form 1 R B

Subject	Comment	Grade	Attitude
Mathematics	Melanie is a hard worker, though when she doesn't want to work, she doesn't work as well	B+	~~2~~ 3
Spelling	Melanie is a good speller although she could do better	A-	2 ~~X~~
Unit Work	Melanie is a reluctant worker in unit work, and only does well in things that interest her	C	~~X~~ 4
Reading	Melanie is a keen reader and is often with a new book.	A++	1
Poetry	Melanie is almost as good in poetry as in reading.	A-	2
English	Melanie enjoys english and wishes to do her best here.	A	1
Clothing	Melanie is a good worker in this area.	A	2

Subject	Comment	Grade	Attitude
Physical Education	Melanie is very reluctant and does not do her best.	C-	5
Music	Melanie misses a lot because of Speech so I cannot say how she works.		
Art	Melanie is a good worker but a little slack on book work.	A-	2
Home Economics	Melanie is a good worker and I'm pleased with her work.	A	~~X~~ 1
Science	Melanie is a little bored in my class and she could do better	~~X~~ C	3
General Comment	Mrs Robilliard Melanie is a good worker though she could do better in some fields. *Mrs Robilliard* Headmistress — Though I have not met your girl, I am pleased with this report. *Headmistress*		

Figure 6–7 Student's Self-Assessment Report Card (by Melanie)

Report for: Greer   Age: 11y
Term 2   Form: 1R

	Grade	Attitude	
Reading	B+	2	Greer I think enjoys reading a lot I think Greer has a good capability although she could do better.
Clothing	B–	3	Greer likes clothing as she said, Although would like to have been faster with her work.
Spelling	C–	3	Greer is not one of the best spellers although she could do better if she tried.
Unit Work	B–	3	Greer likes unit work, but she only does more work when she has to when something interests her.
Religous Studies	A+	2	This is one of her favourite classes, she also tries hard and has a nice neat book always.
Science	A	2	Science is a good subject for Greer because she tries hard and listens well & is fun.

	Grade	Attitude	
P.E.	B	3	Greer likes P.E. a lot although sometimes she has had enough In P.E. she tries hard too.
Maths	C	3	She (Greer) likes maths alot although it can be very frustrating. She tries hard some most of the time and has a good capability to do better.)
Friend-ship		3	In friendship I try to be fair, understanding and appreciative and I get on well with Rebecca D
English	C–	3	I don't usually like English although some times its all right (I suppose)
Art	A	3	I love art. Its fun & interesting although I wish we had more time in ART It is great!!
Home Economics	B	3	Home Economics is so good fun. I think I am a bit noisy some times though.
Teachers Comment			Greer is lovely & cheerful although things like that won't get her anywere in this world. She has to hear brains. She has got the capability, why doesn't she use it? J Robilliard

Figure 6–8 Student's Self-Assessment Report Card (by Greer)

Robilliard, a teacher of Form 1 (in the United States, this would be Grade 6) in the Intermediate Department at St. Margaret's school in Christchurch, New Zealand, shares her students' self-evaluation report cards in Figures 6–7 and 6–8. Note that Mrs. Robilliard's students used the same basic report card format and grading system as the one used at her school. These report cards can be sent home along with the required report card and the teacher's supplementary evaluation or letter to parents.

4. Children can also evaluate the teacher. Analysis of these teacher evaluations can provide additional assessment opportunities, indicating to what extent you are meeting children's individual needs, interests, and goals. Diana Robilliard's students each give their teacher a report card evaluating her effectiveness. Mrs. Robilliard bravely accepts and uses this as part of the reciprocal evaluation and sharing process in her classroom. (Parents could also be invited to give you a report card!) See Figure 6–9 to see what grades Mrs. Robilliard gets.

    It is my belief that children's self-evaluation report cards, as well as the other evaluations by students, provide valuable assessment information for the teacher.

Consider and React 6–10

What do you believe? What can you learn about Greer and Melanie from their self-evaluation report cards? Also consider the report card Catherine wrote on Mrs. Robilliard. What can you learn about Catherine from her evaluation of her teacher? Are these valuable assessment data? Why?

5. Families can also be asked to evaluate their children's progress from one report card period to another. The families' written evaluations can be kept in the children's folders in order to monitor each family's impressions of its child's growth. Teachers may also want to use these evaluations to further document children's growth for school accountability purposes. Teachers can develop their own rating scales, questionnaires, or observation guides for these evaluations, highlighting the areas or strategies they have been emphasizing. Fredericks and Rasinski (1990) designed one such scale asking parents to rate their child's reading growth by responding to such items as "My child understands more of what he/she reads" and "My child enjoys being read to by family members." Parents are asked to indicate the extent that they agree with these statements, and to note any comments, strengths they see, or concerns they have. (See Box 6–6 for my adaptation of this parent/family evaluation material.)

Report for Mrs. D. Rotilliard by Catherine
St. Margareta College
Tuesday 28th June
By kind permission of: Mrs. D. Rotilliard

Subject	Comment	Grades	Attitude
Mathematics	She teaches us very well and is a whole lot more knowledgable in this subject than she says she is. Very good.	B	1
Reading	Mrs. Rotilliard is a very good teacher in this subject. Unfortunately Mrs R. doesn't choose books that interest us much to read aloud to 1R2	C	1
Soc. Studies	Mrs Rotilliard has a wonderful imagination in what activities we accomplish/ accomplish accomplish do in each subject. Excellent!!!	A	1
Oral Work	Mrs. Rotilliard must have liked like games, etc. nearly as much as our daily ton of work because of this unusuary yet brilliant and wonderful of this subject. I think all of from one R look foward to this at the end of the week.	A+	1
Fairness	I think that Mrs. Rotilliard is a reasonably fair person as fair teachers go. Fantastic!!!! Brilliant!!!	A	1
Sympathy	Mrs. Rotilliard is a very sympathetic person if we took approximatley enough as we mournfully stop forward to inform her that our pet budgie just died and our Sikés grandmother had a fit and quietly ate our maths book and you didn't know what on earth a gold fish looked like so you couldn't very easily draw one for Homework !!	B	1
Organization	Mrs. Rotilliard is extremely good at organizing future work, and keeping keeping good order in the classroom, she is readily alert and read to pounce on anyone that whos chatting	A	1
Consideration for others	Mrs Rotilliard considers other in a way that many of FIR like (e.g.- private words, desk arrangements) Keep up the good work.!!!	A+	1
Compatition etc.	Mrs Rotilliard has a range of compatitions and "mark on" lists up one sleeve and a range of chocolate fish up the other, to be frank, Very Good.!!!!	B+	2
Formulness	Mrs Rotilliard is not very formal which I think is absolutly great. It is one of her most fantastic ability. Very, Very, Good.	A+	1
General Comment	This is a very very good report! Keep up the good work Mrs. Rotilliard!		

Figure 6–9 Student's Report Card Evaluation of the Teacher

Box 6–6	Parent/Family observations and evaluation

Name of Student _____ Grade _____

Parents and other family members can play an active role in evaluating their child's reading and literacy development by sharing observations with the teacher. Please circle, under each literacy activity, the words that best describe the extent you've seen your student involved in the activity. Additionally, if you have related comments, these can be very helpful. Please sign, date, and return this form to school. Thank you for your participation in evaluating your student's progress.

1. Reading a book on his/her own for pleasure
   Not at all   **Sometimes**   **More than Sometimes**   **Very Often**
   Comments: _____

2. Asking a family member to read a book to him/her
   Not at all   **Sometimes**   **More than Sometimes**   **Very Often**
   Comments: _____

3. Talking about a book that has been read
   Not at all   **Sometimes**   **More than Sometimes**   **Very Often**
   Comments: _____

4. Writing and sharing his/her own stories or ideas
   Not at all   **Sometimes**   **More than Sometimes**   **Very Often**
   Comments: _____

5. Reading books to younger or other family members
   Not at all   **Sometimes**   **More than Sometimes**   **Very Often**
   Comments: _____

6. Choosing to go to the library to select books
   Not at all   **Sometimes**   **More than Sometimes**   **Very Often**
   Comments: _____

7. Choosing to read rather than watch television or play computer games
   Not at all   **Sometimes**   **More than Sometimes**   **Very Often**
   Comments: _____

8. Seems to understand what has been read
   Not at all   **Sometimes**   **More than Sometimes**   **Very Often**
   Comments: _____

Additional observations or concerns: _____

_____

Signed by _____ Relationship to student _____

Date _____

Source: "Parent/Family Observation and Evaluation" adapted from "Working with Parents: Involving Parents in the Assessment Process" by A. D. Fredericks and T. V. Rasinski in *The Reading Teacher,* 44 (4). Copyright © 1990 by the International Reading Association. All rights reserved. Reprinted by permission.

Strategy Development and Literature Exposure for Whole Class Involvement

The focus of this book is on assessing, planning for instruction, and instructing the individual child based on his or her continuous reading and study strategy assessment information. However, we have seen that in order to accomplish this in a regular classroom, we must also be able to plan for the instruction of the entire class and find ways to organize for that instruction. Therefore, there are times when whole class involvement, activity, and cooperation will be part of every child's individual instructional plan. In the brief sections that follow, several whole class involvement activities will be highlighted. Teachers can use these along with the assessment and other teaching suggestions in this book to plan for full, balanced instruction for every child. For more information on any of these whole class activities, teachers could consult reading methods textbooks and the suggested references.

Sustained Silent Reading

Using **Sustained Silent Reading (SSR)** as part of the everyday classroom routine is an excellent way to emphasize the value you place on reading in your classroom; ensure an absolutely quiet, uninterrupted time for everyone to read; and provide an opportunity for you to model reading behavior. SSR time means that for this particular period of time, everyone in the classroom (including the teacher, visiting parents, guests or observers, teacher aides, etc.) must read. Absolutely nothing is to interrupt this time. Children and teacher take out whatever book or other piece of literature they want to read and read silently. When the time is up, everyone puts that reading material away and continues with other work. It is best to start SSR at the same time each day so that everyone knows what to expect. You might want to begin with a ten- to fifteen-minute time period, and work up to a longer period of time, like twenty to thirty minutes, depending on the age group and what your schedule will allow. (Reutzel and Cooter, 1991, describe their use of SSR as a part of a modified reading workshop [see Atwell, 1998] approach they have designed for use with elementary schoolchildren.)

Registers/Genre Immersion and Comparative Inferencing

The idea and importance of immersion in literary **registers** (the language determined by the circumstances) and **genre** (the type or form of literary content) is fully described in the works of Cambourne (1988) and Brown and Cambourne (1987). Their classroom research in Australia using literature immersion and retelling techniques (and, eventually, comparative inferencing) with elementary grade children have unlimited possibilities for teaching and assessing in the early childhood, elementary, and even middle and high school classrooms. This section will briefly highlight how this whole class activity takes place.

     The teacher selects a narrative genre in which he immerses the entire classroom for about three weeks. For instance, Brown and Cambourne (1987) begin with fables, fairy tales, and myths. The classroom is stocked with a huge collection of this literature, and the children and teacher read nothing but fables for three or four days. Once children have had this experience with fables, the teacher has a whole class meeting, and the children discuss fables. (What makes a fable a fable?, etc.) Then, using large chart paper, the teacher solicits generated knowledge or criteria for a fable. The children are encouraged to compare their generated knowledge with a recognized authoritative source, such as an encyclopedia. Children are encouraged to write their own fables. Then, for another four days, children are immersed in fairy tales. The same procedure is used to generate their learned knowledge of fairy tales. Finally, to conclude this genre, children spend an equal amount of time reading, generating knowledge, and then writing myths.

Throughout the school year, the classroom teacher continues to immerse children in various literature for approximately three-week periods, moving from narrative to expository text. Brown and Cambourne (1987) provide examples of immersion in factual expository text, other expository text that gives directions (such as for arts and crafts projects, science experiments, recipes, etc.). They also provide samples of immersion into literature that provides powerful examples of author techniques like creating a character or developing a setting or atmosphere. Charts with criteria for all the literature studied is maintained and displayed in the classroom.

As the school year progresses, children are encouraged to compare and contrast different registers/genres. Children are given opportunities to rewrite one of their own stories from one type of language or literature into another. For instance, turn your fairy tale into a piece written in an expository factual textbook. How did you do it? What did you have to do to it? What problems did you have? What made it difficult? How did you solve the problems? Obviously, when using this powerful instructional technique, teachers can also use the discussion and children's writing as opportunities to assess each child's strategies and knowledge.

The purpose and steps to a register/genre immersion and suggested follow-up assignments are listed. Cambourne (1988) and Brown and Cambourne (1987) should be read for more depth, details, and examples.

1. The teacher's purpose is to help children develop their literacy (reading and writing) by immersing them in the registers/language (vocabulary, structure of sentences) and structures of various genres/types of literature. It is hoped that children will gain an appreciation and understanding of the literature under study, learn what readers do to read and understand that kind of literature, and learn what writers do to write in a particular register and genre.

2. To facilitate the immersion, the teacher first sets the stage for the genre and models it by demonstrating the literature. (The teacher reads and shares books in the genre with the children.)

3. For several weeks, children are encouraged to read individually in that genre, gaining exposure to other examples and models.

4. Once that is underway, the teacher sets up time for the whole class to share the readings that have been done, retelling and discussing them. This helps the children develop their thoughts, ideas, and insights into the genre.

5. Children are encouraged to write their retellings and keep journals of their insights into the genre they are reading.

6. The teacher uses the written retellings and journals during individual conferences to assess the child's understanding and to help clarify or redirect the child if needed.

7. Near the end of the immersion period, children are encouraged to individually write in the register or genre under study, developing their own story or piece in that register/genre. Children can later share and publish their pieces.

8. The teacher can use this original writing in the genre to assess the child's grasp of the register/genre under study.

9. At the end of the immersion period, the group brainstorms and generalizes a listing of the important criteria for the register/genre. These are kept on display for future discussion, reference, small group work, and comparative inferencing.

10. As the school year continues, various whole group, small group, and individual assignments and study can take place. For example:

    a. Different, previously studied registers/genres can be compared and contrasted so that children can formulate and generate their ideas concerning how reading and writing certain types of literature entails different strategies for the reader and writer.

    b. Children can rewrite their original pieces from one studied genre into another piece to fit another register/genre under study and then reflect on what had to be done to change the piece.

    c. Individual children can contract to publish a minimum of three or four writing pieces from a particular or favorite register/genre.

    d. Individual children can contract to read and share a minimum of three or four pieces of literature, each from different or favorite genres.

    e. Children can select a genre(s) and build an expertise in it by reading intensely in the genre, writing in the register/genre, compiling a reference list of the genre, and sharing their work in the genre for the rest of the class to enjoy through publishing, dramatizing, storytelling, or displaying.

Readers interested in more discussion, research, and activities relating to reading, writing, and genre development might want to read Buss and Karnowski (2000); Chapman (1996); Langer (1992); and Pappas, Kiefer, and Levstik (1999). Cullinan (1992), Rothlein and Meinbach (1996), Savage (2000), and Tomlinson and Lynch-Brown

(2002) are good sources for literature suggestions for various genre studies; and Galda and Cullinan (2002), Lukens (1995) provide extensive discussion and recommended children's literature for different genres and literary devices and registers. Finally, teachers should also be on the lookout for new compilations and books as they are published that could enhance their knowledge of children's literature.

Group Reports, Discussions, and Demonstrations on Content Literature Study

Group reports, discussions, projects, and demonstrations involving content literature study provide excellent activities in which all children in a classroom can be involved. For example, the entire class may be studying services that governments provide as part of a social studies unit. Various groups can be formed to research, study, and report or demonstrate such services. Individual children participating in these whole class projects will be using all of their reading and study strategies and other literacy strategies in order to participate. Other examples abound: Hadaway and Young (1994) discuss ways that reading and writing can be used as avenues of content learning for elementary-age students from diverse language backgrounds. Casteel and Isom (1994) show how the use of reading and writing processes enhances learning in science; and Nelson (1994) helps fifth-grade students develop historical concepts using reading and writing. Many of these ideas involve a combined use of various children's literature, trade books, and content materials to enrich the experiences and learning for students. (Also see the Rogovin, 2001, book for many more ideas.) Whether it is a content area project or a literary project, such as a play, most children will enjoy being part of a group effort and will have an opportunity to practice their strategies in an authentic way. Obviously, there are unlimited possibilities for these types of situations and projects.

Book Binding, Book Writing, and Book Sharing Activities

Children can, individually or in small groups, author and illustrate books, bind books, and share books with each other. Activities such as these provide opportunities for whole class assignments as well as for individual and small group work. Children can also share books they have read and critique or provide a recommendation to others. These activities can be part of an immersion into a specific type of literature, a content area study, or a special interest or author group. Again, there are no limits to the possibilities except those imposed by the teacher's weekly schedule.

Cross-Age Tutoring: A Shared Learning Experience

Older children helping younger children, or **cross-age tutoring** and shared learning, is not a new idea. In fact, it goes back to the one-room schoolhouse of earlier centuries. Like many other tried and true ideas, it works! If you teach an upper-grade class, each of your students can go to a primary-grade classroom each week, or as often as your schedule allows, and work with a youngster on her reading. The older students can listen to younger students read, read stories or chapter books with them, discuss the shared reading with the children, help the younger children with their writing or other literacy-related work, and mentor youngsters on various projects they can do together. The older children will further develop their own reading, learning, and organizational strategies, develop more self-confidence, and take great pride in their teaching of young children.

If you teach a lower-grade class, your children will also benefit from the cross-age tutoring and shared learning arrangement you make with an upper-grade teacher. Each of your students will have her own special buddy and helper, receive a lot of extra help and attention, enjoy the social interaction and shared reading and discussion opportunities, and develop strategies in the areas in which she works with her tutor/mentor. Of course, you will be getting lots of extra help once a week, or whenever scheduled. If you plan accordingly, you and the teacher of the older students can guide the older youngsters to work with the skills, strategies, materials, or books you think will be most helpful for both groups of students. This will be mutually beneficial to the tutors and those being tutored, and would help professionalize the tutors' attitudes to their work with their young learners. Glover and Giacalone (2001); Heath and Mangiola (1991); Leland and Fitzpatrick (1993/1994); Marden, Richard, and Flippo (1991); and many others report many positive results of their cross-age, buddy sharing and learning projects. (For more information on cross-age tutoring and shared reading and learning experiences, also read Morrice & Simmons, 1991, Rekrut, 1994, and Routman, 1994. Readers interested in learning about cross-age tutoring in linguistically and culturally diverse classrooms should consult Heath & Mangiola, 1991, and Samway, Whang, & Pippitt, 1995. Additionally, readers might want to refer to Slavin's, 1987, 1991, research and to Johnson & Johnson, 1999, on cooperative learning, and the summary of research done by Paratore et al., 1991, for findings and recommendations regarding cooperative learning, peer tutoring, and other shared learning possibilities.)

Field Trips and Other Whole Class Activities

Finally, we should not overlook field trips as potential opportunities for study and learning. As in other whole class activities, most children look forward to the excitement and involvement of field trips. Reading, writing, research, and other literacy activities often preface field trips. Field trips can tie into most content areas and many of the literary areas that children study. Children can go to a specialized museum, government service agency (the post office or fire station), a play, and so on. Again, the possibilities can be unlimited, and the potential for learning, making functional and authentic use of skills and strategies, and opportunities for authentic assessment are all there.

Summary

Being a qualitative assessor, planner, and teacher involves being a juggler of time and a super organizer. This chapter has described and illustrated some possible ways to make this happen. However, it all depends on you, the classroom teacher.

You will be the one to design an environment and organization that fits the context of instruction best for you and for all the learners in your classroom. You will do this by carefully considering your beliefs, goals, and needs, along with the special environmental requirements and needs of your students. Then you will make your choices regarding organizing and managing your classroom.

Questions for Reflection and Response

1. What type of environment and organization do you want to create in your classroom? Why? (You might want to refer to your answers for the Context of Instruction Reflection Guide on pp. 204–205.)

2. How much instructional time is really available to the classroom teacher? Using the Finding Available Instructional Times format (Figure 6–1), work it out and see.

3. How can you make the best use of the time, space, and materials available in your classroom?

4. Why are teacher planning, organization, and appropriate grouping procedures critically important in the classroom?

5. Using as many of the grouping ideas suggested in this chapter as you like, develop your own summary list for the various reading and other literacy strategies, skills, and interests you want to emphasize in your classroom. (If you are currently working in a classroom, you might want to observe and assess individual students and later pencil in their names as you make decisions about their strengths, needs, and interests.)

6. Reflect on the various instructional groups your summary list suggests. How will you be able to balance your time and facilitate these various groups?

7. What organizational, classroom management, and record-keeping ideas do you like best? Why?

8. If possible, try out a reciprocal conferencing and sharing session with a student and his/her family. How did you develop opportunities for equal participation? How did it go?

9. Which ideas for reporting and sharing students' progress with parents/families do you like best? Why? If possible, experiment with them.

10. If possible, try out genre immersion with a group of students for three to four weeks. Take notes or keep a journal recording these activities and interactions. What were your results?

CHAPTER 7

ASSESSMENT, INSTRUCTION, AND LEARNING IN THE CLASSROOM

Focus and Goals of the Chapter

- ♦ To present an overview of the circular and ongoing relationship between assessment and instruction and to provide information on beliefs and issues that are pertinent to decisions, assessment/instruction, and learning in the classroom

- • To help teachers develop an overall plan and model for diagnostic instruction in their classrooms

- • To provide guidance to help teachers consider their own specific skill and strategy instruction lessons, including plans for independent student practice and evaluation of student learning, and scaffolding or modifying instruction based on evaluation

- • To present two approaches to diagnostic teaching: the alternative method and the scaffolding method

- • To present "the negotiated curriculum," an approach to facilitate the empowerment of learners

- • To present discussion and details regarding various beliefs, perspectives, and philosophies about assessment and instruction that have permeated the literature

in recent years, including whole language, multicultural education, IRA/NCTE assessment standards, the U.S. Department of Education's position and instructional recommendations, IRA's principles to guide educational policy and practice, and Balanced Reading Instruction

- To help teachers formulate, develop, and justify their own balanced perspective based on their beliefs and learnings, with citations to support their views

- To pull it all together and answer questions relative to qualitative instruction, including questions regarding skills and strategies, learning and instruction, teacher's role, social context, indirect and direct instruction, learners with special needs, culturally diverse and language diverse/ESL learners, materials for instruction, and the use of writing.

Introduction

This second chapter of Part Two focuses on assessment, instruction, and learning in the classroom and on the beliefs, issues, and questions that are pertinent to this focus. Diagnostic teaching based on thoughtful teacher assessments and analyses is the recommended basis for classroom instruction. This diagnostic teaching and instruction is in response to, and part of, the qualitatiive assessments that teachers do every day. Qualitative assessment and instruction go hand in hand. As we observe and assess students' skills and strategy use, we also consider, plan, and implement any needed instruction for them. In fact, assessment and instruction often overlap, and an outside observer might not be able to tell whether the teacher is assessing or instructing. Only the teacher knows whether his overall purpose is to assess, to instruct, or both, since many assessment techniques are also excellent teaching techniques, and vice versa.

Although I acknowledge and promote this circular and ongoing relationship between good assessment and good instruction, I believe it is also important to emphasize that direct instruction is a fundamental part of the classroom teacher's responsibilities. When teachers assess and determine that particular skill and strategy development are necessary, it is important that they know how to proceed. This chapter is designed to help teachers do that. Later, Chapter 8 follows up by presenting the instructional needs of children and some sample strategy lessons developed to address those needs.

"A Model for the Classroom Teacher's Decision Making," Revisited

In Chapter 1, a decision-making model was presented to help you chart your own course regarding assessment options and what you might want to emphasize in your classroom. That model is displayed again in Box 7–1 for your perusal and consideration.

Consider and React 7–1

Review the areas and strategies you noted earlier (see your Chapter 1 reactions) and take a few minutes to reconsider them. Would you add or delete any? Why?

The areas and strategies you select as most important are also most likely the ones you have been observing and assessing in your classroom. When your qualitative analysis leads you to believe that some of your students need some direct instruction in order to further develop these areas and strategies, you will want to proceed accordingly. First, as was illustrated in Chapter 6, you will organize for managing the classroom, including instructional groupings. Next, you will need to make specific instructional plans for working with those groups. In the section that follows, a plan, a focus, and a model for diagnostic instruction are provided to assist you in these next steps of classroom assessment and instruction decision making.

Box 7–1	A model for the classroom teacher's decision making
Question:	What should be assessed? Assessment Options Linguistic Experience and Strategy Use Cognitive Experience and Strategy Use Affective Influences Cultural and Sociocultural Influences Other Options: (Based on individual teacher's professional readings, course, experiences, etc.)
Question:	What do I want to teach or emphasize in my classroom program as it relates to reading?
Answer:	These are the things (areas, skills, or strategies) that I believe are important and I want to emphasize, develop, and teach in my classroom:

A Plan, Focus, and "Model for Diagnostic Instruction"

As we have seen, the classroom teacher reviews his assessment options, considers what he wants to emphasize in his particular classroom, and makes his choices. Based on these choices, he observes and assesses individual children as they do their regular classroom work, read silently and/or orally, reflect on their readings and strategies, write, and do other literacy-related study and work. During the course of these ongoing assessments, the teacher qualitatively analyzes what he observes and keeps a folder, records, notes, or some type of collaborative portfolio collection for each child's reading and strategy development.

These data and analysis, whether formal or informal, regarding children's individual development in the areas and strategies the teacher believes are most important and that the teacher wants to emphasize in his classroom, are used to plan for diagnostic instruction. See the steps and questions that are involved:

Step 1 Develop a list of areas and strategies that you have decided to emphasize in your classroom.

Step 2 Select from this listing the areas and strategies that require your direct instruction (note, you have observed and qualitatively analyzed that some of the children in your classroom need to develop or further develop these particular areas, skills, and strategies).

Step 3 Consider the following questions and use your answers to plan and develop instruction:

Question: Are there several children who need this specific instruction? If so, how can I organize my classroom and group children for this?

Answer: Look at your own data and analysis for individual children in your classroom to determine who would benefit from direct instruction for a given skill or strategy. Also, see Chapter 6 and the appendix for classroom organization ideas and samples.

Question: What are some ideas, lessons, or activities I can develop or promote to provide direct instruction for each of these identified areas, skills, and strategies so that the instruction is functional and not isolated or set apart from real reading and study activities?

Answer: Generate your own ideas based on the specific needs you observed as you assessed the children in your classroom. Also, see Chapter 8 for samples of teaching ideas and strategy lessons developed by other classroom teachers.

Question: Is there a suggested format or lesson plan outline that I could follow to give my direct instruction ideas more shape?

Answer: Really any format or lesson plan outline you feel comfortable with is fine. You don't have to formalize it, as long as you know what your purpose is, how you are going to accomplish it, and how you are going to assess children's development in the particular skill or strategy. However, in order to provide some uniformity, I have listed the strategy lesson and activity format that classroom teachers used when contributing to Chapter 8.

Strategy Lesson/Activity/Game Procedure Format

1. Specific focus of instruction
2. Suggestions for developing background
3. Description of the teaching procedure
4. Suggestions for independent student practice
5. Suggestions for observing and evaluating students' strategy development
6. Ideas for scaffolding or modifying instruction based on evaluation
7. Suggested materials and literature.

Question: What are some things that I should consider as I develop and proceed with my instructional focus and plans?

Answer: This really depends on your own particular philosophy and beliefs regarding teaching and learning. But, based on the ideas suggested in this book, the Analysis of Instruction and Learning Focus Reflection Guide (Box 7–2) should help you focus and delineate your own plans.

When teachers are focusing on both children's instruction and learning, they are continually assessing children as they teach them and as children work independently on their own or with others. The assessing and instructing, and assessing and instructing, and so on, are circular and continuous and should take place as part of the genuine classroom curriculum. Teachers will find that they can teach their regular classroom curriculum, keeping skill and strategy development needs in mind, and can take and

Box 7–2	Analysis of instruction and learning focus reflection guide

Focus

- What is the focus of my instruction?
- What is it that I want my students to learn to do?

Strategies and Background Involved

- What strategies will students need to use in order to learn (or to develop) what I'm asking them to focus on?
- What can I do to develop background or prepare students for this instruction?

Instruction Involved

- What will I need to do to help them use these strategies?
- What will I need to do to make my instruction authentic and a part of real reading and real classroom study and activities?
- How will I proceed and what do I do?
- Is there some related independent practice or work that I could suggest as a follow-up to my instruction?

Observation and Evaluation

- What should I look for to observe and evaluate student's development?
- How can I encourage students to reflect on and evaluate their own development of these strategies and on their learning?
- What can I do to scaffold or modify this instruction based on these evaluations?

Materials and Literature

- What tools, materials, literature, or special arrangements will we need for this strategy instruction or activity?

develop opportunities for direct instruction of needed reading and study strategies within the context of any subjects or units that they teach. Figure 7–1 illustrates this diagnostic instruction model. It should be noted that children and parents/families, as well as the teacher, can take part in monitoring, assessing, and planning skill and strategy development.

Alternative Method Approach

Wixson (1991) indicates that **diagnostic teaching** (or **diagnostic instruction**) integrates assessment and instruction, permitting us to observe the ways in which different reader

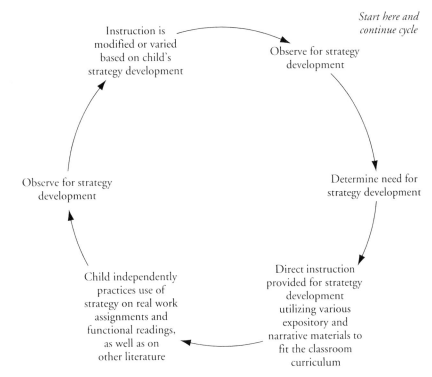

Instruction is modified or varied based on child's strategy development

Start here and continue cycle

Observe for strategy development

Determine need for strategy development

Observe for strategy development

Direct instruction provided for stratetgy development utilizing various expository and narrative materials to fit the classroom curriculum

Child independently practices use of strategy on real work assignments and functional readings, as well as on other literature

Figure 7–1 Model for Diagnostic Instruction

and **contextual factors** (affected by the reading situation and/or by the text itself) may be influencing a student's reading. In other words, as we teach or work with students we are able to continuously assess their strategy use as they read various types of texts and encounter various difficulties with text. This is diagnostic because it allows us to continue to observe and collect information about the reader's strategies in order to further clarify and test our hypothesis about what the reader might need. This is also instructional because it provides opportunities to try out methods for working with a student. Wixson further describes two of the ways to make decisions regarding diagnostic teaching: the alternative method and the scaffolding method approaches.

The **alternative method approach** involves trying out various methods for teaching the needed strategy to see which one is easiest for the child and/or most helpful to her. The child takes part in evaluating which method worked best. Derived from a Wixson (1991) example, here is how Mrs. Davis, Courtney's first-grade teacher, decided to proceed with Courtney's phoneme-grapheme word recognition instruction:

Mrs. Davis first tried a **Language Experience Approach (LEA)**, using language experience activities to promote a stimulus for discussion and dictation of a story. Mrs. Davis would point out letter-sound correspondence (phonics) and configuration within the dictated story, and also use follow-up flashcards of new sight vocabulary from the story.

Then as an alternate method, Mrs. Davis tried letter-sound (phonics) and configuration instruction to teach Courtney how to sound out words from parts to whole using a Dr. Seuss book they read together. Mrs. Davis observed that Courtney learned using both of these methods, although she seemed to learn most easily and enthusiastically using the LEA. When asked which way she preferred learning, Courtney said the LEA was the most fun and that she learned to read lots of new words. Using her own observations and Courtney's evaluation, Mrs. Davis decides to proceed with phoneme-grapheme instruction for Courtney using the LEA.

Consider and React 7–2

Consider Courtney's phonics instruction. How were the two methods different? Do you agree with Mrs. Davis's decision to continue instruction using the Language Experience Approach? Why?

Scaffolding Method Approach

The **scaffolding method approach** involves the teacher presenting a reading task to the student, observing the student's response, and then introducing small modifications of the reading task to see what might help the student become a more **strategic reader** (a reader who consciously uses strategies to make sense of his reading). Each modification, or layer of the task, is based on a hypothesis the teacher makes as to what might help the child be successful. The teacher layers the prompts or supports from the least support to the most support, in order to observe and identify the minimum intervention and prompting necessary for the child's success. Here is an example of the scaffolding method approach derived from another Wixson (1991) example: Katie, a sixth grader, has been observed by Ms. Nguyen, her teacher, to have little metacognitive awareness. When asked how she arrives at her answers to comprehension questions about various reading selections, Katie usually answers, 'I don't know." Ms. Nguyen begins scaffolding by asking a sequence of prompts, planning to note the point at which Katie can respond with the requested information:

1. What could you do to help explain how you arrived at that answer, Katie?
2. Do you think you know how you arrived at it?
3. Can you try to figure it out?
4. Is the information you need in the selection?
5. Where in the selection might you find that information?

Because Katie continues to answer "I don't know," Ms. Nguyen adds the next layer of scaffolding. Now she asks Katie to look in various parts of the selection to see if the answer might have been found there. As she works through the selection with Katie, she determines whether more prompts are necessary. If so, she might scaffold next by modeling how she (Ms. Nguyen) could support the answer to the metacognitive probe. Using scaffolding, Ms. Nguyen is then able to observe how much instructional support Katie needs to develop her metacognitive awareness. Katie also evaluates the helpfulness of the prompts. For example, Katie decides whether the various prompts helped her. Which ones helped her most? And, what might she need the next time she is asked to explain how she arrived at an answer to a reading comprehension question? Ms. Nguyen would then continue to work with Katie, supporting her so that Katie can begin to assume more and more of the responsibility for understanding how she arrives at answers to questions about a reading.

Consider and React 7–3

Consider Katie's metacognitive strategy instruction. How did Ms. Nguyen scaffold the instruction? Why does question 1 require less teacher support than question 5? Why do you think it is important for Katie to also evaluate which prompts helped her most?

Readers interested in more examples of using scaffolding as an approach to reading instruction should see Graves and Graves (1994). Those interested in examples of how text can be used as a means of scaffolding instruction for beginning readers might want to see Brown (1999/2000), and for examples of literacy scaffolds that can be used for both first- and second-language readers, see Boyle and Peregoy (1998). Additionally, studies of **reciprocal teaching** (a term used to describe instructional procedures, including scaffolding, that involve dialogues between the teacher and students as students attempt to gain meaning from text) have been reviewed, and readers interested in these should see Rosenshine and Meister (1994). It should be noted that scaffolding *is* an important guided reading device used to help provide support to youngsters as they read and as they attempt to understand text.

The Negotiated Curriculum: Empowering Your Learners

Garth Boomer (1985), an Australian educator, was an advocate of the negotiated curriculum. Boomer believed in getting children involved in the shaping of plans for instruction. While he indicated that the teacher first needs to develop his or her plans around the kinds of literacy experiences, content, and specific strategies and abilities the teacher values most, he also advocated use of the children's input to later shape and refine these plans. Boomer believed that control must be with the learner if we are to promote independence and personal power. This applies to children learning to read and write, as well as to their teachers. A slightly modified list of ways that Boomer (1985, p. 73) suggested children can contribute or negotiate includes the following:

1. Children suggest some resources they can bring (e.g., a book, a picture, etc.).
2. Children decide on a product they would like to work toward (in addition to the teacher's demands and within the general framework established by the teacher).
3. The group or individuals make suggestions about learning activities.
4. The group or individuals arrange deadlines and timing of the activities.
5. The group or individuals brainstorm with the teacher about possible methods of evaluating how well they have done.
6. The group or individuals suggest or select modifications or extensions to the content.
7. The group or individuals convince the teacher that they already know much of what he has planned for them to learn.
8. Individuals convince the teacher that they be allowed to draw up alternative programs.

Boomer further explained that to begin the negotiating with a group unused to this collaborative effort, start by discussing what you intend and then invite contribution of resources. He also indicated that it is important for the teacher and the children to establish what they already know and can do, and what they do not know and need to be able to do. In this way they will not be covering unnecessary ground.

> ### Consider and React 7–4
>
> How would you get students involved in curriculum and instruction decisions? How would this empower your learners?

Beliefs and Philosophies That Can Balance Assessment and Instruction Decisions

The terms *skill instruction, strategy instruction, direct instruction,* and *diagnostic instruction* are labels for describing instructional practices that can mean different things depending on the context they are in and the actual beliefs and philosophy of the user. Let me illustrate. To Mrs. Lieberman, who believes in functional reading for real purposes, assignments, and entertainment, strategy instruction involves diagnostic, direct instruction for the purpose of developing and expanding children's strengths. Mrs. Lieberman believes that strategy lessons can be developed using real reading materials and events. She dislikes the idea of using workbooks, dittos, and reading kits and does not teach skills in isolation. Furthermore, when she observes that a child lacks certain reading skills or strategies, she first considers whether the lack of the specific skill is causing a loss of comprehension. If so, she plans for instruction. She does not believe in teaching skills just for the sake of learning or showing mastery of the skills.

To Mr. Miller, who believes in systematic instruction, a scope and sequence of skills, the need to control and introduce vocabulary, and the importance of children's performance on all of the **subskills** (subparts of skills), strategy instruction and skills instruction are the same thing. Mr. Miller diagnoses his students to determine their weaknesses and provides direct instruction to fix those weaknesses. He sees nothing wrong with teaching skills one at a time, teaching skills in isolation, and using workbooks, dittos, and various reading kits to drill children on the necessary skills. Mr. Miller believes that this diagnostic, direct, and specific skills instruction is necessary so that every child can perform adequately on each skill and subskill in the scope and sequence chart of the reading program he advocates. While he thinks comprehension is something to work toward, he believes the various skills and subskills must be learned first.

As you can see, while both Mrs. Lieberman and Mr. Miller use the terms *skill* and *strategy instruction, direct instruction,* and *diagnostic instruction* to describe their belief about reading assessment and its relationship to instruction, these terms clearly have different meanings and usage to these two teachers, who obviously have differences in their ideas and philosophies. Cambourne (1994) indicates that those who hold widely divergent views do so because they tend to view the world, and interpret what they see and hear, differently. He says it is as if they filter "information through different frameworks or lenses" that influence their interpretations (p. 2). Where do these differing views and the principles and ideas behind them come from? How do we know which to consider or adopt? How do we defend those philosophies, principles, and ideas we adopt? These are important questions. The rest of this chapter is devoted to answering them.

Although there are probably as many philosophies and positions about assessment and instruction as there are teachers who assess and teach, there are some philosophies and ideas that have permeated the literature. Some of these will be delineated in this chapter. Following the listing of these positions, there is a discussion regarding how to balance these principles, ideas, and standards into a comfortable "fit" with your own beliefs about reading, literacy, and, in fact, about all kinds of learning.

Whole Language Philosophy and Principles

Whole language is described as a philosophy about how children learn. It is not a method or approach to teaching reading, but it does inform the way teachers teach (Newman & Church, 1990). "Whole language" is further described as supporting learning that is realistic, relevant, authentic, and child-centered.

Stephens (1991) discusses characteristics that can be observed in classrooms that are consistent with the whole language philosophy: (1) Children are engaged as learners. They use language to make and test hypotheses, explore possibilities, reflect on what they learn, and decide what they want to learn next. (2) Teachers are engaged as learners.

They see themselves as professionals, read widely, and reflect often. They plan extensively, revise as necessary, and assess continuously. They establish environments that facilitate learning and use demonstration and response as primary teaching tools. (3) Learning is a social process, and transactions between teachers, students, and curriculum significantly contribute to the learning that occurs. (4) Texts that are used are whole and cohesive, serve a purpose for the learner, and have an audience broader than just the teacher (pp. 14–15).

Harp (1994, pp. 48–65) provides a listing of principles of assessment and evaluation for whole language classrooms. Many of these have been included for your review:

1. Assessment and evaluation are first and foremost for the individual learner.
2. Assessment and evaluation strategies should honor the wholeness of language.
3. Reading and writing are viewed as processes.
4. Teacher intuition is a valuable assessment and evaluation tool, and teacher observation is at the center of assessment and evaluation.
5. Assessment and evaluation of reading should reflect what we know about the reading process, including the factors that influence comprehension: prior knowledge, text structure, reading strategies, and interests and attitudes.
6. Assessment and evaluation of writing should reflect what we know about the writing process.
7. Assessment and evaluation tools are varied, and literacy is assessed in a variety of contexts.
8. Assessment and evaluation are integral parts of instruction and occur continuously.
9. Assessment and evaluation are developmentally and culturally appropriate.
10. Assessment and evaluation should reveal children's strengths.

Consider and React 7–5

Which of the whole language principles do you particularly agree with? Why?

(Readers wanting more information on the whole language perspective should also see Church, 1994; Froese; 1996; Goodman, 1986, 1992; Stephens, 1991; and Turbill and Cambourne, 1998).

Multicultural Education Perspective and Characteristics

The multicultural education perspective seeks to provide equal access, opportunities, and respect for all learners. Banks (1999) discusses and details the characteristics and the assessment and teaching practices that should inform school curricula and other decisions. These characteristics of multicultural classrooms and schools have been taken from the work and ideas of Banks (pp. 17–20, 111):

1. Teachers and administrators have expectations for all students and positive attitudes toward them, and they respond to all students in positive, caring ways.

2. Curriculum reflects the experiences, cultures, and perspectives of a range of cultural and ethnic groups as well as of both genders.

3. Teaching styles match the learning, cultural, and motivational styles of the students.

4. Teachers and administrators show respect for all of the students' first languages and dialects.

5. Instructional materials present events, situations, and concepts from the perspective of the full range of cultural, ethnic, and racial groups.

6. Assessment and testing procedures are culturally sensitive and result in students of color and language-minority students being represented proportionately in advanced groups and in classes or programs for the gifted and talented.

7. School and classroom cultures and the actual learnings of the students reflect cultural and ethnic diversity.

8. Teaching strategies should be involvement-oriented, interactive, personalized, cooperative, and student-centered. Banks indicates: "Teacher-centered instruction has serious disadvantages when teaching any kind of content. However, it is especially inappropriate when teaching multicultural content, an area in which diversity is valued and different perspectives are an integral part of the content" (p. 111).

Consider and React 7–6

Which aspects of the multicultural education perspective do you particularly value? Why?

(Readers wanting more information on the multicultural perspective should see Banks, 1999; Faltis, 2001; Garcia, 2002; Tiedt & Tiedt, 2002; on multicultural education sources available on the Internet, see Finegan, Helms, & Gotthoffer, 2000; on teaching using multicultural literature, see Bieger, 1995/1996; Harris, 1997; Hefflin & Barksdale-Ladd, 2001; and Young, Campbell, & Oda, 1995.)

IRA/NCTE Joint Task Force on Assessment Standards
The IRA/NCTE Joint Task Force on Assessment published a set of standards to guide decisions about assessing the teaching and learning of reading and writing (IRA/NCTE, 1994). Members of this task force were representative of a diverse group of literacy researchers with differing philosophies. The standards they developed are intended to reflect what has been learned from the research on language, learning, and literacy

extending several decades back. The following list is taken from these standards or has been derived from these standards to address the assessment and instruction decisions in individual classrooms:

1. The interests of the students are paramount in assessment.
2. The primary purpose of assessment is to improve teaching and learning.
3. Assessment must reflect and allow for critical inquiry into curriculum and instruction; instruction informs assessment and vice versa.
4. Assessment must recognize and reflect the intellectually and socially complex nature of reading and writing and the important roles of school, home, and society in literacy development.
5. Assessment must be fair and equitable.
6. The consequences of an assessment procedure are the first, and most important, consideration in establishing the validity and use of the assessment.
7. The teacher is the most important agent of assessment.
8. The assessment process should involve multiple perspectives and sources of data.
9. All stakeholders must participate in assessment.
10. Parents must be involved as active, essential participants in the assessment process.

Consider and React 7–7

Which of the IRA/NCTE assessment standards do you especially agree with? Why?

(Additionally, readers wanting the details of IRA's position on high-stakes assessments in reading should see IRA, 1999.)

U.S. Department of Education Position and Recommendations for Instruction

The U.S. Department of Education (DOE) has disseminated this position concerning reading instruction (2001b) in a document published through a collaborative effort of the National Institute for Literacy, National Institute of Child Health and Human Development, and the U.S. DOE, and developed for the DOE by the Center for the Improvement of Early Reading Achievement (CIERA). The document focuses on five areas of instruction and how they should be taught: phonemic awareness, phonics, fluency, vocabulary, and text comprehension. The DOE indicates that their conclusions about reading instruction have been drawn from the National Reading Panel report (2000). This section summarizes their position on each area they endorse:

1. Phonemic awareness instruction is important, and it should be taught and developed in small groups in the early grades. It is most effective when children are taught to manipulate phonemes using the letters of the alphabet, and when instruction focuses on only one or two rather than several types of phoneme manipulation.

2. Phonics instruction is important, and it is most effective when it is done systematically and explicitly, beginning in kindergarten or first grade.

3. Fluency instruction is important, and it can be developed by the teacher modeling fluent reading, and by having students engage in repeated oral reading.

4. Vocabulary development is important, and vocabulary can be developed in two ways: **indirectly,** when students engage in discussion, listen to adults read to them, and read extensively on their own; and **directly,** when students are explicitly taught individual words as well as strategies they can use independently to learn new words.

5. Text comprehension instruction is important, and it can be developed by teaching comprehension strategies through explicit instruction, cooperative learning, and by helping readers use strategies flexibly and in combination. Metacognitive strategies are recognized as what good readers use to think about and have control over their reading.

Consider and React 7–8

Which of the U.S. Department of Education areas and recommendations for instruction do you personally support? Why?

IRA's Principles to Guide Educational Policy and Practice

The International Reading Association (IRA) Board of Directors have developed and adopted a set of ten principles to guide the formulation of educational policy and practice (IRA, 2000b). This position statement, which IRA calls "Making a Difference Means Making It Different: Honoring Children's Rights to Excellent Reading Instruction," emphasizes that there can be no single, simple solution to the problem of teaching children to read proficiently. Furthermore, it stresses that policies, practices, and materials that focus on one part of literacy at the expense of other areas are too narrow and may cause children to not understand or enjoy what they read. It urges policy makers and educators to take a broader view. The "Children's Rights" (2002) extrapolated from the larger IRA policy statement appears in *Reading Today,* delineating these principles and rights:

1. Children have a right to appropriate early reading instruction based on their individual needs.

2. Children have a right to reading instruction that builds both the skill and the desire to read increasingly complex materials.

3. Children have a right to well-prepared teachers who keep their skills up to date through effective professional development.

4. Children have a right to access a wide variety of books and other reading material in classroom, school, and community libraries.

5. Children have the right to reading assessment that identifies their strengths as well as their needs and involves them in making decisions about their own learning.

6. Children who are struggling with reading have a right to receive intensive instruction from professionals specifically prepared to teach reading.

7. Children have a right to reading instruction that involves parents and communities in their academic lives.

8. Children have a right to reading instruction that makes skilled use of their first language skills.

9. Children have a right to equal access to technology used for the improvement of reading instruction.

10. Children have a right to classrooms that optimize learning opportunities.

Consider and React 7–9

Which of the IRA principles would you advocate for and why?

(Readers wanting information concerning what literacy experts, reading researchers, and classroom teachers from diverse perspectives agree to concerning contexts and practices for reading instruction should see Flippo, 1999 and 2001a.)

Balanced Reading Instruction Philosophy and Principles

Many reading professors and teachers are calling for a balanced reading philosophy that includes a combination and balance of philosophies, approaches, and methods (Au, Carroll, & Scheu, 2001; Blair-Larsen & Williams, 1999; Fitzgerald, 1999; Pearson, 2001; Pressley, 2001; Reutzel, 1999; Spiegel, 1992, 1994b; Strickland, 1994/1995; Thompson, 1994). In fact, some of these and many others have formulated a special interest group of IRA called "Balanced Reading Instruction" to encourage this philosophy. Thompson (1994, p. 46) provides a listing of the principles this group believes in and promotes.

1. A balance between teaching students and facilitating their learning

2. A balance between using instructional approaches and open reading times

3. A balance between using **code teaching methods** (such as various types of phonic and graphophonic instruction) and meaning emphasis methods

4. A balance between incidental one-on-one intervention and development of planned lessons

5. A balance between use of **trade books** (books published for sale to the general public) and published teaching materials

6. A balance between using informal observations and more formal assessing instruments

7. A balance between use and awareness of language.

Consider and React 7–10

Which of the Balanced Reading Instruction principles do you agree with in particular? Why?

Developing and Defending Your Own Balanced Perspective

It is clear that the lists of standards and principles for assessment and instruction could go on and on. For example, we could produce a list from those supporting the emergent literacy philosophy (as cited in Chapter 3), and a list from those supporting use of authentic assessment (for instance, see Valencia et al., 1994, and others cited earlier in this book), and a list from the work of others supporting more attention to phonological awareness and phonics (for example, Adams, 1990; Chall, 1996; Stanovich, 1986), and so on. However, more lists are really not necessary to convey the idea that reading assessment and instruction decisions are a personal and professional matter. There isn't a one "right way" to proceed. The best way is for the individual teacher to use the standards, ideas, principles, and aspects of the various philosophies that best fit his or her perspective and beliefs about reading to find the balance that suits him or her. Your own personal, professional, balanced perspective is the one you will most likely have the most success with. You will find that your beliefs are based on all you have read and experienced regarding literacy instruction. You will also probably find that your beliefs match many of those on the preceding lists. However, you might find that while you agree with many of the ideas, there are others with which you do not agree. You will probably also notice that many of the lists overlap and often include similar ideas. In fact, several of the lists are developed from reviewing the research from various philosophies.

Rather than force yourself to adopt a group or widely publicized philosophy or position, why not use the best from each? Remember "the best" is a personal and professional choice and will be different for different teachers. My suggestion is that our own set of principles or beliefs should be the basis by which we check the appropriateness of our assessments and our diagnostic, direct instruction, and other skill/strategy development plans. If our assessments, skill/strategy development, and other classroom instruction measure up to our principles, then I believe we will be doing our best to provide qualitative reading instruction based on everything we know about the child and everything we believe in and value about language, literacy, and respect for individuals. (Readers might want to read in-depth some of the literature cited in this section to learn more about the principles, standards, or ideas listed.)

Readers might additionally want to take the time to develop their own list of principles, beliefs, or standards from some of those cited in this section, or earlier in this book, or from other available professional sources. Doing this, and noting the source for each, will provide you with the necessary grounding and defense for your philosophy and the principles and ideas you hold most dear. When asked why you are using the assessments, instruction, or skill and strategy lessons you are implementing, you will be able to provide a justification based on some of the widely published and accepted standards, principles, or ideas. You will also be providing a justification that supports and fits your own personal, professional, and balanced perspective of reading assessment and instruction. Using the format that follows, try developing your own list:

Standards, Principles, or Ideas	Source	Relevant Citations	Justification (or Why I Support This Idea)

Misconceptions and Questions Relative to Qualitative Instruction

Many reading teachers and researchers have been fielding questions and concerns relative to teaching skills, strategies, direct instruction, and diverse learners while at the same time believing in many of the ideas and principles of various perspectives, including emergent literacy, developmental instruction, and more naturalistic or holistic learning (Church, 1994; Crafton, 1994; Kameenui, 1993; Krashen, 1999; McQuillan, 1998; Newman & Church, 1990; Routman, 1996; Samway & McKeon, 1999; Slaughter, 1988; Spiegel, 1992; Strickland, 1994/1995; Strickland & Morrow, 1989b). In this section I will draw on these authors' ideas, and mine, to summarize and react to the most obvious misconceptions and questions.

Consider and React 7–11

Consider and review each question and response. What do you think? Are there other arguments you would add to my reactions?

What About Skills and Strategies Instruction?

Skills involve the ability to perform a task. Sometimes many skills used together form a strategy. **Strategies** involve the way we go about working out a problem. Both skill and strategy instruction have a place in the early childhood, elementary, middle, and high-school classroom. Teachers who believe in ideas from an emergent literacy, whole language, or developmental perspective should not be uncomfortable with skill and strategy instruction, as long as the instruction is not done as something separate from actual reading and writing. Skill and strategy instruction involving real reading, study, and writing are to be valued, especially when the instruction is diagnostic and the result of qualitative assessment. Look for planned instruction that values the learner's input, dialect, language, diversity, interests, choices, sharings, discussions, strengths, skills, and strategies, and that uses real literature and real content materials as much as possible.

What About Learning and Its Relationship to Instruction?

Learning should be an outgrowth of instruction, but learning and instruction are not the same thing. Children often learn from the situation, atmosphere, attitudes, and beliefs prevalent in the classroom, without the teacher ever having specifically implemented any instruction. Banks (1999, p. 19) refers to this as the **hidden curriculum** in the multicultural education literature and indicates that this is the curriculum that no teacher explicitly teaches but that all students learn. Ideally, your hidden curriculum in reading as well as in cultural and ethnic inclusion will give children *learnings* that you would be pleased to have them acquire.

Literacy learning and teaching literacy are also not the same. Children will acquire their literacy learnings from birth on and it will be influenced by their family, culture, environment, and social interactions outside as well as inside school. Au, Mason, and Scheu (1995) remind us that reading is a social process, one that people rely on to accomplish everyday goals and use to make sense out of their everyday interactions. Your teaching should influence literacy learnings, but instruction is only one piece of what is involved.

When learners want to acquire new information and ideas, they use **learning strategies** (self-initiated strategies that help them learn and acquire the desired information). When learners want to read, they use **reading strategies** (self-initiated strategies that help them comprehend what they wish to read and understand). When teachers want to teach specific skills, strategies, or concepts, they use **teaching strategies** (self-initiated strategies that help them present the skills, strategies, or concepts they wish their students to develop). Teachers can focus on teaching students how to learn. If your focus is on developing students' use of learning and reading strategies, then you are teaching students how to learn. Baker and Brown (1984) emphasize that reading is an active thinking process and requires a supportive literacy environment that facilitates the learning of strategies. Short (1991) emphasizes that the continuous monitoring of a student's strategy development, a classroom that provides a literacy environment with differing amounts of support for readers, and teacher/student interactions before, during, and after the reading of whole text are all important characteristics of environments that support the development of reading and learning strategies.

What About the Teacher's Role?

Some might assume that the nonauthoritarian or more holistic teacher doesn't teach. Instead they might assume that she is a facilitator in her classroom, and that the classroom is a very unstructured and free place where children move about reading, writing, and interacting at their leisure and without any particular standards or any planning on the part of the teacher. Yet while this description may on the surface seem true to some observers, its accuracy is not borne out.

Yes, the teacher is a facilitator, but she is a teacher, too. In order for her classroom to look relaxed and user-friendly, the teacher must be highly organized, have realistic but many expectations, and be ready and able to assess and teach in a facilitative and functional way. This means that the teacher plans and implements instruction as needed based on her ongoing assessments and the needs she perceives. The teacher need not be authoritarian in order to provide this instruction.

The teacher's role is a critical one. Students need opportunities to interact using oral and written language (reading and writing) as they construct meaning about what they have read. Raphael and McMahon (1994) show that learning is a social process that involves the teacher's support and design of opportunities for this interaction. Grant, Guthrie, Bennett, Rice, and McGough (1993/1994, p. 338) emphasize that motivation, **cognition** (recognizing, conceiving, judging, and reasoning), and social interaction are equally important to reading development. The teacher's simultaneous support of motivation, cognition, and social interaction enables students to become self-determining readers who can design their own learning. Students need support for their sense of autonomy and competence if they are to develop the necessary intrinsic motivation for learning. Teachers have long acknowledged the value of motivation, and this is supported by a robust research literature that documents the link between motivation and achievement (Gambrell, 2001). The research of Oldfather and Dahl (1994) also indicates that teachers must be aware of the purposes, experiences, and perceptions of learners within the classroom; these should be indicators that help teachers understand the conditions that support each child's desire to learn. An aware and competent teacher can provide this necessary support for students.

What Is Meant by the Social Context of Reading?

Some of the literature, principles, and ideas already cited in this chapter have referred to the social context or social process of reading. In fact, discussions and citations throughout this book support this concept about reading. It seems important, then, to discuss it and its meaning and relevance.

Au (1993) thoroughly describes the view of reading and writing as part of and specific to a **social context.** She indicates that when someone reads or writes, his reading or writing is taking place within a particular social context. Here are some examples: If Lon is reading and taking notes in the school library with a group of other students to get information for an assignment, that is the particular social context of the reading and writing. If Raj is reading a book in his temple, synagogue, or church to study biblical, historical, or ideological references, that is the particular social context of his reading. If Ella is reading a storybook to her younger sister, Elena, that is the particular social context of this particular reading. Readers and writers learn to meet the requirements of the social context of the reading or writing in which they are engaging.

Au (1993) points out how especially important social context is when it comes to the literacy instruction of students with diverse backgrounds. The social contexts of their homes or communities often prepare students to learn in ways quite different from what is expected at school. This must be taken into consideration by the teacher. The parent/family informational interviews (as described in Chapter 3) and the parent/family involvement and communications (as described in Chapter 6) should help teachers learn more about children's emergent literacy and the social contexts for reading and writing with which they are already familiar and competent.

The idea that reading and writing are an outgrowth of and part of social context is often referred to as **social constructivism** in the literature on literacy and learning. This theory also supports the belief that readers actively construct their own understandings about what they read. This is very different from the belief that the information in the text is instead just transmitted to the reader. The work of the Russian social psychologist L. S. Vygotsky (i.e., his work republished in 1978) is often cited as a foundation for this idea. Vygotsky saw the teacher's role as providing just the right amount of support for children's learning, as parents and family provided support in children's earliest years. The teacher talks with children about their reasoning and thinking about their readings and moves children forward, gradually releasing responsibility for the reading task to the children. The scaffolding method is an example of this type of teaching. Another example is asking children questions to draw ideas from them, rather than just telling them the answers (Au et al., 1995). Using these methods and other ideas, such as cross-age tutoring and cooperative learning groups, teachers can help to provide more support for children's learning.

If you believe that reading is a social or a socially complex process, and that it involves the reader's development or construction of his own reading from what he reads, you are holding a social constructivist belief. (Readers wanting more information about reading as a social process might want to read Au, 1993; Raphael & Hiebert, 1996; and the other authors cited in this section and chapter who indicate the importance of the social context of reading and writing.)

What About Indirect and Direct Instruction?

Indirect instruction tends to be more covert instruction. It involves the teacher planning and orchestrating classroom situations that will lead to specific outcomes. An example of this is when the teacher has planned for a quiet reading time, and everyone (children and teacher) quietly reads his or her selected book in any comfortable spot in the room. On the other hand, **direct instruction** implies that the teacher takes a more dominant role, where teacher talk and teacher intervention is more obvious (Duffy & Roehler, 1993). An example of direct instruction is when the teacher and a small group of children predict the possible outcomes to the mystery book they are sharing, and the teacher follows up by soliciting the reasons why individuals have predicted as they did. Children contribute their individual predictions and reasons, but the teacher tends to have the most control.

Both indirect and direct instruction have their place in all classrooms, including the emergent literacy, developmental, and whole language classroom. There are times that more covert instructional planning works best; however, skill and strategy instruction require the teacher's more direct involvement. Whether instruction is indirect or direct should not be the issue; instead, the issue is whether the instruction is learner-centered or not. Learner-centered instruction values the learner—the learner's strategies, ideas, and contributions. If instruction is not learner-centered, then it may be too teacher-centered and too teacher-dominated. If we assume that the teacher already has the skills and strategies, then we do not have to focus instruction on the teacher. Perhaps what some find objectionable is teacher-centered instruction, rather than qualitatively based direct instruction that is learner centered. (Some are referring to this more meaningful, qualitative, and learner-centered approach to skill and strategy instruction, based on students' needs and building on what students already know, as **explicit instruction.** See McIntyre & Pressley, 1996.)

Spiegel (1992) and Flippo (2001b) indicate that there is a need to build bridges, or at least to identify the common ground, between perspectives and approaches, blending the best from each and finding the common threads of agreements. Baumann (1991), Duffy and Roehler (1987), Durkin (1990), and many others believe that a certain amount of direct instruction is necessary and desirable. Heymsfeld (1989) and Mosenthal (1989) recommend that direct instruction, emphasizing strategies as opposed to just skills and using authentic reading materials, is the excellent blend or bridge. Pérez (1994, p. 92) indicates that phonics instruction need not be synonymous with excessive worksheets, nor must it exclude the use of quality literature. Teachers can integrate phonics instruction with use of children's literature and writing if the skills are applied in the context of reading and writing, rather than as isolated exercises. For learners with special needs, Sears et al. (1994) recommend explicit strategy instruction within context, using authentic materials, combined with use of informal assessment procedures. Furthermore, Spiegel and others she cites (Calfee & Piontkowski, 1981; Delpit, 1988, 1991) point out that many minority children and children from lower socioeconomic backgrounds need some direct instruction, as opposed to only indirect learning, to be able to compete and be successful in the expectations and conventions of the majority culture. Spiegel stresses that while many upper- and middle-income children come to school with a background that may make indirect instruction sufficient, this is not the case for many lower-income children. Finally, in his research article, Anderson (1994) suggests that the concept of emergent literacy might be the natural bridge between whole language and more traditional direct instruction. He cites Goodman (1992), an advocate of whole language, and Adams (1990), an advocate of direct instruction and a code emphasis approach, as both supporting the emergent literacy concept of literacy acquisition. (See Chapter 3, p. 48 for a listing of emergent literacy research conclusions. Interested readers might also want to refer to Flippo, 2001a; see McIntyre & Pressley, 1996; read Spiegel, 1992, and review the research cited in support of direct and explicit instruction.)

What About Learners with Special Needs and Diverse Learners?

Qualitative instruction, based on qualitative assessment, tends to be very specific diagnostic instruction. Having assessed children's cue system strategy usage and cognitive strategies during reading, study, and writing activities, and having assessed information learned from them and their parents/families, the classroom teacher is in a good position to know each child's skill/strategy strengths and possible needs. Youngsters who are having difficulty in school because of their special needs should be well served in a classroom where the teacher is dedicated to individualizing instruction based on all children's strengths and perceived needs.

Diverse learners (children who have diverse backgrounds and needs) need to be respected, valued, accepted, and encouraged to take risks. Teachers who encourage strategy development usually encourage risk taking, too. In order to risk making a guess during oral reading, children need to know that taking a guess is valued in the classroom. A good guess is often still a miscue, but it is very possibly a miscue that indicates strength in one or more cue systems. All children should be encouraged by a classroom teaching situation that dignifies their differences and unique qualities, and, for example, recognizes that they may be accustomed to a different syntax if English is not their first language.

The Calero-Breckheimer and Goetz (1993) study with third- and fourth-grade children indicates that Spanish-English bilingual readers can successfully transfer reading strategies from their native language to English and that their comprehension in both languages is positively related to strategy use. These findings support the nurturing of strategy development in **ESL** (English as a Second Language) and in the bilingual students' own native languages. At the very least, it would make sense to assess ESL students as they read materials in their own languages, and to encourage them to retain and use the effective strategies they have already established in their native languages. (This study supports theorists who believe that reading strategies developed in the first language are transferred to the second language [Goodman, 1973; Krashen, 1996; and others].)

I believe that youngsters beginning school in cultures where the language at school is different from their language should initially—if at all possible—be taught to read and be given opportunities to further develop reading strategies in their native languages. This is particularly important when we realize how developed children's linguistic and cognitive strategies are by the time they are school age (see the cited research in Chapter 3 on emergent literacy). Support for this belief can also be found in the literature on language minority and ESL learners (e.g., Carrasquillo & Segan, 1998; Escamilla & Andrade,

1992; Freeman & Freeman, 1993; Krashen, 1996; Samway & McKeon, 1999; and many others cited in this section).

Gersten and Jiménez (1994) found that many instructional practices that teachers employ when teaching reading to students considered at risk also seem to be effective for teaching ESL students to read. The following practices were recommended:

1. Developing new vocabulary, checking students' understanding of the vocabulary, and providing opportunities for meaningful use of the new vocabulary

2. Paraphrasing students' comments and encouraging them to expand their responses, including questioning and activities that require elaborated responses

3. Presenting ideas, verbally and in written form, using consistent language and minimizing use of synonyms and idioms

4. Using scaffolded instruction and cognitive strategy development

5. Instructing students using methods that involve a high level of student interaction, as well as teacher's modeling of comprehension strategies.

Pikulski (1994) reviewed successful reading programs for first-grade **at-risk** children (learners who have been identified as potentially being at risk of having problems learning due to being disadvantaged in some way). He recommends that at-risk children should receive individual or small group instruction; that pull-out programs can be effective but that instruction in the regular classroom is important; that children who are having difficulties with reading should spend more time receiving quality reading instruction; that ongoing assessment is necessary and assessment of oral reading is an informative, effective procedure; that the use of predictable texts has merit; that children should be given the opportunity to write every day and should be allowed to read the same books over and over if they wish; that communication between home and school should be encouraged and children should be provided with materials that they can take home and read daily; and that instructional procedures should ensure that students see reading as an act of constructing meaning.

While many are demanding better quality, better methods, and better provisions for special education students and other unique and diverse learners, we have been reminded by Kameenui (1993) as well as the many reading researchers who contributed to the Expert Study and follow-up dialogue (see Flippo, 2001a), that *there is no one best method or approach to literacy instruction.* Kameenui's concern is that we get on with teacher-directed instruction for learners who need it. He indicates that, while some search for improved methods, many youngsters are getting further and further behind their peers. Kameenui cites Stanovich's (1986) **Matthew effect.** According to the Matthew effect, the literacy-rich get richer, and the literacy-poor get poorer in reading opportunities, vocabulary development, written language, general knowledge, and so on. However, the contributors to the Expert Study dialogue explain how one size doesn't fit all, and therefore it is imperative that teachers know how to plan good qualitative skill/strategy instruction, based on good and ongoing qualitative assessment and analysis. This skilled, knowledgeable, and student-sensitive assessment, instruction, assessment, and analysis should be beneficial for learners with special needs, other diverse learners, and learners from diverse cultures as well.

Jackson (1993/1994) and Moll and González (1994, p. 454) indicate that too little attention is given to helping teachers to recognize the strengths that culturally different students bring to the classroom and to capitalize on these strengths. Jackson suggests that teachers use seven generic teaching strategies in their literacy instruction to enhance multicultural learning in their classrooms. They are (1) building trust; (2) becoming culturally literate; (3) building a repertoire of instructional strategies; (4) using effective questioning techniques; (5) providing effective feedback; (6) analyzing instructional materials; and (7) establishing positive home–school relations. Jackson urges teachers to act now. She indicates that although there is no panacea, the seven time-honored teaching strategies she describes offer a basis for taking a proactive stance toward the problem of miseducating or undereducating whole generations of students from culturally varied backgrounds. (Readers might want to refer to Jackson, 1993/1994, for her specific details, and to Moll & González, 1994, for their summary of research on learning resources and activities. Readers might also want to consult other literature and books that have been written specifically for literacy instruction in multicultural, bilingual, multilingual, and other diverse-student settings [Au, 1993, 2001; Brisk & Harrington, 2000; Carrasquillo & Segan, 1998; Cary, 2000; Freeman & Freeman, 2000; Jiménez, 2001; Opitz, 1998b; Risko & Bromley, 2001; and Samway & McKeon, 1999] for more background and instructional ideas. Those who are interested in developing programs for ESL and bilingual family involvement should also refer to Ashworth & Wakefield, 1994, and Quintero & Huerta-Macias, 1990. Additionally, those interested in studying and learning from the literacy challenges and needs of other culturally unique groups—the urban children and families of poor, white Appalachia—are directed to the work of Purcell-Gates, 1995; and for the migrant children of South Texas, to the work of Hayes, Bahruth, & Kessler, 1998.)

What About Materials for Instruction?

Materials for strategy lessons and assessments should be authentic literature, trade books, content books, and other materials appropriate to the age, interests, and schemata of the children in the class. This genuine literature and material should include various genres, content areas, and texts. If you wish to use leveled books in your classroom, that is fine. As described in Chapter 6, there are many ways of leveling books and working with learners to help them select appropriate books. Your decisions regarding leveled books will have a lot to do with the context of instruction you are most comfortable with. If you want to use a basal series in your classroom, then certainly do so. The newer basals provide a collection of stories, poems, and other pieces of literature that many children will enjoy, and because teachers can easily get multiple copies, groups of children can share their ideas about the commonly read literature. However, other children's literature, like storybooks, trade books, magazines, newspapers, and other collections of good stories and poems should also be used. Even songs and the lyrics in songs can be a good source of instructional material (Dwyer, 1982; Flippo, 1988) if your students are interested in music. Most important of all is that students have *access* to reading material and frequent opportunities to read. McQuillan's review of the research (1998) provides evidence that access to print and the amount of reading students do are the best predictors of reading achievement.

The idea is to use books and materials that children are really interested in reading, and whenever possible to use whole books or stories rather than fragments. Skill and strategy instruction (that supports the learners' strengths, needs, and comprehension) and ongoing assessments should take place "within" these materials so that the focus is on making sense of the text, rather than on just learning or assessing a strategy or skill. For example, let's say you want to work with a child on further developing his semantic cue system. You do this by encouraging the child to guess unfamiliar words when he encounters them in the text or song that seem to make sense with the rest of the text. Any guess that makes sense is considered a very good guess. Or suppose you want to work with another child on both her semantic and phoneme-grapheme cue systems. You encourage this child to narrow her guesses to words that make sense and look like and sound like the unfamiliar word in the text or story. A very good guess here is a word that makes sense in the text and has some of the phoneme and grapheme qualities of the unknown word. A review of research studies (Tunnell & Jacobs, 1989) supports the use of real books for reading instruction, and Peters (1991) urges use of materials with authentic content for authentic assessment purposes. Allen, Freeman, Lehman, and Scharer (1995) point out that when using children's literature for reading instruction, teachers should not forget to also use it as an opportunity to help children observe literary quality and author techniques.

Lim and Watson (1993) indicate that the use of content-rich material for reading, writing, and discussion in a socially based classroom works just as well for second-language learners. Learners learn to read and write naturally by reading and writing about something of substance. Combining authentic language experiences with content learning leads to learning both the language skills and strategies, and learning the content materials. But Lim and Watson caution that the instructional focus cannot be based on an idea of language as an object, and of content as a collection of facts. This would be counterproductive for the learning of the language and content. (Readers interested in materials for second-language learners might also want to review ideas presented in Ashworth & Wakefield, 1994; Hadaway, Vardell, & Young, 2001; Hadaway & Young, 1994; Olivares, 1993; and Opitz, 1998b. Gillespie, Powell, Clements, & Swearingen, 1994, review the Newbery Medal books, noting that they often portray ethnic characters and can be used effectively in multicultural education. Readers could consult the Gillespie et al. article for ideas about using this excellent children's literature as the content for their instructional lessons; also see Harris, 1997, and look for other new ideas in journals like *The Reading Teacher* and in IRA books.)

What About Using Writing?

Emergent literacy research has helped us to better understand children's language development. By the time children come to our classrooms, they are already experienced language users. In fact, most of them have been developing as listeners, speakers, writers, and readers for at least five or six years. Their linguistic and cognitive experiences and existing strategies enable most of them to communicate quite well through speaking and listening. Additionally, many children, by the time they reach kindergarten and first grade, are already well practiced at scribble writing or invented spelling; and some are even using beginning, medial, and/or ending letters fairly correctly to represent some key words. Often they can read or recognize many words as well. If you have any doubt about this, tag along in the grocery store with a five- or six-year-old, or listen to a child's repertoire as you go for a car ride down a typical suburban main street—the words pizza, McDonald's, Burger King, and the like, are often rattled off with hope or anticipation. Additionally, they often engage in **pretend reading,** which is really not pretending at all—in other words, they already know how to hold a book, and turn pages, and that books tell a story. Pretend reading is just modeling what they know they are supposed to do with books. Developing reading and writing strategies is developmental, just as learning to walk and talk are developmental.

So what about writing, and how can it be used to enhance reading development? Writing can be used very naturally. Since children eventually develop an awareness that reading involves making sense of talk and ideas that have been written down, one of the most natural ways to use children's talk and ideas is to use lists they help generate, pictures they describe, letters they write, stories and poems they develop, and so on, as a basis for early reading work. This is very valuable with children from all cultural, ethnic, and linguistic backgrounds.

Karnowski's (1989) article describes this step-by-step approach to using the Language Experience Approach (LEA) for collaborative group or individual writing: (1) provide a stimulus for discussion; (2) discuss the experience or topic; (3) have the child(ren) dictate and the teacher write the exact words; (4) read the story; and (5) use the story as material for teaching reading skills. In the same article, Karnowski indicates that process writing (a systematic process for developing students' writing) can be used in addition to the LEA, and that the two are not mutually exclusive. She provides this simplified format for process writing: (1) prewriting (brainstorming and discussion); (2) sloppy copy (putting down your ideas using scribble writing, invented spelling, or even pictures); (3) revising (reading it to your teacher and deciding whether to change or add anything); and (4) publishing (sharing your story with others). Both the LEA and process writing involve the child's active participation in writing and reading.

In Chapters 3 and 4 of this book, writing was shown as a means of learning more about a child's strategy development and comprehension. Likewise, through writing, children gain another medium for developing their linguistic and cognitive strategies. For example, Pikulski (1994) indicates that when young children have opportunities to write, they attend to the details of the words as they write them, and this supports the development of their word identification and analysis skills. Lewis, Wray, and Rospigliosi (1994) show how content writing done with paragraph frames provides a kind of scaffolding support for students' cognitive learning as well as for their increased understanding of text features. Additionally, the past editors of *The Reading Teacher* journal, Rasinski and Padak and others (2000a) have compiled a collection of strategies to further the development of reading and writing connections in the classroom.

Finally, writing and reading are really inseparable. Together with speaking, listening, and thinking they are the basis for our communication system. Beuchat (1993/1994) indicates that teachers should include family, librarians, publishing houses, booksellers, and writers, if at all possible, in their classrooms. Children need to see that writers are real people like themselves. Self-expression through writing, and sharing by others reading our writing, are what writing and reading books are all about. (There are so many other good articles and books on reading and writing and several that are appropriate to share with parents and others who have questions about the reading and writing relationship. Readers might want to refer to Barron's, 1990, booklet, *I Learn to Read and Write the Way I Learn to Talk*, also available in Spanish, 1993; Clay, 1987; and Strickland & Morrow, 1989b, as well as some of the others suggested in Chapter 6. As pointed out elsewhere, as new books and other materials are published, teachers should be on the alert for them, and the IRA is always a good source.)

Summary

This chapter has focused on instruction and learning in the classroom and on the circular, ongoing relationship between assessment and instruction and learning. In so doing, this chapter has introduced a plan, focus, and model for diagnostic instruction and has described two of the ways that teachers can make decisions regarding methods of instruction: the alternative method approach and the scaffolding method approach. And it was pointed out that children can and should take part in monitoring and evaluating their own development.

The importance of empowering learners was emphasized, and Boomer's (1985) idea of the negotiated curriculum was described, with suggestions for teachers. Additionally, the beliefs, philosophies, principles, and ideas that tend to drive assessment and instruction decisions were discussed, and some were delineated. A suggestion was made that, in order to provide a foundation and justification for their own balanced professional perspectives, teachers can develop their own lists of the principles and ideas from various positions that fit their beliefs.

Finally, many misconceptions and questions were raised and addressed regarding skills and strategy instruction; learning and its relationship to instruction; the teacher's role in the classroom; the idea of reading as a social process; indirect and direct instruction, and learner-centered or teacher-centered instruction; learners with special needs and diverse learners; materials for instruction; and writing and the reading-writing relationship. A case was made for explicit, direct instruction to develop skills and strategies when the classroom teacher has qualitatively assessed that the instruction is necessary or desirable.

This chapter sets the stage for the last chapter, Chapter 8, which presents rationales for instruction and presents teacher-developed strategy lessons for the enhancement of students' linguistic and cognitive strategies. Ideally, the discussions and foundations presented in this chapter will be carried over as you review the teaching ideas presented in the next chapter.

Questions for Reflection and Response

1. Explain the circular and ongoing relationship between good assessment and good instruction. How is diagnostic, explicit, direct instruction a part of this? Can you defend this idea? How?

2. What are some of the ways you will involve students and their parents/families in the ongoing monitoring, assessing/reassessing, and planning of skill and strategy development?

3. Try working through the steps and questions to develop your own overall plan and model for diagnostic instruction. What areas and strategies will you emphasize? Which require your direct instruction? Are there several children who would benefit from this explicit, direct instruction? How will you proceed?

4. Select one of the direct instruction strategy areas you just indicated, and, using the Analysis of Instruction and Learning Focus Reflection Guide provided in this chapter, work through the guide to consider and plan some specific skill or strategy instruction for children. Be able to justify why this instruction and the evaluation you plan are appropriate.

5. Experiment with the alternative method approach and the scaffolding method approach with students. What was the most difficult part of using each approach? What advantages do you perceive in each approach?

6. What are your thoughts concerning Boomer's negotiated curriculum? What are the strengths of these ideas?

7. What do the terms *skill instruction, strategy instruction, direct instruction,* and *diagnostic instruction* mean to you?

8. Can you think of situations in which you have been involved where these terms (*skill instruction, strategy instruction, direct instruction,* and *diagnostic instruction*) have been unclear or have been interpreted differently by different individuals? What problems did this cause? How does this happen? Are there any solutions?

9. Review the philosophies, principles, perspectives, standards, and ideas from the various groups presented in this chapter and earlier in this book (e.g., see the emergent literacy ideas detailed in Chapter 3). Check off each of those with which you agree. Using the format under "Developing and Defending Your Own Balanced Perspective," make a list of principles or ideas in which you believe, citing the source and relevant citations. Next to each, write a justification for why you support each idea.

10. Review the misconceptions and questions presented in this chapter. Are there any other questions you believe should be addressed? What are they? Try answering your questions based on all you know from your readings and experiences.

CHAPTER 8

IDEAS FOR STRATEGY DEVELOPMENT

Focus and Goals of the Chapter

- ◆ To provide an overview of citations and rationales that support the need for explicit, direct, teacher-planned strategy instruction, with many examples modeling teachers' instructional decisions based on assessments of students

- • To help teachers make their own strategy lesson decisions, providing criteria to help guide them

- • To provide a review of the general procedures covered in this book that lead to appropriate instructional decisions for students

- • To summarize information that provides justification for specific skill/strategy instruction in areas that include the linguistic strategies: phoneme-grapheme (including phonics and sight words) and syntax and semantic (including grammatical structure, vocabulary, and other contextual cues)

- • To summarize information that provides justification for specific strategy instruction in areas that include the cognitive strategies of comprehension, metacognition, and schemata, along with various study skills and strategies

- • To provide a range of classroom teachers' observations and instructional decisions, as well as an array of strategy lessons (using explicit, direct instruction) designed to guide and develop fluency, independence, and meet a variety of specific linguistic (phoneme-grapheme, syntax, and semantic) and cognitive (comprehension, metacognitive, and study) skill/strategy needs

- • To reinforce the importance of individual teachers' understandings, actions, and decisions and the importance of teachers' respect for all involved stakeholders.

Introduction

In the previous chapter the need for some explicit, direct instruction was established; in this chapter we look at a sampling of strategy lessons and activities that use this explicit, direct instruction. These strategy lessons were developed by my students and by classroom teachers who had determined, after qualitative assessment, that some students in their classrooms would benefit from explicit instruction to enhance their linguistic (phoneme-grapheme, syntax, and semantic) and/or cognitive (comprehension, metacognitive, and study) skills/strategies. Some of the lessons focus on one particular strategy or aspect of the strategy, while others combine work on more than one skill/strategy. There is no right or wrong way for teachers to combine strategy development. Contributing teachers used the assessed strengths and needs of their students to plan direct instruction. You will need to do the same thing. If you have several children who have difficulty making a logical guess at unfamiliar words, or if you have children who have difficulty focusing on specific facts and details as they read, you might decide to develop separate strategy lessons just for those focuses. On the other hand, if you have students who have problems retelling a story or a content-oriented message, you might decide to develop a strategy lesson to more generically focus on important aspects to consider when retelling what one has read.

The strategy lesson samples are not meant to be prescriptive. They are only meant to provide examples of how various classroom teachers, from the early elementary through upper elementary as well as middle school years, have chosen to guide, develop, and enhance use of a particular skill/strategy (or combination of strategies) for their students in their respective classrooms. It is hoped that by seeing how these strategy lesson ideas can be implemented, you will be encouraged to fashion your own based on assessments of your students' needs, your decisions regarding what you want to emphasize and teach, your philosophy and beliefs, and your students' input regarding what they want to learn (the negotiated curriculum) and what they most want to read (their interests and motivations applied to the curriculum). A review of criteria, a look at general procedures, and some discussion and examples regarding rationales and instructional decisions are presented, then sample strategy lessons are shown.

Strategy Lesson Decisions

We have already seen that instructional decisions are based on our individual knowledge, beliefs and philosophies regarding assessment, instruction, and learning. Even so, readers may be interested in the criteria used to select strategy lessons for this chapter. Although these criteria, and the need for strategy lessons, reflect my knowledge and beliefs, there is support in the literacy education literature for most of these criteria and for explicit strategy lessons (e.g., see Dole, Brown, & Trathen, 1996; Heilman, Blair,

& Rupley, 2002; Hoyt, 2000; IRA, 2000a; Robb, 2000; Tancock, 1994; and many cited in this chapter as well as in Chapters 6 and 7, and throughout this book). These criteria might be meaningful and applicable for you as you review, plan, develop, and implement skill and strategy lessons and other instruction for your students. It should be pointed out that the strategy lessons included in this chapter provide a guided reading experience and fit the generic definition of what takes place in "guided reading groups" (as defined in Chapter 6 of this book). Additionally, the suggested "criteria to guide instruction" that follow present appropriate considerations for decisions about guided reading.

Criteria to Guide Instruction

The following criteria, in the form of reflective questions, were used to review strategy lessons and other instructional decisions for the students cited in this chapter.

1. Would this instruction be viewed as authentic in its purposes, materials, assignments, and readings?

2. Does this instruction focus too much on performing a skill or drilling students and not enough on the application of skills/strategies to authentic reading and other learning situations?

3. Does this instruction allow students to talk about the reading process and reflect on the skills/strategies they use?

4. Do students actually get to read and/or study as part of this instruction (thereby aiding the development of their fluency and their independence as readers and learners)?

5. Does this instruction build on students' existing strengths, strategies, and knowledge and use them to scaffold and develop other needed strategies?

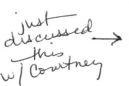

6. Is this instruction short enough, is it to the point, and is it stimulating enough so as to hold students' interest and ensure that they see the point of the activity and instruction?

7. Whenever possible, does this instruction include use of children's literature, personal interests, schemata, and research interests?

8. Will students see this instruction as useful to their purposes and other assignments, or, instead, will they see it as extra work that is keeping them from getting their necessary work done?

9. Does this instruction include opportunities for students to self-assess their reading and/or study strategies?

10. Does this instruction show respect for all learners, including their cultural and other unique characteristics and qualities?

11. Does the activity seem like an actual representation of what readers do and how they do it?

12. Would this instruction, overall, lead students to enjoy the reading/study activity and leave them feeling positive about the experience and about reading/ studying?

Consider and React 8–1

Are you comfortable with these suggested criteria? Considering your own beliefs, what would you add or delete? Why?

Review of General Procedures

How, then, should instruction proceed? While each teacher should proceed based on her own knowledge, philosophy and beliefs, this book has described certain procedures that would lead a teacher to make appropriate instructional decisions for her students.

1. Understand the information from and limitations of standardized testing and be able to help parents/families understand them, too. (See Chapter 2.)

2. Assess students' emergent literacy, interests, motivations, feelings, and other relevant information, as well as information gained from interviews with students, their families, and past teachers. (See Chapter 3.)

3. Assess students' linguistic strategies by sampling their oral reading. Determine what strategies they use for decoding and/or encoding unknown or unfamiliar words in text. Determine whether there is a need for skill/strategy instruction. If so, determine whether the student(s) would benefit from instruction to enhance their use of phonics, sight words, configuration, or structural analysis information. Would they also benefit from instruction to enhance vocabulary, use of punctuation, and use of other semantic or syntactic clues? What about their fluency? Would repeated readings and other word recognition practice enhance their fluency development? (See Chapter 3.)

4. Assess students' cognitive strategies by sampling their comprehension, comprehending strategies, metacognition, and study strategies during oral and silent reading and during various content reading and study. Determine what strategies students use. Determine whether they are successful at understanding text and doing various necessary research and assignments. Determine whether there is a need for strategy instruction. If so, determine which reading and study strategies would be of benefit to them. (See Chapter 4.)

5. Collect, analyze, and use this information to develop and plan instruction that seems prudent and meets individual students' needs, interests, motivations, and schemata. (See Chapter 5.)

6. Group students and organize your classroom to facilitate the program and instruction you believe will serve the needs and interests of all students. (See Chapter 6 and the Appendix.)

7. Design instruction to fit the ideas, principles, and philosophy in which you believe—in other words, your own balanced perspective. (See Chapter 7.)

8. When teaching, continually observe, sample, and assess each student's developing skills and strategies. As part of your instruction, encourage students to self-assess their development, scaffolding and/or modifying instruction when and as needed. (See Chapters 5, 6, 7, and 8.)

9. Involve children and their parents/families in ongoing assessment and evaluation of the children's progress. Do this in meaningful and supportive ways so that all stakeholders are given opportunities for involvement and so that their contributions are respected and used to inform instruction. (See Chapter 6 and the Appendix.)

10. Develop students' reading strategies within the framework of authentic and meaningful reading and study activities in order to facilitate students' fluency and independence as readers and learners. This is the overall goal of all assessment and instruction. (See Chapters 1 through 8.)

Consider and React 8–2

Consider this summary and review of general procedures, and your own philosophy and beliefs, then respond to the question: "How should instruction proceed?"

In the sections that follow, linguistic and cognitive strategy development with rationales for instruction are summarized, and samples of instructional decisions that real teachers made about individual students are provided. These decisions are a result of the qualitative assessment and analysis procedures that are summarized and detailed throughout this book.

Linguistic Strategies

Direct instruction for the purpose of developing and enhancing linguistic strategies and children's fluency as readers is part of word recognition and analysis, as well as a part of comprehension strategies instruction. As children develop these linguistic strategies (phoneme-grapheme, syntax, and semantic), they do so because they are using them to make sense out of what they read. In all situations, teachers encourage children to use these skills/strategies to make more appropriate guesses when they come to unknown or unfamiliar words in text. The more appropriate guesses show development in the strategy. When children attempt to use all three cue systems to guess an unknown word, there is a tremendous likelihood of "the guess" making sense.

Phoneme-Grapheme Strategy Development

Phoneme-grapheme development can include instruction involving phonics, **structural analysis** (word parts), sight words, and configuration cues. A teacher would decide that a student (or several students) needs explicit, direct instruction in one or more aspects of the phoneme-grapheme cue system because an analysis of the student's miscues revealed that she was not attempting, or was unsuccessfully attempting, to use this cue system and the resulting miscues were causing her to lose meaning. Although the teacher would want to call the looks and sounds of words in text to the student's attention when she attempted to guess unfamiliar words, the teacher would also want the student to continue to use syntax and semantic strategies to determine whether the guessed word fits and makes sense. So while the focus of instruction for this student might be on phoneme-grapheme, or an aspect of phoneme-grapheme strategies (such as the use of phonetic analysis), it would not exclude the importance of the other cue systems for help in confirming or eliminating a possible guess. It is recommended that this explicit, direct instruction be done using authentic literature, texts, and purposes, when possible.

Rationale for Instruction Most reading teachers acknowledge the need for some phoneme-grapheme instruction or development. These include researchers and teachers as diverse as Adams (1990), Clay (1993b), Cunningham (2000), Goodman (1986), Heilman (2002), Holdaway (1990), Routman (1996), Stahl (1992), and Strickland (1994/1995). The discussions regarding phoneme-grapheme instruction have not really been "should we" or "shouldn't we" controversies, but instead "how should we" arguments. As pointed out in Chapter 7, many disapprove of instruction involving isolated skills and/or teaching out of context, but even whole language advocates recommend phoneme-grapheme strategy instruction, when necessary, within meaningful text; and advocates of direct instruction suggest that the teacher can best further this skill and strategy development by asking questions, modeling the process and strategies, providing explicit practice, and helping children reflect on content and process.

Instructional Decisions So when are phonics, sight words, configuration, and word parts strategy instruction necessary, and how do teachers decide what aspect of phoneme-grapheme development could be beneficial? This is determined by observing each child's cue system usage. Once the classroom teacher has observed enough to determine that a particular child is not using or is misusing phoneme-grapheme cues to try to identify or pronounce unknown or unfamiliar words, and the teacher has determined that these miscues are causing a meaning loss, some phoneme-grapheme strategy instruction is necessary. The particular emphasis of the instruction can be determined by the classroom teacher when she analyzes the miscues.

Consider and React 8–3

Carefully consider the observations that Mrs. Lim makes about children in her classroom and the instructional decisions she makes for each. What instruction do you think would be appropriate? Think about it, record your ideas, and then compare them to Mrs. Lim's decisions.

Tisha—Observation/Analysis   Tisha often guesses words without regard to their beginning or ending letters and sounds. These miscues have been causing a meaning loss.

Instructional Decision   I'm going to focus more on phonics with Tisha in order to develop an awareness of the beginning letters and sounds and the ending letters and sounds of the words she miscued. This will all be done within context. Additionally, I'm going to remind Tisha to use her strong sense of syntax and her developing semantic strategies to check her phoneme-grapheme guesses. (See the strategy lesson, "Using Children's Literature to Focus on the Phoneme-Grapheme and Semantic Cue Systems" on p. 311 for an example of how a teacher helps students develop phonetic and graphemic awareness and semantic strategies.)

Patrick—Observation/Analysis   Patrick often does not recognize words in text that I believe he should know. For example, Patrick doesn't recognize such words as "boy," "girl," "dog," "cat," "mom," and "dad." I believe that, by now, these words should be in Patrick's sight vocabulary. Of course, sight words are different for each individual, and they are certainly a product of individual schemata, but even so, I think it is unusual that Patrick doesn't recognize these words.

Instructional Decision   I'm going to try some sight word instruction with Patrick, beginning with the words I noted in my qualitative analysis and building on his existing oral vocabulary. The instruction will be done within meaningful text. My hope is to build Patrick's sight vocabulary so that he will "just know" these words when he encounters them, without having to try to sound them out. I want Patrick to gain some fluency and independence as a reader, as well. One good way to develop sight words *and* develop fluency and independence is through use of the LEA. As Patrick repeatedly reads stories he has dictated, he should learn to recognize *his own words*. Using flashcards I will continue to reinforce the recognition of these words. I believe this will help him eventually to *sound* and *feel* more fluent as a reader, so I'll try the LEA method first to see whether Patrick finds it helpful. (Note the way another teacher expands sight vocabulary through literature readings and writings in "Using Children's Literature to Focus on the Phoneme-Grapheme and Semantic Cue Systems" on p. 311.)

Rafael—Observation/Analysis   Rafael successfully uses phonics to guess the beginning and ending sounds of words when he encounters them in text, but he doesn't seem to notice such grapheme cues as the length, shape, or overall looks of words. These miscues have been causing a meaning loss.

Instructional Decision   I'm going to focus on word configuration with Rafael, with particular emphasis on noticing the length, shape, and/or overall look of words he has miscued in text. For example, the word in the text was "bugs" and Rafael guessed "binoculars." I'd like Rafael to notice that the word he guessed, "binoculars," even though it has the same beginning and ending letters/sounds as "bugs," is much longer than "bugs" and has a different shape and look. Of course, I'm going to take special care to remind Rafael to also check out his guess to see whether it sounds right (syntax) and makes sense (semantic strategy) in the context. Additionally, I'm going to let Rafael know that although he was inaccurate, "binoculars" wasn't a very bad guess. It does tell me, and him, that he is using beginning and ending letters/sounds to make guesses about words. He has definitely shown some development in his phoneme-grapheme strategies since the beginning of the school year. (See the strategy lesson "Figure It Out! Using Mutilated Text for Instruction" on p. 314 for an example of an exercise a teacher uses to help students notice graphemic features of words in text while reading for meaning.)

Consider and React 8–4

Did you agree with Mrs. Lim? Can you suggest and justify other instruction that you would also try with one or more of these children?

Syntactic and Semantic Strategy Development

Syntactic and semantic strategy development can include instruction involving grammar, sentence structure, punctuation, vocabulary, meaning, and other contextual cues (even pictures can provide a clue) for the purpose of guessing or figuring out unknown or unfamiliar words encountered in text. Instruction may include a focus on the development of one or more aspects of the syntax and semantic strategy systems, depending on the teacher's qualitative analysis of each child's strategy use. If the teacher determines that a child is often not using, or is unsuccessfully using, his syntax or semantic cue systems and is losing meaning as a result, the teacher would decide that some explicit, direct instruction is necessary. As is the case with all cue system strategy development, even though the focus of instruction may be on one particular cue system, the teacher would encourage the use of all cue systems to confirm or eliminate a possible guess. Additionally, instruction would be done using authentic reading, texts, and purposes, when possible, with an appreciation of the existing insights and strengths that each reader brings to the text.

Rationale for Instruction   Syntax and semantic cues are part of the context of the story or text. When readers encounter unknown or difficult words, phoneme-grapheme cues are usually not enough to help them predict, guess, confirm, or self-correct. Readers need to also make use of the grammar/sentence structure cues (syntax) and the meaning cues (semantic) present in the text. Good readers have learned to do this automatically.

However, some youngsters need guidance and instruction to notice and use the various context cues. Syntax and semantic strategy modeling and instruction can be planned for this type of cue system development.

While most reading teachers and researchers recognize and would support the need for some instruction or development in areas of syntax and semantic strategies for children who need this work, the writings of Goodman and Marek (1996), Goodman, Watson, and Burke (1996), and Constance Weaver (2002) offer insightful examples of instructional support and other teacher-student interactions for syntax and semantic development.

Instructional Decisions   The classroom teacher makes use of assessment information and observations made while interacting with the children in order to make instructional decisions concerning their needs for syntax and semantic strategy instruction. For example, after qualitatively analyzing students' miscues, Mrs. Rosenfeld notes that Angel, Eugene, and Lavonda are substituting words that don't grammatically/structurally fit and that these substitutions are repeatedly causing a meaning loss as they read. Mrs. Rosenfeld decides that some syntactic awareness development instruction is necessary for them. She also notes that Eric frequently omits or inserts words as he reads. These omissions and insertions usually don't fit the structure of the sentence and often throw Eric off. Mrs. Rosenfeld decides that syntactic awareness instruction would help Eric, too.

Some children do better with syntax cues but often substitute a word or words that do not make sense in the sentence, paragraph, or larger context of the text or story. (Remember the example and analysis of Caryl's linguistic strategies in Chapter 3?) These children are losing meaning when this happens. Mrs. Rosenfeld realizes that they are not attentive to the semantic or meaning cues in the text. Semantic strategy instruction is planned to help these children notice how the meaning of surrounding text, punctuation, and other cues can help them predict and guess words that do make sense in the particular story or context.

Like all other cue system strategy instruction, the teacher knows she must take care to encourage use of all the cue systems to predict, guess, confirm, or self-correct unfamiliar or unknown words when encountered in the text. Even though the focus of instruction may be on an aspect of semantic strategies or syntactic awareness, the other cues should not be neglected.

Consider and React 8–5

Consider how several other teachers analyzed their students' strategy needs. What instruction do you think would be appropriate? Think about it, record your ideas, and then compare them to the instructional decisions made by each teacher.

Emily—Observation/Analysis Emily, a non-fluent reader, is weak in all three cue systems, but she *does* attempt to use phonics to decode unknown or unfamiliar words. However, she doesn't seem to realize that she should be reading for meaning, often refusing to even guess a word.

Instructional Decision Ms. Gregg decides to work with Emily on trying to make good guesses (and on not being afraid to do so) using the semantic and syntactic cues in text. Emily can verify her guesses using phonics and other phoneme-grapheme strategies, but Ms. Gregg wants her to focus on the use of the context clues (semantic and syntactic information) first. (See the strategy lesson "Developing a Good Guess," on p. 307 for an example.)

Nicholas—Observation/Analysis Nicholas needs to develop the use of semantic strategies and phonetic and graphemic awareness to make more appropriate guesses at unknown or unfamiliar words he encounters in text. He would also benefit from recognizing more words by sight. Nicholas does seem to have a natural sense for syntax, and even though he miscues often, his miscues are usually syntactically correct.

Instructional Decision Mrs. Langlois decides to work with Nicholas and others who need explicit, direct instruction to develop semantic and phoneme-grapheme verification strategies by reading children's literature and writing text for wordless picture books. She also develops activities that help these children expand their sight-word knowledge. Mrs. Langlois models appropriate strategies so that as the children read selected literature and also write their own text, they can discuss and explain their verification strategies, select new words they want to make their own (sight and vocabulary words), and tell how they remember these words. (See the strategy lesson "Using Children's Literature to Focus on the Phoneme-Grapheme and Semantic Cue Systems" on p. 311 for an example.)

Juan—Observation/Analysis Juan is one of several students who needs explicit, direct instruction and practice to further develop his syntactic and semantic awareness and the use of phoneme-grapheme cues (particularly grapheme) to make more appropriate guesses at unknown or unfamiliar words. These miscues indicate a weakness in all of the cue systems, and cause a loss of meaning.

Instructional Decision Miss Letendre decides to provide instructional activities that help Juan and his group focus on the use of all three cue systems to figure out words in context. She plans for a series of strategy lessons using several methods of text deletions and modified cloze ideas with various types of literature in order to make these students focus on clues in the text. The selected deletions and methods she uses will help the students focus on specific words and clues (see Chapter 4, p. 132, for various possibilities). For example, when she uses mutilated text, blurring or leaving out the bottoms or middles of certain words or lines of words, the students must note the graphemic features of what is left and use syntax and semantic clues to figure out the meaning of the text. (See the strategy lesson "Figure It Out! Using Mutilated Text for Instruction" on p. 314 for an example.)

> **Consider and React 8–6**
>
> Did you agree with these instructional decisions? Can you suggest and justify other instruction that you would want to try with any of these children?

Cognitive Strategies

Direct instruction, for the purpose of developing and enhancing comprehension, metacognition, and study strategies, is part of cognitive learning. The overall goal of this instruction is to help learners understand what they read (comprehension), realize how they arrive at this understanding (metacognition), and become independent learners (application of study strategies). While it is not possible, or desirable, to separate the comprehension and study processes from other aspects of reading (e.g., linguistic processes, interest and motivation factors, textual factors, situational factors, etc.), it may become obvious to the classroom teacher that some children are having difficulty understanding, explaining, and applying what they read. If qualitative analysis leads to the decision that a child would benefit from the development of comprehension, metacognition, or study strategies, the instructional focus would be on those aspects of cognition; but this instruction would not eliminate the reader's attention to other areas, such as linguistic strategies. In other words, cognitive processes are complex; they involve all other aspects of reading. Therefore, good cognitive strategy development should include, when possible, utilizing whole passages, texts or stories, whole concepts and ideas, real issues, interests, and projects with consideration to and in conjunction with all the other aspects of reading.

Comprehension and Metacognitive Strategy Development

Comprehension and metacognitive strategy development can include instruction involving such areas as developing students' schemata, developing students' metacognitive awareness, and developing students' comprehending skills and strategies. These include noting/recalling details, noting sequence of events, understanding cause-and-effect relationships, making inferences, making predictions, drawing conclusions, and summarizing information. The focus of the instruction would always involve understanding what one reads, and the evaluation of students' learning would usually involve a demonstration of that understanding through metacognitive awareness (knowing how one arrived at one's answers and conclusions). Explicit, direct instruction in any of these aspects of comprehension should be done using meaningful readings, texts, and purposes, and building on what students already know.

Rationale for Instruction Most reading teachers acknowledge the need for some aspect of comprehension instruction. In fact, although philosophies differ, the importance of comprehension is probably one of the most agreed-upon areas in the field of literacy education today. Many have written whole books on reading comprehension instruction (Blachowicz & Ogle, 2001; Block & Pressley, 2002; Irwin, 1991; McLaughlin & Allen, 2002; McNeil, 1992; Pearson & Johnson, 1978; Sadler, 2001; Wilhelm, 2001). Overall, there is general agreement that comprehension is a very complex process. Additionally, there is general agreement that comprehension involves many other factors and aspects of reading, literacy, and cognition. Therefore, few would argue with the importance of emphasizing, nurturing, and developing overall comprehension and strategic comprehending strategies in the classroom; the "how" could be the only point of possible contention. As with other aspects of literacy instruction, many would argue against comprehension instruction that drilled skills in isolation or involved teaching outside of context.

Metacognition is an extension of comprehension—I would even argue that it is the cognitive process that confirms one's comprehension. Students who are metacognitively aware not only can understand what they read, but can explain how they arrived at their understandings. Jackson (1993/1994) suggested that metacognitive awareness strategy development is good for multicultural learners. In this chapter, an emphasis on developing metacognitive awareness is interwoven with strategy lessons for other cognitive strategies, as well as for linguistic strategy development. It is difficult to really separate any strategy instruction from metacognition; however, classroom teachers can and do (as you will see in the strategy lessons) often focus on one strategy more than another, based on their analyses of students' development and needs.

Likewise, schemata is important to comprehension. It is clear that without a reasonably well-developed schemata for what is being read, readers will have difficulty understanding. In this chapter, you will see strategy ideas for developing schemata interwoven with strategy lessons for other aspects of comprehension and comprehending skills/strategies, as well as for linguistic strategy development. Because schemata needs to be present before comprehension and metacognition can take place, some teachers will focus on schemata development before involving children in reading the related texts. Other teachers will work on schemata development during reading.

Instructional Decisions Instructional decisions are never made in isolation. The teacher makes instructional decisions based on many factors, including assessment results; things he wants to emphasize in his classroom; his own knowledge, philosophy and beliefs; context of instruction; classroom curriculum and materials; time considerations; and students' interests and motivations. However, certain observations and analyses regarding these factors might promote certain instructional decisions.

Consider and React 8–7

Here are some examples of how various teachers made their instructional decisions about children in their classrooms. As you review the teachers' observations and analyses, think about and record the instruction you would suggest. Then see what instructional decisions the teachers made. How do yours compare?

Yuri—Observation/Analysis   Yuri didn't contribute at all to the small group discussions on families and the different kinds of families and family structures. She usually enjoys small group interaction and is not a shy child. Additionally, Miss Dwyer noticed that she didn't volunteer to work on the family mural for the back of the room. When asked a question about families, she didn't answer. Yuri, a child of Asian ethnicity, is an only child who was adopted when she was a toddler. Her parents are non-Asian and are older than most of the other children's parents in the class. Yuri doesn't have any other relatives nearby. Miss Dwyer suspects that Yuri may not have a schema for different family structures and extended families and may also be uncomfortable because her family is different. This could be what is inhibiting Yuri.

Instructional Decision   Because they are just beginning the family unit, and because students will be expected to do a lot of independent reading, writing, and research on families for the next six weeks, Miss Dwyer decides to prepare a schemata development lesson to define "family" and broaden students' experiences. She will invite Yuri to participate and will also look through her notes to see which other students might particularly benefit from this schemata development lesson. Miss Dwyer will invite them, and any other interested students, to join the group. (See the strategy lesson "Understanding Family," on p. 317 for an example.)

Jaishally—Observation/Analysis   Jaishally is a very good oral reader, seldom making miscues that cause a meaning loss. She also seems to comprehend whatever books she chooses to read, as well as most of the other reading that is done in class. However, when Mrs. Langlois asks Jaishally how she arrived at an answer, she often replies, "I don't know." Mrs. Langlois believes that Jaishally would benefit from some metacognitive development instruction.

Instructional Decision   Mrs. Langlois decides to work on metacognitive development instruction with Jaishally and other students in the class who seem unaware of, or at least are reluctant to explain, how they arrive at their answers. She will begin by selecting a story for the children to discuss and read, something that they all would enjoy. She will encourage the students to make predictions, then she will read the story to the group and ask the children for a retelling. Children will discuss their predictions in light of the actual story, and discuss the strategies they each used to understand the story and confirm or correct their predictions. Everyone will be encouraged to discuss their predictions. If they won't try or if they get stuck, Mrs. Langlois can continue to scaffold and to model how she arrived at her predictions and the strategies she used. (See the strategy lesson "Using Aesop's Fables for Developing Metacognitive Awareness of Reading Strategies" on p. 319 for an example.)

Justin—Observation/Analysis Justin has a great deal of difficulty drawing conclusions and expressing other text-implicit or inferential information. He seems afraid to go beyond anything that hasn't been explicitly stated in the story or text.

Instructional Decision Mrs. Finn decides it is important for Justin to develop strategies for drawing conclusions about what he has read. She wants him to learn to use the text-explicit information to draw conclusions and as support for those conclusions. She decides to design a lesson to help develop these important strategies. Justin and other students who would benefit from this instruction are invited to participate. (See the strategy lesson "Outsmarting Encyclopedia Brown" on p. 321 for an example.)

Max—Observation/Analysis Max has difficulty pulling together the various pieces of information found in text and summarizing that information. For instance, whenever he does a retelling of narrative or expository text, he tells every detail he can recall, but cannot tell what the essence, big idea(s), or overall theme(s) seems to be. He doesn't seem to see the relationship between the isolated details. He also has difficulty writing a report or summary of what he has learned from a unit of study or a field trip. Once again, he provides a string of details, but has difficulty putting those details together into a summary or "big idea(s)" type of statement.

Instructional Decision Miss Beane decides that she will provide instructional support and lessons to help Max and others develop strategies for gathering and then summarizing information. Miss Beane wants to provide this instruction using content material that the students will be working on in science. She believes it is important that students can summarize and support their content reading and learnings; this is the kind of work they must be able to do in the upper elementary and middle school grades. She will try to use various modes of learning to help students be successful at pulling together and summarizing the content material they study. (See the strategy lesson "You Be the Teacher" on p. 323 for an example.)

Sam—Observation/Analysis Sam seems to have good cue system strategies and is a fluent reader. He understands the factual and text-explicit information he reads and does fairly complete retellings. However, when the teacher asks Sam to make inferences from what he has read, he falters. Sam especially has difficulty making inferences about characters in the narratives read and discussed in class.

Instructional Decision Mrs. Langlois decides to develop lessons to work with Sam and others on strategies for analyzing characters and making inferences from the available character information. She uses children's literature along with brainstorming and cooperative learning techniques to develop her lesson. (See the strategy lesson "Using Children's Literature to Develop Strategies for Making Inferences About Characters" on p. 325 for an example.)

Jamal—Observation/Analysis   Jamal is a fairly good and fluent reader, particularly of narrative materials. When he reads these materials orally, he reads rapidly, making miscues, but he usually self-corrects and almost always comprehends and shows metacognitive awareness of what he has read. However, when he tries to read expository text at the same rapid pace, he invariably has problems with comprehension. Mrs. Marchand thinks Jamal needs some guidance and instruction to help him learn how to adjust his pace to the material he is reading.

Instructional Decision   Mrs. Marchand wants to make use of Jamal's strengths (his good comprehension and metacognitive awareness when reading story-type materials) to try out a self-assessment and instructional technique for adjusting reading rate through metacognitive awareness. The technique involves having individual students decide whether they should read certain expository material slowly, moderately, or fast, deciding on just how fast they can read and still understand it. Basically, students try out a material at a certain pace and note whether that pace is "just right" for their understanding of the material. Using rate awareness, individual comprehension, and metacognitive awareness, students adjust their rate for reading (Flippo & Lecheler, 1987). Mrs. Marchand decides to try this out with Jamal and any other students who would like to work on their reading rate and fluency with expository text.

> ### Consider and React 8–8
>
> Do you agree with these teachers' instructional decisions? Is there other instruction that you believe would be particularly helpful for one or more of these students? Why?

Study Skills and Strategy Development

Development and application of study skills and strategies are a vital part of cognitive learning. The overall goal of direct instruction to enhance study skills and strategies is to lead learners toward analysis of the assignment or learning task, and then toward self-appraisal of what they must do and the necessary organizational strategies they could use to accomplish the assignment or learning task. Development of independent learners is of utmost importance. Because of this, teachers should not interfere with students' study strategies unless teachers have observed that some students are having difficulty or would benefit from some explicit, direct instruction.

Study skills and strategy development can include instruction to enhance the way a child uses and reads maps, graphs, tables, and other graphic displays; reads a textbook chapter; outlines information; writes reports; takes notes; studies for a test; uses the dictionary; and uses researching skills, such as in the library. Classroom teachers often make assignments to students involving one or several of these areas. When students know what is expected and how to go about doing these assignments, they have a much better opportunity to be successful. However, the child who does not understand what is involved or how to do it may not be able to do or complete the assignment. A lack of study skills and strategies required for assignments that the teacher frequently makes could cause children to fail or receive poor grades in the content areas involved.

Although I use the terms synonymously and concurrently throughout this chapter, it does seem important to point out the difference and the relationship between a study skill and a study strategy. **Study skill** usually refers to a specific skill or ability to perform a learning-related task. For example, you might consider notetaking to be a study skill. Certainly it involves a specific skill or ability to take notes from either a lecture or written material. On the other hand, studying a textbook chapter is more of a **study strategy** than a study skill. This is because studying a textbook chapter usually involves the use of many study skills in order to have a strategy for learning and/or studying—in this example, for studying and learning from a textbook chapter. For instance, one may need to scan the chapter, take notes, outline important information, summarize other information, read graphs and tables, and so on to study a textbook chapter (Flippo, 2002, & in press).

Once the teacher has analyzed which study skills and strategies the children will need in order to complete assignments in her classroom, she should assess students' abilities to apply these study skills and strategies to the required assignments. Students who have difficulty with these skills and strategies should receive direct instruction to enhance the needed strategy or skill. As with all other instruction, it should be done within the context of authentic reading and study materials, and/or with real assignments and purposes, as opposed to isolated drills. (See Ms. Irizarry's study skill and strategy checklist in Box 8–1.) Ms. Irizarry first analyzed her classroom assignments and then listed all the relevant skills and strategies she believed her students would need to successfully complete assignments. These are the study skills and strategies she will assess and, when necessary, provide instruction in.

Rationale for Instruction   Most reading teachers acknowledge the need for some instruction in study skills and strategies. This instruction should focus on reading and studying to learn. Armbruster (1991) states that "one reason students have difficulty reading to learn is that they have had little practice doing it. According to research, elementary children read little informational text" (p. 324). Holdaway (1990) states, "A great deal of planned teaching and guidance is required to capitalize on these opportunities" (referring to the "practice of the skills associated with study performance," p. 71). Others such as Devine and Kania (2003), Flippo (2000, & in press), and Irvin and Rose (1995) have devoted a chapter or entire books specifically to reviewing or teaching study skills and strategies. Historically, most efforts have been directed toward developing the

Box 8–1	Study skills and strategies checklist			
Name of Student	Reading/ Using Graphs	Reading/ Using Tables	Reading/ Using Maps	Reading Textbook Chapters

Box 8–1	(*Continued*)					
Outlining Information	Writing Reports	Taking Notes	Studying for a Test	Using the Dictionary	Researching Skills	Using the Library

study strategies of older students, but as I point out (in Flippo, in press-a), teachers of elementary-age children are equally responsible and accountable for the students in their classrooms—responsible for their learning, their application of the learning, and for their development into independent, self-assured learners who know what to do, how to do it, and where, when, and how to locate additional assistance as necessary. Study skills and strategy instruction, provided as needed and with children's existing strategies in mind, can enhance this development and independence. As with all other areas of instruction, this instruction should be done in a meaningful, purposeful manner, and not as isolated exercises.

Finally, remember the concern of authors such as Jackson (1993/1994), Kameenui (1993), Spiegel (1992), and others cited in Chapter 7. They suggested that many ethnically/culturally diverse children, children from less privileged backgrounds, and other unique and diverse learners need explicit, direct instruction to compete and be successful in the expectations of the majority culture. Nor should we forget the concerns of Duke (1999), cited in Chapter 4: many such children are not exposed to enough expository text in the early grades. Study skills and strategy instruction using a variety of informational texts can keep these learners from getting further and further behind their peers.

Instructional Decisions   Decisions regarding instruction in study skills and study strategies are usually made after careful observation, analysis, and consideration of assessment information. For instance, we saw how Ms. Irizarry planned to categorize and organize her study strategy assessment information on the students in her classroom. When a student (or students) shows a real need for explicit study skill or strategy instruction, the classroom teacher should develop an appropriate strategy lesson or activity.

Consider and React 8–9

Here are some examples of how several teachers make their instructional decisions. Review each observation/analysis, think about the instruction you would suggest, record your ideas, and note each teacher's instructional decisions. How do yours compare?

Sophie—Observation/Analysis   Sophie seems to have a great deal of trouble reading and using graphs and tables in the various content textbooks Mr. Carlson uses in class. It is often necessary for students to do homework and other independent work using these materials, and this causes Sophie a good deal of frustration.

Instructional Decision   Sophie and Mr. Carlson both agree that some special lessons on graph and table reading would be helpful. Mr. Carlson decides to develop a strategy lesson where children use their personal interests and research to develop their own graphic displays. Those graphs, tables, and strategies will then be shared with each other. Mr. Carlson invites Sophie and other interested students to participate. One student, Alexander, has shown particular interest and skill with the classroom computer(s). He is excited to be included for his computer expertise. (See the strategy lesson "Teaching Graph and Table Reading Strategies by Using Children's Personal Experiences, Interests, Information, and Research" on p. 328 for an example.)

Zoe—Observation/Analysis   Zoe exhibits fairly strong linguistic and comprehending strategies when we read and discuss various narrative materials. She is clearly a fluent and independent reader with these materials. But when content textbooks are used, and she must read various chapters as assigned, Zoe lacks confidence and often cannot retell or discuss important chapter content.

Instructional Decision   Because Zoe is in an upper elementary grade, and Miss Babineau knows she will be required to do more textbook reading and assignments as the school year progresses, she decides to teach Zoe and others needing this instruction a technique for reading textbook chapters. Miss Babineau wants to start with the next required chapter, use cooperative learning, and teach this strategy. (See the strategy lesson "Teaching the SQ3R Procedure with Cooperative Learning" on p. 332 for an example.)

Navy—Observation/Analysis   Navy is a very bright student, but she and others in Mrs. Hale's class often do not do well on tests covering textbook materials, related handouts, and notes from the information Mrs. Hale shares with the class.

Instructional Decision   After talking with Navy and other students who have problems with the tests, Mrs. Hale realizes that she needs to prepare skill/strategy instruction and practice to help students study for these tests. Navy, Chinsan, and others indicated they would like to develop their test preparation and study strategies. (See the strategy lesson "Studying Smart" on p. 335 for an example.)

Martin—Observation/Analysis   Martin, along with several others in Miss DePietro's class, has difficulty noting, selecting, and using important factual information when reading expository materials. Martin often overlooks pertinent details that affect his comprehension of the material.

Instructional Decision   Miss DePietro decides that Martin and others would benefit from instruction and opportunities to practice their notetaking skills within meaningful text reading. Using their current unit of study, Miss DePietro designs a strategy lesson to focus on getting the facts, while making the activities fun and relevant for the students involved. (See the strategy lesson "Getting the Facts: Reporters Take Notes" on p. 337 for an example.)

Gretchen—Observation/Analysis   One of the standing weekly assignments in our classroom involves use of the dictionary. Mrs. Calise has observed that although Gretchen does eventually find the needed words in the dictionary, she has a hard time doing this work within the time allotted. One problem seems to be that Gretchen doesn't use her time efficiently when looking up words. Mrs. Calise's assessment also indicated that

Gretchen doesn't make use of the guide words and is unaware of, or doesn't use, the alphabetical organization of the dictionary beyond the first letter.

Instructional Decision   After a conference about this, Gretchen asked Mrs. Calise to provide supervised practice on dictionary use for her. She is especially interested in learning how to find the words more quickly so that she can finish the assignment when most of the other students do. Mrs. Calise plans to put a small strategy group together to do the actual dictionary assignment. First, Mrs. Calise will demonstrate and model how she finds the first couple of words; then Mrs. Calise will let volunteer students in the group find some of the words and model and tell the group how they found them. Strategies that the teacher and individual students use will be highlighted and discussed by the group as it completes the dictionary assignment together.

> ### Consider and React 8–10
>
> Which instructional decisions did you agree with? Is there other instruction you would plan for any of these students? Why?

Recommendations for Strategy Lessons: Sources and Ideas

How, you may ask, does all of this translate into actual classroom instruction for individual students? This section attempts to demonstrate that connection and also suggest materials and ideas. Although the sample lessons that follow will give you some ideas to stimulate your own strategy lesson development, readers may want to refer to other sources for additional ideas and information.

More information concerning phoneme-grapheme instruction can be found in Adams (1990); Clay (1993b); Cunningham (2000); Dahl, Scharer, Lawson, and Grogan (2001); Fox (2000); Goodman (1993); Heilman (2002); Savage (2001); Stahl (1992); and Strickland (1998). Early childhood teachers, particularly those interested in ideas and books to enhance phonological awareness, might also refer to Ericson and Juliebö (1998) and Opitz (2000). For additional ideas for syntax and semantic strategy development, consult Goodman, Watson, and Burke (1996); consult works by authors like Beck, McKeown, and Kucan (2002); Blachowicz and Fisher (2000); Cudd and Roberts (1993/1994); Heimlich and Pittelman (1986); Johnson (2001); Johnson and Pearson (1984); Marzano and Marzano (1988); Moe (1989); Nagy (1988); Robb (1999); and Towell (1997/1998), for insight into, as well as specific ideas regarding, vocabulary development (part of semantic development and *very* important to students' comprehension). Karnowski (2000) and Robb (2001) provide numerous suggestions to strengthen the grammar and writing of students—many of these can be reconfigured to strengthen syntax strategies during reading as well. Also, Hinkel and Fotos (2002) offer valuable insight regarding the teaching of grammar to ESL students. Finally, Rasinski and Padak (2001) could be consulted for their ideas on fluency development through oral reading, and Opitz and Rasinski (1998) for many effective oral reading activities.

Readers wanting more information about aspects of reading comprehension instruction can consult Block and Pressley (2002) and many of the other books on comprehension cited earlier in this chapter. For a review of the issues and research related to teaching reading comprehension strategies to students with learning disabilities, see Gersten, Fuchs, Williams, and Baker (2001). Robb (2000), Sadler (2001), and Wilhelm (2001), in turn, provide more ideas on developing and using comprehending strategies in the classroom. Readers who would like to focus on developing thinking processes across the curriculum might want to see Hyde and Bizar (1996); Yopp and Yopp (2001) give many examples of literature-based reading activities to enhance pre-, post-, and during-reading comprehension and engagement; Atwell's book (1990) is recommended for using writing as a means of learning in every subject area. More direction and ideas for using retellings in instruction can be found in Brown and Cambourne's (1987) *Read and Retell*. Readers also might want to seek out articles in teacher-oriented journals such as *The Reading Teacher* and *Journal of Adolescent & Adult Literacy* for more ideas and rationales for utilizing various comprehension strategy instruction. For example, Baumann, Jones, and Seifert-Kessell (1993) illustrate how to use think-alouds (a metacognitive development technique), and Ali (1993/1994) explains the use of reader-response for enhancing comprehension and making literature interesting and meaningful for older second-language students; Emery (1996) shows how teachers can use story maps with character perspectives to help children comprehend stories. Also, see the compilation, by Rasinski and Padak and others (2000b), of many comprehension strategy ideas that have been previously published, over the years, in *The Reading Teacher*.

Readers wanting more ideas regarding various study skills and strategies could consult some of the authors previously cited in this chapter, as well as other authors of content reading and strategy books. For example, McKenna and Robinson (2002) and Tierney and Readence (2000) each contains a chapter on study skills/strategies, and the Moore, Moore, Cunningham, and Cunningham (2003) book contains teaching strategies for K–12, some of which include instruction to enhance study skills. Additionally, those interested in developing the learning strategies and related study skills of elementary students are referred to Flippo (in press) and to Flippo (2000) for a book of study skills and test-taking strategies for application in middle and high school settings with students and their actual assignments and tests.

Readers looking for books and other literature they can use with their strategy lessons could consult Barton (2001), Campbell (2001), Peterson (2001), and Williams (2000), for ideas; Freeman and Person (1998) for many informational children's books; Donoghue (2001) for children's literature and activities to enhance content learning; and the 2000 IRA publication, *Celebrating Children's Choices* (Post) for children's favorite books with suggested activities. Also, Beaty (1994) provides an extensive source for picture books to go with children's interests and various genres; many are good for developing schemata and for dealing with certain situations and problems (such as resolving conflicts, finding a friend, etc.). Likewise, Slaughter (1993) is suggested for her annotated bibliography of predictable books, as well as ideas for sharing books with children; Roser and Martinez (1995) are recommended for ideas to encourage and model "book talk" in the classroom; Calkins et al. (2002) and Hill, Noe, and Johnson (2001) provide useful book lists for instructional purposes; and Short (1995) supplies extensive annotated listings of professional resources for teachers. Additionally, Bromley, 1996, provides examples of story maps and webs developed from many children's trade books to illustrate how these can enhance instruction.

Finally, for ideas regarding how computer technology and the Internet can support your strategy instruction, see Grabe and Grabe (2000, 2001); Leu and Leu (2000); Tomei (2001); Valmont (2003); Wepner, Valmont, and Thurlow (2000); Willis, Stephens, and Matthew (1996); and other relevant publications.

Teacher-Developed Lessons for Strategy Development

In this section, samples of strategy lessons for developing, guiding, and enhancing various linguistic and cognitive strategies are displayed. Their titles and focuses of instruction will give you a good idea of the purpose of each. It is hoped that these strategy lessons and activities, designed by classroom teachers, will also give you some new ideas for developing strategy lessons for your own particular students and classroom situations. Contributing teachers all used the strategy lesson format presented in Chapter 7, though you will notice variations in teaching style, philosophy, and the amount of learner input and control. The teachers who designed these strategy lessons are as unique and individual as the students they teach. We readily acknowledge that all learners are individuals and that we must honor their differences and uniqueness; likewise, we must also acknowledge the idea that all teachers are individuals and their differences and uniqueness should be honored as well. Teachers are encouraged to develop skill and strategy lessons and other instructional activities to fit their own styles, philosophies, beliefs, and students.

Developing a "Good Guess"
By Nancy Gregg

Specific Focus of Instruction   This instruction was designed for a second-grade student, Emily, who is weak in all three cueing systems and lacks fluency and independence as a reader. This particular strategy lesson sequence, however, focuses explicitly on developing Emily's semantic and syntactic cueing systems. Throughout this instruction, Emily will be asked to make "good guesses" using semantic and syntactic cues. If efforts to use these cues fail, she will be encouraged to make a "good guess" using phoneme-grapheme cues. My overall plan is to help Emily become more aware that she should be reading to "get meaning." In order to do this, I will try to first activate or "bring to mind" her schema of the topics she is about to read. In this sample, I model the approach I use and my ideas for working with this child.

Suggestions for Developing Background   Choose an appropriate book with stimulating pictures that support the text and contain subject matter or experiences familiar to the student. Before opening the book, ask the student to look at the cover and guess what the book is about. When she gives you an answer, ask her how she knew. Often, a student will say, "I don't know." If you respond in turn by saying, "I think you might know because there are some clues here," the student will be more likely to point them out. Work on reinforcing this connection between clues and meaning.

Use the same approach with the text. Have the student look at the picture and guess what the text is about. Again, reinforce the idea that clues help the reader get meaning. Then have the student read the text to the best of her ability. Praise her efforts to make "good guesses" at words she doesn't know. Discuss why she made a particular guess. What clues did she use? Many of the clues will come from the pictures, but some will come from the textual material itself. If the student does not note these context clues, point them out and model how you found them. By the end of this activity, the student should realize that she is looking for meaning, that there are semantic and syntactic clues in the text, and that it is beneficial to consider how she is getting meaning from the text. Also, if previously she was unwilling to risk guessing at words, this activity should reinforce the idea that it's worthwhile to make "good guesses" using available clues.

Description of the Teaching Procedure   First, obtain a variety of books that will relate to the child's interests and background experience. Next, using slightly sticky tape, removable labels, or post-it notes, block out occasional words in the text. To begin, block out words that will be obvious from the surrounding text so that the student is certain to guess correctly. Before reading any book, always discuss with the student what she knows about a topic. The cover of a book is often a good stimulus for this discussion. Point out that in the earlier activity, having an idea about what the book was about made it easier to get meaning from the text.

Explain to the student that you will read the text and ask her to make a good guess for the missing word. Point out that she will have to listen carefully for clues in the sentence and that the word she chooses should make sense. Next, model what you want her to do. Point out that your "guess" is a good guess because it makes sense using specific clues in the sentence.

As the student makes good guesses, use these opportunities to specifically discuss what clues she found in the sentence to help her and other strategies she uses to find a word that makes sense. For instance, reading beyond the word searching for clues and returning to the beginning of a sentence to try again are both good strategies to use to gather meaning from the text.

Suggestions for Independent Student Practice   Suggest books that the student can read independently. (Some of those I used with Emily are listed at the end of this strategy lesson.) Because this student has been accustomed to reading word for word, it is important to find material that has the appropriate supports and challenges (see Peterson, 1991). The small percentage of words that she cannot read must be words she can guess using semantic and syntactic clues. Highly predictable books that add on a last phrase, such as *There Was an Old Lady Who Swallowed a Fly* (Adams, 1975), can give the student a chance to fluently read the sections she knows and a chance to figure out unknown words using clues in the text. Many other books will also be appropriate, depending on the student's interests and reading ability.

Suggestions for Observing and Evaluating Students' Strategy Development   It is possible to track the student's miscues as she guesses. One method, which allows the teacher to keep pace with the oral reading, is to uncover the word as you go along and place the tape (or label or Post-it note) perpendicular to the word on the page. After the lesson, quickly go back and write any miscues on the tape. The other option is to write miscues on the tape or labels as the student guesses. But be careful, as this may slow down the reading and lead the student to believe she guessed "wrong." Reviewing the miscues reveals valuable information. First, you are able to analyze whether the student is using the semantic and syntactic clues. Second, patterns of words may be revealed that show the kinds of words with which the student is having difficulty.

As the student guesses, and you discuss how she made the guesses, she may begin to make connections not only with clues in the sentence and the surrounding text, but with her entire experience with a topic. These connections are important. They show that the student is beginning to look for meaning and relate new information to existing schema.

Ideas for Scaffolding or Modifying Instruction Based on Evaluation   As the student reads and works with you, she should become more aware that she is reading for meaning, rather than to decode individual words. She will also become aware that she is using clues in the text that enable her to make good guesses. As she becomes more proficient, you can become more critical of her guesses. For example, in the beginning you might accept "*What* candy would you like?" Later, as she becomes more adept, suggest that there is a better guess (*which*). Next, you can block out different kinds of words. In the beginning, many of the words will be obvious or very concrete. Later, increase the difficulty by choosing words that are not so obvious and are more abstract.

By tracking the miscues, patterns of words may appear that show areas in which the student needs more instruction or practice. Follow up by working with the student to gradually provide the additional work and practice she may need. This strategy development can be done using fiction and nonfiction books, magazines, and other types of literature the child likes.

Finally, as the student becomes more and more proficient at using clues in the immediate sentence, have her look in the surrounding text for additional clues. If she misses clues that could have helped her make a better guess, suggest that she reread a passage specifically looking for missed clues. If necessary, make a game out of it (such as a detective game) in order to keep the child interested and stimulated. It is important to mention that students who are weak in all three cueing systems are most likely having difficulty reading. If a student has seriously attempted to use semantic and/or syntactic clues and cannot make a good guess, do not frustrate her. At that point, if you believe it is appropriate, uncover the word and allow the child to use phoneme-grapheme cues to help her with the word.

Suggested Materials and Literature At first, use many relatively easy books with pictures that provide a high degree of support for the meaning. These books should be within a student's schemata and interests. As the student gets better at using semantic and syntactic clues, use books that provide less support in the illustrations. For independent reading, try to provide a large selection of highly predictable books with familiar story structure so that the child has the greatest opportunity to experience success as she reads on her own. Also, the teacher will need some slightly sticky tape, labels, or post-it notes to block out words in text when working with the child.

Peterson, B. (1991). Selecting books for beginning readers: Children's literature suitable for young readers: A bibliography. In D. Deford, C. Lyons, & G. S. Pinnell (Eds.), *Bridges to literacy: Learning from reading recovery* (pp. 119–147). Portsmouth, NH: Heinemann.

Some suggested children's books include the following:

Adams, P. (1975). *There was an old lady who swallowed a fly*. New York: Grosset & Dunlap.

Carle, E. (1993). *Today is Monday*. New York: Philomel Books.

Cole, J. (1981). *Golly Gump swallowed a fly*. New York: Parents Magazine Press.

Fox, M. (1986). *Hattie and the fox*. New York: Bradbury Press.

Hooks, W. (1990). *A dozen dizzy dogs*. New York: Bantam Books.

Lewison, W. (1992). *"Buzz," said the bee*. New York: Scholastic.

Lobel, A. (1970). *Frog and toad are friends*. New York: Harper & Row.

Lobel, A. (1977). *Mouse soup*. New York: Harper & Row.

Mayer, M. (1968). *There's a nightmare in my closet*. New York: Dial Press.

Minarik, E. H. (1968). *A kiss for Little Bear*. New York: Harper & Row.

Wells, R. (1973). *Noisy Nora*. New York: Dial Press.

Using Children's Literature to Focus on the Phoneme-Grapheme and Semantic Cue Systems
By Nellie Anne Kwasny Langlois

Specific Focus of Instruction　　The focus of this strategy lesson is the development of children's phoneme-grapheme and semantic strategies along with continued support for their stronger syntax strategies. Particular emphasis will be on the development of phonetic and graphemic awareness, expansion of sight words, and development of semantic strategies.

Suggestions for Developing Background　　The teacher conducts a shared reading of a book that calls for children's predictions— for example, *If You Give a Mouse a Cookie* by Laura Joffe Numeroff (1985). The teacher shows the cover of the book and asks students to make predictions from the cover and title. The teacher reads the book. During and after the reading, the teacher involves all students by asking them questions, asking for their predictions, asking them to describe why things happened, and asking for their favorite parts of the story.

Description of the Teaching Procedure　　The teacher suggests, "Let's read this story again. This time I have covered up some of the author's actual words, and we'll have to choose from several possibilities which word would be the best to use." If available, the teacher uses a "big book" version of the story and covers selected words with colored paper or sticky notes, listing at least three possible choices, including the covered word. If a big book is unavailable, the teacher can copy the text on chart paper. Consider some examples from our story:

　　Page 2—"He's going to ask for a *glass* of milk." On this page, cover the word "glass" and list the possibilities: "glad," "grass," and "glass." Ask the students to make observations about the way these words look, choose the best word for the sentence, and explain their choice. (The words all begin with the same first letter and are the same length, but the second and last letters make these words look and sound different. "Glad" and "grass" make no sense. We know he needs a "something" of milk; "glass" is the only word that makes sense using this clue.) Verify the answer against the actual text. Encourage students to notice that our selected word, "glass," matches the looks and sounds of the uncovered word, and it makes sense, too.

　　Page 3—"He'll probably *ask* you for a straw." On this page, cover the word "ask" and list "ask," "all," and "answer." Again, ask the students to make observations about the way the word choices look, choose the best word, and explain. ("All" and "answer" make no sense. "Ask" makes sense both syntactically and semantically. Also, point out that "ask" has been used previously in this story. Have a student locate it.) Verify his/her answer against the actual text. Continue reading with the students; part way through, cover up a word—but now, offer no possible choices. Instead, ask students what words would fit. For example:

Page 13—"He'll probably ask you to _____ him a story." Write student responses on the board (encourage guessing). If a student guesses the actual word deleted from the text, include it on the list. Discuss all suggestions with the group. Why do some words make sense while others do not? How do some words in the sentence suggest what the missing word could be? Look at the actual missing word to see whether we are right. (If more than one word "fits," ask which one looks and sounds the most like the one in the text? How did you figure it out?)

Page 15—"When he looks at the pictures, he'll get so _____ he'll want to draw one of his own." Again, encourage students to make suggestions and predictions for the missing word. If no one suggests "excited," print the first two letters and the last two letters of the word on the board and allow more guessing. Again, discuss why some guesses make more sense in the sentence. How do the first and last two letters help narrow the possibilities? (Being aware of the sounds and looks of a word [phoneme-grapheme] gives you more clues.)

Suggestions for Independent Student Practice   The teacher asks the students to form small cooperative learning groups and distributes to each group *If You Give a Moose a Muffin* (Numeroff, 1991) and paper. The small group will read the book together. In each book, the teacher has covered selected words offering three possibilities for each. The students work together to decide what is the best choice for each of the missing words and to defend their answers. Then they uncover the words to verify their guesses by checking whether the uncovered words match their choices based on the looks and sounds of the words. Students are encouraged to make a list of any new words they have learned.

Suggestions for Observing and Evaluating Students' Strategy Development   While students are working in small groups, the teacher visits each group, checking for understanding, offering support, and modeling the verification process as necessary. She reviews the group's answers and listens as they explain. She may select subsequent pages and ask individual students to consider sentences containing missing words and then give their special guesses, explanations of them, and verification processes. Students are encouraged to share their lists of new words and tell how they remember them.

Ideas for Scaffolding or Modifying Instruction Based on Evaluation   If a student is experiencing real difficulty with the phoneme-grapheme and semantic cue systems, provide him with some special practice that may make him more confident at predicting and confirming new words in the text using these strategies. For example, the teacher and student may read *The Little Engine That Could* (Piper, 1990) together. The teacher should encourage the student to use the context as much as possible to help guess words as he reads the book and to verify them with phoneme-grapheme information. All the child's guesses that fit and make sense should be encouraged. If the child also verifies by the look and sound of the word, that is excellent. If a guess doesn't make sense, the teacher could ask for another guess and continue until a guess does make sense, and then again encourage verification with phoneme-grapheme cues.

Alternatively, the teacher may conceal some letters in a word (for example, "coo_ie" for "cookie") in order to help the student practice making initial predictions using the phoneme-grapheme cue system along with syntax and semantic cues.

Sometimes students can write part of the text for a book. For example, in Jan Brett's *Berlioz the Bear* (1991) and *Annie and the Wild Animals* (1985), a pictorial subplot frames the text and principle illustrations. Students may use their understanding of the story to write text with logical syntax and semantic features for these subplots.

Wordless books provide an additional source of potential text. For example, students may write the text for *Good Dog, Carl* (Day, 1985), *The Snowman* (Briggs, 1978), or *Dr. Anno's Magical Midnight Circus* (Anno, 1972). Students can demonstrate their understandings of semantic and syntactic logic while writing the texts. This also provides an excellent opportunity both for students to use phonemic and graphemic awareness to write new words and for students to further develop their own lists of new words they know. It would be useful and fun to gather together students who have done text writings of these books in order to compare and contrast their texts. Students should learn to appreciate each other's choice of words and developing vocabulary, as well as to see the various connotations of meaning that different readers can get from a book.

Suggested Materials and Literature Big book, or text written on chart paper; colored paper or sticky notes cut to cover selected words; teacher-prepared choices for missing words; other selected book(s) for independent practice; paper and pencils for students' lists of new words.

Some suggested books include the following:

Anno, M. (1972). *Dr. Anno's magical midnight circus*. New York: John Weatherhill.

Brett, J. (1985). *Annie and the wild animals*. Boston: Houghton Mifflin.

Brett, J. (1991). *Berlioz the bear*. New York: Putnam's Sons.

Briggs, R. (1978). *The snowman*. New York: Random House.

Day, A. (1985). *Good dog, Carl*. Hong Kong: Green Tiger Press.

Numeroff, L. J. (1985). *If you give a mouse a cookie*. New York: Scholastic.

Numeroff, L. J. (1991). *If you give a moose a muffin*. New York: HarperCollins.

Piper, W (1990). *The little engine that could*. New York: Platt & Munk/Putnam.

Figure It Out! Using Mutilated Text for Instruction
By Kimberly Letendre

Specific Focus of Instruction   This activity is designed to help develop syntactic and semantic awareness and the use of phoneme-grapheme cues (particularly grapheme), through use of mutilated text. Students are encouraged to guess appropriate words, after seeing only part of the words, by checking to see whether the words look right, fit, and make sense in the sentence and paragraph or story.

Suggestions for Developing Background   Try to begin by mutilating only words that you know your students are familiar with. To prepare your students for this activity, model and practice reading with them a couple of examples of mutilated text. As you do this with the students, solicit the clues that helped each guess the mutilated words. The teacher can use both expository and narrative text.

Description of the Teaching Procedure   Find a selection or short story your students haven't read that is within the schemata and general interests of the group and is authentic text that students would have to read for their work in class. Prepare copies of the selection with some of the words mutilated—that is, part of the lines of print would be missing, blurred, or smudged. For example, the bottoms or middles of some of the words and lines of text would be missing. It is not advisable to eliminate the tops of the words, as those grapheme clues are most helpful to students. (To picture what I'm describing, visualize copies you've seen that are misprinted or unclear, showing only parts of words or lines of text. Also, see Figure 8–1.) Ask students to try to read the selection using their sharpest visual (grapheme) skills combined with help from the context of the selection. Tell them to fill in the mutilated words with words that both fit the shape of the letters that are shown and that make sense and fit grammatically into the sentence, paragraph, and story or selection. When the students have read the selection, and have made corrections to the mutilated words, encourage a discussion about what clues led to their particular corrections. Use this opportunity to generate ideas concerning how good readers can figure out unfamiliar words when they encounter them in text.

Suggestions for Independent Student Practice   Students can select stories and other textual materials they have to read for their assignments in class and then prepare their own examples of mutilated text. Later they can exchange them with each other. As their partners figure out the corrections, they are asked to explain any clues that led them to encode the mutilated words.

Suggestions for Observing and Evaluating Students' Strategy Development   You will have opportunities to observe your students' syntax, semantic, and phoneme-grapheme strategies as they work on the mutilated text. Note their reasonings as they explain the clues that led to their corrections. Listen to ideas they generate regarding how good readers can often figure out unfamiliar words from clues in the text. Ask what clues help them the most. Ask what clues are hardest to find or use. Ask why.

Ideas for Scaffolding or Modifying Instruction Based on Evaluation To make the activities easier, you could provide students with two or three words to choose from. The words could have strong grapheme similarities, but very different meanings and parts of speech (for example, "plant" and "bland"). Students must use their syntax and semantic strategies to select the appropriate words mutilated in the text.

To make the use of mutilated text more fun, the teacher could encourage the idea of a detective game. Each day or every few days, students can be given another mutilated clue (mutilated because the detective found it crinkled up in the garbage or in the victim's pocket, etc.). Once figured out, the clues could lead students toward their assignment for the day or toward developing another piece in a group add-on mystery.

The teacher may decide to actually use a mystery story or novel for this activity, mutilating key parts of the story and giving students the next photocopied sections or chapters to read every few days or so. Every so often the group can meet to discuss the story, plot, and events along with the syntax, semantic, and grapheme clues they used to figure out the mutilated parts.

As an alternate but similar activity, the teacher and students can try a modified cloze exercise, deleting (rather than mutilating) selected words in the text.

Scott found a piece of wood and a huge rock and made a giant ramp for us to jump off of with our bikes. The ramp was so high! At first I was a little scared. I pretended to tie my shoe so that Scott would have to go first. He started showing off, racing up to the ramp at top speed, then doing a wheelie as he flew off the ramp. "Come on Caine! I'll bet you can't jump as high as I did or as far!" he bragged. He made a mark in the dirt with his heel where his back tire had landed.

I decided it was easier to go along with Scott than to try to reason with him for the zillionth time, and I headed for the ramp as fast as I could. I did a wheelie over the ramp just like Scott did. I didn't jump as far as Scott did, but I came close. I think Scott was surprised at how close I came because he sped toward the ramp peddling as hard as he could. He jumped higher than ever! But when he started to lift the front of his bike to do a wheelie, he lost control. The bike flipped over his head and Scott landed flat on his back under his bike. Luckily, he was okay, just a few bumps and bruises. But geez! He could have been seriously hurt. He's lucky he wasn't bleeding to death! After that he decided we should head on home.

Figure 8–1 Example of Mutilated Text

Suggested Materials and Literature   A few samples of mutilated text for initial modeling/practice; one complete teacher-prepared mutilated short story or expository selection (multiple copies for each student's use); many books and stories for students to read and use for creating their own mutilated text selections or stories; a good mystery story or novel. (The teacher can prepare mutilated text by using a straight-edge ruler, correction fluid, and a copy machine, or use a computer and its page layout or graphic software. See sample provided in Figure 8–1.)

Understanding "Family"
By Kryss Dwyer

Specific Focus of Instruction   Development of schemata by broadening students' experiences and definitions of "family."

Suggestions for Developing Background   Read aloud the picture book *Mama One, Mama Two* (1982) by Patricia MacLachlan (or another selected picture book). Stop reading at a provocative point, such as when Maudie packs her pens and drawing pencils to go to her "for-a-while" foster home. Invite the children to take out their literature log and to "freewrite" (Elbow, 1998) about what is on their minds, what they visualize, what they feel. From the student responses discuss concepts of family and whether they identify with Maudie. Continue to read aloud, stopping to write or talk about the tensions that Maudie feels and her final acceptance of two Mamas in her life.

Description of the Teaching Procedure   The teacher may continue to read picture books that describe many kinds of families. (See the suggested bibliography at the end of this strategy lesson.) Frequent discussion and written responses should follow so that students develop an inclusive definition of family, providing rich schemata for future readings related to this theme.

Suggestions for Independent Student Practice   Independently, or in small groups, students will read additional picture books, noting the range of family structures in which children live. They will reread to identify the ways in which the author lets the reader know how the children cope with family issues in their lives. Students may lift statements that touch them personally, combining these to create a bulletin board of literary language that describes a range of family issues, organizations, and feelings.

Suggestions for Observing and Evaluating Students' Strategy Development   Records and responses should be kept by students in their logs. Teacher may note the number and the range of books that individual students read. Also note changes in the comments they make during group discussions and in their written responses as they look for evidence of personal connections to the text and increasingly complex insights into family roles, issues, and resolutions or acceptance of problems. Teachers may also make notations of comments that show growth in patterns of thinking about families.

Ideas for Scaffolding or Modifying Instruction Based on Evaluation   Read a chapter book about family life, such as *Sarah Plain and Tall* (MacLachlan, 1985), so that students may "live through" the experience in a longer text of the coming together of a new family.

Students may create webs that illustrate their expanding knowledge and literary experiences with families.

They may revisit texts to develop readers' theater or choral readings of particularly powerful scenes.

Suggested Materials and Literature   Literature logs, paper, pencils, selected literature.

Elbow, P. (1998). *Writing with power: Techniques for mastering the writing process* (2nd ed.). New York: Oxford University Press.

Bibliography of family stories include the following:

Bunting, E. (1991). *Flyaway home*. New York: Clarion Books.

Cairnes, J. (1977). *Daddy*. New York: Harper & Row.

Crews, D. (1991). *Bigmamas*. New York: Greenwillow.

Crews, D. (1992). *Shortcut*. New York: Greenwillow.

Garland, S. (1992). *Billy and Belle*. New York: Viking.

Jenness, A. (1990). *Families: A celebration of diversity, commitment, and love*. Boston: Houghton Mifflin.

Keats, E. J. (1967). *Peter's chair*. New York: Harper & Row.

Levinson, R. (1985). *Watch the stars come out*. New York: Dutton.

MacLachlan, P, (1982). *Mama one, mama two*. New York: Harper & Row.

MacLachlan, P. (1985). *Sarah plain and tall*. New York: Harper & Row.

Rylant, C. (1985). *The relatives came*. New York: Bradbury Press.

Williams, V B. (1982). *A chair for my mother*. New York: Greenwillow.

Williams, V B. (1983). *Something special for me*. New York: Greenwillow.

Williams, V B. (1984). *Music, music, for everyone*. New York: Greenwillow.

Yarborough, C. (1979). *Cornrows*. New York: Dutton.

Using Aesop's Fables for Developing Metacognitive Awareness of Reading Strategies
By Nellie Anne Kwasny Langlois

Specific Focus of Instruction   Development of metacognitive awareness through making predictions about events in Aesop's and other fables.

Suggestions for Developing Background   The teacher displays a picture of a tortoise and a hare or writes the words on chart paper. She invites students to brainstorm words that they associate with each animal, recording their ideas. The teacher asks students to envision a foot race between the two animals and predict the winner. She demonstrates one possible prediction and how she justifies it: "The hare will win the race because his strong hind legs permit him to run fast."

Students then contribute their own predictions and supporting statements. The word associations on the chart are available as prompts.

Description of the Teaching Procedure   The teacher reads the fable of "The Tortoise and the Hare." After the oral reading, she invites the students to join in retelling the fable, recording the student text for later revision, editing, and class publication. During this time, the teacher observes and supports the students in developing a sequential and cohesive retelling. The teacher then demonstrates how readers become aware of the strategies they use to develop meaning. Example: "I was able to predict that the hare would win the race because I knew something about this animal's body, but when I read, 'how ridiculous,' I thought that the hare might be overconfident, and I had to change my prediction. Let's think together about how you made your predictions." The teacher solicits students' discussion about how they arrived at their individual predictions.

Suggestions for Independent Student Practice   Teacher and students revisit students' predictions, noting how they used their experiences and knowledge of animals and races. Students may read an additional fable independently, noting their predictions, the corrections to their predictions, and the strategies they used on blank bookmarks. They may then compare and contrast their prediction strategies with those of others during a small group discussion.

Suggestions for Observing and Evaluating Students' Strategy Development   To observe students' awareness of the strategies that they use while reading, the teacher may distribute copies of the text and ask the students to mark the words in the text that support or help them correct their predictions. Additional questions might include the following: How did the writer provide clues as to character? (For example, with words like "boastful," "boldly," "never slackened," "plodding.") Did you need to change your prediction? Where? Why? How did you know your prediction needed changing? How did the writer organize the events in the story? How did this help you? How does insight into the vocabulary and other language clues and the structure of the text help you to read?

Ideas for Scaffolding or Modifying Instruction Based on Evaluation   The teacher may read additional fables by Aesop, fables from other cultures, and modern fables such as those by Arnold Lobel. Each reading provides opportunity for further discussion of the strategies that effective readers use to monitor the developing meaning. Extensions of these readings may include writing original fables, acting in a dramatization, preparing a readers' theatre version, and creating original murals and paintings. These translations into other modes serve as indicators of students' comprehension, ability to construct new meanings, and overall strategy development. For further assessment, the teacher may eavesdrop during paired reading or talk with children, searching for and noting comments and ideas that show students' awareness and thinking about the strategies they use. She may also probe with questions to help students reflect on their strategy use, as needed.

Suggested Materials and Literature   Chart paper, markers, blank bookmarks, copies of "The Tortoise and the Hare," from B. Bader, (1991), *Aesop & company with scenes from his legendary life* (Boston: Houghton Mifflin) and A. Lobel, (1980), *Fables* (New York: Harper & Row).

Other suggested sources of fables include:

Clark, M., & Voake, C. (1990). *The best of Aesop's fables*. Boston: Little, Brown.

Haviland, V. (1963). *Favorite fairy tales told in Poland*. Boston: Little, Brown.

Jones, H. (1981). *Tales from Aesop*. New York: Frank Watts.

Kennerly, K. (1973). *Hesitant wolf and scrupulous fox: Fables selected from world literature*. New York: Random House.

Outsmarting Encyclopedia Brown
By Jacqueline L. Finn

Specific Focus of Instruction   Development of strategies for drawing conclusions.

Suggestions for Developing Background   The teacher reads one of the mysteries from #10, *Encyclopedia Brown Takes the Case* (Sobol, 1988). Students need individual copies of the text. Each Encyclopedia Brown mystery is interrupted when the reader has sufficient information to draw conclusions about the criminal. At this point, in small groups of two or three, the students write their conclusions on large charts and write supporting information under their conclusions.

Description of the Teaching Procedure   The teacher and students then reread the text to uncover the elements of a mystery, described in Hebert (1976): (1) There must be a crime, or at least a crime-in-the-making. (2) The crime, or crime-in-the-making must be discovered. (3) There must be a crime solver. (4) There must be witnesses who observed the crime with varying degrees of accuracy. (5) There must be suspects. (6) There must be a motive. (7) The mystery solver finds clues that implicate, or lead him to, the criminal. (8) There must be a chase that moves the story to a high pitch of excitement. In the chase, the mystery solver and the criminal try to outwit each other. (9) The criminal confesses and the true story emerges.

The students will find the wording in the text that reveals the elements of the mystery. With this added information, they read the conclusion to the story and verify or modify their own conclusions. Discussion to justify students' conclusions based on the evidence found in the text is encouraged.

The teacher will invite students to select a mystery of their choice from the same collection. Students read independently and revisit the text, following the guidelines to the structure of a mystery, and attempt to solve the problem and write justifying statements. They then read the solution, comparing their conclusions and logic to the author's, and discuss their reasoning.

Suggestions for Independent Student Practice   Students may want to read several more mysteries in their small groups, then guess and write their conclusions in a journal before proceeding to the actual conclusion in the mystery story they selected. They should be encouraged to share their conclusions before and after they read the author's ending.

Suggestions for Observing and Evaluating Students' Strategy Development   The teacher observes the students' abilities to draw conclusions while they are in the process of finding evidence in the text to support their conclusions, as they discuss their logic, and in their written conclusions.

Ideas for Scaffolding or Modifying Instruction Based on Evaluation   The teacher can model how she draws conclusions while reading a mystery.

Students may translate their knowledge of the mystery genre to a cartoon form, creating an original cartoon mystery.

Some students may want to create a visual map of one of the mysteries, illustrating all of the important clues that support the conclusion. In this way, they can document their thinking.

Suggested Materials and Literature   Chart paper, markers, pens, journals.

Hebert, K. (1976). *Teaching and writing popular fiction: Horror, adventure, mystery and romance*. New York: Teachers and Writers Collaborative.

Sobol, D. (1988). *#10, Encyclopedia Brown takes the case*. New York: Bantam.

You Be the Teacher
By Lisa A. Beane

Specific Focus of Instruction   The development of strategies for summarizing information, and the extension of students' schemata and knowledge regarding insects.

Suggestions for Developing Background   The teacher will discuss natural variations in preferred modes for learning: visual, auditory, kinesthetic, and tactile. Students can reflect on their own preferences and contribute to the discussion.

Description of the Teaching Procedure   Over a period of time, the teacher shares Big Books, nonfiction trade books, and videos that describe the life cycles of insects. She demonstrates the many ways in which authors present their knowledge. Students are instructed to write in list form, in their science journals, as many important facts as they can remember about the life cycles that were shown in the books or videos, and to supplement their factual information with illustrations, labels, diagrams, or cutaways just as they have seen done in books.

The teacher makes available a "text set" (Short & Harste, 1996) or set of varied textual material on life cycles. In cooperative groups, students select one insect they will study. The teacher discusses and demonstrates numerous modes of presenting information: charts, drama, transparencies, original Big Books, picture books, narratives. Students may refer to the books in the text set, to videos, and to their own science journals to prepare a short presentation to the class of the life cycle of one insect, selecting appropriate modes for presenting their own information to a group.

Suggestions for Independent Student Practice   Students will create their own evaluation instrument, arriving at criteria for assessing their own work. They can then, in their groups, assess and discuss their work and progress.

Suggestions for Observing and Evaluating Students' Strategy Development   The teacher monitors and assesses constantly. She observes students' ability to select and summarize information accurately in their journals, summarize and use information from trade books, and translate their knowledge into effective presentation modes. Additionally, the students' own evaluation instruments and criteria for assessing their own work will provide valuable insights into their understandings.

Ideas for Scaffolding or Modifying Instruction Based on Evaluation   As needed, the teacher will model how she or he selects and summarizes information and scaffolds the students toward the desired responses and skills.

The basic processes used here—listening, reading, viewing, and then summarizing—can be used with any content area. The quality of many current nonfiction books provides models for students so that they can present their knowledge in varied and interesting ways.

Suggested Materials and Literature   Science journals and pencils; a set of textual materials on life cycles; various art materials for students' supplements and presentations.

Freeman, E. B., & Person, D. G. (Eds.). (1992). *Using nonfiction trade books in the elementary classroom: From ants to zeppelins.* Urbana, IL: National Council of Teachers of English.

Short, K. G., & Harste, J. C. (with Burke, C.). (1996). *Creating classrooms for authors and inquirers* (2nd ed.). Portsmouth, NH: Heinemann.

Using Children's Literature to Develop Strategies for Making Inferences About Characters
By Nellie Anne Kwasny Langlois

Specific Focus of Instruction   The purpose of this lesson is the development of comprehension strategies by focusing on inferences about characters. In this lesson, the students practice making inferences while reading Wende and Harry Devlin's (1971) *Cranberry Thanksgiving*.

Suggestions for Developing Background   The teacher selects a book in which the meaning and entertainment is enhanced by inferences, such as *Cranberry Thanksgiving*. The teacher shows the front and back cover of the book, which displays a cranberry recipe and the title. She asks the students to predict what the book might be about.

Description of the Teaching Procedure   The teacher shows the portraits of the four central characters found on the inside cover of the book and asks the students for their first impressions of the characters. The teacher tapes chart paper to the chalkboard on which she has written the characters' names at the top and the subdivisions for the following categories: first impressions, final impressions, and story facts. Children brainstorm their "first impressions" of the characters:

Uriah Peabody/Mr. Whiskers: hairy, pirate, bad guy

Grandmother: sweet, smart, good

Maggie: young, pretty, nice

Mr. Horace: handsome, clean, good guy

The teacher reads the book and, as often as possible during and after the reading, elicits predictions and impressions from the students. She discusses the element of surprise and the outcomes. The teacher returns to the character charts and, under the category "final impressions," lists the conclusions reached by the students as they reconcile their predictions with the facts presented in the story.

The teacher invites a second reading, this time to try to understand the facts in the story and how they help the reader infer meaning. For example, on page 9, "[Grandmother] was not [very fond of Mr. Whiskers]. Too many whiskers and not enough soap." The teacher asks the students what they know about Mr. Whiskers, judging from this statement. She asks first for the story facts and then for what they imply. In this instance, the facts are that he has too many whiskers and does not use enough soap. The implication is that he is not very clean, and this created an unfavorable impression of the character (as viewed by Grandmother).

On page 11, Grandmother is "fuming" and calls Mr. Whiskers "clamdigging." While she hides her secret recipe behind a brick, children read, "Strange how he always showed up when she took down the great yellow bowl and all the good things that went into it."

The fact here is that "strangely" Mr. Whiskers shows up when Grandmother makes cranberry bread from her highly prized recipe. The teacher asks the students what the sentence suggests to them about Mr. Whiskers: One implication is that there is something sneaky and devious about his intentions, especially towards her cranberry bread.

On page 12, "'Scat! Shoo!' She would call out the window every time he came too close to the house." The teacher may help the students infer that Grandmother believes she must chase Mr. Whiskers away and that the words she uses imply that she considers him animal-like.

On page 14, the teacher focuses on the description of Mr. Horace: "He actually bows, and he has a gold cane and smells of lavender." The teacher asks the students what facts they know about Mr. Horace. Then she asks what they can infer from these facts; they infer that his manners, gold cane, and personal hygiene indicate that he is probably very classy and rich, and he certainly makes a good first impression.

On page 15, the teacher points out how the two characters are contrasted: "There they were, Mr. Horace, pink-cheeked and starched, and Mr. Whiskers in his old captain's hat. As they came in, trailing behind was the smell of lavender in an aura of clams and seaweed." Again, the teacher asks the students to express their inferences.

As the story is reread, the teacher continues to point out significant facts, asking students to state their inferences and the impressions they have formed from the facts. The teacher and students work together in this way until page 26, when the recipe is stolen.

Suggestions for Independent Student Practice   The teacher asks the students to form pairs or small groups and gives each a copy of *Cranberry Thanksgiving*. Each pair also receives character charts on which they are to work together to list facts and inferences about Mr. Whiskers and Mr. Horace, beginning on page 26, when the recipe is stolen.

Suggestions for Observing and Evaluating Students' Strategy Development   While students are working, the teacher should observe for understanding, model, and, when necessary, provide advice. The teacher reviews the character sheets and asks students to explain their answers. She may refer to pages yet to be considered by the children and inquire about facts and inferences.

Ideas for Scaffolding or Modifying Instruction Based on Evaluation   The teacher may invite children to interpret the story by acting out or pantomiming significant portions of the text.

Students may work individually or in pairs on character sheets for the character Grandmother, analyzing story information for all the previously stated categories, as well as describing how Grandmother's opinions of the two characters changed, referring to specific facts from the book to support their findings.

Students may rewrite the end of the story. Perhaps Mr. Whiskers could indeed be the thief, and Mr. Horace the noble man. The students should use facts that convey specific implications to readers. Even Maggie could be the thief. How could the students use facts to convince us that she is not a sweet, naive future heiress to a cranberry bread recipe but, instead, a calculating criminal?

Students may consider other favorite characters from other books and analyze the character for a few pages to see how the author uses facts and implications to portray characters.

Suggested Materials and Literature   Chart paper, paper, pencils, pens.

Devlin, W. & Devlin, H. (1971). *Cranberry Thanksgiving*. New York: Parents Magazine Press.

Teaching Graph and Table Reading Strategies by Using Children's Personal Experiences, Interests, Information, and Research
By Richard B. Carlson and Denise Djerbaka

Specific Focus of Instruction   The development of graph and table-reading skills and strategies.

Suggestions for Developing Background   Children are exposed to great quantities of information as they go about their daily and school-related activities. Much of this information can lend itself to graphing and other visual displays, such as tables. Children can be introduced to the idea that graphs and tables are a way of organizing and displaying information and that reading graphs requires the reader to understand how the information has been organized.

Provide a few examples for the children. For instance, gather data about their shoes. How many are made of leather or a leather-like material? How many are made of canvas or some type of fabric? What about color? How many are wearing black shoes? Brown shoes? Red shoes? White shoes? Blue shoes? Multicolor shoes? Or, some other solid color shoes? The teacher solicits the information and notes on chart paper the numbers next to each category. Using these categories as headings (or any other categories from examples that the children or teacher conjure up), the teacher draws a simple chart or graph, verbalizing and pointing to the numbers represented for each category so that the children specifically see where the table or graphed information is coming from. After the graph is drawn, the teacher removes the previous chart paper so that only the graphed information is now available.

Children in the group are encouraged to read the graph and answer such questions as these: Do more people in our group wear leather or leather-like shoes, or do more wear canvas shoes? How do you know? What color shoes do most people have? How do you know?

Try to develop a discussion relative to the usefulness of tables and graphs. Allow children to consider all the possibilities they can think of as to how tables and graphs can be used and what kind of information can be found in them.

Description of the Teaching Procedure   Make various age-appropriate textbooks and other content-area and research books that contain graphs and tables available to the children. Let them browse through the books and look for graphs and tables. When they find one, encourage them to try to figure out what information is presented by the display. Suggest that the caption under the graph or table, its title, and the labels on it will provide clues.

Children who want to try to read these graphs or tables should be encouraged to do so. Be willing to assist by asking probing questions and helping children discover how to read the graphic materials. Allow other children to help. Model the reading of a difficult graph or table. Explain how you arrived at your conclusion as to what information the graph/table is presenting.

Children may find graphs that are very different from the examples you developed in class; point out that there are many kinds of graphs (bar graphs, line graphs, cluster graphs, stacked graphs, pie graphs, etc.) and that some are better to use than others for certain kinds of information and graphic displays.

Suggestions for Independent Student Practice   Allow students to form their own working partnerships or small groups. Encourage children to research or gather data from any areas in which they are interested. They can use data based on their own experiences, interests, personal information, or any area of content study from your classroom work or from their own readings or other research.

Once they gather their data, their assignment is to develop a graphic display of the data, develop questions that can be answered by reading the table or graph, and share their table or graph with the larger group. The sharing will involve a discussion of the information presented, what it means, and how it was collected. Students can also share the problems they had in gathering and displaying their data. The larger group will then be questioned by the graph/table authors to see whether the children in the larger group can read the graphic display. All children will be encouraged to tell how they arrived at their answers to the graph/table questions. The classroom computer(s) and printer can be used by the children to display and print their tables and graphs, or the children can draw them on graph paper.

See Figure 8–2 for examples of a graph and a table, with questions, that were developed by participating children. There is no limit to the kinds and numbers of graphs or tables children can develop from their inquiry. These graphic displays, based on children's personal research conducted in and out of the classroom, are an excellent way to introduce and develop skills and strategies for reading graphic materials.

Suggestions for Observing and Evaluating Students' Strategy Development   The graph and table development, questions and answers, and presentations and discussions regarding tables and graphs provide many assessment opportunities for the teacher. Use all of these opportunities to observe and monitor children's developing strategies.

Additionally, as children browse through texts, discovering new tables and graphs, you will be able to assess their skills and sophistication as they try to read them and learn what information each contains. Children also can contribute significantly by self-assessing their understanding, strategies, and development. Just ask!

Ideas for Scaffolding or Modifying Instruction Based on Evaluation   When you ascertain that individual children seem able to read and understand the graphs and tables as developed by their peers, you might want to expand their practice toward the reading of graphs and tables in content-area texts you use in the classroom. Suggest that such a

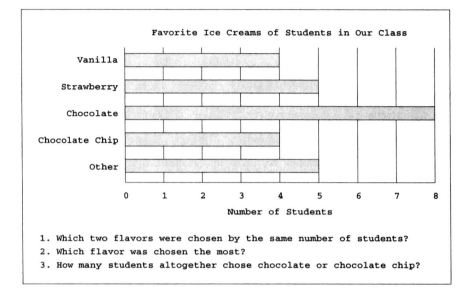

1. Which two flavors were chosen by the same number of students?
2. Which flavor was chosen the most?
3. How many students altogether chose chocolate or chocolate chip?

Number of Birthdays in Mr. Carlson's and Ms. Djerbaka's Classes

| Mr. Carlson | | Ms. Djerbaka | |
Month	Birthdays	Month	Birthdays
January	4	January	2
February	1	February	3
March	0	March	2
April	2	April	4
May	2	May	3
June	0	June	1
July	4	July	0
August	3	August	2
September	2	September	3
October	0	October	2
November	4	November	3
December	3	December	1

1. Which class has more May birthdays?
2. How many September birthdays are there altogether in both classes?
3. Which months have the most birthdays altogether?

Figure 8–2 Sample of the Graph and Table Research of Children

child try explaining to you a graph or table in his social studies text. If the child can read
and explain these graphs and tables, use the child as a peer tutor to help others as they
encounter published graphs in their texts.

If children have trouble making the transition to understanding the graphs published in their texts, take time to help them see how the graphs in their texts can be
read more easily once they read and use the background information provided by the

text itself. This background information, into which the graph is inserted, usually helps students get a better grasp of the context of the research data displayed. It, along with the graph title and other obvious information on the graph, should provide more clues to what the graph is about, what it is showing, and how it relates to the text. This is often difficult reading for even the best of readers, so you should provide children with as many opportunities as possible to work with you as you model and encourage interpretation of these graphic displays.

Suggested Materials and Literature   Chart paper; paper and pencils for gathering information, developing drafts of tables and graphs, and developing accompanying questions; age-appropriate textbooks and other content-area books that contain tables and graphs; graph paper and rulers and/or classroom computers and printers; children's own textbooks.

Teaching the SQ3R Procedure with Cooperative Learning
By Tracie L. Babineau

Specific Focus of Instruction   To help students develop an approach to previewing and reading their textbook chapters.

Suggestions for Developing Background   Children in fourth, fifth, and sixth grades often need guidance and instruction in order to handle the increasing amount of textbook reading expected of them. In this strategy lesson I describe how an elementary teacher can make use of the SQ3R procedure (Robinson, 1946) to provide this guidance and instruction, as well as to provide some structure for her content-area teaching. The teacher might want to begin by discussing what is commonly found in a textbook chapter, demonstrating with a textbook that children are already familiar with. She can solicit these attributes from the children, pointing out such things as headings, diagrams, bold and italic print, and so on. If possible, encourage discussion that would lead to children providing the purposes for each of these in a chapter.

Description of the Teaching Procedure   The teacher introduces the SQ3R procedure by writing the words "Survey, question, read, recite, and review" on the board. The teacher briefly describes each step and later models each one for the students. Some brief explanations and ideas for using each step follow:

Survey: Without reading the chapter, look over the text. Examine pictures, take notice of italic and bold print, and read all headings. In a nutshell, have students familiarize themselves with the chapter, asking themselves, "What is this chapter about?"

Question: Go back through the chapter and try to turn headings into questions. Record the questions that are generated. These questions can set a purpose for reading.

Read: Take time to read the chapter. Students may read silently, aloud, individually, with a partner, or as a group to answer the questions they generated.

Recite: Encourage students to restate in their own words the important information from each of the various text sections. This may be done individually, with a partner, or as a group. Children can restate this information in written form or orally.

Review: Encourage students to review important information and summarize. If possible, see whether they can develop a summary sentence for each big idea in the chapter. This could give students a summary listing for all or most of the important ideas. This also will help them pull the concepts and information from the whole chapter together. See whether they want to restate the answer to the initial survey question, "What is this chapter about?"

Suggestions for Independent Student Practice   Divide the group into two or three smaller groups. Ask each group to work on the same chapter. Have each group choose a recorder to record the outcome of the following steps: survey, question, read, recite, and review. Try to find a role for each member of the group. Create jobs if necessary.

The recorder for each section should be responsible for leading the group through each step. Of course, the teacher will be available, as needed, to facilitate this and to help guide groups. Here's an example of how the first step might proceed in a small group: The recorder for "survey" will ask the group to look over and discuss the chapter. The recorder will write comments and questions the group may have, such as, "We liked the picture of the walrus," or "The heading on page 63 reminded Zoe of . . ." This step helps activate schemata students may have for a particular idea or topic.

After each small group has completed all five steps, encourage a larger group discussion. Encourage talk about how the survey step went, what they each learned from the pictures, and whether it gave them an idea of what the chapter was about. Compare the questions the groups generated from the headings. Ideally, the questions will be fairly close in meaning. When they differ, discuss how they are different and why the information may have been interpreted or expressed in a different way. Discuss how each group chose to recite the chapter. What ideas did they focus on? Compare the important and big ideas generated by the students in each group. Ask students to judge whether the listed sentences adequately represent each big idea.

Suggestions for Observing and Evaluating Students' Strategy Development   Monitor small and large group participation. Observe whether individual students grasp each step and whether each student seems to understand the ideas and content of the chapter. At the recite step, listen to see how well each made sense of the information. Ask probing questions, if needed, to facilitate understanding. As a group, students should be able to help one another to understand. Encourage students to evaluate their own and their small group's success at understanding the material by applying each step. Ask them to evaluate what was most helpful, what was least helpful, and what they each might want to leave out of future chapter readings because it was not helpful to them personally. Students can develop their own personal steps (their modified SQ3R) to try out in future chapter readings. Encourage individuals and/or groups to evaluate their success with their invented procedure.

Ideas for Scaffolding or Modifying Instruction Based on Evaluation   Model each of the steps (again) for individual students, as needed. Work in this way, modeling and then guiding students who need additional support until the students can work through the text chapter on their own.

The questions generated from the headings could be divided and answered in the small groups. Ask each group to select a question or two that they will be responsible for answering and, later, for presenting to the larger group.

Have students think of other aspects of the chapter topics that they would like to learn more about. Discuss how to go about finding the desired information. Allow interested children or groups to pursue the information and report it to the larger group in any way they choose.

Suggested Materials and Literature   Any subject-area textbook with chapters that is currently used in your classroom. (In order to authentically use this strategy lesson with a group, teachers are strongly encouraged to do this activity with a textbook chapter that children are or will be responsible for reading in the social studies, science, or other subject-area curriculum. In other words, this strategy lesson should be viewed by the children in this group as useful, rather than as just an exercise.)

Robinson, F. P. (1946). *Effective study*. New York: Harper & Brothers.

Studying Smart
By Virginia Hale

Specific Focus of Instruction Studying for a test using real content material, notes, and study strategy techniques.

Suggestions for Developing Background The teacher will survey students to find out how each studies for tests. The teacher and students will then, as a group, discuss these findings and develop a list of important techniques and things to consider when preparing for a test, such as prep time, organization, reading materials (textbooks, notes, and handouts), note preparation, and memorization techniques.

Description of the Teaching Procedure The teacher and students will complete a mock study exercise for a pretend test on a real topic/area they are working on in social studies, science, or other content study. The students will study one or two textbook chapters and notes from the teacher. Together the teacher and students will organize this information for study preparation. The teacher and students may use the following techniques, or any others that they listed as a result of their initial discussion: (1) organizing resources/class notes according to importance of information; (2) making study notes, including topic cards, lists, outlines, and diagrams; and (3) memorization techniques, using association, mnemonic devices such as acronyms, whole learning, and recite and write.

Suggestions for Independent Student Practice Students will practice using their own organization and study techniques (as previously noted). For example, making study notes could be practiced by using the students' class notes on a given topic and organizing them into topic cards, lists, outlines and/or diagrams. Students can work individually, in small groups, or with a partner.

Suggestions for Observing and Evaluating Students' Strategy Development The teacher will observe individual students in the process of organizing resources, developing their study notes, and using other test preparation techniques. This opportunity to observe students prepare for a mock test should provide insight into each student's study skills and strategies. Following the mock test preparation, students will also be asked to evaluate their own strategies. What worked for each of them? What was difficult to do? What was easy? How can they use this information to make their next test preparation go smoother or be more successful?

Ideas for Scaffolding or Modifying Instruction Based on Evaluation Students needing additional support can work individually with the teacher. Model whatever organization, note study, or memorization technique is problematic for the student. Then have the student model it back for you. Continue to work together in this way until the student is able to study independently.

Students can pair up and use their test organization and studying techniques by testing each other with the pretend test. The students will take turns being the tester and the test taker. Students can be encouraged to give each other feedback and evaluate each other's study strategies, continuing to reflect on their own.

Suggested Materials and Literature   Textbooks, paper, class notes, pencils and pens, note cards, mock test.

Flippo, R. F. (2000). *TestWise: Strategies for success in taking tests* (2nd ed.). Grand Rapids, MI: Good Apple (an imprint of McGraw-Hill Children's Publishing).

Getting the Facts: Reporters Take Notes
By Catherine DePietro

Specific Focus of Instruction This strategy development project has been designed to provide opportunities to encourage and help students develop, over time, their note-taking skills. Notetaking is an important skill for recording, gathering, and organizing information efficiently.

Suggestions for Developing Background Have the students role-play that they are reporters for a new children's magazine focusing on science, geography, history, or the environment. (The teacher may plan the focus to include a particular theme or unit of study.) These reporters give the managing editor their notes on the stories they're writing (these could be based on information found in a unit chapter, in one of their textbooks, or in other content reading material). The managing editor (teacher in the beginning, but later this could be a student) wants the reporters to stick to the facts (who, what, where, when, why, and how), cite all sources of information, be concise yet thorough, and have a good idea of their topics by relying on their notes. Children pick various parts or sections on different aspects of the topic; these are their "assignments" as reporters. Reporters brainstorm an appropriate title for their magazine. Students who are very interested may also want to volunteer to design a cover for this issue of the magazine, organize the contents, take photographs or develop illustrations, and assume various other publication responsibilities.

Description of the Teaching Procedure After the teacher presents this scenario to the students, she will ask them to read material on their particular aspect of the topic—their "assignments." The students will take notes and prepare their notes to share with the managing editor. The teacher should not require any specific method to use for notetaking. Students should be allowed to develop their own method, one that is comfortable for them and also effective for their purposes. (If students need more help to proceed, the teacher should model the method(s) that she uses for notetaking, verbalizing her thinking and strategies during the process.)

The managing editor will look over the notes with each student and discuss them. The students will be encouraged to use their notes and will be invited to write a story for the magazine using these notes. If they wish, students can find or draw pictures to enhance the content information presented in their magazine stories.

Next, the students can submit their stories for publication. The teacher and volunteer staff will arrange to photocopy or print out each story for the class, collate the materials, and give each student a copy of the new magazine. Each story can be read aloud by its author and discussed. Students can peer- and self-critique. Were all the facts there? How did students use the text to effectively take notes? Were all sources of information properly cited? This discussion is very constructive and, through self-reflection and discussion with their peers as well as through other techniques used by other students,

students should be able to grasp what seemed particularly effective. Students might want to incorporate new ideas into their personal method for notetaking. With continued opportunities for practice, students can continue to develop their notetaking skills.

Suggestions for Independent Student Practice   The students can organize the next issue of their magazine and, working in pairs and small groups, repeat the activities just described. Students can take turns playing various roles in the writing and publication process.

The group can produce a monthly magazine or topical magazine to distribute to their class, to other classes in the school, and to their own families. The students can choose the publishing, story writing, and reporting roles they find most interesting. The focus should continue to be on getting the facts from notetaking and then using the facts to effectively convey information in a story.

Suggestions for Observing and Evaluating Students' Strategy Development   As students work on their selected topic and story, they will be developing and practicing their notetaking skills. By observing individual students as they develop and use these skills, the teacher is in an excellent position to assess each child's development, strategies, and efficiency. Additionally, the teacher is in an excellent position to offer assistance and instructional support as needed. As students share their notes and the resulting stories, both the teacher and the student can reflect on and assess the student's strategy development.

Ideas for Scaffolding or Modifying Instruction Based on Evaluation   If the teacher notices a student is having difficulty with notetaking, she can do some reading with the student and together they can talk about the relevance of the reading material. She would want to encourage him to state his opinions about what is important, to read summaries of topics or written material with him and talk about their importance, or to perhaps point out headings and subtitles to the student and ask him to predict what content under the headings or subtitles might be about.

Suggested Materials and Literature   Textbooks; a wide selection of other materials related to the subject or unit of study; writing materials; art supplies, and/or photo supplies/camera, for cover design and illustrations; access to a copy machine; available computer and printer.

Summary

This chapter has presented some discussion and examples regarding instructional decisions and an array of sample strategy lessons developed by classroom teachers for students in their own classrooms. The overall purposes of these strategy lessons has been to guide and enhance students' word recognition and analysis strategies, their understanding of what they read, and their independence as learners in order to develop their individual strategies for and fluency with reading and studying to learn. The lessons that focused on linguistic strategies (phoneme-grapheme, syntax, and semantic) were designed to help students use these strategies to figure out unfamiliar or unknown words encountered in text. The emphasis was on strengthening students' skill and strategy use while building on their existing strengths and insights. Explicit, direct instruction is recommended when students have lost comprehension due to particular miscues and when their developing fluency and independence as readers are affected. It is hoped that skill and strategy development will lead to success at predicting, guessing, confirming, and self-correcting words in text, so that students will self-monitor their reading.

The lessons that focused on cognitive abilities and strategies included ideas for developing schemata, comprehending strategies, and metacognitive awareness, and emphasized instruction for developing students' comprehension and their schemata while building on their existing strategies, strengths, and insights. Explicit, direct instruction is recommended when the teacher and/or student have observed the need. It is hoped that strategy development will lead to students' further understanding of text and their independence as readers who can self-monitor, self-pace, self-correct, and self-justify their responses and rationales.

Finally, the lessons that focused on study skills and strategies included ideas for developing students' reading and understanding of tables and graphs, textbook reading strategies, and strategies for notetaking from textual materials and for studying for a test. Explicit, direct instruction is recommended when the classroom teacher and/or student has observed the need. When teacher intervention seems needed, the teacher should implement instruction with respect for a student's current strategies and insights.

This chapter concludes Part Two, the organization and instruction section of this book. Readers might also be interested in reviewing the materials in the appendix, which includes additional ideas, forms, portfolio inserts, rubrics, and the like for organizing and implementing classroom assessment and instruction.

Closing Remarks

This book has been about your role as assessor and instructor in your classroom. It has been stressed that "the teacher is the most important agent of assessment" (IRA/NCTE, 1994, p. 27) and that the most powerful assessments are those that occur in the daily activity of the classroom. Much of the cited research and literature has emphasized the importance of the teacher's knowledge, beliefs, philosophy, and goals for her students. It really all depends on you, how you perceive your role, and how you elect to implement assessment and instruction. You might have heard it said that you are king or queen of your classroom, and when you close that door, you can do almost anything you please. Regardless of how true this may be, I hope that "what you please" will in any case be to nurture, guide, teach, and develop a balanced reading, study, and learning skill/strategy program, one that will be based on the qualitative assessment, analysis, and instruction of kids doing meaningful work and assignments, and reading pertinent and/or pleasurable literature, both narrative and expository. I also hope that "what you please" will include respect for the child, respect for the child's family, respect for the child's culture and emergent literacy, respect for your own professional know-how, and love and respect for reading and other literacy endeavors. Good luck, and good assessment and instruction!

Questions for Reflection and Response

1. Using the guidelines in the "Criteria to Guide Instruction" section presented in this chapter, and any other criteria you would add, review the skill and strategy instruction you may have planned for children (see question number 4 at the end of Chapter 7). How does your strategy instruction measure up? Is there something you would add or change? Why?

2. Using the information in the "Review of General Procedures" section presented in this chapter, can you recall and list the different procedures and activities that would lead to your making appropriate instructional decisions for students? If asked to, how would you explain and justify each?

3. Using some of the citations and rationales presented in this chapter, try making a case for developing phoneme-grapheme skills/strategies for children in need with teacher-planned, explicit, direct instruction.

4. Using some of the citations and rationales presented in this chapter, try making a case for developing syntactic and semantic strategies for children in need with teacher-planned, explicit, direct instruction.

5. Using some of the citations and rationales presented in this chapter, make a case for developing comprehension and metacognitive strategies for children in need.

6. Using some of the citations and rationales presented in this chapter, make a case for developing study skills and strategies for children in need.

7. If possible, further develop, fine-tune, and detail your own strategy lesson for the specific area or skill/strategy you identified in question number 4 at the

end of Chapter 7. Be sure to refer back to your notes regarding any necessary changes to be made after you compared your ideas to the delineated criteria (see your response to question number 1 in this chapter's "Questions for Reflection and Response").

8. How can you ensure that your instruction is truly an outgrowth of your assessment and that your instruction provides more opportunities for continued assessment in your classroom?

9. What does the idea "You are king or queen of your classroom, and when you close that door, you can do almost anything you please" mean to you? How can you combine "what you please" with what is most important for and respectful of each student and his/her family in your class?

10. If you were asked to pose one question that could be used to evaluate a classroom teacher's understanding of literacy assessment and instruction, what would it be? Why is the question a good one to ask? How would *you* answer it?

PORTFOLIO, RUBRIC, AND OTHER IDEAS FOR REFLECTION, ONGOING ASSESSMENT, AND ORGANIZING FOR INSTRUCTION

Portfolio Sample for Reading

My Name _____ Date _____

What I selected:

How I selected it:

Why it was selected:

Portfolio Sample for Writing

My Name _____ Date _____

*What I selected:

How I selected it:

Why it was selected:

*Note: I attached it to this writing sample form.

Name _____   Date _____

My Portfolio

My portfolio is organized in this way:

I organize it this way because:

My best work is:

My work that needs "more work" is:

My work that has shown the most improvement is:

Why:

I am proudest of:

Why:

Organizing My Portfolio

My Name _____   Date _____

I have looked through everything I have collected for my portfolio. I have organized it all into separate piles. Each pile contains a certain kind of work and certain kinds of examples. Each pile is like a chapter of my portfolio. Below I have named and listed all my chapters and drawn a picture to represent each. I have also explained what is in each chapter and why it is there.

My Chapter Titles	What is in each chapter?	Why it is here?
Chapter 1: _____		
Picture of Chapter 1		
Chapter 2: _____		
Picture of Chapter 2		
Chapter 3: _____		
Picture of Chapter 3		
Chapter 4: _____		
Picture of Chapter 4		
Chapter 5: _____		
Picture of Chapter 5		

Portfolio Contents

My Name _____ Date _____

List of Included Items:
(in the order they have been included)

Why I Included Them:
(For example: favorite book/story; favorite
writing I've done; sample of . . .)

1. _____ | _____
2. _____ | _____
3. _____ | _____
4. _____ | _____
5. _____ | _____
6. _____ | _____
7. _____ | _____
8. _____ | _____
9. _____ | _____
10. _____ | _____
11. _____ | _____
12. _____ | _____
13. _____ | _____
14. _____ | _____
15. _____ | _____
16. _____ | _____
17. _____ | _____
18. _____ | _____
19. _____ | _____
20. _____ | _____
21. _____ | _____
22. _____ | _____
23. _____ | _____
24. _____ | _____
25. _____ | _____

A Title for My Portfolio

After reviewing my entire portfolio, I think a good title for it is:

_____

_____

_____

This is why: _____

_____

_____

_____

_____

_____

_____

_____

_____

_____

_____

_____

_____

_____

_____

_____

My signature _____ Date _____

A picture to illustrate what I like best about my portfolio:

_____

My Signature

_____

Date

My Portfolio Reading and Writing Summary

Here's what is best about my reading:

Here's what I think I could do better on my reading:

Here's what is best about my writing:

Here's what I think I could do better on my writing:

My Name _____ Date _____

Warning! Beware! If you read my portfolio you are going to find out a lot about me. Like . . .

How I read: _____
_____
_____
_____

What I like to read: _____
_____
_____
_____

How I write: _____
_____
_____
_____

What I like to write: _____
_____
_____
_____

What I like to do: _____
_____
_____
_____
_____

And, who I am: _____
_____
_____
_____
_____

_____   _____
My Signature   Date

Portfolio Evaluation Form

Name of Portfolio Author _____
Name of Evaluator _____
Date of Evaluation _____

After a careful review of this portfolio, this is my evaluation:

Samples of reading are _____

Because _____

Samples of writing are _____

Because _____

Overall, the best thing(s) I liked about this portfolio is/are _____

Because _____

If I were the portfolio author I would _____

Because _____

Rubric for
Self-Evaluation · Teacher Evaluation of Reading   Skills · Strategies · Comprehension
(circle one of these)   (circle one of these)

Goal: _____

Scoring Criteria	Objective: ___	Objective: ___	Objective: ___	Objective: ___	Objective: ___
5	Criteria: ___	Criteria: ___	Criteria: ___	Criteria: ___	Criteria: ___
4	Criteria: ___	Criteria: ___	Criteria: ___	Criteria: ___	Criteria: ___
3	Criteria: ___	Criteria: ___	Criteria: ___	Criteria: ___	Criteria: ___
2	Criteria: ___	Criteria: ___	Criteria: ___	Criteria: ___	Criteria: ___
1	Criteria: ___	Criteria: ___	Criteria: ___	Criteria: ___	Criteria: ___

KEY: 5 – Excellent; 4 – Good; 3 – Satisfactory; 2 – Fair; 1 – Needs Improvement

Rubric for
Self-Evaluation · Teacher Evaluation of Writing
(circle one of these)

Conventions · Organization ·
Content
(circle one of these)

Goal: _____

Scoring Criteria	Objective: _____	Objective: _____	Objective: _____	Objective: _____	Objective: _____
5	Criteria: _____	Criteria: _____	Criteria: _____	Criteria: _____	Criteria: _____
4	Criteria: _____	Criteria: _____	Criteria: _____	Criteria: _____	Criteria: _____
3	Criteria: _____	Criteria: _____	Criteria: _____	Criteria: _____	Criteria: _____
2	Criteria: _____	Criteria: _____	Criteria: _____	Criteria: _____	Criteria: _____
1	Criteria: _____	Criteria: _____	Criteria: _____	Criteria: _____	Criteria: _____

KEY: 5 – Excellent; 4 – Good; 3 – Satisfactory; 2 – Fair; 1 – Needs Improvement

Student Conference Record for Reading

Date _____

Student's Name _____

What is the title of the book you are reading? _____

Who wrote it? _____

Have you read other books by this author? If so, what books? _____

_____

_____

Why did you choose this book? _____

Tell something about the story so far: _____

_____

_____

_____

What would you like to do when you finish this book? (For example: write a report, draw a poster, give an oral report to the class, write a letter to the author, etc.) Why? _____

_____

_____

_____

Would you like to read another book by this same author? Why? _____

_____

_____

_____

_____

Teacher and student comments: _____

_____

_____

_____

_____

Student Conference Record for Writing

Date _____

Student's Name _____

What is the title of the piece you are writing now? _____

What kind of piece is it (story, poem, essay, report, etc.)? _____

How far have you gotten in the writing process (rough draft, self-editing, peer editing, polishing)?

_____

_____

_____

What do you plan to do next with this piece? _____

_____

_____

_____

What do you like best about this piece? _____

_____

_____

_____

Is there anything you would like to change in this piece? _____

_____

_____

_____

Teacher and student comments: _____

_____

_____

_____

_____

My Chapter Book Review

Title _____

Author _____

Why did I choose this book? _____

Main character(s)	**The setting(s)**

State the main problem(s) or situation(s): _____

_____

_____

Tell about the ending—giving the climax and/or resolution: _____

_____

_____

Was there a theme? Do you have a question for the author? _____

_____

_____

Rename the chapters
(Carefully choose your words to entice the reader.)

What book do you want to read next?

Title _____

Author _____

Why? _____

To become a better reader I need to [write or list your ideas]:

Checklist

1. 5 morning journal entries _____

2. Favorite book of the week

    _____
    title   author

3. Writing workshop _____

    _____

    _____
    title/idea of my piece

4. Completed science activities _____

5. Made an entry in science log _____

6. Completed math homework _____

7. Made an entry in social studies log _____

8. I shared _____ this week with:

    _____ the whole class   _____ a small group

    _____ the teacher   _____ another student

9. Interest group (s) _____

    _____

10. Idea of the week _____

    _____

11. Strategy group idea(s) of the week _____

    _____

12. Attended and shared at class meetings _____

    _____

13. My ideas about the week _____

    _____

    _____

    _____

    _____

Using the Computer to Organize for Instruction

Teachers can use computers to assist in organizing for instruction. It requires an initial investment of time on the part of the teacher, but the benefits are twofold. After the system is learned, the computer can save the teacher a lot of time; as well, the teacher can serve as a model for his students in using a computer for authentic purposes.

In organizing students for instruction, the computer can be used to create grids listing the name of each child in the class and the areas or strategies in which the children need assistance or development. It is easy to move a name from one group or designation to another, and children's names can be noted for many and various groups or designations. Viewing these grids and lists can be helpful to the teacher in planning instruction and making decisions regarding appropriate groupings and purposes. Schedules, assignments, and evaluations can also be recorded on the computer. See the Strategy Group Chart and the Work Completed Chart generated on the computer to illustrate examples of organizational possibilities.

Strategy Group Chart

Names	Reading with purpose	Using prior knowledge	Predicting	Using all language cues	Confirming and correcting	Monitoring own comprehension	Reviewing and retaining information	Adjusting rate for material/ purpose	Reading graphic displays	Researching skills	Pursuing special reading interests
Aaron	✓	✓				✓		✓			
Becca						✓			✓		
Domingo			✓						✓		
Elizabeth	✓					✓		✓		✓	
Jessica		✓		✓						✓	✓
Kai				✓					✓		
Kaycie		✓		✓	✓						
Kit					✓		✓				✓

Work Completed Chart

Names	Journal Entry	Book Review	Story Response	Writing Workshop	Group Assignments	Handwriting Sample	Research Project	Write to Spell	Sharing
Aaron									
Becca									
Domingo									
Elizabeth									
Jessica									
Kai									
Kaycie									
Kit									

Qualitative Analysis of Linguistic Systems Summary Sheet

Student _____   Date _____

			Cue System Usage	
Miscue in Full Sentence	Meaning Change*	Phoneme - Grapheme	Syntax	Semantic

* Was this a change of author's intended meaning?

GLOSSARY

Affective influences The child's interests, motivations, attitudes, self-image, feelings, and needs.

Age-level equivalent scores These are norm-referenced scores derived from the average raw scores of children in the norming group who took the test under consideration at a particular age; the scores are reported in years and months. Derived and used very much like grade-equivalent scores.

Alphabetic principle The concept that spoken words are represented by written spellings (or symbols).

Alternative method approach A teaching approach that involves trying out various methods for teaching the needed strategy to see which one is easiest, or most helpful, for the child.

Analysis As used in this book, an open, flexible, reflective, and ongoing type of evaluation process.

Anchor papers Actual models or samples of student work to correspond to the scoring criteria for each performance level of the rubric.

Anecdotal notes General and specific notes about what you observe or what the child is doing as it relates to your purpose for observing the child.

Assessment All observations, samplings, and other informal and formal, written, oral, or performance-type testing that a teacher might do in order to gather information about a child's abilities, interests, motivations, feelings, attitudes, strategies, skills, and special cultural or sociocultural considerations. Assessment is ongoing and includes information from multiple sources, including children's reflections and those of their parents/families.

At-risk Learners who have been identified as potentially being at risk of having problems learning due to being disadvantaged in some way.

Authentic assessments Assessments of many kinds of literacy abilities in contexts that closely resemble the actual situations in which those abilities are used.

Authentic purposes "Real" purposes for reading and study, as opposed to contrived purposes and assignments.

Authentic reading materials "Real" reading materials, as opposed to the contrived materials used in workbooks and in other contrived assignments.

Automaticity The ability to automatically or with little effort identify, decode, or know words.

Balanced perspective   One that makes use of the most appropriate ideas from various philosophies.

Benchmarks   Describe or provide examples of student behavior, growth, or performance that may be useful in judging various stages of development. (See "markers.")

Blends   Combinations of letters that blend to make one sound, with minimal change to the sounds of the individual letters.

Cloze assessment   A method of determining a student's ability to read specific textual materials by having him fill in words that have been deleted from the text.

Code teaching methods   Various types of phonic and graphophonic instruction.

Coded comprehension questions   Each question is designated by the kind of question; for example: recalling of details, making an inference, drawing conclusions, and so forth. These designations help the teacher evaluate the student's comprehension skills.

Coefficient of equivalence   A type of reliability that reports parallel or alternate form reliability so that test users can know what to expect if they use an alternate form of the same test. (See "test reliability.")

Coefficient of stability   An indication of a test's stability over time. (See "test reliability.")

Cognition   The process of recognizing, conceiving, judging, and reasoning; also "knowing."

Cognitive experience   A child's existing knowledge and related experience.

Comprehension   The process by which we read and get information and/or meaning from text; also, the result (product) of our reading of text.

Concurrent validity   A type of criterion-related validity. Reported with a validity coefficient.

Configuration   Shape of words.

Congruent validity   A type of construct validity. (See "construct validity.")

Construct validity   The relationship between the test and a specific trait. No single validity coefficient can report the construct validity of a test.

Content reading inventories   An informal assessment usually based on the silent reading of expository text material, involving students answering questions based on the reading; sometimes called "group reading inventories."

Content validity   The extent to which a test measures something explicitly relevant to the population being tested and to the purpose of the testing. The most important validity for the classroom teacher. Not reported with a validity coefficient.

Context   Reading situation, surrounding text.

Context clues   Syntax and semantic clues found in the text.

Context of instruction   This includes teachers' beliefs and the classroom environment, classroom organization, grouping patterns, and classroom interactions.

Contextual factors   Factors affected by the reading situation and/or by the text itself.

Conventions   Spelling, punctuation, capitalization, presentation, layout, style, structure, and coherence.

Convergent validity   A type of construct validity. (See "construct validity.")

Cooperative learning groups   Students working together in a group small enough that everyone can participate on a collective task that has been clearly assigned. Students are expected to carry out their task without direct and immediate supervision of the teacher. Examples include interest and content groups, literature and author preference groups, and peer and authoring groups.

Criterion-referenced scores   Scores that are determined from the quantitative results of commercially prepared tests by comparing a student's raw score to the predetermined passing score for the test or subtest.

Criterion-referenced tests   Test developers base the scores for passing the tests on comparisons of students' scores to certain predetermined "criteria."

Criterion-related validity   A predictive validity measure that involves correlating the test with an accepted index or criterion. Reported with a validity coefficient.

Cross-age tutoring   Older children helping younger children; shared learning.

Cue (cues, plural)   A synonym for clue (clues).

Cultural and sociocultural considerations   Unique qualities, lifestyles, and values.

Cultural difference paradigm   A paradigm that supports the idea of teachers using strategies that are consistent with children's cultural characteristics, showing respect for their cultures, lifestyles, and values, as opposed to a deficit (fix-it) theory of children's needs.

Cut-off score   On criterion-referenced tests, this score separates those that pass from those who fail a particular test.

Data   Meaningful information gathered by the teacher concerning or impacting the child's reading of school-related and recreational materials.

Decoding   A definition of word recognition and analysis that indicates it (word recognition and analysis) starts with symbols and involves getting the intended meaning of words by identifying and analyzing symbols of familiar language.

Derived scores   Scores such as percentile ranks, grade equivalents, and stanines that have been developed or "derived" from raw scores.

Developmental punctuation   Children's use of punctuation based on their evolving knowledge of how written language works.

Diagnostic instruction   See "diagnostic teaching."

Diagnostic teaching   The integration of assessment and instruction, permitting teachers to observe the ways in which different reader and contextual factors may be influencing a student's reading. Teachers continuously assess students' strategy use as students read a variety of texts and encounter various difficulties with text. Same as "diagnostic instruction."

Diagnostic tests   Tests that are designed to assess strengths and weaknesses.

Direct instruction   Instruction that involves the teacher taking a more dominant role, where teacher talk and teacher intervention is more obvious; also see "direct instructional activities."

Direct instructional activities   Planned and specific teacher-directed instruction; same as "direct instruction."

Discrete reading skills   Separate reading skills. Sometimes presented in isolation on many norm-referenced and criterion-referenced tests.

Discriminant validity   A type of construct validity. (See "construct validity.")

Diverse learners   Children who have diverse backgrounds and needs.

Emergent literacy   A point of view that supports the idea that because of the complexity of each child's literacy development, it is productive to observe children's understandings about reading and writing by viewing the strategies they use. These strategies involve many skills, but the skills are not necessarily linear or in hierarchical order.

Encoding   A definition of word recognition and analysis that indicates it (word recognition and analysis) starts with an idea or with meaning and involves bringing meaning to the symbols to arrive at the message.

Environmental print   The words on objects and places in our environment, which seem to be all around us as we move through our daily lives, routines, and activities.

Error analysis   See "miscue analysis."

ESL   The abbreviation for English as a Second Language.

Evaluation   This involves making use of assessment information to make judgments and decisions about the quality of children's work and performance.

Explicit instruction   A meaningful, qualitative, and learner-centered approach to instruction; skill and strategy instruction that is based on students' needs and builds on what students already know.

Expository text   Most content and informational-type texts. Uses five types of text structures.

Extrapolate   A procedure that involves inferring an unknown score from a known score.

Face validity   This is determined by a somewhat superficial examination of test content; does this test look like it measures what it claims to measure?

Family literacy   The ways that parents, children, and extended family members use literacy at home and in their communities.

Flexible grouping   Classroom groupings of students that are fluid and that are called together for a focus on particular skills, strategies, interests, motivations, literature, and other purposes, but *not* with a particular focus on ability levels.

Fluency   The ability to read both smoothly and accurately.

Formal assessments   Measurements such as standardized tests, basal workbooks and tests, and teacher-made objective tests dominated by multiple choice, true/false, and other questions to which there is only one correct or acceptable answer.

Frustration level   The reading level at which the child reaches complete frustration.

Genre   The type or form of literary content; for example, novels, poems, fairy tales, histories, biographies, and so on.

Graded passages Reading materials that have been identified as written at certain grade-level designations.

Graded word lists Groups of words ranked by grade-level designations.

Grade-level equivalent scores These are norm-referenced scores derived from the average raw scores of children in the norming group who took the test under consideration in a particular month of school; the school year is divided into ten-month increments and scores are reported for each grade and month. Derived and used very much like age-level equivalent scores.

Graphophonic The term that many reading experts use when they refer to sound and sight clues and strategies rather than using the term *phoneme-grapheme*.

Group reading inventories See "content reading inventories."

Guided reading groups Flexible reading groups in which the teacher guides students through the reading of the text or story for a meaningful reading experience and provides necessary support and modeling along the way.

Hidden curriculum The curriculum that no teacher explicitly teaches but that all students learn (as cited in the multicultural education literature).

High-stakes assessment When one test or assessment instrument is used to make important decisions about students, teachers, and their schools.

Implicit detail Detail derived from information implied, but not explicitly stated, in the text.

Independent level The reading level at which the child is able to function independently in reading.

Indirect instruction More covert instruction that involves the teacher planning and orchestrating classroom situations that will lead to specific outcomes.

Individualization The adjustment of teaching-learning activities to students' skills/ strategies, interests, and needs.

Informal assessments These include observations, interviews, and samplings orchestrated by the classroom teacher to assess skills/strategies, approaches, and processes children use.

Informal Reading Inventories (IRIs) An informal assessment instrument which involves having children read from graded word lists and passages, then answer comprehension questions to determine their reading levels.

Instructional context The setting and conditions of instruction.

Instructional level The reading level at which the child can profit from teacher-directed reading instruction.

Internal consistency reliability A type of reliability that reports the consistency of performance among various test items. (See "test reliability.")

Invented spelling Writers' own spellings. Recognized as being based on their individual knowledge of language.

Item clusters Groups of items measuring specific objectives on standardized tests.

Language experience activities   Teaching/learning activities that involve the teacher taking dictation from a child as the child tells a story; later the child is asked to read back his story. Stories often are used as springboards to highlight sight word development, as well as for other skill/strategy instruction. (See "Language Experience Approach (LEA).")

Language Experience Approach (LEA)   A method of teaching reading that uses language experience activities to promote a stimulus for discussion and dictation of a story or paragraph. (See "language experience activities.")

Large-scale testing   Testing of students in an entire school, district, or state.

Learning strategies   Self-initiated strategies that help learners learn and acquire the desired information.

Leveled texts   Books and texts that have been ordered according to their difficulty for readers. The texts are then usually "matched" to particular readers.

Linguistic cueing systems   Three cue systems that include the phoneme-grapheme, syntax, and semantic systems.

Linguistic experience   A child's experience with language, including syntax, semantic, and phoneme-grapheme experience.

Markers   Signs of a child's growth. Represents the same idea as "benchmarks." (See "benchmarks.")

Matthew effect   According to the Matthew effect, the literacy-rich get richer, and the literacy-poor get poorer in reading opportunities, vocabulary development, written language, general knowledge, and so on.

Mean   The average raw score of a group. Determined by adding all the students' raw scores and dividing by the number of students in the group.

Medial sounds   Sounds in the middle position of a word.

Metacognitive awareness   An advanced cognitive process that involves the reader's awareness of his own comprehension.

Metacognitive probing   Part of metacognitive assessment/instruction involving asking students many questions or "probes" to find out about their cognitive processes.

Miscue analysis   A procedure for observing, evaluating, and monitoring oral reading errors to assess children's use of reading strategies. Some reading authorities refer to this as "error analysis."

Miscues   Deviations from the actual wording of the text that a child makes when reading orally.

Modified cloze   A modification (such as accepting synonyms, using less frequent deletions, or deleting only certain types of words) to the traditional cloze assessment procedure. (See "cloze assessment.")

Mutilated text   Text that has been altered so that part of the lines of text are missing, blurred, or smudged.

Narrative text   Text that includes most story-type materials and has common text structure and features.

Naturalistic data   Data that have emerged from authentic reading, writing, and assignments, and from other real classroom study and work.

Negotiated curriculum   The curriculum developed when children are involved in the shaping and refining of plans for instruction.

Norm group   The group to which your students' scores will be compared on a norm-referenced test.

Normal distribution curve   The classic bell-shaped curve, which indicates that test scores are distributed symmetrically around the mean.

Norm-referenced scores   Scores derived from the quantitative results of standardized survey, achievement, or diagnostic tests, by comparing a student's raw score to the derived raw scores of the norm group.

Norm-referenced tests   Tests that report norms to which your students are compared.

Omissions   The miscues that occur when a reader leaves out words or skips them, without attempting to guess.

Open-ended questions   Questions without one correct answer. By using them, a teacher solicits students' opinions and personal responses to their readings.

Paragraph frames   An open-ended sentence completion technique, similar to story frames, but used with content material. Uses specific signal words to solicit the information from a reading.

Passage dependent   When reading and understanding a test passage are essential to getting the items correct.

Passage independent   When the ability to answer a test question is not based on information in the test passage alone.

Peer groups   Children of the same age who meet to help each other with specific work, readings, or assignments.

Percentile ranks   Norm-referenced scores, usually reported from 1 through 99. These ranks indicate students' relative positions in a group.

Phoneme-grapheme   Sound and sight clues and strategies. Also referred to as "graphophonic" by many reading experts.

Phonemes   The individual speech sounds that make up words.

Phonemic awareness   An awareness or understanding that spoken words are made up of a sequence of individual sounds.

Phonics   Letter-sound correspondence in written language.

Phonological awareness   Refers to an awareness of *many* aspects of spoken language, including words within sentences, syllables within words, and phonemes within syllables and words. (Phonemic awareness is just one part of the broader concept known as "phonological awareness.")

Portfolios   Collections of selected samples of different types and aspects of students' work and other assignments that provide the teacher and child with material to reflect on, discuss, and monitor.

Predictive validity   A type of criterion-related validity. Reported with a validity coefficient.

Pretend reading   When children use what they know about reading (like how to hold a book, turn pages, that books tell a story) to model what they know they are supposed to do with books.

Prior knowledge   The knowledge (vocabulary and other background knowledge) that students bring to the text before reading it; familiarity and background knowledge.

Process writing   A systematic process for developing students' writing.

Process-oriented   An interest in the strategies, approaches, and processes children use as they read, write, and do their assignments.

Product-oriented   An interest in the outcomes, and in the number right or wrong.

Progress notes   Ongoing notations that a teacher might make regarding a child's progress as the teacher works with the child.

Qualitative analysis (analyses, plural)   Carefully and systematically analyzing a child's use of strategies to figure out words and get meaning from text, as in the modified miscue analysis procedure used and explained by the author of this book. A qualitative analysis may also include the student's interests, motivations, feelings, and comprehension and related strategies, as well as his or her study skills/strategies. (Also see "qualitatively analyze" and "qualitative emphasis.")

Qualitative data   Data that emerge based on studying the "quality" of children's responses and their work.

Qualitative emphasis   This involves the teacher observing many samples of students' motivations, work, and strategies to get a more complete view of each student in order to decide the most useful ways of helping the student develop effective reading strategies.

Qualitatively analyze   A focus on the quality of the child's responses, strategies, or work. To look for more information beyond the score, grade, or number correct when analyzing quantitative data.

Quantitative data   Data that emerge based on counting or extrapolating from the "quantity" of children's correct responses.

Raw data   This usually refers to the data gathered from tests by noting students' responses on their answer sheets, along with information regarding the students' school, grade, date of birth, and the month of testing; these are data that have not yet been converted into norm-referenced or criterion-referenced scores.

Raw score   Number correct on a test.

Readability levels   The designation of materials as appropriate for the interests, schemata, and vocabulary of most children at specified grade levels. Various formulas and considerations are typically used to try to determine readability levels.

Readiness tests   Tests that assumed a group of isolated, but related, sequential skills— skills that were deemed essential before a child could begin to learn to read.

Reading rate   This can be estimated by counting the number of words per minute read with comprehension, in several different types of reading selections at students' independent reading levels.

Reading strategies   Self-initiated strategies that help readers comprehend what they wish to read and understand.

Reciprocal conferencing and sharing   A process that involves the sharing of information and perceptions between two or more mutually interested individuals for the purpose of benefiting the child and empowering the family, child, and teacher.

Reciprocal teaching   Instructional procedures, including scaffolding, that involve dialogues between the teacher and students as students attempt to gain meaning from text.

Registers   The language determined by literary or social circumstances, such as argumentative, explanatory, and so forth.

Reliability   See "test reliability."

Reliability coefficient   How information about a test's reliability is reported; statistically calculated.

Retell the passage   The act of telling everything a child can remember about what he reads. (See "retellings.")

Retellings   An informal assessment of comprehension involving retelling all that can be remembered from a reading. Can be done with expository as well as narrative materials. (See "retell the passage.")

Retrospective miscue analysis   An instructional strategy that involves readers reflecting on their own miscues.

Rubrics   The specific criteria or standards that will be used to score and evaluate students' performance, work, or skills. Rubrics can help the students and teacher determine to what extent students have met the goals of a particular assignment, project, or task.

Running records   A procedure for analyzing oral reading miscues or errors; similar to miscue analysis.

Scaffolding method approach   A teaching approach that involves the teacher presenting a reading task to the student, observing the student's response, and then introducing small modifications of the reading task to see what might help the student become a more strategic reader; the teacher tries to scaffold from least support to most support, depending on the reader's needs.

Schema (schemata, plural) A person's concept or mental picture and organization for a given idea, topic, event, person, or thing.

Scriptally implicit Questions that involve the reader using his background knowledge and schema to answer the questions. The information is not stated or implied in the text or story; "in my head" questions.

Self-corrections The miscues that a child notices and fixes or self-corrects on his own. Self-corrections are an indication of reading strategy strengths.

Semantic Meaning clues and strategies.

Sight words Words recognized by sight without a need for analysis.

Skills The ability to perform a task; sometimes many skills used together form a strategy. Skill instruction involves the teacher helping children develop their skills.

Social constructivism A theory about learning that includes the ideas that reading and writing are an outgrowth of and part of social context, and that readers actively construct their own understandings about what they read.

Social context The idea that when someone reads or writes, his reading or writing is taking place within a particular social context.

SQ3R A textbook study procedure involving the steps "survey, question, read, recite, and review."

Stakeholders All those who have a stake in a student's assessment, teaching, and learning (most usually the children and their parents/families).

Standardized tests Commercially prepared formal assessments that are to be given under prescribed conditions.

Stanine scores Standard scores developed from norm-referenced scores by dividing the norming group's scores into nine fairly equal groupings, ranging from a low of stanine 1 through a high of stanine 9.

Story frames An open-ended sentence completion technique used to solicit children's written response to literature; provides information concerning students' understanding of and response to characters, setting, and other features of the story.

Strategic reader A reader who consciously uses strategies to make sense of his reading.

Strategies The way we go about working out a problem. Strategy instruction involves the teacher helping children develop and become aware of the strategies they use.

Strategy use How a child seems to go about trying to figure out a word or the meaning of something the child has read or how to do an assignment.

Structural analysis The study of word parts.

Structured questions Systematic questions focused by the teacher's purpose.

Study skill A specific skill or ability to perform a learning-related task; for example, notetaking is a study skill.

Study strategy The use of many study skills in order to have a strategy for learning and/or studying; for example, studying a textbook chapter is a study strategy which could involve scanning the chapter, taking notes, outlining, summarizing, reading graphs and tables, and so on.

Subskills   Subparts of skills.

Subtests   Subparts of a larger test, such as a part of a survey, group diagnostic or criterion-referenced test.

Survey tests   General tests yielding information on a student's overall achievement.

Sustained Silent Reading (SSR)   A particular period of time when everyone in the classroom must read.

Syntax   Structure/phrasing clues and strategies.

Teaching strategies   Self-initiated strategies that help teachers present the skills, strategies, or concepts they wish their students to develop.

Test reliability   A report of how consistently a test measures whatever it is measuring.

Test-retest reliability   An indication of a test's stability over time. (See "test reliability.")

Test validity   The extent to which a test is measuring what it claims to measure.

Text-explicit   Questions that can be answered by finding the information that is explicitly stated in the text or story; "right there" or literal questions.

Text-implicit   Questions that involve inferring information from the text or story; the information is not explicitly stated; "think and search" or inferential questions.

Think-aloud reading protocols   Verbalizations of a reader's thoughts before, during, and after reading.

Total reading score   A score based on the number correct on a commercially prepared, standardized reading test.

Trade books   Books published for sale to the general public.

Validity   See "test validity."

Whole language   A philosophy about how children learn that informs the way teachers teach. Advocates of whole language indicate they support learning that is realistic, relevant, authentic, and child-centered.

Word bank   A collection of personal words that children learn to "know by sight."

PROFESSIONAL REFERENCES
AND SUGGESTED READINGS

Adams, M. J. (1990). *Beginning to read: Thinking and learning about print*. Cambridge, MA: MIT Press.

Ali, S. (1993/1994). The reader-response approach: An alternative for teaching literature in a second language. *Journal of Reading, 37* (40), 288–296.

Allen, V. G., Freeman, E. B., Lehman, B. A., & Scharer, P. L. (1995). Amos and Boris: A window on teachers' thinking about the use of literature in their classrooms. *The Reading Teacher, 48* (5), 384–390.

Allington, R. L. (1980). Poor readers don't get to read much in reading groups. *Language Arts, 57* (8), 872–876.

Allington, R. L. (1983). The reading instruction provided readers of differing ability. *Elementary School Journal, 83* (5), 548–559.

Allington, R. L. (1994). What's special about special programs for children who find learning to read difficult? *Journal of Reading Behavior, 26* (1), 95–115.

Allington, R. L. (1995). Literacy lessons in the elementary schools: Yesterday, today, and tomorrow. In R. L. Allington & S. A. Walmsley (Eds.), *No quick fix: Rethinking literacy programs in America's elementary schools* (pp. 1–15). New York: Teachers College Press.

Allington, R. L. (2001). *What really matters for struggling readers: Designing research-based programs*. New York: Addison Wesley Longman.

Alvermann, D. E., & Phelps, S. F. (2002). *Content reading and literacy: Succeeding in today's diverse classrooms* (3rd ed.). Boston: Allyn and Bacon.

American Educational Research Association (2001). *AERA position statement concerning high-stakes testing in pre k–12 education* [On-line]. Available: http://www.aera.net/about/policy/stakes.htm

Andersen, S. R. (1994). Trouble with testing. In K. M. Paciorek & J. H. Munro (Eds.), *Early childhood education 94–95* (pp. 147–149). Guilford, CT: Dushkin.

Anderson, J. (1994). Parents' perceptions of emergent literacy: An exploratory study. *Reading Psychology, 15* (3), 165–187.

Applebee, A. N., Langer, J. A., & Mullis, I. (1988). Who reads best? *Factors related to reading achievement in grades 3, 7, and 11*. Princeton, NJ: NAEP/Educational Testing Service.

Armbruster, B. B. (1991). Using literature in the content areas. *The Reading Teacher, 45* (4), 324–325.

Ashworth, M., & Wakefield, H. P. (1994). *Teaching the world's children: ESL for ages three to seven.* Marham, Ontario: Pippin.

Atwell, N. (Ed.). (1990). *Coming to know: Writing to learn in the intermediate grades.* Portsmouth, NH: Heinemann.

Atwell, N. (1998). *In the middle: New understandings about writing, reading, and learning* (2nd ed.). Portsmouth, NH: Heinemann.

Au, K. H. (1993). *Literacy instruction in multicultural settings.* Ft. Worth, TX: Harcourt Brace.

Au, K. H. (2001). What we know about multicultural education and students of diverse backgrounds. In R. F. Flippo (Ed.), *Reading researchers in search of common ground* (pp. 101–117). Newark, DE: International Reading Association.

Au, K. H., Carroll, J. H., & Scheu, J. A. (2001). *Balanced literacy instruction: A teacher's resource book* (2nd ed.). Norwood, MA: Christopher-Gordon.

Au, K. H., Mason, J. M., & Scheu, J. A. (1995). *Literacy instruction for today.* New York: HarperCollins.

Au, K. H., Scheu, J. A., Kawakami, A. J., & Herman, P. A. (1990). Assessment and accountability in a whole literacy curriculum. *The Reading Teacher, 43* (8), 574–578.

Azwell, T., & Schmar, E. (Eds.). (1995). *Report card on report cards: Alternatives to consider.* Portsmouth, NH: Heinemann.

Baker, L., & Brown, A. (1984). Metacognitive skills and reading. In P. D. Pearson (Ed.), & R. Barr, M. L. Kamil, & P. Mosenthal (Section Eds.), *Handbook of reading research* (pp. 353–394). New York: Longman.

Banks, J. A. (1999). *An introduction to multicultural education* (2nd ed.). Boston: Allyn and Bacon.

Barr, R. (1989). The social organization of literacy instruction. In S. McCormick & J. Zutell (Eds.), *Cognitive and social perspectives for literacy research and instruction* (pp. 19–33). The thirty-eighth yearbook of the National Reading Conference. Chicago: National Reading Conference.

Barron, M. (1990). *I learn to read and write the way I learn to talk: A very first book about whole language.* Katonah, NY: Richard C. Owen.

Barron, M. (1993). *Aprendo a leer y a escribir de la manera en que aprendo a hablar: Mi primer libro acerca del lenguaje integrado.* Katonah, NY: Richard C. Owen.

Barton, J. (2001). *Teaching with children's literature.* Norwood, MA: Christopher-Gordon.

Baumann, J. F. (1991). Of rats and pigeons: Skills and whole language. *Reading Psychology, 12* (1), iii–xiii.

Baumann, J. F., Jones, L. A., & Seifert-Kessell, N. (1993). Using think-alouds to enhance children's comprehension monitoring abilities. *The Reading Teacher, 47* (3), 184–193.

Beach, S. A. (1994). Teacher's theories and classroom practice: Beliefs, knowledge, or context? *Reading Psychology, 15* (3), 189–196.

Beaty, J. J. (1994). *Picture book storytelling: Literature activities for young children.* Ft. Worth, TX: Harcourt Brace.

Beck, I. L., McKeown, M. G., Hamilton, R. L., & Kucan, L. (1997). *Question the author: An approach for enhancing student engagement with text.* Newark, DE: International Reading Association.

Beck, I. L., McKeown, M. G., & Kucan, L. (2002). *Bringing words to life: Robust vocabulary instruction.* New York: Guilford.

Behm, M., & Behm, R. (1993). *¡Leamos! Prepare a sus hyos a leer y escribir: 101 ideas (Let's read! 101 ideas to help your child learn to read and write).* Bloomington, IN: ERIC Clearinghouse on Reading, English, and Communication, and EDINFO Press.

Berghoff, B., & Egawa, K. (1991). No more "rocks": Grouping to give students control of their learning. *The Reading Teacher, 44* (8), 536–541.

Betts, E. A. (1946). *Foundations of reading instruction.* New York: American Books.

Beuchat, C. E. (1993/1994). The writer: Another agent in the development of literacy. *The Reading Teacher, 47* (4), 312–315.

Bieger, E. M. (1995/1996). Promoting multicultural education through a literature-based approach. *The Reading Teacher, 49* (4), 308–312.

Blachowicz, C. L., & Fisher, P. (2000). Vocabulary instruction. In M. L. Kamil, P. B. Mosenthal, P. D. Pearson, & R. Barr (Eds.), *Handbook of reading research* (Vol. 3, pp. 503–523). Mahwah, NJ: Erlbaum.

Blachowicz, C., & Ogle, D. (2001). *Reading comprehension: Strategies for independent learners.* New York: Guilford.

Blachowicz, C. L. Z., Sullivan, D. M., Cieply, C. (2001). Fluency snapshots: A quick screening tool for your classroom. *Reading Psychology, 22* (2), 95–109.

Blair-Larsen, S. M., & Williams, K. A. (Eds.). (1999). *The balanced reading program: Helping all students achieve success.* Newark, DE: International Reading Association.

Blevins, W. (1997). *Phonemic awareness activities for early reading success.* New York: Scholastic.

Block, C. C., & Pressley, M. (Eds.). (2002). *Comprehension instruction: Research-based best practices.* New York: Guilford.

Boomer, G. (1985). *Fair dinkum teaching and learning.* Upper Montclair, NJ: Boynton/Cook.

Bormuth, J. R. (1968). The cloze readability procedure. *Elementary English, 55,* 429–436.

Box, B. J. (2000). *Word identification strategies: Phonics from a new perspective.* Upper Saddle River, NJ: Merrill/Prentice Hall.

Boyle, O. F., & Peregoy, S. F. (1998). Literacy scaffolds: Strategies for first- and second-language readers and writers. In M. F. Opitz (Ed.), *Literacy instruction for culturally and linguistically diverse students* (pp. 150–157). Newark, DE: International Reading Association.

Brabham, E. G., & Villaume, S. K. (2002). Leveled text: The good news and the bad news. *The Reading Teacher, 55* (5), 438–441.

Brisk, M. E., & Harrington, M. M. (2000). *Literacy and bilingualism: A handbook for all teachers.* Mahwah, NJ: Erlbaum.

Bromley, K. D. (1996). *Webbing with literature: Creating story maps with children's books* (2nd ed.). Boston: Allyn and Bacon.

Brown, F. G. (1983). *Principles of educational and psychological testing* (3rd ed.). New York: Holt, Rinehart and Winston.

Brown, H., & Cambourne, B. L. (1987). *Read and retell.* Sydney, New South Wales: Methuen.

Brown, H., & Cambourne, B. (1991). Evaluation in the whole language classroom: A collaborative research project. In E. Daly (Ed.), *Monitoring children's language development: Holistic assessment in the classroom* (pp. 82–102). Portsmouth, NH: Heinemann.

Brown, K. J. (1999/2000). What kind of text—For whom and when? Textual scaffolding for beginning readers. *The Reading Teacher, 53* (4), 292–307.

Buehl, D. (2001). *Classroom strategies for interactive learning* (2nd ed.). Newark, DE: International Reading Association.

Burns, P. C., & Roe, B. D. (2002). *Informal Reading Inventory* (6th ed.). Boston: Houghton Mifflin.

Buss, K., & Karnowski, L. (2000). *Reading and writing: Literary genres.* Newark, DE: International Reading Association.

Butler, D. (1988). *Babies need books* (Rev. ed.). Portsmouth, NH: Heinemann.

Butler, D., & Clay, M. (1987a). *Reading begins at home* (Updated ed.). Portsmouth, NH: Heinemann.

Butler, D., & Clay, M. (1987b). *Writing begins at home.* Portsmouth, NH: Heinemann.

Calero-Breckheimer, A., & Goetz, E. T. (1993). Reading strategies of biliterate children for English and Spanish texts. *Reading Psychology, 14* (3), 177–204.

Calfee, R. C., & Perfumo, P. (1993). Student portfolios: Opportunities for a revolution in assessment. *Journal of Reading, 36* (7), 532–537.

Calfee, R. C., & Piontkowski, D. C. (1981). The reading diary: Acquisition of decoding. *Reading Research Quarterly, 16* (3), 346–373.

Calkins, L., & Teachers College Reading and Writing Project Community. (2002). *A field guide to the classroom library (Guides A–G).* Portsmouth, NH: Heinemann.

Cambourne, B. (1988). *The whole story.* Auckland, New Zealand: Ashton Scholastic.

Cambourne, B. (1994). Why is evaluation of learning such a "hot" issue? What's the problem? In B. Cambourne & J. Turbill (Eds.), *Responsive evaluation: Making valid judgments about student literacy* (pp. 1–8). Portsmouth, NH: Heinemann.

Campbell, J. R., Kapinus, B. A., & Beatty, A. S. (1995). *Interviewing children about their literacy experiences*. Washington, DC: U.S. Government Printing Office, National Center for Education Statistics, Office of Educational Research and Improvement.

Campbell, R. (Ed.). (1998). *Facilitating preschool literacy*. Newark, DE: International Reading Association.

Campbell, R. (2001). *Read-alouds with young children*. Newark, DE: International Reading Association.

Carr, J. C. (1999). *A child went forth: Reflective teaching with young readers and writers*. Portsmouth, NH: Heinemann.

Carrasquillo, A., & Segan, P. (Eds.). (1998). *The teaching of reading in Spanish to the bilingual student* (2nd ed.). Mahwah, NJ: Erlbaum.

Cary, S. (2000). *Working with second language learners: Answers to teachers' top ten questions*. Portsmouth, NH: Heinemann.

Casteel, C. P., & Isom, B. A. (1994). Reciprocal processes in science and literacy learning. *The Reading Teacher, 47* (7), 538–545.

Castle, J. M. (1999). Learning and teaching phonological awareness. In G. B. Thompson & T. Nicholson (Eds.), *Learning to read: Beyond phonics and whole language* (pp. 55–73). Newark, DE: International Reading Association, and New York: Teachers College Press.

Chall, J. S. (1979). The great debate: Ten years later, with a modest proposal for reading stages. In L. B. Resnick & P. A. Weaver (Eds.), *Theory and practice of early reading* (Vol. 1, pp. 29–55). Hillsdale, NJ: Erlbaum.

Chall, J. S. (1996). *Learning to read: The great debate* (3rd ed.). Fort Worth, TX: Harcourt Brace.

Chapman, M. L. (1996). More than spelling: Widening the lens on emergent writing. *Reading Horizons, 36* (4), 317–339.

Children's rights. (2002, February/March). *Reading Today, 19* (4), 38.

Chomsky, C. (1971). Invented spelling in the open classroom. *Word, 27,* 499–518.

Chomsky, C. (1972). Write now, read later. In C. B. Cazden (Ed.), *Language in early childhood education* (pp. 119–126). Washington, DC: Association for Education of Young Children.

Chomsky, C. (1979). Approaching reading through invented spelling. In L. B. Resnick & P. A. Weaver (Eds.), *Theory and practice of early reading* (Vol. 2, pp. 43–65). Hillsdale, NJ: Erlbaum.

Church, S. M. (1994). Is whole language really warm and fuzzy? *The Reading Teacher, 47* (5), 362–370.

Clark, C., Chow-Hoy, T. K., Herter, R. J., & Moss, P. A. (2001). Portfolios as sites of learning: Reconceptualizing the connections to motivation and engagement. *Journal of Literacy Research, 33* (2), 211–241.

Clay, M. M. (1968). A syntactic analysis of reading errors. *Journal of Verbal Learning and Verbal Behavior, 7*, 434–438.

Clay, M. (1987). *Writing begins at home: Preparing children for writing before they go to school.* Portsmouth, NH: Heinemann.

Clay, M. M. (1993a). *An observation survey of early literacy achievement.* Portsmouth, NH: Heinemann.

Clay, M. M. (1993b). *Reading Recovery: A guidebook for teachers in training.* Portsmouth, NH: Heinemann.

Clay, M. M. (2000a). *Concepts about print: What have children learned about the way we print language?* Portsmouth, NH: Heinemann.

Clay, M. M. (2000b). *Running records for classroom teachers.* Portsmouth, NH: Heinemann.

Cohen, E. G. (1994). Restructuring the classroom: Conditions for productive small groups. *Review of Educational Research, 64* (1), 1–35.

Come, B., & Fredericks, A. D. (1995). Family literacy in urban schools: Meeting the needs of at-risk children. *The Reading Teacher, 48* (7), 566–570.

Cox, B. E., Fang, Z., & Otto, B. W. (1997). Preschoolers' developing ownership of the literate register. *Reading Research Quarterly, 32* (1), 34–53.

Crafton, L. (1994). *Challenges of holistic teaching: Answering the tough questions.* Norwood, MA: Christopher-Gordon.

Craig, M. T., & Yore, L. D. (1995). Middle school students' metacognitive knowledge about science reading and science text: An interview study. *Reading Psychology, 16* (2), 169–213.

Cramer, E. H., & Castle, M. (Eds.). (1994). *Fostering the love of reading: The affective domain in reading education.* Newark, DE: International Reading Association.

Cramer, R. L. (2001). *Creative power: The nature and nurture of children's writing.* New York: Addison Wesley Longman.

Cudd, E. T., & Roberts, L. (1989). Using writing to enhance content area learning in the primary grades. *The Reading Teacher, 42* (6), 392–404.

Cudd, E. T., & Roberts, L. L. (1993/1994). A scaffolding technique to develop sentence sense and vocabulary. *The Reading Teacher, 47* (4), 346–349.

Cullinan, B. E. (Ed.). (1992). *Invitation to read: More children's literature in the reading program.* Newark, DE: International Reading Association.

Cunningham, P. M. (2000). *Phonics they use: Words for reading and writing* (3rd ed.). New York: Addison Wesley Longman.

Cunningham, P. M., Hall, D. P., & Defee, M. (1998). Nonability-grouped, multilevel instruction: Eight years later. *The Reading Teacher, 51* (8), 652–664.

Curtis, S. (1991). Whole language evaluation strategies: Examining the doughnut instead of the hole. In E. Daly (Ed.), *Monitoring children's language development: Holistic assessment in the classroom* (pp. 34–51). Portsmouth, NH: Heinemann.

Dahl, K. L., & Farnan, N. (1998). *Children's writing: Perspectives from research.*

Newark, DE: International Reading Association, and Chicago: National Reading Conference.

Dahl, K. L., Scharer, P. L., Lawson, L. L., & Grogan, P. R. (2001). *Rethinking phonics: Making the best teaching decisions.* Portsmouth, NH: Heinemann.

Daly, E. (Ed.). (1991). *Monitoring children's language development: Holistic assessment in the classroom.* Portsmouth, NH: Heinemann.

Daniels, H. (2002). *Literature circles: Voice and choice in book clubs & reading groups* (2nd ed.). Portland, ME: Stenhouse.

Davey, B. (1983). Think-aloud modeling the cognitive processes of reading comprehension. *Journal of Reading, 27* (1), 44–47.

Day, J. P., Spiegel, D. L., McLellan, J., & Brown, V. B. (2002). *Moving forward with literature circles.* New York: Scholastic.

Deford, D. E. (1986). Classroom contexts for literacy learning. In T. E. Raphael (Ed.), *The contexts of school-based literacy* (pp. 163–180). New York: Random House.

Delpit, L. D. (1988). The silenced dialogue: Power and pedagogy in educating other people's children. *Harvard Educational Review, 58* (3), 280–298.

Delpit, L. D. (1991). A conversation with Lisa Delpit. *Language Arts, 68,* 541–547.

Devine, T. G., & Kania, J. S. (2003). Studying: Skills, strategies, and systems. In J. Flood, D. Lapp, J. R. Squire, & J. M. Jensen (Eds.), *Handbook of research on teaching the English language arts* (2nd ed., pp. 942–954). Mahwah, NJ: Erlbaum.

Díaz-Rico, L. T., & Weed, K. Z. (1995). *The crosscultural, language, and academic development handbook.* Boston: Allyn and Bacon.

Doiron, R. (1994). Using nonfiction in a read-aloud program: Letting the facts speak for themselves. *The Reading Teacher, 47* (8), 616–624.

Dole, J. A., Brown, K. J., & Trathen, W. (1996). The effects of strategy instruction on the comprehension performance of at-risk students. *Reading Research Quarterly, 31* (1), 62–88.

Dombey, H., Moustafa, M., and others (1998). *W(hōle) to part phonics: How children learn to read and spell.* London: Center for Language in Primary Education, and Portsmouth, NH: Heinemann.

Donoghue, M. R. (2001). *Using literature activities to teach content areas to emergent readers.* Boston: Allyn and Bacon.

Duffelmeyer, F. A. (1994). Effective Anticipation Guide statements for learning from expository prose. *Journal of Reading, 37* (6), 452–457.

Duffy, G. G., & Roehler, L. R. (1987). Teaching reading skills as strategies. *The Reading Teacher, 40* (4), 414–418.

Duffy, G. G., & Roehler, L. R. (1993). *Improving classroom reading instruction: A decision-making approach* (3rd ed.). New York: McGraw-Hill.

Duffy, G., Roehler, L., & Herrmann, B. A. (1988). Modeling mental processes helps poor readers become strategic readers. *The Reading Teacher, 41* (8), 762–767.

Duke, N. K. (1999). *The scarcity of informational texts in first grade* (Center for the Improvement of Early Reading Achievement Rep. No. 1–007). Ann Arbor, MI: CIERA/University of Michigan.

Durkin, D. (1990). Dolores Durkin speaks on instruction. *The Reading Teacher, 43* (7), 472–476.

Dwyer, E. J. (1982). Writing musicals in the classroom. *The Reading Teacher, 35* (6), 729.

Edwards, P. A., McMillon, G. T., Turner, J. D., & Laier, B. (2001). Center for the Improvement of Early Reading Achievement: Who are you teaching? Coordinating instructional networks around the students and parents you serve. *The Reading Teacher, 55* (2), 146–150.

Elbow, P. (1998). *Writing with power: Techniques for mastering the writing process* (2nd ed.). New York: Oxford University Press.

Elley, W. B. (1992). *How in the world do students read?* Hamburg, Germany: International Association for the Evaluation of Educational Achievement.

Elliott, S. N. (1980). Children's knowledge and uses of organizational patterns of prose in recalling what they read. *Journal of Reading Behavior, 12,* 203–212.

Emery, D. W. (1996). Helping readers comprehend stories from the characters' perspectives. *The Reading Teacher, 49* (7), 534–541.

Ericson, L., & Juliebö, M. F. (1998). *The phonological awareness handbook for kindergarten and primary teachers*. Newark, DE: International Reading Association.

Escamilla, K., & Andrade, A. (1992). Descubriendo la lectura: An application of Reading Recovery in Spanish. *Education and Urban Society, 24* (2), 212–226.

Escamilla, K., Andrade, A. M., Basurto, A. G. M., & Ruiz, O. A. (with Clay, M. M.). (1996). *Instrumento de observación de los logros de la lecto-escritura inicial*. Portsmouth, NH: Heinemann.

Falk, B. (2000). *The heart of the matter: Using standards and assessment to learn*. Portsmouth, NH: Heinemann.

Fallon, I., & Allen, J. (1994). Where the deer and the cantaloupe play. *The Reading Teacher, 47* (7), 546–551.

Faltis, C. J. (2001). *Joinfostering: Teaching and learning in multilingual classrooms* (3rd ed.). Upper Saddle River, NJ: Merrill/Prentice-Hall.

Farr, R. (1992). Putting it all together: Solving the reading assessment puzzle. *The Reading Teacher, 46* (1), 26–37.

Farr, R., & Carey, R. F. (1986). *Reading: What can be measured?* (2nd ed.). Newark, DE: International Reading Association.

Farr, R., & Tone, B. (1998). *Portfolio and performance assessment: Helping students evaluate their progress as readers and writers* (2nd ed.). Fort Worth, TX: Harcourt Brace.

Fawson, P. C., & Reutzel, D. R. (2000). But I only have a basal: Implementing guided reading in the early grades. *The Reading Teacher, 54* (1), 84–97.

Fenstermacher, G. D. (1994). The knower and the known: The nature of knowledge in research on teaching. In L. Darling-Hammond (Ed.), *Review of research in education* (pp. 3–56). Washington, DC: American Educational Research Association.

Fiderer, A. (1998). *35 Rubrics & checklists to assess reading and writing* (Grades K–2). New York: Scholastic.

Fiderer, A. (1999). *40 Rubrics & checklists to assess reading and writing* (Grades 3–6). New York: Scholastic.

Finegan, C., Helms, R. G., Gotthoffer, D. (2000). *Quick guide to the Internet for multicultural education*. Boston: Allyn and Bacon.

Fitzgerald, J. (1999). What is this thing called "balance"? *The Reading Teacher, 53* (2), 100–107.

Flippo, R. F. (1988). The use of music, songs, and lyrics in reading instruction. In C. Anderson (Ed.), *Reading: The abc and beyond* (pp. 55–61). London: Macmillan Education.

Flippo, R. F. (1998). Points of agreement: A display of professional unity in our field. *The Reading Teacher, 52* (1), 30–40.

Flippo, R. F. (1999). *What do the experts say? Helping children learn to read*. Portsmouth, NH: Heinemann.

Flippo, R. F. (2000). *TestWise: Strategies for success in taking tests* (2nd ed.). Grand Rapids, MI: Good Apple an imprint of McGraw-Hill Children's Publishing.

Flippo, R. F. (Ed.). (2001a). *Reading researchers in search of common ground*. Newark, DE: International Reading Association.

Flippo, R. F. (2001b). The "real" common ground: Pulling the threads together. In R. F. Flippo (Ed.), *Reading researchers in search of common ground* (pp. 178–184). Newark, DE: International Reading Association.

Flippo, R. F. (2002). Study skills and strategies. In B. Guzzetti (Ed.), *Literacy in America: An encyclopedia of history, theory, and practice* (Vol. 2, pp. 631–632). Santa Barbara, CA: ABC-CLIO.

Flippo, R. F. (in press). *Strategies for studying and learning from text*. Portsmouth, NH: Heinemann.

Flippo, R. F., & Branch, H. (1985). A program to help prepare pre-schoolers for reading. *Reading Horizons, 25* (2), 120–122.

Flippo, R. F., & Lecheler, R. (1987). Adjusting reading rate: Metacognitive awareness. *The Reading Teacher, 40* (7), 712–713.

Flippo, R. F., & Schumm, J. S. (2000). Reading tests. In R. F. Flippo & D. C. Caverly (Eds.), *Handbook of college reading and study strategy research* (pp. 403–472). Mahwah, NJ: Erlbaum.

Flippo, R. F., & Smith, J. A. (1990). Encouraging parent involvement through home letters. *The Reading Teacher, 44* (4), 359.

Flood, J., Lapp, D., Flood, S., & Nagel, G. (1992). Am I allowed to group? Using flexible patterns for effective instruction. *The Reading Teacher, 45* (8), 608–616.

Flynt, E. S., & Cooter, R. B. (1999). *English-Español Reading Inventory for the Classroom.* Upper Saddle River, NJ: Merrill/Prentice Hall.

Fountas, I. C., & Pinnell, G. S. (1996). *Guided reading: Good first teaching for all children.* Portsmouth, NH: Heinemann.

Fountas, I. C., & Pinnell, G. S. (1999). *Matching books to readers: Using leveled books in guided reading, K–3.* Portsmouth, NH: Heinemann.

Fox, B. J. (2000). *Word identification strategies: Phonics from a new perspective* (2nd ed.). Upper Saddle River, NJ: Merrill/Prentice Hall.

Fredericks, A. D., & Rasinski, T. V. (1990). Involving parents in the assessment process. *The Reading Teacher, 44* (4), 346–349.

Freeman, D. E., & Freeman, Y. S. (1993). Strategies for promoting the primary languages of all students. *The Reading Teacher, 46* (7), 552–558.

Freeman, D. E., & Freeman, Y. S. (2000). *Teaching reading in multilingual classrooms.* Portsmouth, NH: Heinemann.

Freeman, E. B., & Person, D. G. (Eds.). (1992). *Using nonfiction trade books in the elementary classroom: From ants to zeppelins.* Urbana, IL: National Council of Teachers of English.

Freeman, E. B., & Person, D. G. (1998). *Connecting informational children's books with content area learning.* Boston: Allyn and Bacon.

Fresch, M. J., & Wheaton, A. (2002). *Teaching and assessing spelling.* New York: Scholastic.

Froese, V. (Ed.). (1996). *Whole-language: Practice and theory* (2nd ed.). Boston: Allyn and Bacon.

Fry, E. (2001). Instant Word Comprehensive Test. In *Informal reading assessments k–8* (pp. 27–33). Westminster, CA: Teacher Created Materials.

Fuhler, C. J. (1994). Response journals: just one more time with feeling. *Journal of Reading, 37* (5), 400–405.

Gahagan, H. S. (1994). Whole language assessment and evaluation: A special education perspective. In B. Harp (Ed.), *Assessment and evaluation for student centered learning* (2nd ed.; pp. 179–211). Norwood, MA: Christopher-Gordon.

Galda, L., & Cullinan, B. E. (2002). *Literature and the child* (5th ed.). Belmont, CA: Wadsworth/Thomson Learning.

Galda, L., Cullinan, B. E., & Strickland, D. S. (1997). *Language, literacy, and the child* (2nd ed.). Ft. Worth, TX: Harcourt Brace.

Gambrell, L. B. (2001). What we know about motivation to read. In R. F. Flippo (Ed.), *Reading researchers in search of common ground* (pp. 129–143). Newark, DE: International Reading Association.

Gambrell, L. B., Koskinen, P. S., & Kapinus, B. A. (1991). Retelling and the reading comprehension of proficient and less-proficient readers. *Journal of Educational Research, 84* (6), 356–362.

Gambrell, L. B., Palmer, B. M., Codling, R. M., & Mazzoni, S. A. (1996). Assessing motivation to read. *The Reading Teacher, 49* (7), 518–533.

Garcia, E. (2002). *Student cultural diversity: Understanding and meeting the challenge* (3rd ed.). Boston: Houghton Mifflin.

Gentry, J. R. (1997). *My kid can't spell: Understanding and assisting your child's literacy development.* Portsmouth, NH: Heinemann.

Gentry, J. R., & Gillet, J. W. (1993). *Teaching kids to spell.* Portsmouth, NH: Heinemann.

Gersten, R., Fuchs, L. S., Williams, J. P., & Baker, S. (2001). Teaching comprehension strategies to students with learning disabilities: A review of research. *Review of Educational Research, 71* (2), 279–320.

Gersten, R., & Jiménez, R. T. (1994). A delicate balance: Enhancing literature instruction for students of English as a second language. *The Reading Teacher, 47* (6), 438–449.

Gibson, P. S., & Flippo, R. F. (1996). Metacognitive assessment and exercises to develop and enhance metacognitive awareness. *Balanced Reading Instruction, 3* (1), 19–25.

Gillespie, C. S., Powell, J. L., Clements, N. E., & Swearingen, R. A. (1994). A look at the Newbery Medal books from a multicultural perspective. *The Reading Teacher, 48* (1), 40–50.

Glazer, S. M. (1994). Authentic assessment, evaluation, portfolios: What do these terms really mean, anyway? *Reading Today, 12* (1), 3–4.

Glover, M. K., & Giacalone, B. (2001). *Surprising destinations: A guide to essential learning in early childhood.* Portsmouth, NH: Heinemann.

Goldman, S. R., & Rakestraw, J. A. (2000). Structural aspects of constructing meaning from text. In M. L. Kamil, P. B. Mosenthal, P. D. Pearson, & R. Barr (Eds.), *Handbook of reading research* (Vol. 3, pp. 311–335). Mahwah, NJ: Erlbaum.

Good, T. L., & Marshall, S. (1984). Do students learn more in heterogeneous or homogeneous achievement groups? In P. L. Peterson, L. C. Wilkinson, & M. Hallinan (Eds.), *The social context for instruction* (pp. 15–38). San Diego: Academic Press.

Goodman, K. S. (1969). Analysis of oral reading miscues: Applied psycholinguistics. *Reading Research Quarterly, 5* (1), 9–30.

Goodman, K. S. (1973). Psycholinguistic universals in the reading process. In F. Smith (Ed.), *Psycholinguistics and reading* (pp. 21–27). New York: Holt, Rinehart and Winston.

Goodman, K. S. (1977, May 5). New evidence for a psycholinguistic theory of reading: A single reading process. Speech given at the Twenty-Second Annual Convention of the International Reading Association, Miami Beach, FL.

Goodman, K. S. (1982). *Language and literacy: The selected writings of Kenneth S. Goodman* (Vol. 1). Boston: Routledge & Kegan Paul.

Goodman, K. S. (1984). Unity in reading. In A. C. Purves & O. Niles (Eds.), *Becoming readers in a complex society* (pp. 79–114). Chicago: National Society for the Study of Education.

Goodman, K. S. (1986). *What's whole in whole language?* Portsmouth, NH: Heinemann.

Goodman, K. S. (1992). I didn't found whole language. *The Reading Teacher, 46* (3), 188–199.

Goodman, K. (1993). *Phonics phacts.* Portsmouth, NH: Heinemann.

Goodman, Y. (1978). Kidwatching: An alternative to testing. *Journal of National Elementary Principals, 57* (4), 41–45.

Goodman, Y., & Burke, C. (1972). *RMI manual: Procedures for diagnosis and evaluation.* Katonah, NY: Richard C. Owen.

Goodman, Y. M., & Marek, A. M. (1996). *Retrospective miscue analysis: Revaluing readers and reading.* Katonah, NY: Richard C. Owen.

Goodman, Y. M., Watson, D. J., & Burke, C. L. (1987). *Reading Miscue Inventory: Alternative procedures.* Katonah, NY: Richard C. Owen.

Goodman, Y. M., Watson, D. J., & Burke, C. L. (1996). *Reading strategies: Focus on comprehension* (2nd ed.). Katonah, NY: Richard C. Owen.

Grabe, M., & Grabe, C. (2000). *Integrating the Internet for meaningful learning.* Boston: Houghton Mifflin.

Grabe, M., & Grabe, C. (2001). *Integrating technology for meaningful learning* (3rd ed.). Boston: Houghton Mifflin.

Grant, R., Guthrie, J., Bennett, L., Rice, M. E., & McGough, K. (1993/1994). Developing engaged readers through concept-oriented instruction. *The Reading Teacher, 47* (4), 338–340.

Graves, D. H., & Sunstein, B. S. (Eds.). (1992). *Portfolio portraits.* Portsmouth, NH: Heinemann.

Graves, M., & Graves, B. (1994). *Scaffolding reading experiences.* Norwood, MA: Christopher-Gordon.

Guthrie, J. T. (1996). Educational contexts for engagement in literacy. *The Reading Teacher, 49* (6), 432–445.

Guthrie, J. T., Schafer, W., Wang, Y. Y., & Afflerbach, P. (1995). Relationships of instruction to amount of reading: An exploration of social, cognitive, and instructional connections. *Reading Research Quarterly, 30* (1), 8–25.

Guthrie, J. T., & Wigfield, A. (Eds.). (1997). *Reading engagement: Motivating readers through integrated instruction.* Newark, DE: International Reading Association.

Hadaway, N. L., Vardell, S. M., & Young, T. A. (2001). Scaffolding oral language development through poetry for students learning English. *The Reading Teacher, 54* (8), 796–806.

Hadaway, N. L., & Young, T. A. (1994). Content literacy and language learning: Instructional decisions. *The Reading Teacher, 47* (7), 522–527.

Hallinan, M. (1984). Summary and implications. In P. L. Peterson, L. C. Wilkinson, & M. Hallinan (Eds.), *The social context of instruction: Group organization and group processes* (pp. 229–240). San Diego: Academic Press.

Hansen, J. (1992). Students' evaluations bring reading and writing together. *The Reading Teacher, 46* (2), 100–105.

Hansen, J. (1998). *When learners evaluate.* Portsmouth, NH: Heinemann.

Harman, S. (1992). Snow White and the seven warnings: Threats to authentic evaluation. *The Reading Teacher, 46* (3), 250–252.

Harp, B. (1989). When the principal asks: "What do we know now about ability grouping?" *The Reading Teacher, 42* (6), 430–431.

Harp, B. (1994). Principles of assessment and evaluation in whole language classrooms. In B. Harp (Ed.), *Assessment and evaluation for student-centered learning* (2nd ed., pp. 47–66). Norwood, MA: Christopher-Gordon.

Harp, B. (2000). *The handbook of literacy assessment and evaluation* (2nd ed.). Norwood, MA: Christopher-Gordon.

Harris, T. L., & Hodges, R. E. (Eds.). (1995). *The literacy dictionary: The vocabulary of reading and writing.* Newark, DE: International Reading Association.

Harris, V. J. (1997). *Using a multiethnic literature in the K–8 classroom.* Norwood, MA: Christopher-Gordon.

Harste, J. (1990). Jerry Harste speaks on reading and writing. *The Reading Teacher, 43* (4), 316–318.

Harste, J. C., Woodward, V. A., & Burke, C. L. (1984). *Language stories & literacy lessons.* Portsmouth, NH: Heinemann.

Hayes, C. W., Bahruth, R., & Kessler, C. (1998). *Literacy con cariño* (New ed.). Portsmouth, NH: Heinemann.

Heath, S. B., & Mangiola, L. (1991). *Children of promise: Literacy activity in linguistically and culturally diverse classrooms.* Washington, DC: National Education Association, Center for the Study of Writing and Literacy, and American Educational Research Association.

Hebert, K. (1976). *Teaching and writing popular fiction: Horror, adventure, mystery and romance.* New York: Teachers and Writers Collaborative.

Heddens, J. W., & Speer, W. R. (2001). *Today's mathematics: Concepts and classroom methods, Part 1* (10th ed.). New York: John Wiley and Sons.

Hefflin, B. R., & Barksdale-Ladd, M. A. (2001). African American children's literature that helps students find themselves: Selection guidelines for grades k–3. *The Reading Teacher, 54* (8), 810–819.

Heilman, A. W. (2002). *Phonics in proper perspective* (9th ed.). Upper Saddle River, NJ: Merrill/Prentice Hall.

Heilman, A. W., Blair, T. R., & Rupley, W. H. (2002). *Principles and practices of teaching reading* (10th ed.). Upper Saddle River, NJ: Merrill/Prentice Hall.

Heimlich, J. E., & Pittelman, S. D. (1986). *Semantic mapping: Classroom applications.* Newark, DE: International Reading Association.

Heller, M. F. (1995). *Reading-writing connections: From theory to practice* (2nd ed.). White Plains, NY: Longman.

Henk, W. A., & Melnick, S. A. (1995). The Reader Self-Perception Scale (RSPS): A new tool for measuring how children feel about themselves as readers. *The Reading Teacher, 48* (6), 470–482.

Henk, W. A., & Selders, M. L. (1984). A test of synonymic scoring of cloze passages. *The Reading Teacher, 38,* 282–287.

Herrmann, B. A. (1992). Teaching and assessing strategic reasoning: Dealing with the dilemmas. *The Reading Teacher, 45* (6), 428–433.

Heymsfeld, C. (1989). Filling the whole in whole language. *Educational Leadership, 46,* 65–68.

Hiebert, E. (1983). An examination of ability grouping for reading instruction. *Reading Research Quarterly, 18* (2), 231–255.

Hiebert, E. H. (1991). Research directions: Literacy contexts and literacy processes. *Language Arts, 68,* 134–139.

Hiebert, E. H., & Calfee, R. C. (1992). Assessing literacy: From standardized tests to portfolios and performances. In A. E. Farstrup & S. J. Samuels (Eds.), *What research has to say about reading instruction* (2nd ed., pp. 70–100). Newark, DE: International Reading Association.

Hiebert E. H., Valencia, S. W., & Afflerbach, P. P. (1994). Definitions and perspectives. In S. W. Valencia, E. H. Hiebert, & P. P. Afflerbach (Eds.), *Authentic reading assessment: Practices and possibilities* (pp. 6–21). Newark, DE: International Reading Association.

Hill, B. C., Noe, K. L. S., & Johnson, N. J. (2001). *Literature circles resource guide.* Norwood, MA: Christopher-Gordon.

Hill, S. (1991). Goal-based assessment in literacy. In E. Daly (Ed.), *Monitoring children's language development: Holistic assessment in the classroom* (pp. 118–127). Portsmouth, NH: Heinemann.

Hinchman, K. A., & Michel, P. A. (1999). Reconciling polarity: Toward a responsive model of evaluating literacy performance. *The Reading Teacher, 52* (6), 578–587.

Hinkel, E., & Fotos, S. (Eds.). (2002). *New perspectives on grammar teaching in second language classrooms.* Mahwah, NJ: Erlbaum.

Hoffman, J. L. (1995). The family portfolio: Using authentic assessment in family literacy programs. *The Reading Teacher, 48* (7), 594–597.

Holdaway, D. (1990). *Independence in reading* (3rd ed.). Portsmouth, NH: Ashton Scholastic/Heinemann.

Holmes, B. C., & Roser, N. L. (1987). Five ways to assess readers' prior knowledge. *The Reading Teacher, 40* (7), 646–649.

Hoyt, L. (2000). *Snapshots: Literacy mini-lessons up close.* Portsmouth, NH: Heinemann.

Hyde, A. A., & Bizar, M. (1996). *Thinking in context: Teaching cognitive processes across the elementary school curriculum* (2nd ed.). New York: Longman.

Indrisano, R., & Paratore, J. R. (1991). Classroom contexts for literacy learning. In J. Flood, J. Jensen, D. Lapp, & J. Squire (Eds.), *Handbook of research on teaching the English language arts* (pp. 477–488). New York: Macmillan.

International Reading Association. (1981). *International Reading Association position on the misuse of grade equivalent scores.* Newark, DE: Author.

International Reading Association. (1991). *Resolutions on assessment.* Newark, DE: Author.

International Reading Association. (1999). *High-stakes assessments in reading: A position statement of the International Reading Association.* Newark, DE: Author.

International Reading Association. (2000a). *Excellent reading teachers: A position statement of the International Reading Association.* Newark, DE: Author.

International Reading Association. (2000b). *Making a difference means making it different: Honoring children's rights to excellent reading instruction.* Newark, DE: Author.

International Reading Association. (2002). *Family–school partnerships: Essential elements of literacy instruction in the United States: A position statement of the International Reading Association.* Newark, DE: Author.

International Reading Association, & National Council of Teachers of English Joint Task Force on Assessment. (1994). *Standards for the assessment of reading and writing.* Newark, DE: Author.

Irvin, J. L., & Rose, E. O. (1995). *Starting early with study skills: A week-by-week guide for elementary students.* Boston: Allyn and Bacon.

Irwin, J. W. (1991). *Teaching reading comprehension process* (2nd ed.). Englewood Cliffs, NJ: Prentice-Hall.

Irwin, J. W., & Doyle, M. A. (1992). *Reading/writing connections: Learning from research.* Newark, DE: International Reading Association.

Jackson, F. R. (1993/1994). Seven strategies to support a culturally responsive pedagogy. *Journal of Reading, 37* (4), 298–303.

Jenkins, C. B. (1996). *Inside the writing portfolio: What we need to know to assess children's writing.* Portsmouth, NH: Heinemann.

Jiménez, R. T. (2001). "It's a difference that changes us": An alternative view of the language and literacy learning needs of Latina/o students. *The Reading Teacher, 54* (8), 736–742.

Johns, J. (2001). *Basic Reading Inventory* (8th ed.). Dubuque, IA: Kendall/Hunt.

Johns, J. L., & Berglund, R. L. (2002a). *Fluency: Questions, answers, evidence-based strategies.* Dubuque, IA: Kendall/Hunt.

Johns, J. L., & Berglund, R. L. (2002b). *Strategies for content area learning.* Dubuque, IA: Kendall/Hunt.

Johns, J. L., Lenski, S. D., & Elish-Piper, L. (1999). *Early literacy assessments and teaching strategies.* Dubuque, IA: Kendall/Hunt.

Johnson, D. D. (2001). *Vocabulary in the elementary and middle school*. Boston: Allyn and Bacon.

Johnson, D. D., & Moe, A. J. (with Baumann, J. F.). (1983). *The Ginn word book for teachers: A basic lexicon*. Lexington, MA: Ginn.

Johnson, D. D., & Pearson, P. D. (1984). *Teaching reading vocabulary*. New York: Holt, Rinehart and Winston.

Johnson, D. W., & Johnson, R. T. (1999). *Learning together and alone* (5th ed.). Boston: Allyn and Bacon.

Johnson, M. S., Kress, R. A., & Pikulski, J. J. (1987). *Informal reading inventories* (2nd ed.). Newark, DE: International Reading Association.

Johnston, P. H. (1984). Prior knowledge and reading comprehension test bias. *Reading Research Quarterly, 14*, 219–239.

Johnston, P. H. (1992). *Constructive evaluation of literate activity*. White Plains, NY: Longman.

Jongsma, K. S. (1991). Rethinking grading practices. *The Reading Teacher, 45* (4), 318–320.

Juel, C. (1988). Learning to read and write: A longitudinal study of fifty-four children from first through fourth grade. *Journal of Educational Psychology, 80*, 437–447.

Kameenui, E. J. (1993). Diverse learners and the tyranny of time: Don't fix the blame; fix the leaky roof. *The Reading Teacher, 46* (5), 376–383.

Karlsen, B., & Gardner, E. F. (1995). *Stanford Diagnostic Reading Test* (4th ed.). San Antonio, TX: The Psychological Corporation.

Karnowski, L. (1989). Using LEA with process writing. *The Reading Teacher, 42* (7), 462–465.

Karnowski, L. (2000). *Great grammar lessons that work*. New York: Scholastic.

Keegan, S., & Shrake, K. (1991). Literature study groups: An alternative to ability grouping. *The Reading Teacher, 44* (8), 542–547.

Koch, R., & Schwartz-Petterson, J. (2000). *The portfolio guidebook: Implementing quality in an age of standards*. Norwood, MA: Christopher-Gordon.

Kohn, A. (2000). *The case against standardized testing: Raising the scores, ruining the schools*. Portsmouth, NH: Heinemann.

Krashen, S. D. (1996). *Under attack: The case against bilingual education*. Culver City, CA: Language Education Associates.

Krashen, S. D. (1999). *Three arguments against whole language & why they are wrong*. Portsmouth, NH: Heinemann.

Kuhs, T. M., Johnson, R. L., Agruso, S. A., & Monrad, D. M. (2001). *Put to the test: Tools and techniques for classroom assessment*. Portsmouth, NH: Heinemann.

LaBerge, D., & Samuels, S. J. (1974). Toward a theory of automatic information processing in reading. *Cognitive Psychology, 6*, 293–323.

Langer, J. A. (1992). Reading, writing, and genre development. In J. W. Irwin &

M. A. Doyle (Eds.), *Reading/writing connections: Learning from research* (pp. 32–54). Newark, DE: International Reading Association.

Leal, D. J. (1993). The power of literary peer-group discussions: How children collaboratively negotiate meaning. *The Reading Teacher, 47* (2), 114–120.

Leland, C., & Fitzpatrick R. (1993/1994). Cross-age interaction builds enthusiasm for reading and writing. *The Reading Teacher, 47* (4), 292–301.

Leslie, L., & Caldwell, J. (2001). *Qualitative Reading Inventory–3.* New York: Addison Wesley Longman.

Leu, D. J., & Leu, D. D. (2000). *Teaching with the Internet.* Norwood, MA: Christopher-Gordon.

Lewis, M., Wray, D., & Rospigliosi, P. (1994). "And I want it in your own words." *The Reading Teacher, 47* (7), 528–536.

Lim, H-J. L., & Watson, D. J. (1993). Whole language content classes for second-language learners. *The Reading Teacher, 46* (5), 384–393.

Lipson, M. Y., & Wixson, K. K. (1997). *Assessment and instruction of reading and writing disability: An interactive approach* (2nd ed.). New York: Addison Wesley Longman.

Lloyd, L. (1999). Multi-age classes and high ability students. *Review of Educational Research, 69* (2), 187–212.

Lukens, R. J. (1995). *A critical handbook of children's literature* (5th ed.). New York: HarperCollins.

MacGinitie, W. H., MacGinitie, R. K., Maria, K., & Dreyer, L. G. (2000). *Gates-MacGinitie Reading Tests* (4th ed.). Itasca, IL: Riverside.

Marden, M. R., Richard, M., & Flippo, R. F. (1991). Fifth grade/kindergarten mentor program: Beginnings. *New England Reading Association Journal, 27* (2), 2–4.

Martens, P. (1996). *I already know how to read: A child's view of literacy.* Portsmouth, NH: Heinemann.

Marzano, R. J., & Marzano, J. S. (1988). *A cluster approach to elementary vocabulary instruction.* Newark, DE: International Reading Association.

McGee, L. M., & Richgels, D. J. (2000). *Literacy's beginnings: Supporting young readers and writers* (3rd ed.). Boston: Allyn and Bacon.

McIntrye, E., & Pressley, M. (Eds.). (1996). *Balanced instruction: Strategies and skills in whole language.* Norwood, MA: Christopher-Gordon.

McKenna, M. C. (1980). *An introduction to the cloze procedure: An annotated bibliography.* Newark, DE: International Reading Association.

McKenna, M. C., & Kear, D. J. (1990). Measuring attitude toward reading: A new tool for teachers. *The Reading Teacher, 43* (9), 626–639.

McKenna, M. C., Kear, D. J., & Ellsworth, R. A. (1995). Children's attitudes toward reading: A national survey. *Reading Research Quarterly, 30* (4), 934–956.

McKenna, M. C., & Robinson, R. D. (2002). *Teaching through text: Reading and writing in the content areas* (3rd ed.). Boston: Allyn and Bacon.

McLaughlin, M., & Allen, M. B. (2002). *Guided comprehension: A teaching model for grades 3–8*. Newark, DE: International Reading Association.

McNeil, J. D. (1992). *Reading comprehension: New directions for classroom practice* (3rd ed.). New York: HarperCollins.

McQuillan, J. (1998). *The literacy crises: False claims, real solutions*. Portsmouth, NH: Heinemann.

Meyer, B. J. F., & Freedle, R. O. (1984). Effects of discourse type on recall. *American Educational Research Journal, 21*, 121–143.

Michel, P. A. (1994). *The child's view of reading: Understandings for teachers and parents*. Boston: Allyn and Bacon.

Mitchell, J. N., & Irwin, P. A. (2002). *The reader retelling profile: Using retellings to make instructional decisions*. Manuscript submitted for publication.

Moe, A. J. (1989). Using picture books for reading vocabulary development. In J. W. Stewig & S. L. Sebesta (Eds.), *Using literature in the elementary classroom* (2nd ed., pp. 23–34). Urbana, IL: National Council of Teachers of English.

Moll, L. C., & González, N. (1994). Lessons from research with language-minority children. *Journal of Reading Behavior, 26* (4), 439–456.

Monson, R. J., & Monson, M. P. (1994). Literacy as inquiry: An interview with Jerome C. Harste. *The Reading Teacher, 47* (7), 518–521.

Moore, D. W., Moore, S. A., Cunningham, P. M., & Cunningham, J. W. (2003). *Developing readers and writers in the content areas k–12* (4th ed.). Boston: Allyn and Bacon.

Morrice, C., & Simmons, M. (1991). Beyond reading buddies: A whole language crossage program. *The Reading Teacher, 44* (8), 572–577.

Morrow, L. M. (1988). Retelling stories as a diagnostic tool. In S. M. Glazer, L. W. Searfoss, & L. M. Gentile (Eds.), *Reexamining reading diagnosis: New trends and procedures* (pp. 128–149). Newark, DE: International Reading Association.

Morrow, L. M. (Ed.). (1995). *Family literacy: Connections in schools and communities*. Newark, DE: International Reading Association.

Morrow, L. M. (1997). *The literacy center: Contexts for reading and writing*. York, ME: Stenhouse.

Morrow, L. M., Paratore, J., Gaber, D., Harrison, C., & Tracey, D. (1993). Family literacy: Perspective and practices. *The Reading Teacher, 47* (3), 194–200.

Mosenthal, P. B. (1989). The whole language approach: Teachers between a rock and a hard place. *The Reading Teacher, 42* (8), 628–629.

Murphy, S., & Underwood, T. (2000). *Portfolio practices: Lessons from schools, districts, and states*. Norwood, MA: Christopher-Gordon.

Nagy, W. E. (1988). *Teaching vocabulary to improve reading comprehension*. Newark, DE: ERIC Clearinghouse on Reading and Communication Skills, National Council of Teachers of English, and International Reading Association.

National Reading Panel (2000). *Teaching children to read: An evidence-based assessment of the scientific research literature on reading and its implications for reading instruction. Reports of the subgroups*. Bethesda, MD: National Institute of Health. [On-line] Available: http://www.nichd.nih.gov/publications/nrp/

Nelson, C. S. (1994). Historical literacy: A journey of discovery. *The Reading Teacher, 47* (7), 552–556.

Newman, J. M., & Church, S. M. (1990). Myths of whole language. *The Reading Teacher, 44* (1), 20–26.

Ogle, D. M. (1986). K-W-L: A teaching model that develops active reading of expository text. *The Reading Teacher, 39* (6), 564–570.

Oldfather, P., & Dahl, K. (1994). Toward a social constructivist reconceptualization of intrinsic motivation for literacy learning. *Journal of Reading Behavior, 26* (2), 139–158.

Olivares, R. A. (1993). *Using the newspaper to teach ESL learners*. Newark, DE: International Reading Association.

Olson, M. W., & Gee, T. C. (1991). Content reading instruction in the primary grades: Perceptions and strategies. *The Reading Teacher, 45* (4), 298–306.

Opitz, M. F. (1998a). *Flexible grouping in reading: Practical ways to help all students become stronger readers*. New York: Scholastic.

Opitz, M. F. (Ed.). (1998b). *Literacy instruction for culturally and linguistically diverse students*. Newark, DE: International Reading Association.

Opitz, M. F. (2000). *Rhymes and reasons: Literature and language play for phonological awareness*. Portsmouth, NH: Heinemann.

Opitz, M. F., & Ford, M. P. (2001). *Reaching readers: Flexible & innovative strategies for guided reading*. Portsmouth, NH: Heinemann.

Opitz, M. F., & Rasinski, T. V. (1998). *Good-bye round robin: 25 effective oral reading strategies*. Portsmouth, NH: Heinemann.

Palincsar, A. S., & Brown, A. L. (1984). Reciprocal teaching of comprehension-fostering and comprehension-monitoring activities. *Cognition and Instruction, 1* (2), 117–175.

Pappas, C. C. (1991). Fostering full access to literacy by including information books. *Language Arts, 68*, 449–462.

Pappas, C. C. (1993). Is narrative "primary"? Some insights from kindergartners' pretend readings of stories and information books. *Journal of Reading Behavior, 25* (1), 97–129.

Pappas, C. C., Kiefer, B. Z., & Levstik, L. S. (1999). *An integrated language perspective in the elementary school: An action approach* (3rd ed.). New York: Addison Wesley Longman.

Paratore, J. R., Fountas, I. C., Jenkins, C. A., Ouellette, J. M., & Sheehan, N. M. (1991). Grouping students for literacy learning: What works. *Massachusetts Primer, 20* (1), 2–19.

Pardo, L. S., & Raphael, T. E. (1991). Classroom organization for instruction in content areas. *The Reading Teacher, 44* (8), 556–565.

Paris, S. (1991). Portfolio assessment for young readers. *The Reading Teacher, 44* (9), 680–682.

Paris, S. G., Calfee, R. C., Filby, N., Hiebert, E. H., Pearson, P. D., Valencia, S. W., & Wolf, K. P. (1992). A framework for authentic literacy assessment. *The Reading Teacher, 46* (2), 88–98.

Pearson, P. D. (2001). Life in the radical middle: A personal apology for a balanced view of reading. In R. F. Flippo (Ed.), *Reading researchers in search of common ground* (pp. 78–83). Newark, DE: International Reading Association.

Pearson, P. D., & Johnson, D. D. (1978). *Teaching reading comprehension.* New York: Holt, Rinehart and Winston.

Pérez, B. (1994). Spanish literacy development: A descriptive study of four bilingual whole-language classrooms. *Journal of Reading Behavior, 26* (1), 75–93.

Peters, C. W. (1991). You can't have authentic assessment without authentic content. *The Reading Teacher, 44* (8), 590–591.

Peterson, B. (1991). Selecting books for beginning readers: Children's literature suitable for young readers: A bibliography. In D. Deford, C. Lyons, & G. S. Pinnell (Eds.), *Bridges to literacy: Learning from Reading Recovery* (pp. 119–147). Portsmouth, NH: Heinemann.

Peterson, B. (2001). *Literacy pathways: Selecting books to support new readers.* Portsmouth, NH: Heinemann.

Piaget, J. (1959). *The language and thought of the child* (3rd ed.). (Marjorie Gabain, Trans.). London: Routledge & Kegan Paul.

Pikulski, J. J. (1990a). Informal reading inventories. *The Reading Teacher, 43* (7), 514–516.

Pikulski, J. J. (1990b). The role of tests in a literacy assessment program. *The Reading Teacher, 43* (9), 686–688.

Pikulski, J. J. (1994). Preventing reading failure: A review of five effective programs. *The Reading Teacher, 48* (1), 30–39.

Pikulski, J. J., & Tobin, A. W. (1982). The cloze procedure as an informal assessment technique. In J. J. Pikulski & T. Shanahan (Eds.), *Approaches to the informal evaluation of reading.* Newark, DE: International Reading Association.

Pinnell, G. S., Pikulski, J. J., Wixson, K. K., Campbell, J. R., Gough, P. B., & Beatty, A. S. (1995). *Listening to children read aloud.* Washington, DC: Office of Educational Research and Improvement, U.S. Department of Education.

Plake, B. S., & Impara, J. C. (Eds.). (2001). *The fourteenth mental measurements yearbook.* Lincoln, NE: The Buros Institute of Mental Measurements, University of Nebraska–Lincoln: University of Nebraska Press.

Post, A. D. (with Scott, M., & Theberge, M.). (2000). *Celebrating Children's Choices: 25 years of children's favorite books.* Newark, DE: International Reading Association.

Power, B. (1999). *Parent power: Energizing home-school communication.* Portsmouth, NH: Heinemann.

Pressley, M. (2001). Balanced teaching of elementary literacy competencies: An update. *Balanced Reading Instruction, 8* (1), 1–7.

Purcell-Gates, V. (1995). *Other people's words: The cycle of low literacy.* Cambridge, MA: Harvard University Press.

Purcell-Gates, V., L' Allier, S., & Smith, D. (1995). Literacy at the Harts' and the Larsons': Diversity among poor, inner-city families. *The Reading Teacher, 48* (7), 572–578.

Quintero, E., & Huerta-Macias, A. (1990). All in the family: Bilingualism and biliteracy. *The Reading Teacher, 44* (4), 306–312.

Radencich, M. C., & McKay, L. J. (1995). *Flexible grouping for literacy in the elementary grades.* Boston: Allyn and Bacon.

Raphael, T. E. (1986). Teaching questions-answer relationships, revisited. *The Reading Teacher, 39,* 516–522.

Raphael, T. E., & Hiebert, E. H. (1996). *Creating an integrated approach to literacy instruction.* Fort Worth, TX: Harcourt Brace.

Raphael, T. E., & McMahon, S. I. (1994). Book Club: An alternative framework for reading instruction. *The Reading Teacher, 48* (2), 102–116.

Rasinski, T. V. (1994). Making parental involvement work. *Reading Today, 11* (6), 31.

Rasinski, T. V. (Ed.). (1995). *Parents and teachers: Helping children learn to read and write.* Fort Worth, TX: Harcourt Brace.

Rasinski, T. V., & Padak, N. D. (2001). *From phonics to fluency: Effective teaching of decoding and reading fluency in the elementary school.* New York: Addison Wesley Longman.

Rasinski, T. V., Padak, N. D., Church, B. W., Fawcett, G., Hendershot, J., Henry, J. M., Moss, B. G., Peck, J. K., Pryor, E., & Roskos, K. A. (Eds.). (2000a). *Developing reading-writing connections: Strategies from The Reading Teacher.* Newark, DE: International Reading Association.

Rasinski, T. V., Padak, N. D., Church, B. W., Fawcett, G., Hendershot, J., Henry, J. M., Moss, B. G., Peck, J. K., Pryor, E., & Roskos, K. A. (Eds.). (2000b). *Teaching comprehension and exploring multiple literacies: Strategies from The Reading Teacher.* Newark, DE: International Reading Association.

Rauch, S. J. (1994). The balancing effect continues: Whole language faces reality. *Balanced Reading Instruction, 1* (1), 41–44.

Read, C. (1971). Pre-school children's knowledge of English. *Harvard Educational Review, 41,* 1–34.

Readence, J. E., Moore, D. W., & Rickelman, R. J. (2000). *Prereading activities for content area reading and learning* (3rd ed.). Newark, DE: International Reading Association.

Rekrut, M. D. (1994). Peer and cross-age tutoring: The lessons of research. *Journal of Reading, 37* (5), 356–362.

Reutzel, D. R. (1999). On Welna's sacred cows: Where's the beef? *The Reading Teacher, 53* (2), 96–99.

Reutzel, D. R., & Cooter, R. B. (1991). Organizing for effective instruction: The reading workshop. *The Reading Teacher, 44* (8), 548–554.

Reutzel, D. R., & Wolfersberger, M. (1996). An environmental impact statement: Designing supportive literacy classrooms for young children. *Reading Horizons, 36* (3), 266–282.

Revie, A. (1991). Using the Pathways document to optimise the conditions of learning. In E. Daly (Ed.), *Monitoring children's language development: Holistic assessment in the classroom* (pp. 140–152). Portsmouth, NH: Heinemann.

Rhodes, L. K., & Nathenson-Mejia, S. (1992). Anecdotal records: A powerful tool for ongoing literacy assessment. *The Reading Teacher, 45* (7), 502–509.

Richards, J. C., & Gipe, J. P. (1992). Activating background knowledge: Strategies for beginning and poor readers. *The Reading Teacher, 45* (6), 474–476.

Richgels, D. J. (1995). Invented spelling ability and printed word learning in kindergarten. *Reading Research Quarterly, 30* (1), 96–109.

Richgels, D. J. (2001). Phonemic awareness. *The Reading Teacher, 55* (3), 274–278.

Rickards, D., & Cheek, E. (1999). *Designing rubrics for k–6 classroom assessment.* Norwood, MA: Christopher-Gordon.

Risko, V. J., & Bromley, K. (Eds.). (2001). *Collaboration for diverse learners: Viewpoints and practices.* Newark, DE: International Reading Association.

Robb, L. (1998). *Easy-to-manage reading & writing conferences.* New York: Scholastic.

Robb, L. (1999). *Easy mini-lessons for building vocabulary.* New York: Scholastic.

Robb, L. (2000). *Teaching reading in middle school.* New York: Scholastic.

Robb, L. (2001). *Grammar lessons & strategies.* New York: Scholastic.

Robinson, F. P. (1946). *Effective study.* New York: Harper and Brothers.

Robinson, V. B., Ross, G., & Neal, H. C. (2000). *Emergent literacy in kindergarten: A review of the research and related suggested activities and learning strategies.* San Mateo, CA: California Kindergarten Association.

Rockwell, R. E., Andre, L. C., & Hawley, M. K. (1996). *Parents and teachers as partners: Issues and challenges.* Fort Worth, TX: Harcourt Brace.

Rog, L. J., & Burton, W. (2001/2002). Matching texts and readers: Leveling early reading materials for assessment and instruction. *The Reading Teacher, 55* (4), 348–356.

Rogovin, P. (2001). *The research workshop: Bringing the world into your classroom.* Portsmouth, NH: Heinemann.

Rosenbaum, J. E. (1980). Social implications of educational grouping. In D. C. Berliner (Ed.), *Review of research in education* (pp. 361–401). Washington, DC: American Educational Research Association.

Rosenshine, B., & Meister, C. (1994). Reciprocal teaching: A review of the research. *Review of Educational Research, 64* (4), 479–530.

Roser, N. L., & Martinez, M. G. (Eds.). (1995). *Book talk and beyond: Children and teachers respond to literature.* Newark, DE: International Reading Association.

Rothlein, L., & Meinbach, A. M. (1996). *Legacies: Using children's literature in the classroom.* New York: HarperCollins.

Routman, R. (1994). *Invitations: Changing as teachers and learners K–12* (Rev. ed.). Portsmouth, NH: Heinemann.

Routman, R. (1996). *Literacy at the crossroads: Crucial talk about reading, writing, and other teaching dilemmas.* Portsmouth, NH: Heinemann.

Routman, R. (2000). *Conversations: Strategies for teaching, learning, and evaluating.* Portsmouth, NH: Heinemann.

Sadler, C. R. (2001). *Comprehension strategies for middle grade learners: A handbook for content area teachers.* Newark, DE: International Reading Association.

Samway, K. D., & McKeon, D. (1999). *Myths and realities: Best practices for language minority students.* Portsmouth, NH: Heinemann.

Samway, K. D., Whang, G., & Pippitt, M. (1995). *Buddy reading: Cross-age tutoring in a multicultural school.* Portsmouth, NH: Heinemann.

Sanacore, J. (1991). Expository and narrative texts: Balancing young children's reading experiences. *Childhood Education, 67,* 211–214.

Savage, J. F. (2000). *For the love of literature: Children & books in the elementary years.* Boston: McGraw-Hill.

Savage, J. F. (2001). *Sound it out! Phonics in a balanced reading program.* Boston: McGraw-Hill.

Schmitt, M. C. (1990). A questionnaire to measure children's awareness of strategic reading processes. *The Reading Teacher, 43* (7), 454–461.

Searfoss, L. W. (1993). Assessing classroom environments. In S. M. Glazer & C. S. Brown, *Portfolios and beyond: Collaborative assessment in reading and writing* (pp. 11–26). Norwood, MA: Christopher-Gordon.

Shanahan, T., Mulhern, M., & Rodriguez-Brown, F. (1995). Project FLAME: Lessons learned from a family literacy program for linguistic minority families. *The Reading Teacher, 48* (7), 586–593.

Shannon, P. (1985). Reading instruction and social class. *Language Arts, 62* (6), 604–613.

Shepard, L. A. (2000). The role of assessment in a learning culture. *Educational Researcher, 29* (7), 4–14.

Shockley, B. (1994). Extending the literate community: Home-to-school and school-to-home. *The Reading Teacher, 47* (6), 500–502.

Shockley, B., Michalove, B., & Allen, J. (1995). *Engaging families: Connecting home and school literacy communities.* Portsmouth, NH: Heinemann.

Short, K. G. (1991). Literacy environments that support strategic readers. In D. E. DeFord, C. A. Lyon, & G. S. Pinnell (Eds.), *Bridges to literacy: Learning from Reading Recovery* (pp. 97–118). Portsmouth, NH: Heinemann.

Short, K. G. (Ed.). (1995). *Research & professional resources in children's literature: Piecing a patchwork quilt.* Newark, DE: International Reading Association.

Short, K. G., & Harste, J. C. (with Burke, C.). (1996). *Creating classrooms for authors and inquirers* (2nd ed.). Portsmouth, NH: Heinemann.

Silvaroli, N. J., & Wheelock, W. H. (2001). *Classroom Reading Inventory* (9th ed.). Boston: McGraw-Hill.

Siu-Runyan, Y. (1994). Holistic assessment in intermediate classes: Techniques for informing our teaching. In B. Harp (Ed.), *Assessment and evaluation for student-centered learning* (pp. 143–177). Norwood, MA: Christopher-Gordon.

Skillings, M. J., & Ferrell, R. (2000). Student-generated rubrics: Bringing students into the assessment process. *The Reading Teacher, 53* (6), 452–455.

Slaughter, H. B. (1988). Indirect and direct teaching in a whole language program. *The Reading Teacher, 42* (1), 30–34.

Slaughter, J. P. (1993). *Beyond storybooks: Young children and the shared book experience.* Newark, DE: International Reading Association.

Slavin, R. E. (1987). Ability grouping and student achievement in elementary schools: A best-evidence synthesis. *Review of Educational Research, 57* (3), 293–336.

Slavin, R. E. (1991). Are cooperative learning and "untracking" harmful to the gifted? *Educational Leadership, 48* (6), 68–71.

Slosson, R. L. (1981). *The Slosson Oral Reading Test.* Monterey, CA: Publishers Test Service.

Smith, C. B. (Ed.). (1991). *Alternative assessment of performance in the language arts: Proceedings.* Bloomington, IN: ERIC Clearinghouse on Reading and Communication Skills.

Snow, C. E., Burns, M. S., & Griffin, P. (Eds.). (1998). *Preventing reading difficulties in young children.* Washington, DC: National Research Council, National Academy Press.

Spandel, V. (2001). *Creating writers* (3rd ed.). New York: Addison Wesley Longman.

Spiegel, D. L. (1992). Blending whole language and systematic direct instruction. *The Reading Teacher, 46* (1), 38–44.

Spiegel, D. L. (1994a). A portrait of parents of successful readers. In E. H. Cramer & M. Castle (Eds.), *Fostering the love of reading: The affective domain in reading education* (pp. 74–87). Newark, DE: International Reading Association.

Spiegel, D. L. (1994b). Finding the balance in literacy development for all children. *Balanced Reading Instruction, 1* (1), 6–11.

Spiegel, D. L., Fitzgerald, J., & Cunningham, J. (1993). Parental perceptions of preschoolers literacy development. *Young Children, 48* (5), 74–79.

Squire, J. R. (1987). Introduction: A special issue on the state of assessment in reading. *The Reading Teacher, 40* (8), 724–725.

Stahl, S. A. (1992). Saying the "p" word: Nine guidelines for exemplary phonics instruction. *The Reading Teacher, 45* (8), 618–625.

Stanovich, K. E. (1986). Matthew effects in reading: Some consequences of individual differences in the acquisition of literacy. *Reading Research Quarterly, 21,* 360–407.

Stephens, D. (1991). *Research on whole language: Support for a new curriculum*. Katonah, NY: Richard C. Owen.

Stephens, E. C., & Brown, J. E. (2000). *A handbook of content literacy strategies: 75 practical reading and writing ideas*. Norwood, MA: Christopher-Gordon.

Strickland, D. S. (1994/1995). Reinventing our literacy programs: Books, basics, balance. *The Reading Teacher, 48* (4), 294–302.

Strickland, D. S. (1998). *Teaching phonics today: A primer for educators*. Newark, DE: International Reading Association.

Strickland, D. S., & Morrow, L. M. (1989a). Developing skills: An emergent literacy perspective. *The Reading Teacher, 43* (1), 82–83.

Strickland, D. S., & Morrow, L. M. (1989b). Young children's early writing development. *The Reading Teacher, 42* (6), 426–427.

Strickland, K., & Strickland, J. (1998). *Reflections on assessment: Its purposes, methods and effects on learning*. Portsmouth, NH: Boynton/Cook, Heinemann.

Stroll, D. R. (Ed.). (1997). *Magazines for kids and teens* (Rev. ed.). Newark, DE: International Reading Association, and Educational Press Association of America.

Sulzby, E. (1985). Children's emergent reading of favorite storybooks: A developmental study. *Reading Research Quarterly, 20* (4), 458–481.

Sulzby, E. (1991). Assessment of emergent literacy: Storybook reading. *The Reading Teacher, 44* (7), 498–500.

Sulzby, E. (1992). Research directions: Transitions from emergent to conventional writing. *Language Arts, 69* (4), 290–297.

Sulzby, E., & Teale, W. H. (1987). *Young children's storybook reading: Longitudinal study of parent-child interaction and children's independent functioning. Final report to the Spencer Foundation*. Ann Arbor: University of Michigan.

Sunstein, B. S., & Lovell, J. H. (Eds.). (2000). *The portfolio standard: How students can show us what they know and are able to do*. Portsmouth, NH: Heinemann.

Sweet, A. P., & Guthrie, J. T. (1996). How children's motivations relate to literacy development and instruction. *The Reading Teacher, 49* (8), 660–662.

Tancock, S. M. (1994). A literacy lesson framework for children with reading problems. *The Reading Teacher, 48* (2), 130–140.

Taylor, B. M., Pressley, M. P., & Pearson, P. D. (2000). *Research-supported characteristics of teachers and schools that promote reading achievement*. Washington, DC: National Education Association, Reading Matters Research Report.

Taylor, B. M., & Samuels, S. J. (1983). Children's use of text structure in the recall of expository material. *American Educational Research Journal, 20*, 234–237.

Taylor, D. (Ed.). (1997). *Many families, many literacies*. Portsmouth, NH: Heinemann.

Taylor, D. (1998). *Family literacy: Young children learning to read and write*. Portsmouth, NH: Heinemann.

Teale, W. H., & Sulzby, E. (1986). Emergent literacy as a perspective for examining how children become writers and readers. In W. H. Teale & E. Sulzby (Eds.), *Emergent literacy: Writing and reading* (pp. vii–xxv). Norwood, NJ: Ablex.

Temple, C., Nathan, R., Temple, F., & Burris, N. A. (1993). *The beginnings of writing* (3rd ed.). Boston: Allyn and Bacon.

Templeton, S. (1995). *Children's literacy: Contexts for meaningful learning.* Boston: Houghton Mifflin.

Templeton, S. (1997). *Teaching the integrated language arts* (2nd ed.). Boston: Houghton Mifflin.

Thomas, A., Fazio, L., & Stiefelmeyer, B. L. (1999a). *Families at school: A guide for educators.* Newark, DE: International Reading Association.

Thomas, A., Fazio, L., & Stiefelmeyer, B. L. (1999b). *Families at school: A handbook for parents.* Newark, DE: International Reading Association.

Thompson, R. A. (1994). The origin of Balanced Reading Instruction: An IRA special interest group. *Balanced Reading Instruction, 1* (1), 45–46.

Tiedt, P. L., & Tiedt, I. M. (2002). *Multicultural teaching: A handbook of activities, information, and resources* (6th ed.). Boston: Allyn and Bacon.

Tierney, R. J., Carter, M. A., & Desai, L. E. (1991). *Portfolio assessment in the reading-writing classroom.* Norwood, MA: Christopher-Gordon.

Tierney, R. J., & Readence, J. E. (2000). *Reading strategies and practices: A compendium* (5th ed.). Boston: Allyn and Bacon.

Tobias, S. (1994). Interest, prior knowledge, and learning. *Review of Educational Research, 64* (1), 37–54.

Tomei, L. A. (2001). *Teaching digitally: A guide for integrating technology into the classroom.* Norwood: Christopher-Gordon.

Tomlinson, C. M., & Lynch-Brown, C. (2002). *Essentials of children's literature* (4th ed.). Boston: Allyn and Bacon.

Tompkins, G. E. (2002). *Language arts: Content and teaching strategies* (5th ed.). Upper Saddle River, NJ: Merrill/Prentice-Hall.

Towell, J. (1997/1998). Fun with vocabulary. *The Reading Teacher, 51* (4), 356–358.

Trumbull, E., & Farr, B. (Eds.). (2000). *Grading and reporting student progress in an age of standards.* Norwood: Christopher-Gordon.

Tunnell, M. O., & Jacobs, J. S. (1989). Using "real" books: Research findings on literature based reading instruction. *The Reading Teacher, 42* (7), 470–477.

Turbill, J., & Cambourne, B. (Eds.). (1998). *The changing face of whole language* [Reprinted from the May 1997 themed issue of *The Australian Journal of Language and Literacy, 20* (2)]. Newark, DE: International Reading Association.

Unwin, C. G. (1995). Elizabeth's story: The potential of home-based family literacy intervention. *The Reading Teacher, 48* (7), 552–557.

U.S. Department of Education. (2001a, September). *Community Update, 91,* 1–8.

U.S. Department of Education. (2001b). *Put reading first: The research building blocks for teaching children to read* (Kindergarten through Grade 3). Washington, DC: Partnership for Reading/National Institute for Literacy, National Institute of Child Health and Human Development, and U.S. Department of Education.

U.S. Department of Education, International Reading Association, & HCI The Life Issues Publisher Joint Project. (2000). *A practical guide to reading assessments.* Newark, DE: Author.

Vacca, R. T., & Vacca, J. L. (2002). *Content area reading: Literacy and learning across the curriculum* (7th ed.). Boston: Allyn and Bacon.

Valencia, S. (1990). A portfolio approach to classroom reading assessment: The whys, whats, and hows. *The Reading Teacher, 43* (4), 338–340.

Valencia, S. W. (1998). *Literacy portfolios in action.* Fort Worth, TX: Harcourt Brace.

Valencia, S. W., Hiebert, E. H., & Afflerbach, P. P. (Eds.). (1994). *Authentic reading assessment: Practices and possibilities.* Newark, DE: International Reading Association.

Valencia, S., & Pearson, P. D. (1987). Reading assessment: Time for a change. *The Reading Teacher, 40* (8), 726–732.

Valencia, S. W., & Place, N. (1994). Portfolios: A process for enhancing teaching and learning. *The Reading Teacher, 47* (8), 666–669.

Valencia, S. W., & Wixson, K. K. (2000). Policy-oriented research on literacy standards and assessment. In M. L. Kamil, P. B. Mosenthal, P. D. Pearson, & R. Barr (Eds.), *Handbook of reading research* (Vol. 3, pp. 909–935). Mahwah, NJ: Erlbaum.

Valmont, W. J. (2003). *Technology for literacy teaching and learning.* Boston: Houghton Mifflin.

Vygotsky, L. S. (1962). *Thought and language.* Cambridge, MA: MIT Press.

Vygotsky, L. S. (1978). *Mind in society: The development of higher psychological processes.* Cambridge, MA: Harvard University Press.

Wade, S. E. (1990). Using think-alouds to assess comprehension. *The Reading Teacher, 43* (7), 442–451.

Walp, T. P., & Walmsley, S. A. (1995). Scoring well on tests or becoming genuinely literate: Rethinking remediation in a small rural school. In R. L. Allington & S. A. Walmsley (Eds.), *No quick fix: Rethinking literacy programs in America's elementary schools* (pp. 177–196). New York: Teachers College Press.

Wasik, B. H., Hermann, S., Berry, R. S., Dobbins, D. R., Schimizzi, A. M., Smith, T. K., & Herman, P. (2000). *Family literacy: An annotated bibliography.* Washington, DC: U.S. Department of Education, Office of Educational Research and Improvement, National Institute on Early Childhood Development and Education.

Weaver, B. M. (2000). *Leveling books k–6: Matching readers to text.* Newark, DE: International Reading Association.

Weaver, C. (2002). *Reading process & practice* (3rd ed.). Portsmouth, NH: Heinemann.

Weber, R. (1968). The study of oral reading errors: A survey of the literature. *Reading Research Quarterly, 4,* 96–119.

Weber, R. (1970). A linguistic analysis of first-grade reading errors. *Reading Research Quarterly, 5* (3), 427–451.

Weinstein, R. S. (1976). Reading group membership in first grade: Teacher behaviors and pupil experience over time. *Journal of Educational Psychology, 68* (1), 103–116.

Wepner, S. B., Valmont, W. J., & Thurlow, R. (Eds.). (2000). *Linking literacy and technology: A guide for k–8 classrooms.* Newark, DE: International Reading Association.

Wiesendanger, K. D. (2001). *Strategies for literacy education.* Upper Saddle River, NJ: Merrill/Prentice Hall.

Wilde, S. (1992). *You kan red this! Spelling and punctuation for whole language classrooms, k–6.* Portsmouth, NH: Heinemann.

Wilde, S. (1997). *What's a schwa sound anyway? A holistic guide to phonetics, phonics, and spelling.* Portsmouth, NH: Heinemann.

Wilde, S. (2002). *Testing and standards: A brief encyclopedia.* Portsmouth, NH: Heinemann.

Wilhelm, J. D. (2001). *Improving comprehension with think-aloud strategies.* New York: Scholastic.

Wilkinson, I. A. G., & Townsend, M. A. R. (2000). From Rata to Rimu: Grouping for instruction in best practice New Zealand classrooms. *The Reading Teacher, 53* (6), 460–471.

Williams, N. (2000). *Children's literature selections and strategies for students with reading difficulties: A resource for teachers.* Norwood, MA: Christopher-Gordon.

Willis, J. W., Stephens, E. C., & Matthew, K. I. (1996). *Technology, reading, and language arts.* Boston: Allyn and Bacon.

Winograd, P. (1994). Developing alternative assessments: Six problems worth solving. *The Reading Teacher, 47* (5), 420–423.

Winograd, P., Paris, S., & Bridge, C. (1991). Improving the assessment of literacy. *The Reading Teacher, 45* (2), 108–116.

Wixson, K. K. (1991). Diagnostic teaching. *The Reading Teacher, 44* (6), 420–422.

Wixson, K. K., Valencia, S. W., & Lipson, M. Y. (1994). Issues in literacy assessment: Facing the realities of internal and external assessment. *Journal of Reading Behavior, 26* (3), 315–337.

Wolf, K. P. (1993). From informal to informed assessment: Recognizing the role of the classroom teacher. *Journal of Reading, 36* (7), 518–523.

Wood, K. D., Roser, N. L., & Martinez, M. (2001). Collaborative literacy: Lesson learned from literature. *The Reading Teacher, 55* (2), 102–111.

Woods, M. L., & Moe, A. J. (1995). *Analytical Reading Inventory* (5th ed.). Upper Saddle River, NJ: Merrill/Prentice Hall.

Woods, M. L., & Moe, A. J. (2003). *Analytical Reading Inventory* (7th ed.). Upper Saddle River, NJ: Merrill/Prentice Hall.

Worthy, J., & Broaddus, K. (2001/2002). Fluency beyond the primary grades: From group performance to silent, independent reading. *The Reading Teacher, 55* (4), 334–343.

Yopp, H. K. (1995). A test for assessing phonemic awareness in young children. *The Reading Teacher, 49* (1), 20–29.

Yopp, R. H., & Yopp, H. K. (2000). Sharing informational text with young children. *The Reading Teacher, 53* (5), 410–423.

Yopp, R. H., & Yopp, H. K. (2001). *Literature-based reading activities* (3rd ed.). Boston: Allyn and Bacon.

Young, T. A., Campbell, L. C., & Oda, L. K. (1995). Multicultural literature for children and young adults: A rationale and resources. *Reading Horizons, 35* (5), 375–393.

Youngs, S. (2002). Parents as reflective partners. *Primary Voices K–6, 10* (4), 24–30.

Zuttell, J., & Rasinski, T. V. (1991). Training teachers to attend to their students' oral reading fluency. *Theory Into Practice, 30,* 212–217.

CHILDREN'S LITERATURE REFERENCES

Adams, P. (1975). *There was an old lady who swallowed a fly*. New York: Grosset & Dunlap.

Anno, M. (1972). *Dr. Anno's magical midnight circus*. New York: John Weatherhill.

Bader, B. (1991). *Aesop & company with scenes from his legendary life*. Boston: Houghton Mifflin.

Brett, J. (1985). *Annie and the wild animals*. Boston: Houghton Mifflin.

Brett, J. (1991). *Berlioz the bear*. New York: Putnam's Sons.

Briggs, R. (1978). *The snowman*. New York: Random House.

Bunting, E. (1991). Fly *away home*. New York: Clarion Books.

Cairnes, J. (1977). *Daddy*. New York: Harper & Row.

Carle, E. (1993). *Today is Monday*. New York: Philomel Books.

Clark, M., & Voake, C. (1990). *The best of Aesop's fables*. Boston: Little, Brown.

Cole, J. (1981). *Golly Gump swallowed a fly*. New York: Parents Magazine Press.

Crews, D. (1991). *Bigmama's*. New York: Greenwillow.

Crews, D. (1992). *Shortcut*. New York: Greenwillow.

Day, A. (1985). *Good dog, Carl*. Hong Kong: Green Tiger Press.

Devlin, W., & Devlin, H. (1971). *Cranberry Thanksgiving*. New York: Parents Magazine Press.

Fox, M. (1986). *Hattie and the fox*. New York: Bradbury Press.

Galdone, P. (1972). *The three bears*. New York: Clarion Books/Houghton Mifflin.

Garland, S. (1992). *Billy and Belle*. New York: Viking.

Goodall, J. (1977). *The surprise picnic*. New York: McElderry Books/Atheneum.

Haviland, V. (1963). *Favorite fairy tales told in Poland*. Boston: Little, Brown.

Hawes, J. (1964). *Bees and beelines*. New York: Thomas Y. Crowell.

Hooks, W. (1990). *A dozen dizzy dogs*. New York: Bantam Books.

Jenness, A. (1990). *Families: A celebration of diversity, commitment, and love*. Boston: Houghton Mifflin.

Jones, H. (1981). *Tales from Aesop*. New York: Frank Watts.

Keats, E. J. (1967). *Peter's chair*. New York: Harper & Row.

Keen, B. (Trans.). (1992). How the first skirmish between the Indians and the Christians took place in Samaná Bay on the Island of Española. In B. Keen (Trans.), *The life of the Admiral Christopher Columbus by his son Ferdinand* (Rev. ed.) (pp. 88–90). New Brunswick, NJ: Rutgers University Press.

Kennerly, K. (1973). *Hesitant wolf and scrupulous fox: Fables selected from world literature.* New York: Random House.

Levinson, R. (1985). *Watch the stars come out.* New York: Dutton.

Lewison, W. (1992). *"Buzz," said the bee.* New York: Scholastic.

Lobel, A. (1970). *Frog and toad are friends.* New York: Harper & Row.

Lobel, A. (1977). *Mouse soup.* New York: Harper & Row.

Lobel, A. (1980). *Fables.* New York: Harper & Row.

MacLachlan, R (1982). *Mama one, mama two.* New York: Harper & Row.

MacLachlan, P. (1985). *Sarah plain and tall.* New York: Harper & Row.

Mayer, M. (1968). *There's a nightmare in my closet.* New York: Dial Press.

Minarik, E. H. (1960). *Little Bear's friend.* New York: Harper & Row.

Minarik, E. H. (1968). *A kiss for Little Bear.* New York: Harper & Row.

Numeroff, L. J. (1985). *If you give a mouse a cookie.* New York: Scholastic.

Numeroff, L. J. (1991). *If you give a moose a muffin.* New York: HarperCollins.

Piper, W. (1990). *The little engine that could.* New York: Platt & Munk/Putnam.

Rylant, C. (1985). *The relatives came.* New York: Bradbury Press.

Sobol, D. (1988). *#10, Encyclopedia Brown takes the case.* New York: Bantam.

Thaler, M. (1993). Hippo makes a wish. In *Make a wish* (136–146). Needham, MA: Silver Burdett Ginn.

Wells, R. (1973). *Noisy Nora.* New York: Dial Press.

White, E. B. (1952). *Charlotte's web.* New York: Harper & Row.

Williams, V. B. (1982). *A chair for my mother.* New York: Greenwillow.

Williams, V. B. (1983). *Something special for me.* New York: Greenwillow.

Williams, V. B. (1984). *Music, music, for everyone.* New York: Greenwillow.

Yarborough, C. (1979). *Cornrows.* New York: Dutton.

AUTHOR INDEX

SUBJECT INDEX